Commander
Steven Haines
Royal Navy

SMALL NAVIES

Corbett Centre for Maritime Policy Studies Series

Series editors:
Professor Greg Kennedy, Dr Tim Benbow and Dr Jon Robb-Webb,
Defence Studies Department, Joint Services Command and Staff College, UK

The Corbett Centre for Maritime Policy Studies Series is the publishing platform of the Corbett Centre. Drawing on the expertise and wider networks of the Defence Studies Department of King's College London, and based at the Joint Services Command and Staff College in the UK Defence Academy, the Corbett Centre is already a leading centre for academic expertise and education in maritime and naval studies. It enjoys close links with several other institutions, both academic and governmental, that have an interest in maritime matters, including the Developments, Concepts and Doctrine Centre (DCDC), the Naval Staff of the Ministry of Defence and the Naval Historical Branch.

The centre and its publishing output aims to promote the understanding and analysis of maritime history and policy and to provide a forum for the interaction of academics, policy-makers and practitioners. Books published under the eagis of the Corbett Centre series reflect these aims and provide an opportunity to stimulate research and debate into a broad range of maritime related themes. The core subject matter for the series is maritime strategy and policy, conceived broadly to include theory, history and practice, military and civil, historical and contemporary, British and international aspects.

As a result this series offers a unique opportunity to examine key issues such as maritime security, the future of naval power, and the commercial uses of the sea, from an exceptionally broad chronological, geographical and thematic range. Truly interdisciplinary in its approach, the series welcomes books from across the humanities, social sciences and professional worlds, providing an unrivalled opportunity for authors and readers to enhance the national and international visibility of maritime affairs, and provide a forum for policy debate and analysis.

Small Navies
Strategy and Policy for Small Navies in War and Peace

Edited by

MICHAEL MULQUEEN
Liverpool Hope University, UK

DEBORAH SANDERS
King's College, London, UK

IAN SPELLER
National University of Ireland Maynooth, Ireland

ASHGATE

© Michael Mulqueen, Deborah Sanders and Ian Speller 2014

All rights reserved. No part of this publication may be reproduced, stored in a retrieval system or transmitted in any form or by any means, electronic, mechanical, photocopying, recording or otherwise without the prior permission of the publisher.

Michael Mulqueen, Deborah Sanders and Ian Speller have asserted their right under the Copyright, Designs and Patents Act, 1988, to be identified as the editors of this work.

Published by
Ashgate Publishing Limited
Wey Court East
Union Road
Farnham
Surrey, GU9 7PT
England

Ashgate Publishing Company
110 Cherry Street
Suite 3-1
Burlington, VT 05401-3818
USA

www.ashgate.com

British Library Cataloguing in Publication Data
A catalogue record for this book is available from the British Library

The Library of Congress has cataloged the printed edition as follows:

Small Navies: Strategy and Policy for Small Navies in War and Peace / edited by
    Michael Mulqueen, Deborah Sanders and Ian Speller.
        pages   cm. – (Series: Corbett Centre for Maritime Policy Studies Series)
    Includes bibliographical references and index.
    1. Navies. 2. Sea-power – Case studies. 3. Naval strategy. 4. Naval art and science – Case studies. I. Mulqueen, Michael, editor of compilation. II. Sanders, Deborah, 1968–, editor of compilation. III. Speller, Ian, 1969-, editor of compilation. IV. Title: Strategy and policy for small navies in war and peace.
    VA40.S54 2016
    359'.03–dc23   2013039382

ISBN   9781472417596 (hbk)
ISBN   9781472417602 (ebk-PDF)
ISBN   9781472417619 (ebk-ePUB)

Printed in the United Kingdom by Henry Ling Limited, at the Dorset Press, Dorchester, DT1 1HD

Contents

Series Editors' Preface		*vii*
Preface *Michael Mulqueen, Deborah Sanders and Ian Speller*		*ix*
Notes on Contributors		*xi*
Introduction Ian Speller, Deborah Sanders and Michael Mulqueen		1
1	The Ranking of Smaller Navies Revisited Eric Grove	15
2	Are Small Navies Different? Geoffrey Till	21
3	Small Navies in Perspective: Deconstructing the Hierarchy of Naval Forces Basil Germond	33
4	Transforming Small Navies by Systematic Innovation: A Framework for Productivity, Efficiency and Effectiveness Michael Mulqueen and Terry Warburton	51
5	Adaptive Dynamic Capabilities and Innovation: The Key for Small Navies Protecting National Interests at and from the Sea Mark Mellett	67
6	Small Navies in Asia: The Strategic Rationale for Growth Michael McDevitt	81
7	The Republic of Korea Navy – A 'Big' Small Navy Ian Bowers	95
8	'Best Little Navy in Southeast Asia': The Case of the Republic of Singapore Navy Swee Lean Collin Koh	117

9	Small Navies and Border and Immigration Control: Frontex Operations in the Mediterranean *Giampiero Giacomello and Chiara Ruffa*	133
10	Small Navies in the Black Sea: A Case Study of Romania's Maritime Power *Deborah Sanders*	151
11	A Small Navy in a Changing World: The Case of the Royal Swedish Navy *Niklas Granholm*	167
12	The Strategic Value of Small Navies: The Strange Case of the Confederate Navy *Christopher Tuck*	185
13	Learning to Be Small: The Experience of the British Pacific Fleet, 1944–45 *Jon Robb-Webb*	201

Appendix A	*213*
Bibliography	*215*
Index	*237*

Series Editors' Preface

This collection of essays on small navies comes at a most opportune time. In the West, shrinking defence budgets and unclear strategic focus sees many nations considering naval reductions, both in terms of numbers and capability. The question on many of those nations' minds is will this move them into the small navy category, and if so what is the impact of that re-categorisation. In the Asia-Pacific area naval power is growing, as resurgent or emergent powers attempt to utilise maritime power for their own strategic ends. Some nations in that region are perfectly happy with 'small' navies, as they know that is enough to buy into a bigger maritime strategic environment, such as the American 2007 Maritime Strategy, which put an emphasis on global maritime cooperation and collaboration. Globally, therefore, debates are on-going on what as to what defines a strong naval power from a weak naval power.

Part of that discussion revolves around the relative worth of small navies versus larger navies, particular with respect either to providing access in the maritime domain, or being a useful part of any scheme which seeks to implement a denial strategy to expeditionary naval power. More importantly than general, conventional war-fighting considerations, is the expansion of the concept of security and the role navies play in providing security for their respective nations. A myriad range of tasks, from search and rescue, drugs and human trafficking, fisheries protection, disaster relief, intelligence and cyber operations, as well as hydrographic and scientific support to private and other government agencies, all are now a part of a modern navy's remit. This convergence of economic, security and geo-strategic forces creates the need to understand what navies are, what they are capable of and how to use them as a gauge of national will and power.

The essays within provide a sophisticated model of analysis for that purpose which can be used as an aid to grappling with the question of what constitutes a small navy and how do you recognise it from a large or medium navy. The collection also challenges the reader to work through such issues as to whether or not small navies can be strategic. Though not endowed with organic capabilities that allow strategic effect to be delivered on their own, small navies can act as a conduit or critical enabler for inter-agency and inter-governmental cooperation that can achieve strategic effect. Finally, in the age of austerity and fiscal uncertainty, do small navies present an opportunity for nations to use new and cheaper technologies, in innovative ways that can challenge the established hierarchy of nations possessing 'full-spectrum' large navies? All of these issues are dealt with in a series of sophisticated and scholarly chapters that provide a template for policy-makers interested in gaining an understanding of how to measure naval power not just in terms of hulls and kinetic capability, but through a more holistic and informative process of evaluation.

Preface

Michael Mulqueen, Deborah Sanders and Ian Speller

This book is based on a selection of papers given at an international conference held in October 2012 at the National University of Ireland Maynooth. The conference was the result of a project established through a partnership involving the Centre for Military History and Strategic Studies at Maynooth, the Centre for Applied Research in Security Innovation at Liverpool Hope University and the Corbett Centre for Maritime Policy Studies at King's College London. The aim of the project is to examine the role and activity of small navies, in the past and in the present, through an inter-disciplinary approach that engages with empirical and theoretical methodologies to further our understanding of a subject that has received relatively little scholarly attention to date. An early result of that project was a joint panel at the 2012 International Studies Association conference in San Diego and this was followed, later in the year, by the conference in Maynooth. The conference proved to be a great success, with over 30 papers given by speakers from 17 different countries and covering a wide variety of topics that included historical studies, an examination of contemporary policy and practice and other papers that had a more theoretical focus. The speakers included a mix of established academics, new researchers and naval personnel (both serving and retired) and this allowed for a very creative environment and some very useful discussions. It would be fair to say that all involved were delighted with the quality of the papers and with the range of subjects examined.

Unfortunately it is not possible to publish all of the conference papers in a single publication, much though we would like to have done so. This volume provides a selection of contributions, some from well-established commentators and others from those relatively new to this field. They have been chosen for the quality of their analysis and also because they provide an insight into the range of topics discussed and the type of issues addressed. Sadly many other excellent papers could not be included. Nevertheless, it is hoped that the selection presented here will inform and also challenge, and thus will contribute to our original aim of sponsoring discussion and debate on the subject matter. It is not intended that this book should represent the end of the process but rather it is intended to be the beginning, a step forward in an on-going project that will continue to focus on the role and activity of small navies.

Thanks are owed to all of the contributors to the conference, including those that we could publish here and also those who, unfortunately, we could not. Particular mention must be made of Professor Eric Grove and Professor Geoffrey Till who gave our keynote speeches and managed to set the tone for the conference and also to challenge us with some searching questions. Thanks also are due to the Irish Tánaiste (Deputy Prime Minister) and Minister for Foreign Affairs and Trade, Mr Eamonn Gilmore TD, for launching the conference and for giving us his own views on the importance of the Irish Naval Service within the context of both Irish and European security.

While academics spend a large amount of time travelling from one conference to another, sharing ideas and sipping wine, it is sometimes more difficult for serving naval personnel and coastguard officials to break free from their very busy schedules and thus we are especially grateful that Rear Admiral Mark Mellett (Deputy Chief of Staff, Irish Defence Forces), Lt Col Wallace Camilleri (Commanding Officer, Armed Forces of Malta Maritime Squadron), Cdr Con Burns RN (EUNAVFOR) and Mr Chris Reynolds (Director, Irish Coast Guard) were able to give papers that focused on their own activity and experiences. Thanks are also due, of course, to all of those who attended the conference and thus contributed to a very enjoyable and stimulating event. The entire event would not have been possible without the assistance of a number of people at NUI Maynooth. There are too many to mention here by name but Dr David Murphy, Robert McCabe, Patrick Finnegan and Colleen Stewart all made a contribution that was clearly above and beyond the call of duty.

The Centre for Applied Research in Security Innovation (CASI) provided the editors of this book with a small grant towards the costs of production and marketing. By extension, this was an investment made in building international recognition of new research capacity at our respective institutions and among our contributors more generally. Thanks are also due to those who directly contributed to the production process. Alex Mulqueen collated and compiled the bibliography while Bill Jack compiled the index. A final word of thanks is due to Thomas Gray and to all the staff at Ashgate for their assistance in taking the book from concept to manuscript to shelf.

Notes on Contributors

Ian Bower is a Senior Research Fellow at the Norwegian Institute for Defence Studies in Oslo. Prior to this he completed a PhD in the Department of War Studies at King's College London. In this capacity he has acted as PhD Coordinator for the 'Asian Security and Warfare' and 'Laughton Naval History' Research Groups. Prior to this he completed an MA in War Studies, also at King's College London. His research focuses on the creation of the Republic of Korea Navy.

Chiara Ruffa is a Marie Curie Research Fellow at the Department of Peace and Conflict Research, Uppsala University and was formerly a Research Fellow on the International Security Program at the Belfer Center for Science and International Affairs at Harvard. She has published numerous articles on European security and contemporary security challenges.

Basil Germond is a Lecturer in Diplomacy and Foreign Policy in the Department of Politics, Philosophy and Religion at Lancaster University. His teaching and research interests include European security, maritime security and sea power. He is the author of *Les Forces Navales Européennes Dans La Période Post-Guerre Froide* (2008), co-editor of the *Routledge Handbook of Transatlantic Security* (2010) and author of the forthcoming book, *The Maritime Dimension of European Security*.

Giampiero Giacomello is Assistant Professor of International Relations at the University of Bologna and also Adjunct Professor of European Studies at the James Madison University EU Policy Studies MA programme, Florence. He is the co-editor of *Security in the West* (Cornell University Press, 2009) and co-author of *Italian Military Operations Abroad*, (Basingstoke: Macmillan, 2012).

Niklas Granholm is Deputy Director of Studies at FOI, the Swedish Defence Research Agency. He is an Associate Fellow of the UK Royal United Services Institute, Fellow of the Royal Swedish Naval Society and the Royal Swedish Academy of War Sciences. He has published works on Swedish defence policy and contributed to a number of defence and strategy related publications, including the *RUSI Journal* and the *IISS Strategic Survey*.

Eric Grove is Professor of Naval History and a Senior Fellow of the Centre for Applied Research in Security Innovation at Liverpool Hope University. Previously, he held the Chair in Naval History and was Director of the Centre for International Security and War Studies at the University of Salford. Recognised internationally as a leading expert on naval history and security affairs he has published many books on these topics including, most recently, *The Royal Navy Since 1815, A New Short History*, (2005). A Fellow of the Royal Historical Society he is also Vice President of the Society for Nautical Research and the Navy Records Society.

Swee Lean Collin Koh is an Associate Research Fellow at the Rajaratnam School of International Studies (RSIS) Military Studies Program, part of the Institute of Defence and Strategic Studies at the RSIS. He is also a doctoral candidate in strategic studies at the RSIS. He is an expert on naval developments in Southeast Asia and the concepts of non-provocative defence and naval arms control.

Rear-Admiral Michael McDevitt (retd.) is a Senior Fellow and former Director of the Center for Naval Analyses in Virginia. He has published numerous works on security in the Indo–Pacific Region and on Chinese maritime strategy and policy. During a career that included 34 years of service with the US Navy he rose to the rank of Rear Admiral, commanded a carrier battle group, was Director of the East Asia Policy Office for the Secretary of Defence under George Bush Snr, served two years as Director of Strategy, War Plans and Policy for US CINCPAC and was Commandant of the National War College in Washington DC.

Rear-Admiral Mark Mellett DSM is Deputy Chief of Staff (Support) of the Irish Defence Forces. Previously he served as the Flag Officer Commanding the Irish Naval Service and held, in a personal capacity, a Visiting Professorship in Maritime Security at the Centre for Applied Research in Security Innovation at Liverpool Hope University. In addition to his experience of extensive military service at home and overseas Admiral Mellett is an expert in maritime security, oceans governance and innovation. He has a keen interest in Public Service Transformation and is a founding champion and governor of the Irish Maritime and Energy Resource Cluster. He holds a PhD in Oceans Governance and an MA in Government and Public Policy and is a graduate of the US Naval War College, Newport RI, the Irish Command and Staff School and the Royal Naval College, Greenwich.

Michael Mulqueen is Professor of Media and Security Innovation and Head of the Department of Media and Communication at Liverpool Hope University where he is also Director of the Centre for Applied Research in Security Innovation. His current research focuses on the development of security innovation as an approach to realising more effective and efficient business outcomes from defence and intelligence organisations and from national security networks. A particular focus is on balancing innovation and ethics of Big Data for security. He is the author of *Re-evaluating Irish National Security Policy: Affordable Threats (2009)*, which is the first academic evaluation of Irish national security, as well as numerous articles on defence and security policy and management.

Jon Robb-Webb is a Lecturer in the Department of Defence Studies at King's College London and the UK Joint Services Command and Staff College. His research interests include naval history and maritime strategy, with a particular interest in the modern Royal Navy and the US Navy since 1945. He has published numerous articles and other scholarly works on these topics and his first book, *The British Pacific Fleet Experience and Legacy, 1944–50,* was published by Ashgate in the Corbett Centre for Maritime Policy Studies Series in 2013.

Deborah Sanders is a Senior Lecturer in the Department of Defence Studies at King's College London and the UK Joint Services Command and Staff College and she is a member of the Corbett Centre for Maritime Policy Studies. She specialises in relations between Russia and Ukraine and has a particular interest in maritime security in the Black Sea region. She has published numerous works relating to these topics including *Maritime Security in the Black Sea: can regional solutions work?* (2009), *Between Rhetoric and Reality: The decline of Russian maritime power in the Black Sea?* (2012) and in 2014 will publish a book on Maritime Power in the Black Sea with Ashgate.

Ian Speller is a Senior Lecturer in the Department of History and the Director of the Centre for Military History and Strategic Studies at the National University of Ireland Maynooth where his responsibilities include teaching at the Irish Defence Forces Military College. Prior to this he was a Senior Lecturer in the Defence Studies Department at King's College London. His research interests include maritime strategy, naval warfare, expeditionary operations and post-war British defence policy. He has published numerous books and articles on these topics and is currently completing a book entitled *Understanding Naval Warfare,* to be published by Routledge in 2014.

Geoffrey Till is Professor of Maritime Studies at King's College London and is Director of the Corbett Centre for Maritime Policy Studies. Until retirement in 2006 he was Dean of Academic Studies at the UK Joint Services Command and Staff College and prior to this was Professor of History at the Royal Naval College Greenwich. Recognised as one of the foremost commentators on maritime strategy and contemporary naval affairs, in 2007 he was a Senior Research Fellow at the Rajaratnam School of International Studies (RSIS), Singapore, and in 2008 the inaugural Sir Howard Kippenberger Visiting Chair in Strategic Studies at the Victoria University of Wellington. In 2009 he returned to the Maritime Security Programme of the RSIS as Visiting Professor. His has written extensively on naval history, strategy and policy and the third edition of his *Seapower. A Guide for the Twenty-First Century* was published in 2013.

Christopher Tuck is a senior lecturer in the Defence Studies Department at King's College London and at the UK Joint Services Command and Staff College. Prior to this he lectured at the Royal Military Academy Sandhurst. His research interests include the American Civil War, land warfare, conflict termination and amphibious operations. A co-author of *Understanding Modern Warfare* in 2008, his most recent book, *Confrontation, Strategy and War Termination: Britain's Conflict with Indonesia, 1963–66,* was recently published by Ashgate in 2013.

Terry Warburton is a specialist in the field of enterprise and innovation and a co-founder of the Centre for Applied Research in Security Innovation at Liverpool Hope University. Prior to this he was Director of the Centre for Enterprise Education at Manchester Metropolitan University. He is a Fellow of the Royal Society of Arts and has contributed to a range of publications on entrepreneurship, enterprise and innovation.

List of Plates and Figures

Plates

1   Port side view of the Norwegian guided missile patrol craft *Skjold* (P 690) underway. The craft is painted in a splinter camouflage scheme. Craft such as these, designed to deny sea control within coastal waters, reflect a well-established task for many small navies. (US Navy Photo by Don Montgomery)   109

2   An example of more recent preoccupations is provided here as the crew of Royal Norwegian Coast Guard patrol boat KV *Tor* (W334) simulates being a skiff taken over by pirates as Royal Norwegian Marinejaggers use rigid hull inflatable boats and a helicopter to storm the skiff and regain control. (US Navy photo by Mass Communication Specialist 1st Class Peter D. Lawlor)   109

3   The crisis management team aboard the Republic of Singapore Navy Formidable-class multi-role frigate RSS *Supreme* (FFG 73) directs firefighters from the machinery control room as part of a shipboard fire-fighting exercise during multi-national Rim of the Pacific (RIMPAC) exercises in 2010. (US Navy Photo provided by Singapore Navy)   110

4   The Republic of Singapore Navy frigate RSS *Supreme* (FFG 73), leads the USS *Chung-Hoon* (DDG 93), the RSS *Vigour* (FFG 92), and RSS *Stalwart* (FFG 72) in a formation during Cooperation Afloat Readiness and Training (CARAT) exercises off Singapore in 2011. CARAT is a series of bilateral exercises held annually in Southeast Asia to strengthen relationships and enhance force readiness. (US Navy photo by Mass Communication Specialist 3rd Class Andrew Ryan Smith)   110

5.   The Republic of Korea Navy destroyer *Munmu the Great* (DDH-976) moves into formation during a trilateral exercise with US Navy and Japan Maritime Self Defense Force ships in the East China Sea in June 2012. The exercise is designed to improve interoperability and readiness among the three navies. (US Navy photo)   111

6. The South Korean Navy submarine *Nae Dyong* (SS 069) underway during multinational Rim of the Pacific (RIMPAC) exercises in 2012. Twenty-two nations, forty-two ships, six submarines, more than 200 aircraft and 25,000 personnel were scheduled to participate in the biennial exercise, RIMPAC is the world's largest international maritime exercise. (US Navy photo provided by Japan Maritime Self-Defense Force)   111

7. Small craft suspected to be from the Islamic Republic of Iran Revolutionary Guard Navy, manoeuvre aggressively in close proximity of US Navy vessels in the Strait of Hormuz in 2008. Vessels such as these offer one way for a small navy to harass its larger counterparts and can contribute to a multi-faceted anti-access strategy. (US Navy photo)   112

8. In 2008 Somali pirates in small boats hijacked the MV *Faina*, a Belize-flagged ship carrying a cargo of Ukrainian T-72 tanks and related equipment. The ship was forced to proceed to an anchorage off the Somali Coast and was released after a ransom was paid. Sometimes the absence of an effective small navy can have serious consequences. (US Navy photo)   112

9. The Armed Forces of Malta counter-piracy vessel protection detachment demonstrates aerial boarding procedures during Eurasia Partnership Capstone (EPC) in 2011. Participants for EPC 2011 included approximately 100 representatives from Azerbaijan, Bulgaria, Georgia, Greece, Malta, Romania, Ukraine and the United States, who focused on strengthening maritime relationships between Eurasian nations. (US. Navy photo by Mass Communication Specialist 3rd Class Caitlin Conroy)   113

10. The Offshore Patrol Vessel HSwMS *Carlskrona* (P04) of the Royal Swedish Navy which operated as HQ ship for EU NAVFOR in 2010. Converted from a minelayer in 2002, the *Carlskrona* reflects the changes in Swedish naval policy since the end of the Cold War. (EU NAVFOR image)   113

11. Personnel from the Belgian Navy Ship *Godetia* (A960) provide weapons familiarisation training to sailors from the Cameroon Navy at Douala (Cameroon) as part of a five-day port visit to kick off the European Africa Partnership Station (APS) West engagement. (US Navy photo by Mass Communication Specialist 1st Class Gary Keen)   114

List of Plates and Figures xvii

12 The Royal Danish Navy frigate HDMS *Iver Huitfeldt* (F361) underway in the Arabian Sea in January 2013. *Iver Huitfeldt* was assigned to Commander, NATO Task Force 508 supporting Operation Ocean Shield, maritime interception operations and counter-piracy missions in the region. (US Navy photo by Mass Communication Specialist 2nd Class Deven B. King) 114

13 Officers from the Vietnamese People's Navy on USS *Chafee* (DDG 90) learn search and rescue plotting techniques during the annual Naval Exchange Activity between Vietnam and the US. The event, held annually since 2010, promotes cooperation and understanding between US and Vietnamese Navy participants. (US Navy photo by Mass Communication Specialist 2nd Class Joy Kirch-Kelling) 115

14 Chilean fast attack craft *Teniente Serrano* (LM 38), *Teniente Orella* (LM 37) and *Teniente Uribe* (LM 39), and patrol craft *Guadiamarina Riquelme* (LM 36) proceed in formation of the coast of Iquique. Vessels such as these are typical amongst many small navies. (US Navy photo by Mass Communication Specialist 1st Class Darryl Wood) 115

15 The L.É. *Niamh* (P52) leads four other Irish patrol vessels during annual exercises. *Niamh* is one of two *Róisín*-class large patrol vessels that were built for the Irish Naval Service in Appledore (UK) in the late 1990s/early 2000s, based on a design adapted from the Mauritanian Vigilant class. (Image provided by Irish Naval Service) 116

16. L.É. *Emer* (P21) is one of three Irish offshore patrol vessels built in the now defunct Verlome yard in Cork in the 1970s and early 1980s, procured with the assistance of funding from the European Union. After decades of service in rough seas these ships are at the end of their useful lives and *Emer* is due to be replaced by one of two new OPVs currently under construction for the Irish Naval Service in the UK. (Image provided by Irish Naval Service) 116

Figures

3.1 'Small' navies' natural 'evolution' 45

5.1 The von Clausewitz Trilogy with Market Perspective 76

8.1	Singapore's Total Fertility Rate per Woman	122
8.2	Geographical Spread of Singapore's External Security Cooperation	126
8.3	Scope of Singapore's External Security Cooperation	126
9.1	SAR Areas in the Mediterranean . [Wikicommons: http://en.wikipedia.org/wiki/File:Area_SAR_IT.svg]	139

Introduction

Ian Speller, Deborah Sanders and Michael Mulqueen

> Historians and naval thinkers have only slowly begun to understand that small navies have distinctive purposes, functions and characteristics in and of their own, and that they are neither the remnants of a past great power nor a curious emblem created on the way to great power status.[1]

A number of years ago the US Navy sponsored an international symposium intended to contribute towards the development of what became their new Maritime Strategy. At that event, held in the UK in 2007, one academic contributor, on hearing a suggestion by another that more could be done to meet the concerns of smaller countries, responded with the bold statement that one should not worry too much about the concerns of '*nations of no account*'. It may be unfair to recall an off-the-cuff remark made in the context of a free-flowing debate but it is relevant here because it began a process that resulted in this book. That comment was made with reference to the Republic of Ireland, a small country with a small navy. It is easy to see how the views of such a state might be ignored by those who prefer to think of maritime strategy in Mahanian terms. A service with only eight patrol boats, all optimised for constabulary duties within the Irish EEZ, might not excite the interest or respect of those whose vision of maritime power is defined by a focus on sea control and global force projection. As will be shown, the comment was rather ill-informed, but it did leave at least one participant wondering why it was that the actions and ideas of smaller nations, and smaller navies, could be so easily dismissed. This then caused some reflection on what exactly it was that smaller navies do and how they do it. Unfortunately the attempt to pursue this line of enquiry was hampered by a paucity of literature devoted to the subject, leading to the logical conclusion that something should be done about this situation. Thus it was that the 'Small Navies Project' was born.

The project is based on a partnership between the Centre for Military History and Strategic Studies at the National University of Ireland Maynooth, the Corbett Centre for Maritime Policy Studies at King's College London, and the Centre for Applied Research in Security Innovation at Liverpool Hope University. The project is designed to examine the role and activities of small navies, both past and present, in order to shed light on an important topic that has too often been

---

[1] John B. Hattendorf, 'The US Navy and "Freedom of the Seas", 1775–1917' in Rolf Hobson & Tom Kristiansen, *Navies in Northern Waters 1721*–2000, (London: Frank Cass, 2004) pp. 151–2.

ignored. From the outset we had a number of general aims. Firstly we sought simply to 'shine a light' on the activity of smaller navies. In terms of their size, capabilities and aspirations most navies are small. Large navies dominate the headlines and receive ample coverage in both popular and academic publications but they are the exception not the rule. Their smaller counterparts have a lower profile except when they emerge as potential allies or enemies and there is a tendency to approach them in such terms, defining them by their relationship to larger navies regardless of whether this actually provides the most useful way in which to understand them. Thus, we sought to examine smaller navies in their own right and on their own terms.

In addition to the above we aimed to question whether the traditional concepts and theories of maritime strategy applied to smaller navies in the same way that they did to the large ones. Historically there has been a tendency for people to approach maritime strategy from a perspective built upon an examination of the activity of larger navies on the assumption that the resultant concepts and principles will apply to small navies as much as to large ones. While this may indeed be the case the relative paucity of literature devoted specifically to smaller navies makes it difficult to draw firm conclusions and the assumption at least deserves to be tested. This question relates closely to our final aim which was to assess whether or not it was actually worthwhile to think of 'Small Navies' as a separate category at all. The intention here was to ascertain whether small navies share sufficient characteristics to make it even worthwhile to think of them in such a way. Is it necessary and is it possible to make meaningful generalisations about small navies?

Contemporary events in the shape of the financial instabilities which, from 2008 affected many states and had direct implications on defence budgets, seemed to bring this question of the specific or the general into sharper focus. Could it be argued that seemingly modest cuts (e.g. cuts to sea days of a single ship) would cause a disproportionally negative impact upon a small navy's capacity? Conversely, would it be easier, because of their smallness, to develop small navies so that they could more nimbly adapt to evolving networked challenges including environmental degradation and struggles for ideas? If smaller navies could not stimulate the impressive port economies on which major cities hosting large fleets prospered, would they face a higher risk when governments made decisions about where to make cuts? These and others provided contestable ground on which the case for a distinctive treatment of small navies could be made.

In pursuit of these objectives the partner institutions jointly held an international conference at the National University of Ireland Maynooth in October 2012 and this book contains a selection of papers presented at this event. Unfortunately we were not able to include all of the conference submissions and a full list of speakers and presentations is provided at appendix A. The papers included here provide a useful cross-section of the topics addressed and they offer an insightful examination of a range of subjects of relevance to the aims noted above. As will be seen, we generated as many questions as we did answers. Some speakers adopted a traditional approach to maritime power and strategy while others came at the subject from a different angle. Some believed that there was utility in thinking differently about small navies, others were less convinced. Agreement on this issue was elusive. This was exactly what we had hoped for and was, we think, the sign of a very productive gathering. The conference thus represented a useful first step in a project that, we hope, will continue to investigate these issues.

Nations and Navies of No Account?

It is worth noting that as the aforementioned maritime strategy symposium was underway, in July 2007, and Ireland and other small countries were described as being of no account, the Irish Naval Service was helping to intercept 62 bales of cocaine, worth some €500m, in Dunlough Bay off County Cork. The following year, in another major interdiction operation, the Irish Naval Service seized a second massive haul of drugs, this time 200 miles off the southwest coast of Cork. The total amount of cocaine recovered in these two operations was 3.2 tonnes with an estimated street value of €1.2 billion ($1.5 billion).[2] Given the size of these seizures it appears likely that the final destination for most of the drugs was not the streets of Cork, Galway or Dublin (in Ireland) but rather Liverpool, Birmingham and London (in the UK), making the interdiction operations as important for the security of Britain as they were for Ireland. This *'nation of no account'*, with no aircraft carriers, cruisers, destroyers, frigates or submarines was making an important contribution to national and international security, even if some chose not to recognise it. Others, of course, did recognise it. One of the laudable features of the new US Maritime Strategy, published in October 2007, was that it made explicit reference to the contribution that all navies make towards the maintenance of maritime security and it articulated a desire to find ways to foster and sustain cooperative relationships with other navies, both large and small, in a collaborative exercise to protect the maritime commons.[3]

The emphasis currently placed on maritime security, the maintenance of good order at sea, anti-piracy operations and the like, and the recognition that large navies alone cannot meet all of the challenges that these pose, gives small navies a relevance that may not previously have been so obvious. It seems clear that the contribution that they make should be examined and understood. Certainly this has been reflected in US policy, notably through the emphasis placed on engagement with international partners and on capability building initiatives such as the Africa Partnership Station (APS). Facilitated by the US Naval Forces Europe–Africa, the APS is designed to build African maritime security and safety capability and

---

[2] Deputy Alan Shatter (Minister of Defence), 'Naval Service Operations', Dáil Éireann debate, 7 February 2013. http://oireachtasdebates.oireachtas.ie/ (accessed 01 May 2013).

[3] US Navy, US Marine Corps, US Coastguard, *A Co-operative Strategy for the 21st Century*, (October, 2007)

capacity, to the mutual advantage of all engaged. This is not limited to US–African cooperation. In early 2013, for example, the Belgian command and logistic support ship BNS *Godetia* participated in multi-national exercises under the auspices of the APS and, in collaboration with the US Navy, assisted in training personnel from Benin, Gabon and the Republic of Congo in boarding operations.[4] This is a good example of a small navy helping a large navy to help other small navies.

The imperative to help small African navies to help themselves (and each other) has been reinforced by the experience of Somali piracy, which demonstrates what can happen when a state is not in a position to police its own waters. Sometimes the absence of a small navy can have rather serious consequences. The Somali experience does, of course, also show how small navies can contribute to major international operations. This has been manifest in the European Union's first naval mission, Operation Atalanta, launched in 2008 to deal with the growing threat of piracy off the coast of Somalia. Although enabled by some 'big navy' capabilities, and with its headquarters in Northwood in the UK, EU NAVFOR has been supported by a number of the smaller EU navies, including those of Belgium, the Netherlands, Malta and Sweden and has included vessels from non-EU navies including Norway.[5] The Maltese contribution to Op Atalanta included the provision of a staff officer to the HQ at Northwood and also two Vessel Protection Detachments deployed on the Dutch ships HMNLS *Johann De Witt* and HMNLS *Zuiderkrui*.

The Maltese involvement in Op Atalanta is noteworthy. The Armed Forces Malta (AFM) have a relatively modest Maritime Squadron equipped with 11 offshore and inshore patrol vessels, and an equally modest Air Wing, with which to protect and police Malta's maritime domain, meet Maltese responsibilities for search and rescue, cooperate in enforcement operations with police and customs agencies and contribute to international commitments such as Frontex and Atalanta. Nevertheless, the AFM Maritime Squadron has still found the time, energy and resources to pioneer useful links with it near neighbour Libya, helping to train the post-Gaddafi navy to meet its own obligations to police and protect Libyan waters.[6]

Swedish participation in Operation Atalanta was reflective of a major change in policy since the end of the Cold War. While the Royal Swedish Navy was once preoccupied by the clear and identifiable danger posed by Soviet forces, and thus emphasised coastal defence and sea denial in the Baltic, the removal of that

---

[4] US Naval Forces Africa-Europe/US 6th Fleet Public Affairs, 'Belgian Ship Assists Africa Partnership Station', http://1.usa.gov/1khUF1c (accessed 16 May 2013).

[5] Non-EU navies including Croatia, Montenegro, Serbia and Ukraine have contributed staff officers to the Operational Headquarters and to the Force Headquarters. See the EUNAVFOR website, http://eunavfor.eu/

[6] Lt Col Wallace Camilleri, (Commanding Officer of the AFM Maritime Squadron) 'The Maltese Maritime Squadron', presentation to the 'Small Navies Conference', 20 October 2012. 'AFM in Tripoli to train Libyan Navy' in *Malta Today* (27 August 2012).

threat has left it free to focus on a broader range of tasks that include making a contribution to crisis management operations far from home.[7] In different seas other navies still feel threatened by their neighbours or by extra-regional powers and thus continue to focus on a mix of sea denial, coastal defence and perhaps also on attacks on merchant shipping as a means of protecting their interests or of deterring attack. While the means by which they may do this could be novel, exploiting both new technologies and old in pursuit of anti-access and area denial strategies, the basic rationale is well established and conforms to a very traditional idea of what small navies do when threatened by a more powerful rival. Not even the mighty US Navy can safely ignore the potential challenge posed by a foe such as the Iranian Navy who might, given the opportunity, be able to inflict some very costly damage even in a battle that it would lose. Similarly, in East and Southeast Asia the growth of Chinese naval strength has been met (but not matched) by a growth in the size of other navies within the region. These have an impact on regional balances that it would be imprudent to ignore. The lesson is clear: small navies can and do matter. It would appear foolish to describe them, or the states that deploy them, as being of no account.

What is a Small Navy?

It is surprisingly difficult to define clearly what one means by the term 'small navy'. The definitional challenge is not helped by the fact that so little has been written about small navies as a group. Perhaps the easiest approach would be to state that a small navy is one that is not large. Unfortunately this simply shifts but does not resolve the problem. What is a large navy or a medium sized navy? The US Navy is clearly large, and when measured against it all others seem small, but this is not entirely helpful. The situation is complicated by the fact that many navies might prefer not to be called 'small', whether for reasons of pride, politics, or delusion. It may be significant that some commentators, including Jacob Borresen, have written about small navies without actually employing that phrase.[8] For many navies acceptance of the tag 'small' would represent an intolerable affront to their sense of self and might serve to undermine their position within the national institutional hierarchy. The Royal New Zealand Navy has found an interesting way around this, describing their aspiration to be the best 'small nation navy' in the world.[9] Unfortunately this is not very helpful either. Small nations have often deployed rather large navies, as did Venice, Portugal and Oman in

---

[7] See chapter 11.

[8] For example see Jacob Borresen, 'Coastal Power: The Sea Power of the Coastal State and the management of Maritime Resources' in Hobson & Kristiansen, *Navies in Northern Waters*, pp. 249–275.

[9] See the Royal New Zealand Navy *RNZN 148, Strategic Plan 2008–2025* available online at http://bit.ly/1dO6Xtg

the past, and large nations or states have often had small navies, as did Germany before Tirpitz and China until recently. Geoffrey Till, in one of the few scholarly articles to address this topic directly, reflected on the difficulty of categorisation in a situation where a small navy is not necessarily a weak one and a large navy is not necessarily powerful. He suggested that definitions need to take account of the size and nature of the fleet, geographic range, function and capability, access to high-grade technology, and reputation.[10]

As Till suggests, a focus on size alone is insufficient given that quantitative measures provide a very unreliable guide to capability and no guide at all to intended roles and missions. Is a fleet with 12 old, unreliable and badly maintained Soviet-era missile boats really 'larger' than one with six modern offshore patrol boats backed up by a well-developed shore infrastructure? Is size absolute or is it relative? In some areas of the world, i.e. Europe, a navy of a half a dozen patrol boats might seem rather small while in others, such as in sub-Saharan Africa, it might be relatively large. Navies of equal size might seem either large or small depending on what is expected of them or who or what they are up against. Is a fleet of 12 vessels capable of contributing to international operations far from home really smaller than one with 18 ships able only to operate in their own EEZ? It is also necessary to remember that one really ought not to think of navies as separate institutions but rather as one element in a state's wider maritime power. A 'small' navy backed up by a large air force devoted to maritime operations might, in reality, be less small than another force with more ships but less support from its friends in light blue. In addition, a small, but professional and well-trained navy is likely to be more effective than a larger navy that is reliant on conscripts and which neglects the training and education of its naval personnel. Similarly, a small navy operated by service personnel who are justly rewarded within society for their service, through the provision of good pay and conditions, is also likely to be more effective than a larger navy afflicted by low morale. All of these factors suggest that a focus on numbers alone is not helpful.

There have, of course, been numerous attempts to define hierarchies of naval power and these are examined in Chapter 3 of this book. Notable examples were provided by Morris, Booth, Till and, perhaps most famously, by Eric Grove in 1990.[11] Grove's nine-fold system of categorisation focused on the size, roles, range and overall capabilities of a navy to develop a hierarchy that ranged from the major global force projection navy (complete) at the top down to constabulary navies (rank 8) and token navies (rank 9) at the bottom. The system has proven popular and Professor Grove re-visited his categories in the opening address of

---

[10] Geoffrey Till, 'Can small navies stay afloat?' in *Jane's Navy International*, May 2003.

[11] Ken Booth, *Navies and Foreign Policy*, (New York: Holmes & Meier, 1979) pp. 120–121. Geoffrey Till, *Modern Seapower. An Introduction*, (London: Brassey's, 1987) p. 47. Michael Morris, *Expansion of Third World Navies*, (London: Macmillan, 1987) p. 87. Eric Grove, *The Future of Seapower*, (London: Routledge, 1990), pp. 237–240.

the Small Navies Conference (see Chapter 1). Where the dividing line between small or large navies might sit in his original model was not made clear. One might suggest that navies in ranks five (adjacent force projection navies) down to rank nine (token navies) tend to be small. Whether they are small because they aspire only to fill these roles or fill these roles because they are small will, presumably, vary according to circumstances and history is full of examples of navies that moved from one category to another and, in the process, became either large or small. Such movement, however, is not inevitable and it would be erroneous to believe that a small navy is simply a large navy in waiting or in decline. Grove's system focuses less on the size of the navy per se (although this is clearly a relevant factor) than on the role that it fulfils, implying that it is the latter rather than the former that is most important. This general point is reinforced by Geoffrey Till in Chapter 2 of this book, challenging the idea that it is even worth thinking about small navies as a distinct category.

Unfortunately this all leaves us no nearer to a precise definition. For practical purposes, when planning the conference, we borrowed from Till the suggestion that a small navy is one with both '*limited means and aspirations*'.[12] This has the advantage of being flexible and of allowing individuals to choose for themselves what they thought of as 'small'. The result was a broad range of case studies that included the modest navies of Ireland and Malta, through to the Republic of Korea Navy, which might be said to be on the large side of small. It also included an examination of the British Pacific Fleet of 1944–45, perhaps the most powerful fleet that Britain has ever deployed overseas and one that was far more capable than any other navy in the world at that time, with the exception of the US Navy. The British Pacific Fleet could thus only be considered as being small when compared to its (much) larger US ally, but its inclusion allowed for some reflection on the extent to which it may, or may not, have experienced similar dynamics to other navies that found themselves operating as a junior partner to a larger and more capable force. This approach also allowed for the inclusion of the concept of distinct small navies existing within a larger force, such as the US brown-water fleet that operated in Vietnam in the 1960s, an intriguing topic worthy of further research.[13]

Does Size Matter?

It seems clear that any more precise definition of what a 'small navy' is requires one to answer the question of whether or not small navies are indeed different, the difference then furnishing the definition. The traditional approach is to suggest that

---

[12] Till, 'Can small navies stay afloat'.
[13] For example see Jonathan Chavanne, 'Boats, rivers and mines. The brown water culture of the US Navy in Vietnam', in the *International Journal of Naval History* (forthcoming) at http://www.ijnhonline.org/

the differences are more those of degree than of kind, that small navies face the same kind of challenges as their larger counterparts even if they are forced to seek different solutions. Thus Geoffrey Till has argued that the conceptual differences between large navies and small ones are '*more a matter of degree than of kind*' and that '*[t]here is in fact little that is special or distinctive about a smaller navy*'.[14] He developed this line of argument at the conference and makes a persuasive case to this effect in this book.

On the other hand, one can question the extent to which the inputs and outputs of maritime strategy really are the same for smaller navies, or at least argue that they affect small navies in markedly different ways. For example, it is true that all navies face resource constraints but small navies, denied economies of scale, need to deal with these in particular ways. Traditional approaches include multi-national collaboration, role specialisation, the development of niche capabilities, design compromises and the abandoning of roles and/or capabilities that no longer appear vital (in the eyes of the government if not necessarily to those of the navy). Matters may be complicated by the competing desire to buy the best equipment at the lowest price and a political requirement to be seen to support domestic construction and thus jobs. One potentially smart route through this – using forms of corporate innovation systems to stimulate low cost/high value solutions for naval needs – may be an important breakthrough but one at an early stage of development. More commonly, second-hand equipment provided by friends and allies will offer a short cut towards capability, but such equipment is often sub-optimal for local needs or conditions and may come at the cost of dependency. Compromise is a familiar consequence for those with shallow pockets. Equally, however, the particular needs of a smaller navy may not match those of a larger ally and this may spur investment and initiative such as the Norwegian Navy's sponsorship of the Penguin anti-ship missile or the Israeli development of the Gabriel missile.[15] It is true that all of these problems affect larger navies as much as they do smaller ones. The fact that Britain currently has no long-range fixed wing maritime patrol aircraft after this capability was abandoned by the Royal Air Force, while its smaller neighbour, Ireland, has retained such a capability, offers a stark reminder of this. Nevertheless, it may still be the case that smaller navies have to deal with these challenges in particular ways and that these may be worthy of investigation to identify areas of commonality and of difference.

Small navies clearly face particular personnel challenges. It may be difficult to maintain an appropriate training structure at a reasonable cost, implying dependence on an ally or perhaps some form of partnership with the merchant marine. The Irish Naval Service provides an excellent example of the latter, maintaining state of the art training and educational facilities adjacent to the Naval Base at Cork

---

[14] Till, op. cit.

[15] For an example see Christopher Chant, *Small Craft Navies*, (London: Arms and Armour Press, 1992) also see the discussion in David Wilson (ed.), *Maritime War in the Twenty-First Century*, (Canberra: RAN Seapower Centre, 2001).

through a public private partnership with Cork Institute of Technology and Focus Education.[16] Even with such initiatives it may be difficult to ensure appropriate systems of promotion within a small navy in which opportunities for advancement are more limited and it may also be difficult to ensure an appropriate balance of ship to shore duties, with serious implications for both recruitment and retention. As Jacob Borresen has noted, it can be difficult to gain appropriate command experience in a navy with few ships and even the provision of sufficient sea-time may be difficult in a navy built around missile boats and fast attack craft, vessels that, by design, necessarily spend less time at sea than do larger ships.[17] This may increase the importance of multi-national collaborations and missions if these provide the opportunity for exercises on a scale and command roles of a type that cannot be provided at a national level. Limited size may, in some cases, be a spur to close and fruitful joint cooperation, or it could see the navy subsumed within a larger defence organisation that is generally unsympathetic to its needs.

Of course, and as Till argues in Chapter 2, many of the apparently unique challenges facing small navies are also faced by larger ones in some form or another and it is not difficult to identify obvious differences between small navies. This may suggest that broad generalisations are problematic. It may indeed be the case that small navies share the same roles and concerns of larger navies but they face different challenges in meeting them. Alternately one might argue that the problems that they face and the solutions that they seek are unique and cannot usefully be examined using the same model as applied to larger navies. Further research is required to identify which is the case. Unfortunately, small navies have received relatively little attention from naval historians and maritime strategists, and this is particularly true of those writing in the English language. The scholar of naval history is blessed with an abundance of published material focusing on the two major navies of the past three hundred years, the British and US Navies and, by extension, there is a lesser but still significant body of work that studies their main rivals. Much less is written on the rest, that is to say, on the majority of world navies. In choosing to focus on small navies this book aims to help address this situation.

Structure

The book is divided into two parts: part one focuses on the idea of the small navy, with Chapters 1, 2 and 3 tackling this and the issue of definitions. Chapters 4 and 5 concentrate on the idea of innovation, challenging existing assumptions and addressing an aspect of the experience of small navies that is rarely if ever discussed in the existing literature. Part two examines the experience of small

---

[16] For details see the National Maritime College of Ireland website, http://www.nmci.ie/. Also see Chapters 4 and 5.

[17] Borresen, op. cit. pp. 249–275.

navies through a series of case studies that explore the history, role and activity of a number of navies from East Asia, Europe and North America in order to draw out issues of enduring importance. Each chapter stands on its own merits and offers an authoritative discussion of the matter at hand whilst also contributing to the central theme of the book.

The opening address of the conference was provided by Eric Grove who revisited his 1990 typology of navies and this is reproduced here as Chapter 1. Grove notes that the removal of the old Soviet Fleet means that one of his original categories (rank 2: global force projection (partial)), is no longer relevant but argues for the continuing utility of the overall model and he identifies a number of changes in where navies now sit within this hierarchy. In his concluding remarks, he stresses three key points. First, that the ranking of navies has been squeezed up and down as many smaller navies have developed greater reach and capability while others have become little more than constabulary navies. Second, that the US political and fiscal crisis could see the beginning of a greater medium-term decline and rebalancing of US naval forces and lastly, that although we have not seen the development of a European navy (anticipated in his earlier work), we have witnessed greater European naval cooperation within both the EU and NATO.

In Chapter 2 Geoffrey Till examines two closely related and important questions: whether small navies are different from medium or large navies and whether small navies are in fact different from each other generically. Till argues that small navies are not actually that much different from larger navies. The key issue for Till, is not so much the number of assets a navy has, small or large, but how it balances these against its roles and commitments. He also argues that the specialisation provided by small navies often makes them invaluable to larger navies and that the 'skilful combination of geographical position and asymmetric technology could well make a notionally small navy (in number terms) disproportionately effective strategically'. As has already been noted, he considers the extent to which it is possible to generalise about small navies and questions the use of the term as an organising concept, suggesting that the differences between 'large' and 'small' navies are no greater than the many differences between various small navies.

Basil Germond discusses the practical implications of the classification of navies along a 'small'/'large' line in Chapter 3. His aim is to highlight the links between the production of knowledge (i.e. navies' binary identities and categorisation) and the dominant discourse on power projection. Germond begins by examining the criteria used to classify navies, so as to show what a 'small navy' is according to the generally accepted representation in the specialised academic literature and naval establishments. Germond then shows how this representation contributes to the dominant discourse on the projection of security. He argues that by reproducing the structure and capabilities of the larger navies, 'smaller navies' perform both traditional tasks (such as 'out-of area' deployments) and can 'find salvation' through their participation in large scale operations (such counter-piracy operations) far away from home.

In Chapter 4 Michael Mulqueen and Terry Warburton examine how small navies can survive in an age of austerity. They argue that by the careful rolling out of systemic innovation – an approach to organisational management, derived from industrial economics, which promotes user, lead user and open sources problem solving models – small navies can increase their productivity, efficiency and military effectiveness. For Mulqueen and Warburton, small navies which adapt to incorporate systemic innovation can be reconfigured from being expensive standing assets that consume national income to become actively engaged generators of national wealth. They argue that while there are many challenges facing small navies in adopting systematic innovation, this approach can awaken latent innovation, expand the potential for problem solving, de-conflict decision making and, generally, help make small navies more adaptive organisations. Mark Mellett develops some of these ideas in Chapter 6 where he examines how the growing realisation of the important link between Ireland's maritime wealth and its national interests has led to the transformation of the Irish Naval Service (INS), in particular the development of a survival ethos that has 'helped institutionalise agility and innovation'. Mellett argues that small navies, like the INS, can play a crucial role in optimising the sea as a resource for their governments and society while at the same time protecting national interests at and from the sea. In conclusion, he argues that as a result of these fundamental shifts in focus and orientation, the INS 'seeks to justify the resources it is allocated, add value through its development process, game change through the creation process of innovation and transform the services it delivers'.

In the first of the case studies in part two Michael McDevitt explores the strategic rationale and budgetary arguments for the ongoing modernisation and expansion of the South Korean, Vietnamese and Australian navies. For McDevitt, the South Korean decision to build a modestly sized multi-mission navy can be traced to North Korean belligerency, lingering antipathy towards Japan, latent worries about China, dependence on international trade and a desire to be seen as a responsible global actor. He argues that Vietnamese naval modernisation, fuelled by its economic growth, can be explained by the desire to develop a credible deterrent against China. Despite what McDevitt identifies as the very real requirement to develop a naval hedge against the power projection capabilities of the Chinese navy, the decision by the Australian government to focus on reducing the national debt has led to a delay in the implementation of its ambitious naval force modernisation plans.

Undertaking a detailed examination of just one of these regional navies, in Chapter 7, Ian Bowers examines the expansion and modernisation of the Republic of Korea Navy (ROKN), tracing its growth from a limited small navy to a medium force able to operate on a regional level performing both blue water and traditional deterrent operations. Bowers argues that although the ROKN has traditionally been a small navy, subsequent force modernisation plans represented a 'major step change' in operational thinking for the ROKN given its previous focus on littoral operations and deterrence. Bowers argues that although the transformation process has been complex it has given the ROKN a regional operating capability and a much greater range of war fighting options. However, as Bowers points out the ROKN faces two key challenges in maintaining its drive for a regional maritime capability: the shifting political winds in Seoul and the unpredictable threat from North Korea.

Swee Lean Collin Koh examines the prospects for and challenges facing the 'Best Little Navy in Southeast Asia', the Singapore Navy (RSN) in Chapter 8. He argues that the RSN has demonstrated an ability to 'punch above its weight' through the effective utilisation of technology, human capital and diplomacy. However, as Koh points out practical and geopolitical challenges have affected both the RSN's force development and cooperation with regional and international partners. Despite these challenges, Koh argues that the RSN is 'arguably the best-equipped navy in Southeast Asia' and provides an interesting case study of the ability of a small navy to transcend its physical limitations and make an important contribution to regional and international security.

While Chapters 7 and 8 focus on individual navies in Asia, in Chapter 9 Giampiero Giacomello and Chiara Ruffa examine the challenges facing small navies in Europe as they seek to cooperate under the auspices of Frontex, an EU agency set up in 2004 to promote, coordinate and develop European border management. By comparing the maritime operations launched by France, Italy and Spain within the Frontex framework, they argue that these maritime operations (often with a humanitarian focus) have been largely ineffective. The ability of small navies to address humanitarian issues through Frontex is hampered by severe coordination problems among states and within states tasked with border control in the Mediterranean. For Giacomello and Ruffa, small navies can play an important role in combined humanitarian operations if other law enforcement agencies are provided with more and better guidelines and there is closer cross-national coordination.

Chapters 10 and 11 focus on navies in the Black and Baltic seas, respectively. In Chapter 10 Deborah Sanders examines Romania's maritime power and argues that while Romania has important security and economic interests in the Black Sea, it has struggled to develop a small professional navy. She argues that the challenges of Romania's post-communist transformation, in particular the lack of economic reform and restructuring, political infighting and instability and the lack of defence reform, all delayed the building of a small well-equipped navy. As Sanders points out, a number of quantitative and qualitative changes introduced since 2001 have created the enabling conditions for the development of an increasingly effective Romanian navy. Romania's maritime power in the Black Sea is, however, likely to be adversely affected by poor relations with two Black Sea neighbours, the Russian Federation and Ukraine.

In Chapter 11 Niklas Granholm examines the development of the Royal Swedish Navy (RSwN) from a force focused on coastal defence and local sea denial to one able to contribute to international operations overseas. In common with the Irish example discussed in Chapters 4 and 5, the issues of affordability and cost effectiveness are paramount when exploring future options. In order to determine which type of small navy would best meet Sweden's security needs,

Granholm develops three alternative models for the RSwN which must all address what he identifies as three essential future maritime roles: protection of Sweden's territorial waters, constabulary operations away from home waters and maintaining good order at sea in the Arctic Ocean.

While the preceding chapters focus largely on contemporary concerns Chapters 12 and 13 examine small navies from a historical perspective. In Chapter 12 Christopher Tuck examines the Confederate Navy as a case study for assessing the strategic value of small navies. Tuck argues that the Confederate Navy constitutes a paradoxical example of a small navy. Whilst the Confederate States Navy (CSN) was undoubtedly a small navy especially when compared to its adversary, the United States Navy, it began the war with a 'big navy' mentality; it embraced sea control, decisive battle and the navy as an independent instrument of victory. Paradoxically, as the Confederate Navy got bigger its ambitions dwindled, and it began to prioritise the sorts of roles often associated with small navies such as sea denial and coastal defence. Tuck argues that while the CSN largely failed to meet its early objectives, it was successful in meeting more moderate goals making an important contribution to the ability of the Confederate state to protract the war, creating opportunities for Confederate success. His examination is under-pinned by a belief that one needs to think 'strategically' when assessing the value of a small navy.

In the final chapter, Chapter 13, Jon Robb-Webb examines the experience of the British Pacific Fleet in 1944–45. This fleet, perhaps the most powerful naval force ever deployed overseas by the British, was dwarfed in size and strength by the US Navy and experienced a range of challenges when trying to operate alongside its ally, not least due to the requirement to sustain operations at great range from its bases. The experience provides an interesting insight into the difficulties facing a large navy having to adjust to a reduction in relative size and status, learning to operate with a larger, more capable and, in some respects, more advanced partner. It also sheds light on a neglected yet important aspect of the history of the Royal Navy in the Second World War. The manner in which a great navy can find itself struggling to keep up with a peer offers an interesting perspective on what one might mean by the term 'small'.

Hopefully, when considered together, these chapters meet our first objective, to 'shine a light' on some of the various activities of small navies. They may also go some way towards the process of addressing our other aims, questioning whether it is possible to make meaningful generalisations about such navies, although clearly more work needs to be done on this matter. Regardless of whether or not it is possible to generalise about small navies, and whether or not they share many common characteristics (and the jury is still out on this matter), it is still useful to focus our attention on the activities of such navies. We believe that to ignore them is to fail to truly understand maritime power and strategy. We hope that you enjoy reading this book and also that it may prompt you to dig a little deeper into the activity of navies that, while small, do appear to be of some account.

Chapter 1
The Ranking of Smaller Navies Revisited
(Opening address to the conference)

Eric Grove

When I was commissioned to write my book 'The Future of Sea Power' by Routledge in the late 1980s[1] I was asked to produce 'quite an academic' book with a bit of theory in it. Most of my approach in the book was empirical, a methodology with which I am much happier, but at the end I developed three theoretical frameworks based on the previous analysis. In the first I tried to bring up to date Mahan's analysis of the foundations of sea power, something that itself had been produced at the request of the great man's publishers. In the second I based a revised triangular analysis of the roles of navies on the seminal work of Ken Booth.[2] This has been further developed by the Royal Navy in its latest iteration of British Maritime Doctrine.[3]

The third was 'A Typology for Navies'. Again this owed much to existing literature, notably M.A. Morris in his book *Expansion of Third World Navies* and Steve Haines in his article 'Third World Navies, Myths and Realities'.[4] I sought to go further than these authors to produce a global naval hierarchy that would form the basis of 'some speculative remarks about the future balance of naval power'. I classified as navies 'all those forces capable of exerting force at sea, not necessarily just those bureaucratically organised into a 'navy'.[5] I also used the concept of '*force* projection' that implied 'a capacity to engage in "sea control" and "sea denial" as well as "*power*" projection'. My criteria were not only the sheer number of available assets but their types and sophistication and, crucially,

---

[1] Eric Grove, *The Future of Sea Power* (London: Routledge, 1990). This book was also simultaneously published by the Naval Institute Press. In the event this proved to be a very bad time to attempt such a work as the Soviet Union's collapse and the end of the Cold War undermined significant parts of my analysis.

[2] Ken Booth, *Navies and Foreign Policy* (New York: Holmes and Meier, 1979).

[3] Joint Doctrine Publication 0-10, British Maritime Doctrine, 2011, Chapter 2, Section 2.

[4] Michael Morris, *Expansion of Third World Navies* (London, Palgrave Macmillan, 1987); Haines, Steve. 'Third World Navies, Myths and Realities' *Naval Forces*, April 1988.

[5] Grove, *Future of Sea Power*, p. 237.

the level of afloat support. This provided 'reach' that would also be reflected in the geographical extent of routine deployment.

I came up with nine rungs on the ladder. Top was the only 'Major Global Force Projection Navy – Complete' that of the United States. Next was the only rank two navy, that of the other super power, the Soviet Union, which at that time deployed a 'Major Global Force Projection Navy – Partial'. Third were the 'Medium Global Force Projection Navies' which at that time were only two, Britain and France, both of which possessed nuclear powered submarines, both ballistic missile and attack, sea control surface forces, an amphibious squadron and afloat support. Both were, to a greater or lesser extent capable of operating globally, the first on the basis of group deployments based in Europe, the latter with a more global permanent stationing of assets.

Fourth were the 'Medium Regional Force Projection Navies' able in Morris's words 'to project force into the adjoining ocean basin'.[6] These were the three main Asian navies at this level: India, Japan and China plus the major NATO navies of Canada, Italy, the Netherlands, West Germany and Spain. Both NATO and the Western European Union had provided both force and reach multiplication. Even Belgium had deployed vessels with organic support to the Gulf. South America had two such navies, Brazil and Argentina, both of which had aircraft carriers.

Fifth were 'Adjacent Force Projection Navies' with 'some ability to project force well offshore'.[7] These included Portugal, Greece, Turkey, Chile, Peru, Israel, South Africa, Taiwan, Pakistan and New Zealand. I noted that the two Koreas might be moving into this category along with the major Gulf navies: Iran, Iraq and Saudi Arabia. These were, however, still in rank six 'Offshore Territorial Defence Navies' with high levels of capability in operations up to about 200 miles from the shore. These included most remaining European and North African navies, the mid-level Latin American navies, Bangladesh, Indonesia, Malaysia, Thailand and the Philippines and, in Africa, Nigeria. These navies had the sustainability offered by frigates or large corvettes and/or a submarine force.

Rank seven were 'Inshore Territorial Defence Navies', navies capable of coastal combat rather than just constabulary duties. Rank eight were those navies only capable of constabulary duties. Some countries of course, then as now, deployed specialist coastguards in this role but other navies in Africa, Latin America and Africa, (and Ireland in Europe) had few, if any capabilities beyond the policing function. Finally came Rank nine, the 'token navies' those of the poorest countries with 'a formal organisational structure and a few coastal craft, but little else'.[8]

In my conclusions, I expected that 'the naval balance' would change more towards the top than further down the scale. I thought that the US Navy would not maintain quite the level of supremacy it had in 1990 and the Soviet, Chinese and Japanese navies would approach it more closely as global navies as would

---

[6] Ibid. p. 25.
[7] Ibid.
[8] Ibid. p. 33.

a collective European navy. Then, in the next rank would come the 'significant regional navies': India, the larger South American fleets and Australia. Below these would be 'the lesser African and Asian navies, and the two mavericks in Israel and South Africa; then would come the longer-ranged and the shorter-ranged coast defence navies, the coastguards; and finally the mass of token navies'.[9]

Things have not quite gone as expected, although navies have indeed moved towards the top of the scale. Most notably the end of the Soviet Union abolished rank two as it existed in 1990. The old rank three navies now became rank two medium global force projection navies, a group that now includes a diminished Russian fleet. France remains here as does Britain, despite its temporary abandonment of aircraft carriers, given the UK's powerful nuclear submarine fleet and still significant amphibious 'Response Force Task Group' and afloat support capacity. Carriers will soon be back. China and India are both now coming into this level with carriers, nuclear powered submarines, major amphibious units and the beginnings of afloat support. China has projected force into the Mediterranean and India has gone both to the limits of the Indian Ocean and beyond and its wider ambitions are clear.

Japan is a difficult navy to classify. It is still deliberately kept limited in reach, although perhaps paradoxically, it has used its tankers to support coalition forces in the Indian Ocean. Its coastguard also utilises its large patrol vessels as escorts for plutonium transport ships on distant voyages. There will soon be four helicopter carriers (euphemistically referred to as 'destroyers') and its MSDF has some of the most sophisticated surface combatants in the world. It does not yet have nuclear powered submarines, although it has perhaps the finest fleet of conventional boats in the world, the latest of which have air independent propulsion, useful at shorter ranges. The three LPDs are designed for regional contingencies. On balance, therefore, I would put Japan at the head of rank three 'Medium Regional Force Projection Navies', although more by choice than sheer national potential.

Other rank three medium navies 'on the up' are South Korea that has jumped from moving into the old rank five in 1990 to this elevated status with its Aegis destroyers, large submarine flotilla and growing amphibious and replenishment force. North Korea has moved down a rank. Other rank threes are Australia with its impressive Canberra class LHDs, Hobart class destroyers and Brazil with its carrier and nuclear submarine plans (rank two by the 2020s?). Singapore has also moved rapidly up the order from the old rank seven to the current rank three with its frigates, general purpose LPDs and growing submarine force. Few navies get more capability from 4,500 personnel. Singapore is perhaps the world's most powerful 'small navy'.

The other major NATO and European navies remain at the new rank three: Canada, especially if it replaces its support vessels; Italy with its new carrier; Spain with its new strategic projection ship, LPDs and missile frigates; and Germany with its Berlin class auxiliaries giving useful reach. The combined Dutch/Belgian

---

[9] Ibid., p. 240.

fleet is still there despite cut-backs. Both the Danish and Norwegian navies have in their different ways made considerable improvements in force posture and are now in rank three. Sweden is moving into it with a remarkably wide-ranging fleet of conventional submarines and corvettes, but it requires the delivery of the much discussed support/logistic vessels to be firmly in the category.

We are now coming to what I would describe as the 'small navies' in terms of capability, although some are quite large in terms of personnel. My new ranks four to eight begin with the adjacent force protection navies, those navies able to project force well off shore. These include NATO's Eastern Mediterranean rivals: Turkey and Greece (currently the former in much better shape than the latter); Portugal and Poland; Romania (on the way up); Chile and Peru; Israel and South Africa (the former perhaps with nuclear armed submarines aimed at Iran, based in East Africa). Taiwan and Pakistan remain powerful fleets in this category, while Thailand and Indonesia have moved up into it, the latter with its five innovative multi-role vessels. Malaysia may move up too once she acquires similar vessels. Despite cut-backs and given its requirement for extended Pacific reach outside its own 200-mile zone New Zealand still makes new rank four. The capabilities of HMNZS Canterbury are particularly noteworthy in this regard. Its victories against the Tamil Tiger rebels and its decisive blockade of the territories they held, that required operations at some distance, also argue for putting the brave and battle hardened Sri Lankan Navy in at rank four, moving up two categories. Saudi Arabia's auxiliaries have indeed put that country on the cusp of rank four but her dalliance with the American littoral combat ship and her slowness in adopting submarines keep her in rank four.

These rank five offshore territorial defence navies, capable of combat operations out to 200 miles have lost members up and down since 1990. In Europe the navies have either moved up, or in East Germany's and Yugoslavia's case, disappeared (the latter to be succeeded by the lesser rank six Croatian navy). Bulgaria remains here. Along the North African littoral, Morocco, Algeria and Egypt also remain, although Algeria appears to be going up in the world with its ambitious LHD plans. Iran remains quite powerful at the top of this category, although it has not moved up, as expected. Other Gulf members are Bahrain, the UAE and Oman. In South America this category still includes Colombia, Ecuador and Venezuela and now also includes Mexico which has moved up and Argentina that has moved down. In South Asia Bangladesh remains here but Philippines is more rank seven, effectively a coastguard. Vietnam is, however moving up into rank five, especially with its submarine programme.

Unsurprisingly, perhaps, economically stricken North Korea has now moved down to the sixth rank, the inshore territorial defence navies. Kuwait with its powerful flotilla of missile small craft is a classic example of the type. Finland also remains stolidly here with a similar fleet. Other navies have moved down, however, because of difficulties in maintaining and supporting sufficient assets in service.

Sensibly, a large number of countries have decided to concentrate on constabulary navies/ coastguards and they remain in rank seven. Classic examples are, of course Ireland with its very effective Naval Service, and Iceland with its equally effective coastguard. Brunei has moved down into this category with the non-delivery of its frigates and the post-war Iraq navy is also now to be found here, Saddam's ambitions for higher status having disappeared with his defeats. The dissolution of the Nigerian navy and attempts to rebuild its capacity with constabulary vessels make it definitely of this category while the growing threat of piracy in West African waters is also countered by a very constabulary Ghana Navy. In East Africa the formerly combatant navy of Kenya has become a constabulary force. The standard Caribbean and South Pacific naval force is in this category (the latter often maintained by successful Australian support in capacity building), as are the lesser Latin American navies such as Uruguay. The main priority for such countries is safeguarding their offshore zones. As noted above, the Philippines has come down to the constabulary category with the acquisition, like Nigeria, of large second-hand American coastguard cutters (offshore patrol vessels) as their core surface units. Myanmar's also remains a constabulary fleet. Rather than the move up a rank I thought would happen, if anything the movement here has been in the opposite direction.

As for rank nine, the token navies, we must probably include, perhaps temporarily, the Libyan Navy that could do little about the maritime power projection that brought down Gaddafi and which suffered serious losses. Another navy getting over losses is Georgia, whose vessels were grouped into a coastguard after the 2008 conflict with Russia. Some of the smallest constabulary navies, such as the Gambia that used to have to pay for itself out of fines levied on arrested fishing vessels probably qualify as such, also with assets in need of repairs. Its support by Taiwan, however, that abruptly replaced Communist Chinese support, may maintain some limited patrol capacity. The maritime forces of Belize remain exiguous with a national Coastguard Service only equipped with very small craft. Benin is, however, building up its patrol forces with 100-ton French-built vessels – as well it might with a growing pirate threat and ambitious 200-mile territorial sea claims.

Returning to these assessments demonstrates how the ranking of the world's navies has been squeezed up and down as smaller navies of my older ranks six and seven have grown into forces of greater reach and capability while others have declined to purely constabulary fleets as the priorities of maintaining order and safeguarding resources have prevailed over the deployment of the apparent 'equalisers' of missile armed fast attack craft. Everyone has moved up of course with the departure of the old rank two and in general at least some of my predictions have come true. The USA, however, does still retain its supremacy by some considerable margin – for the time being at least. The American political and fiscal crisis and the resulting sequestration promise major cuts in capability that will take time to overcome and could be the beginning of a greater medium term decline and rebalancing. The European navy I optimistically predicted has not come about although the close cooperation of European navies has occurred, in NATO and EU contexts, extending collective reach, sometimes with US support, sometimes not. One cannot rule out future operations by European carrier and amphibious forces as increasingly important global substitutes for the Americans as the USA increasingly concentrates upon China.

My 1990 conclusion has certainly stood the test of time:

> 'Whatever the pecking order, ... sea power will still be more than a mere slogan. It will be a vital factor in the world political order. Countries will have good reason to care about what goes on at sea and they will want, within their means, to have some way of exerting some level of force there. Maritime forces will continue to absorb large amounts of resources, depending on the capacity of nation to invest in them and its perception of the various uses of the sea, military and civilian, to its overall policy. Certain countries may choose to dismantle their maritime capabilities but others will build them up to compensate. Both seaborne transport and seaborne military power projection will remain of key importance. There will be plenty of scope for the threat or use of force from the sea. Sea power, in short, has a sound and secure future.'[10]

And I must say, in helping launch this conference, small navies, however defined, have key roles to play, both individually and collectively, in applying it.

---

[10] Grove, p. 241.

Chapter 2
Are Small Navies Different?

Geoffrey Till

Are small navies different? The question is deliberately ambiguous and this chapter will address it in two ways, dealing first of all with the issue of the extent to which small navies are different from medium and large ones in anything apart from the simple matter of the number of platforms and/or people they have. Here the essential question is whether small navies are different in kind, or merely in scale from medium and large ones.

The second angle to be explored of course is whether they are different from each other generically. Can one usefully generalise about small navies in any way other than that they all have smaller 'orders of battle' than medium and large navies?

The two questions are of course closely linked and answering them is likely to require something of a review of that hoary old issue of naval classifications that will be covered in other parts of this book.

Distinctive Problems?

So, then, to the distinctiveness of small navies, as opposed to medium or large ones. First of all, the term not infrequently has pejorative overtones of regret or dismissal, as though the smallness of a navy simply reflects the fact that the country in question cannot afford something bigger, and by inference something better able to serve national purposes. It is certainly not difficult to identify some of the particular vulnerabilities and weaknesses that small navies are usually said to have. Of these one of the most obvious is the extent to which small navies are often reliant on other countries for the supply of the platforms, weapons and sensors they need.

These dependencies always come with a price, a price that all too often prejudices national independence of decision. For instance, both Vietnam and the Philippines are looking for technical assistance from the United States in their bid to bolster their capacity to defend national interests in the South China Sea. The Philippines, for example, has allowed its naval and coastguard forces to atrophy to an extent that most observers looking at the country's manifestly maritime nature find surprising. This long period of neglect is due partly to the country's political and constitutional frailties and partly to the greater priority necessarily attached to insurgency now mainly in Mindanao and internal security generally. But faced with what it considers to be encroachments into the 'West Philippine Sea' by the Chinese it has taken delivery of two large refurbished US Coastguard cutters and, anxious not to be the victim of strategic surprise as it was in 1995 over Mischief Reef and was again in April 2012 over Scarborough Shoal, has called for the US to provide assistance in the shape of P3 maritime reconnaissance aircraft.[1] Welcome though US support in this situation most certainly is, the Philippines has nonetheless sought to diversify its strategic dependence by seeking closer relationships with other countries external to the region – most obviously Australia and Japan. The Japanese therefore are now engaged in a significant programme designed to modernise the Philippines' coastguard forces, presumably as a way of bolstering the country's capacity to defend its interests in the 'West Philippine Sea'.

Vietnam likewise is anxious to diversify from its previous dependence on Russia by making use of American equipment and American skills in another attempt to defend its position over the Paracel and Spratly Islands against what it too sees as an increasingly assertive China.[2] It also is seeking to expand its relationships with other countries in a way which might be thought to 'internationalise' the South China Sea problem in a way that may help Vietnam achieve its aims.

But there are clearly problems and dangers with this strategy. The first is that significant domestic political elements in both countries dislike the American connection for a variety of historic and cultural reasons, as exemplified by the closure of the Subic Bay base in the first case and by the long Vietnam War on the other. Neither Government can afford simply to ignore such sentiments. Both, and especially Vietnam given the absence of a formal treaty between them and the Americans, necessarily have their doubts about the extent to which they could rely on the United States support if the situation in the South China Sea deteriorates further. Both must be aware that the American association goes down badly in China and may therefore make the situation tenser than it need be. Both must be also aware of the danger of getting sucked into other issues that the Americans may have with China, say in the East China Sea, especially given their high levels of economic dependence on their large, immediate and permanent neighbour to the north. Both, but especially Vietnam, have to expect a degree of tiresome lecturing about democracy and human rights from Washington.[3] Of course cooperation with the United States *is* growing despite these disadvantages but they are disadvantages nonetheless. All navies that cannot produce what they need themselves have the vulnerabilities that come with dependence and that dependence gets worse the more they need.

---

[1] *Agence France Presse,* 'Philippines may ask the U.S for Air Surveillance', 2 July 2012.

[2] 'Vietnam seeks U.S. equipment to close military gaps' The Editors, *Global Insider,* 6 July 2012.

[3] Patrick Bartra and Vu Trong Khan, 'Clinton presses Vietnam on Human Rights' *The Wall Street Journal* 10 July.

These are the problems facing Taiwan in a still more acute form. Confronting the rising naval power of a potential adversary which does not even recognise Taiwan's formal right to exist and yet unable to supply much of the equipment the country thinks it needs in order to secure a reasonable bargaining capacity, (most obviously fast jets and F16Cs and Ds, and submarines) its need for American help is paramount. But for its part, the United States is very anxious neither to antagonise China more than it has to, nor to encourage separatist adventurism in Taipei for fear of their possible consequences not just in the Taiwan Strait but across the Western Pacific. It would be a dangerous for anyone to assume total convergence of view between Washington or Taipei and to act accordingly.[4] The Taiwanese are well aware that some prominent Americans for example have stated a need to stop arms supply to Taiwan and to revise the Taiwan Relations Act.[5]

In sum, these kind of dependencies mean that small navies, and more precisely, the small countries they help defend, are likely to have only limited independence of strategic decision when up against, or operating in the presence of, much larger ones with incongruent national interests.

An equally obvious problem that all smaller navies are likely to have is the lack of what might be termed 'critical mass'. They may only be able to operate platforms and systems in penny packets like for example the Royal New Zealand Navy's two frigates or Malaysia's two *Scorpene* submarines. Of course this necessarily makes the unit cost of equipping, manning and maintaining these platforms much more expensive since economies of scale are much harder to achieve. Moreover, the iron law of necessary refits will mean that it will be extremely difficult to extract a *continuous* and cost-effective capability out of such small numbers and this complicates the kind of overall mission planning which assumes such availability. Larger navies have this problem too of course, especially when the numbers of platforms associated with a particular capability fall to low levels.

This is important for accountants, sceptical politicians and treasuries like to be sure of the past, present and estimated future cost-effectiveness of the programmes they are funding. Smaller navies which do not seem to be delivering *reliable* value for money in this way, become subject to further pressure which exacerbates their problems and contributes to the danger of a downward spiral in their capability and fortunes.

There is a more insidious aspect to this too. Navies survive and prosper partly through their ability to have an appreciable impact on the defence decision-making processes which define a country's maritime policy. But low numbers, cuts and outsourcing damage morale and retention by reducing promotion prospects, and adversely affect sea–shore employment ratios. This means that there are fewer people with the necessary professional experience to influence, even help shape,

---

[4] Staff Writers, *Agence France Presse,* 'Taiwan plans to buy four warships from the US. Report' 22 April 2012.

[5] For example Admiral William Owens, former Vice Chief of the Joint Chiefs of Staff, 'America must start treating China as a friend' *Financial Times* 17 Nov 2009.

policy at the national level. Policy made without this kind of professional input becomes less likely to serve naval purposes. Instead the navy simply gets told what its policy is.

In the same way, small navies, and indeed small militaries, find it difficult to afford NATO-standard cradle-to-grave professional military education (PME) systems able to deliver all the necessary staff/academic skills needed to able to fight, to argue the maritime case and indeed to procure, 'smartly'. They have to send their best and their brightest abroad, or to be satisfied with manifestly less-than-perfect solutions which do not aspire to the levels achieved by France and other NATO allies – where PME may well take twenty per cent of an officer's career. This matters because, over and over again, the key characteristic of naval effectiveness has been found in the quality of a navy's training.

Some Corrections

But lest this catalogue of woe appear too depressing, a number of corrective points need to be made. First of all, medium and even larger navies are by no means immune to these kinds of pressures and problems either. The critical thing is not the simple number of assets a navy has, but how that balances against the commitments that it has to meet and the roles that this requires it to perform.

Large navies struggle with this just as smaller ones do. For all its world dominance, the US Navy, for example, has a range of commitments that means it has to meet possible contingencies around the world that are varied geographically and may range in requirement from protection against terrorists on jet skis at one end of the spectrum through the swarming tactics of the Iranian republican guard to the DF-21D 'carrier-killing' ballistic missiles of a near peer competitor like China. This makes a Mahanian concentration of force extremely difficult for the Americans and their problem is likely to get worse in the years to come.[6] The differences between the assets/commitments balance between small and large navies accordingly appears much more a question of degree than of kind. It is manifestly *not* a simple matter of numbers. The same is equally true of medium navies.[7]

Secondly, some of the less intense tasks that are often associated with small navies *do* matter at least to them and in fact increasingly to the larger navies too. Classification systems for navies are often based less on what a navy has and more on what it does – and where it does it – its operational range in other words (both in terms of mission and of geographic extent) – and, indeed, its reputation.

---

[6] Joshua Stewart, 'Mideast Crises Force U.S. navy to Keep Carriers at Sea longer' *Defense* News 30 July 2012; Sam Fellman, 'World Crises Challenge U.S. Navy Deployments' *Defense News* 1 Oct 2012.

[7] Pierre Tran, 'Hollande to review "Survival," "Apocalyptic" Budgets', *Defense News International* 1 April 2013.

For instance, a recent sophisticated re-working of the Michael Morris/Eric Grove classification system distinguishes between navies capable of force projection (and then looking at the extent and the range at which the navy in question can do this) at 'territorial defence' (inshore or offshore) and, finally at constabulary roles. But this doesn't quite fit the navies of Southeast Asia and so a revised hierarchy has been proposed:

Rank 1: Adjacent Shipping Protection: Singapore, Malaysia, Thailand
Rank 2: Offshore Territorial Defence: Indonesia, Vietnam
Rank 3: Inshore Territorial Defence: Brunei, Burma
Rank 4: Constabulary: Philippines, Cambodia.[8]

This usefully focuses on the fact that there is a marked tendency for smaller navies to be primarily focused on the protection of their offshore estate and interests – or on what is increasingly now known as Maritime Security with capital letters. A glance at the priority attached in the latest Chinese and Vietnamese Five Year Plans, or at the importance of the potential oil revenues and fishing catch to the Philippines economy certainly helps explain the efforts now being attached to the build-up of their naval and coastguard forces. This plus questions of sovereignty and national pride also helps explain why the Taiwanese for all their other preoccupations are so determinedly engaged in the East and South China Seas disputes.[9]

It might be objected at this point that coastguard forces of various kinds are usually at the forefront of such activities because they are often regarded as less provocative than naval forces, but this is often a distinction without much difference. The relationship of coastguard forces with their navies differ from one country to another, their ships are often armed and, in the case of the Japanese Coastguard, their rules of engagement seem more robust than the Navy's. It will be remembered that the ships responsible for the aggressive harassment of the USNS *Impeccable* in March 2009 were in fact from China's State Oceanic Administration and the Coastal Maritime Safety Agency, not the PLA Navy. On the departure of the Taiwanese flotilla for the Diaoyu/Senkaku Islands, for example, Minister Wang Jinn-Wang of the Coast Guard Administration warned that his units would be guided by the precepts of 'no provocation, no conflict and no evasion' but '.[i]f the Japanese spray water at the Taiwanese fishing boasts, we will spray water back at them' and that he would not rule out the use of arms if 'the other side resorts to it first'.[10] This kind of coastguard activism (which may be partly inspired by competition for responsibility and budgetary resources between the various

---

[8] James Goldrick and Jack McCaffrie, *Navies of South-East Asia: A Comparative Study* (London: Routledge, 2013) pp. 11–13. See also, Geoffrey Till, *Sea Power: A Guide for the 21st Century* (3rd Ed) (London: Routledge, 2013) pp. 116–122.

[9] 'Taiwanese flotilla sails to Diaoyutais' and 'Chinese ships spotted near disputed islands' in *Taipeh Times* 25 September 2012.

[10] 'Taiwanese flotilla sails...' op cit.

agencies of a particular state) could in fact lead to more provocative behaviour simply because their use seems less escalatory than the use of naval forces.

Moreover, many of the world's navies are in effect coastguards. The current Philippine Navy flagship the PS *Gregorio del Pilar* for instance is a refurbished US Coast Guard Cutter and nicely illustrates the cross-over and the intimate connections between navies and coastguard agencies of one sort or another. For all these reasons it seems wrong to exclude coastguard forces from this consideration simply because their ships are painted a different colour from naval ones.

Moreover, the attention that larger navies pay to disputes of this kind in places like the South and East China Sea reinforces the critical importance of the Maritime Security mission, either because of the vigorous way in which the mission is being prosecuted in the Western Pacific, or because it is not being prosecuted vigorously enough, for example off much of Africa (most obviously Somalia) to the detriment of sub-Saharan Africa's own Maritime Security interests. The true importance of small navies and effective coastguards becomes very clear when they are absent, as unfortunately is largely the case off Africa. For a variety of reasons, sea-blindness and a continental mind-set are characteristic of much of the African establishment's approach to policy-making. The result has been a long neglect of its maritime forces.

The impact of piracy in the Gulf of Aden has been variously estimated and has become considerable in financial terms even given the sheer size of the global trade system as a whole.[11] Certainly, it has an adverse impact on economic development and social stability in East and West Africa, an impact reinforced by the consequences of such other forms of maritime crime as illegal oil bunkering and fishing, the drugs trade, human trafficking and pollution, all which reduce the continent's capacity to resolve its developmental problems through effective exploitation of its huge maritime interests. Fortunately there are some signs of a maritime consciousness slowly emerging, even within the African Union, thanks in large measure to the efforts of South Africa.[12]

For all these reasons, the main mission of most small navies is of critical importance to themselves and to the world community generally. They do most certainly *matter*, therefore, and their fortunes intertwine with those of the greater navies at every level. Navies of every sort, great, medium and small, therefore have therefore seen the need to come together to deal with the growing variety of

---

[11] Admiral Lin, Chief of the Defence Staff, ROC estimated the annual cost of Somalia-based piracy at $8 billion rising to a likely $14.3 if current trends continue. Keynote address at 17th International Sea Lines of Communication Conference, Taipei. ROC Sep 25–26th 2012.

[12] Brenthurst Foundation, 'Maritime development in Africa: An independent specialists' framework' Brenthurst Discussion Paper No 3, 2010; RSA Department of Defence, 'Speech by L.N. Sisulu, Minister of Defence and military Veterans, on the Occasion of the Department of Defence Budget Vote.' Good Hope Chamber, Cape Town, 13 April 2011. www.info.gov.za/speech.

non-traditional threats. This also explains why the US Navy and other large navies devote such considerable efforts to Maritime Security capacity building around the world, deliberately aimed at narrowing the operational gaps between the great and small in this area of operation at least, as, for example, through the efforts of the American Africa Command.

Nor can it possibly be concluded that small navies somehow do not matter in the larger more conventionally military scheme of things, an assumption that the sweeping aside of the Iraqi navy in 1991 and 2001, and the Libyan navy in 2011 might seem to suggest. Small navies often *do* matter especially if they are able to achieve strategic effect by being able to exploit either military-technological possibilities or their political alternatives. This last is a point worth emphasising in a world in which the weak seem sometimes able to bully the strong. Even getting into a position where the stronger power may run the danger of universal opprobrium through being forced to fight the brave little forces of a weaker adversary can be a severe deterrent for a stronger forces as the British found out during the Icelandic Cod Wars, a factor which limited the Royal Navy's ability to exploit its potentially overwhelming operational advantages at the time.[13]

On top of this, a militarily skilful combination of geographic position and asymmetric technology could well make a notionally small navy (in numbers terms) disproportionately effective strategically. The Navy and Republican Guard of Iran, for example, might well conclude that new technology in the shape of modern mines, naval missiles and coastal submarines could give the US 7th Fleet considerable pause for thought if used intelligently and resolutely in the circumstances of a distinctive 'narrow seas' environment. For all its carrier battle groups, the US Navy could find itself at a distinct disadvantage when dealing with swarms of small suicide boats, like the two-man terrorist boat that rammed the USS *Cole* in October 2000 in Aden harbour, immobilising a one billion dollar warship for two years of repairs, killing 17 US sailors, and injuring 35. This operation cost al-Qaida 10,000 dollars (as shown in documents evidently seized from an al-Qaida safe house in Kabul after US troops captured the city in October 2001).[14] It has been reported that US Internal Look war games conducted in March in 2012 indicated that the Navy "would have considerable problems dealing with Iranian offensive operations" in the narrow waters of the strait with '...a high probability that Americans vessels will be sunk, with considerable loss of life'.[15] Whether these assessments prove right or wrong in action they are bound

---

[13] The best guide to this remains the now de-classified Naval Staff History (BR 1736(57) *The Cod War: Naval operations off Iceland in Support of the British Fishing Industry (1958–1976)* (London, MOD, 1990).

[14] Arnaud De Borchgrave, *Commentary Alarm bells in the US,* Washington (UPI) 29 May 2012.

[15] Staff Writers, UPI, Manama, 11 June 2012. US Braces itself for Action in Persian Gulf.

to be a consideration in the mind of planners on both sides when deciding their response to a dispute over Iran's alleged nuclear policy, for example.

It may well reflect the capacity of a navy, or its state, to exploit strategic possibilities in a way which might even up the odds even in some putative encounter with a much greater navy. The Vietnamese, Taiwanese and Philippine navies all know they would have no hope of prevailing, or even of surviving, against a much more powerful and implacably resolute Chinese navy. But they also know that things are not so simple. The political and economic costs of victory for the Chinese would be extremely high: such a victory would simply confirm what Beijing calls 'the China threat theory' and undermine its claim to be rising peacefully. It could spark counteractions by others that could worsen its long-term position leading to the very kind of strategic encirclement that it most worries about. Moreover all three navies know that in any such calculation, were such an extremely unlikely event ever to come to pass, PLAN campaign planners would have to keep back, or to keep safe, the bulk of their naval forces to guard against the possibility of American intervention. Such was also the thinking by the navies, armies and air forces of Scandinavia when confronting the adverse 'correlation of forces' apparently set by the Soviet Navy during the Cold War. Vietnam with its acquisition of six *Kilo* submarines is plainly investing in its own version of an Anti-Access/Area Denial (A2/AD) strategy, presumably less in the expectation of winning than of deterring through the prospect of punishment. (There is some doubt though about how effective this would be given the fact that *Kilos* were originally designed for cold water operation and are a little noisy in warmer ones, and that the Chinese have them too and so presumably are well aware of their operational characteristics.) The Taiwanese with their recent development and acquisition of the supersonic Hsiung Ffeng (Brave Wind) III 'carrier–killer missile' and its fitting to their patrol boats and frigates seems to be following the same sea-denial path.[16]

But intrinsically such sea-denial tactics, both political and military, seem no different in principle from those likely to be followed by a detachment of a much larger navy when operating in the presence of more powerful enemy forces. The choice of a sea denial strategy is usually a characteristic of a relationship between two naval forces, not a permanent and defining attribute of either. For example, the re-equipped Vietnamese navy would probably behave very differently if it was taking on the Philippine navy for some bizarre reason. Moreover, the operations of even the smallest naval forces, such as the United Nations river squadrons operating on the rivers of the Democratic Republic of the Congo, for example, seem to perform exactly the same missions (sea control, force projection, the protection of trade, deterrence and coalition building) as their larger oceanic brethren. The differences lie in scale, not principle.

---

[16] 'Taiwan deploying more "carrier killers": report' by Staff Writers, Taipei (AFP) 14 May 2012.

Finally, a small navy's capacity to matter just as do medium and large ones can be increased by the number of strategic devices that are commonly deployed. The most obvious one of these is their ability to profit from specialisation. By eschewing investment in some, or even much, of the full spectrum of naval capability they may well be able to achieve high levels of operational performance in specific areas. Such niche capabilities can offer considerable benefits to larger partners, both directly and indirectly, in terms of burden-sharing. This in turn provides them with a certain amount of political influence, even leverage over the policies of their larger partners and allies. This has indeed been the policy of the Royal Navy in regard to the much larger US Navy for decades.

The small boat experience of the New Zealand Navy, for example, is of considerable interest to Australia and the United States, especially when applied to the troubled island states of the South Pacific. The same can be true in the more traditional naval disciplines: the inshore and SSK experience of the Norwegian and Swedish navies have proved of great operational value to the US Navy and so forth. In a more general way, the US Navy's emphasis on the 'Global Maritime Partnership', also illustrates the extent to which the evident strategic impact of what is still the world's greatest navy depends on the support of many others, both medium and small.

Small navies can moreover reasonably compensate for their smallness, if they feel they need to, by banding together and learning best practice from each other. This appears to be the approach of the new navies of the Baltic and always has been of the closely associated Belgian and Dutch navies. Interestingly, in this they seem to be following the example set by the emerging Forum of Small States at the United Nations, which, in the light of the paralysis of the Security Council over Syria seeks to reform UN procedures as a whole. 'Being small does not mean an absence of big ideas' as Ban Ki Moon told them on 1st October 2012. In an increasingly multipolar world we can expect smaller nations to be more important, and that goes for their navies too.

Conscious investment in the development of key naval defence capabilities can confer strategic as well as commercial and economic benefits for smaller states. The Navy of Chile, though probably best seen as a medium rather than a small navy, has decided to invest in the construction of a national defence industry by designing and building its own patrol boats and a Crocodile 250 submarine as a research vessel and technology demonstrator, for example.[17] Malaysia, Indonesia and other countries of Southeast Asia are likewise encouraging indigenous production for a variety of social, economic and strategic purposes. Thus the Malaysian Defence Minister Dr Ahmad Zahid Hamidi:

> Much of the economies of Europe and America are generated by the defence industry while we and other countries in this region are the end users…Rather

---

[17] 'Chile advances plan to build submarine' by Staff Writers, Santiago, Chile (UPI) 17 May 2012.

than allow the country to be a dumping ground for near obsolete defence products and services, it's time for us to produce our own using the latest technology and at more competitive prices.[18]

Many of these methods of self-improvement apply equally well to medium and large navies, reinforcing the impression that fundamentally all these navies differ in scale but not in kind.

A Second Variety of Difference?

To a considerable extent the second angle on the question of 'are small navies different?' – namely the extent to which they are different from each other has already been dealt with, because the examples given in the course of the analysis of the differences between them and medium and larger navies have already demonstrated the very different forms that 'small navies' can take. The Vietnamese and Philippine navies across either side of the 'East/West Philippine Sea'[19] differ markedly in their traditional aspirations and effectiveness. Such differences illustrate the extent and the impact of distinct cultural and historical backgrounds, strategic contexts and budgetary resources. Again, all the navies that developed through their association with the Royal Navy, for example, share and indeed sustain certain characteristics (uniforms, standard operating procedures, the exchange of personnel, the sharing of intelligence and so forth) that others do not.

Moreover, the detailed study of almost any 'small navy' is likely to show considerable variation over time in response to their changing domestic and international context. Accordingly, such a small navy is likely to be different from itself over the years. This is very evident for example in the Israeli Navy's transition from being a kind of maritime wing of its paramilitary forces in the late 1940s to the compact modern force it is today.[20] In like vein, the Finnish Navy's historic focus on contributing to territorial defence has in recent years, with the ending of the Cold War, taken aboard a developing interest in participating in collective maritime missions abroad, on the basis that 'there are Finnish citizens all over the

---

[18] Quoted in 'Local Firms Can Show their Power' and 'Getting into its Stride' *New Straits Times* 3 December 2009.

[19] Known as the South China Sea to everyone else!

[20] For a historic review of the Israeli Navy see Moshe Tzalel, *From Ice-breaker to Missile Boats: The Evolution of Israel's Naval Strategy* (Westport ,CT: Greenwood Press, 2000). For some of its current preoccupations, Barbara Opall-Rome, 'Israel Eyes S. Korean OPVs for EEZ-Defense', *Defense News,* 14 January 2013.

world so we need to be part of global crisis management'.[21] The growing unease around much of Scandinavia with the pace of and intentions behind Russia's naval modernisation programmes, plus the growth in strategic and commercial importance of the Arctic may well result, however, in some future scaling back of such extra-regional preoccupations with consequence for the mission priorities of all the navies of Scandinavia, Finland's included.[22]

Small navies could, perhaps, be justified as a generic term from the perspective of preferred missions, that is they have some characteristics in common that derive simply from the fact that they often seem to have the same kind of mission priorities, and so their commonality derives from the fact that many of them are trying to do the same kind of thing. Thus many small navies are preoccupied with the defence of the EEZ, especially now that changes in the Law of the Sea reflect the growing strategic and commercial value of their offshore estates. Hence in the Asia Pacific region, as indeed elsewhere, there is expanding interest in new platforms such as offshore patrol craft and in ways of using them effectively. [23] The fact, though, that medium and big navies have exactly the same kinds of mission-derived characteristics (even if many of them divert these into coastguard agencies of one sort or another) robs this approach of its utility as a descriptor of the 'small navy'.

For all these reasons, it is clear that in many respects small navies are simply big navies in miniature. They share many of the prospects and the challenges of their larger equivalents, in terms of balancing resources against commitments and in the objective importance of the varied tasks they are called upon to perform, not only to the nations they serve but very often to the international community as a whole. They do, however, face particular problems in their relative inability to offset these challenges by seeking economies of scale; given this, their requirements for cost-effectiveness have to be particularly high. Sadly, many of them currently fail this test – but, also, many do not. This underscores the sheer diversity of the world's small navies. They are markedly different from each other, and in many cases different from themselves over time. The US Navy, after all, was clearly a small navy at the end of the eighteenth century! One thing they do have in common though is that their success or failure *matters*; accordingly they warrant serious attention and study.

---

[21] Jyri Hakamies, Finland's Minister of Defence, Interview, *Jane's Defence Weekly*, 10 November 2010.

[22] Gerard O/Dwyer, 'Norway Eyes Next-Gen Submarine Acquisition' *Defense News International* 18 February 2013.

[23] Wendell Minnick and Paul Kallender-Umezu, 'Open Asian Market: Vessels, UAVs Sought for Coastal Security,' *Defense News,* 14 January 2013.

Chapter 3
Small Navies in Perspective: Deconstructing the Hierarchy of Naval Forces

Basil Germond

Introduction: Categorisation and the Dominant Discourse

The very phrase 'small navies' raises interesting questions. Classifying is not a neutral act; it creates categories and hierarchies. A 'small navy' is 'small' as opposed to something else, i.e. a 'large', 'big', 'powerful' or 'global' navy. These dualisms structure navies' identities along an either/or line (binary identities). In other words, one knows what a 'small navy' is by knowing what it is not (i.e. a 'large navy'). The first term (i.e. 'small') is seen (and constructed) as inferior and the second term (i.e. 'large') as superior. Such binary identities imply that the construction of the first term (i.e. 'small') depends on the construction of the second term (i.e. 'large' or 'powerful'), which results in mutually exclusive identities. 'Large' being represented as superior, it is constructed as 'better', or, in other words, as an ideal towards which each navy should tend, at least to some extent. This instils the idea that a 'small navy' is not 'small' on purpose but as a result of extrinsic factors (e.g. financial and technological resources limitations, geographical factors, external political pressures, etc.), and that the normal path is to evolve linearly from 'small' to 'large', or at least to tend towards that aim.

The importance of representation and the link between knowledge (claims) and power has been discussed by post-structuralist scholars, first in the field of philosophy and then in International Relations (IR).[1] According to post-structuralism, the connection between the production of knowledge and power (to define and then to control) needs to be revealed and knowledge claims deconstructed. Representations along binary identities contribute to the dominant discourse, reinforce it, and eventually have practical policy implications (through the power to define what is 'normal'). Similarly, critical geopolitics highlights the link between the production of geographical knowledge (i.e. the spatialisation of world politics) and the power to define (i.e. the construction of 'one' world

---

[1] Since the 1980s, IR scholars have been influenced by the works of post-structuralist philosophers such as Michel Foucault and Jacques Derrida. See for example James Der Derian and Michael J. Shapiro (eds), International/intertextual relations: postmodern readings of world politics (Lexington Books: Lexington, 1989).

and its naturalisation).² For example, the representation of a safe 'inside' versus a threatening 'outside' contributes to the normalisation of policies promoting the projection of security beyond one's own boundary.³ Framed within this theoretical context, the chapter discusses the practical implications of the classification of navies along an either/or line, with a focus on Western navies.

The hypothesis is that the current representation and construction of small navies contributes to the dominant discourse on power projection. The aim is to highlight the links between the production of knowledge (i.e. navies' binary identities and categorisation) and the dominant discourse on power projection. The chapter thus offers an innovative perspective on the topic using an analytical framework which is very rarely applied to naval studies where strategic studies and military history methodologies are prominent. Firstly, the chapter examines the criteria used to classify navies, so as to show what a 'small navy' is according to the generally accepted representation in the specialised academic literature and within naval establishments. Then, based on the analysis of Western official documents detailing naval missions,⁴ it shows how this representation contributes to the dominant discourse on the projection of security. On the one hand, 'small navies' tend to reproduce the structure and capabilities of the larger ones, which aim at power projection. On the other hand, to opt out of the either/or conundrum, 'small navies' can find 'salvation' in multilateral naval cooperation. While this allows 'small navies' to perform tasks that were not traditionally associated with them (such as 'out-of-area' deployments) and to participate in large scale operations (such as counter-piracy operations) far away from home, the chapter shows that naval multilateralism also contributes to the normalisation of the practice of projecting security beyond one's own boundary as a way to contribute to the stability of the liberal international order.

Categorising Small Navies

*Ranking Navies: a Literature Review*⁵

Various naval scholars have elaborated criteria to rank navies and methods to establish a hierarchy. In 1987, Michael Morris developed a hierarchy of Third

---

² Gearóid Ó Tuathail and John Agnew, 'Geopolitics and discourse: practical geopolitical reasoning in American foreign policy', *Political Geography*, 11/ 2 (1992): pp. 190–204.

³ Basil Germond, 'The European Union at the Horn of Africa: The Contribution of Critical Geopolitics to Piracy Studies', *Global Policy*, 4/1 (2013): pp. 80–85.

⁴ These include the totality of the European navies as well as the US Navy and a choice of other extra-European 'Western' navies, which is sufficient to avoid any selection bias.

⁵ This discussion is adapted from one of my previous works in French; Basil Germond, *Les Forces Navales Européennes Dans La Période Post-Guerre Froide* (L'Harmattan:

World navies that rapidly became seminal.[6] He devised four classification criteria: the number of different kinds of ships (supposed to indicate navies' functional capabilities), the state of modernity of the fleet and weapon equipment (a somewhat qualitative criteria), supplementary naval power criteria (such as tonnage, naval aviation, Marine Corps, a separate coastguard service and a national naval industry), and finally the broader national resources that can support naval power (i.e. military budget, infrastructure, overall economic performance).[7] With the exception of the second criterion they are rather quantitative and thus fail to take into account qualitative indicators such as the level of sailors' education or their motivation and disposition. Morris concedes that the last three criteria do not substantially modify the hierarchy obtained using the first, purely quantitative, criterion (i.e. the order of battle).[8] Based on those four criteria, Morris established six ranks. The first rank comprises the token navies, i.e. those that possess a formal organisational structure but cannot practically fulfil any naval mission. The second rank groups navies performing only police and constabulary missions. The third and fourth ranks concern navies able to perform defensive combat tasks, in coastal zones (third rank) or offshore (fourth rank). The fifth and sixth ranks include navies possessing enough forces to operate beyond territorial defence, conducting projection operations beyond their EEZ (fifth rank) or in the regional theatre (sixth rank). Due to the absence of any superior rank, this model is not universal and applies to the so-called 'Third World' navies only. That said, Morris's classification is interesting as the established ranks correspond to different types of missions, that is, a functional hierarchy. However, Morris did not envisage cases where missions (and thus capabilities) could be limited by the political decision-makers on a voluntary basis (as in the case of Ireland for example); it thus contributes to the construction of a 'reality' where naval missions (and capabilities) are only limited by the resources at states' disposal. This model has nevertheless been seminal and various authors have subsequently used it as a basis for establishing their own classification criteria and hierarchy.

British naval historian Eric Grove was influenced by Morris when he established his global typology for navies in 1990.[9] He did not actually define new classification criteria, since he used the types of forces deployed, the sophistication of the equipment, the level of afloat support, and the number of vessels. His classification

---

Paris, 2008), pp. 212–222.

[6] Michael A. Morris, *Expansion of the Third World Navies* (The Macmillan Press: London, 1987), pp. 22–56.

[7] The importance of the global power of states in determining the role/capabilities of their navy has also been discussed in 1986 by Hill, who defined three types of states; superpowers, medium powers and small powers. J.R. Hill, *Maritime Strategy for Medium Powers* (Naval Institute Press: Annapolis, MD, 1986), pp. 14–50.

[8] Morris, *Third World Navies*, p. 24.

[9] Eric Grove, *The Future of Sea Power* (Naval Institute Press: Annapolis, MD, 1990), pp. 236–241.

is thus also mainly based on quantitative criteria (types and number of ships and equipment). Grove then established nine ranks in an inverted order compared to Morris. The first three ranks group navies able to project forces at the global level, the fourth and fifth ranks navies limited to regional projection, the sixth and seventh ranks navies confined to a role of territorial defence, the eighth rank, navies with only police and constabulary capabilities, and finally the ninth rank, token navies. In fact, the first three ranks comprising the USA (1), the USSR (2) and the UK and France (3) add up to the six lesser ranks established by Morris. Grove's ranks also correspond to the types of feasible missions (e.g. forces projection, coastal defence, police operations), although putting a stronger emphasis on the range (which will later be endorsed by other authors). That said, the excessive number of ranks (nine) does not favour comparison. The difference between ranks 2 and 3 is ambiguous; indeed how to differentiate a *Global* Force Projection Navy – *Partial* (rank 2) from a *Medium* Force Projection Navy (rank 3)? Actually, the creation of those two distinct ranks (established by the author at the end of the 1980s) was certainly done (a bit artificially) to differentiate the Soviet Navy (rank 2) from the British and French navies (rank 3).

In 1998, the naval geographer Michael S Lindberg established another type of ranking based on two main criteria, i.e. the geographical reach (global, regional, EEZ, territorial waters, internal waters) and the primary missions (power projection, territorial integrity, police duties, and symbolic presence).[10] Lindberg established five ranks: global power projection navy, regional power projection navy, coastal defence navy, constabulary navy, and token navy. Navies can move up the ranks depending on the extent to which they possess the following elements of naval power: force structure (i.e. order of battle), sustainability and reach, flexibility, personnel' quality, and national support infrastructure. Those elements can thus be understood as indicators of reach and capabilities.

In 2002, the French strategist Hervé Coutau-Bégarie, in his *Traité de Stratégie*, has also discussed how to classify navies.[11] He criticised Morris's lack of consideration for qualitative criteria, stating that it results in a misleading hierarchy. In addition to the types of forces, the afloat support and the age/sophistication of ships/equipment (already taken into account by Morris and Grove), he introduced the following qualitative criteria: the level of training of the fleet, the sailors' educational qualifications, as well as the degree of adaptation to the missions assigned. Despite the introduction of new qualitative criteria, Coutau-Bégarie ended up with similar results (i.e. a functional hierarchy) when he formulated his hierarchy. He established a distinction between ranks 1 and 2 (global navies), ranks 3 and 4 (regional navies), rank 5 (coastal navies) and rank 6 (coast-guard navies). Here again, the ranks mainly depend on the types of missions that can be fulfilled and the range of navies.

[10] Michael S. Lindberg, *Geographical Impact on Coastal Defence Navies* (Macmillan: Basingstoke, 1998), pp. 14–37.

[11] Hervé Coutau-Bégarie, *Traité de Stratégie* (Economica: Paris, 2002), pp. 617–621.

In his book *Seapower* Geoffrey Till also established criteria to classify navies[12]. He began by discussing the criteria employed by other authors in the past. As to the size and nature of the fleet (i.e. the number of ships of each type) he specified that this has no value in absolute terms; it can barely be an indicator of relative power. He favours the range or geographical reach, not only looking at where a ship can sail, but also what it can do once arrived and for how long. As to the criterion employed when looking at the types of missions that are assigned to the navies, Till stressed that very often the same missions are assigned to navies having very different capabilities. Finally, when it comes to the technological criteria, he said that acquiring those technologies is not enough; they must be assimilated and operated effectively, i.e. translated into operational activities. Although classifying navies requires taking all of the above-mentioned criteria into account, Till stated that certain criteria are more important than others, notably the one that looks at the types of feasible missions (functions), since projecting forces requires more capabilities than coastal police operations. In summary, Till thinks that navies should be classified according to their relative effectiveness, which can be estimated according to the following criteria: geographical reach, sailors' professional qualifications and skills, readiness of the fleet, afloat support, and the navy's versatility, that is not limited to missions of one type (a balanced fleet). Interestingly, Till specified that a 'small navy' may be more efficient than a 'large' one in some instances, notably when it comes to coastal defence. Also, a navy specialised in one particular task can be very useful within a multinational structure. Till did not carry on with the establishment of a proper hierarchy; – he did not devise any ranking; however, his work allows us to pinpoint many important elements: the range (geographical reach) must be taken into account alongside the capacity for sustained operations; being assigned a mission (and having the necessary types and number of ships to fulfil it) does not presuppose the actual capacity to perform this mission effectively (e.g. are sailors educated and trained to do so?).

In 2004, Josh Barber and Joe Sipos (from the Canadian Navy) projected an estimate for 2025.[13] Their ranking is based on the capacity to perform as many missions as possible, as far away from home as possible and for as long as possible. In addition, they emphasised the difference between operating autonomously versus within a coalition. Starting from that, they established five ranks: rank 1 (capabilities 'to conduct major operations on a global scale without allied support'), rank 2 (capabilities 'to undertake one major "out-of-area" operation'), rank 3 (capabilities 'to conduct limited, independent global expeditionary operations,

---

[12] Geoffrey Till, *Seapower: A Guide for the Twenty-First Century* (Frank Cass: London, 2004), pp. 113–120.

[13] Josh Barber and Joe Sipos, 'The Future Maritime Security Environment', in Robert H. Edwards (ed.), *The Future of Canada's Maritime Capabilities: the Issues, Challenges and Solutions in a New Security Environment* (Centre for Foreign Policy Studies, Dalhousie University: Halifax, 2004), pp. 165–175.

but [only] able to conduct sustained expeditionary operations in cooperation with other navies, good capacity in traditional naval domains'; possess ;the full range of capabilities in all aspects of naval warfare'), rank 4 (capabilities 'to project limited force into adjacent ocean areas; however, it will not be a usual part of their national strategies to do so on a regular basis. They will have sufficient capability to permit sustained medium intensity operations in their own coastal waters'), then rank 5 (all the rest). This classification clearly puts the emphasis on projection/ expeditionary capabilities and thus constructs 'global navies' (such as the US Navy, and to a lesser extent, the British and French ones) as an 'ideal'.

In 2007, ex-Canadian Navy commander turned academic Peter T. Haydon stressed that previous hierarchies have failed to take into account states' foreign and defence policy orientations, that is the decision to voluntarily limit naval missions to coastal defence whatever the resources at disposal.[14] He thus proposed a three-level classification 'based on the actual functions, as a reflection of the states' maritime strategies and thus foreign policies':[15] major naval powers (global responsibilities and interests); medium power navies (widespread interests and collective approach to security); small and coastal navies (no interest beyond their EEZs). The result is still a functional hierarchy, but not based on the order of battle, rather on states' foreign policy objectives. This is an original approach, but it is doubtful that foreign policy objectives are not, at least partially, based on the actual resources at states' disposal.

Table 3.1   Classification criteria employed in the literature

Authors	Classification criteria adopted
Morris (1987)	Order of battle State of modernity Afloat support
Grove (1990)	Variety of forces and number of ships Sophistication Afloat support Range
Lindberg (1998)	Geographical reach Types of missions
Coutau-Bégarie (2002)	Types of forces Afloat support Age of ships Sailors' training Adaptation to the missions assigned

---

[14] Peter T. Haydon, 'Naval Diplomacy: Is it Relevant in the 21st Century?', in Andrew T.H. Tan (ed.), *The Politics of Maritime Power* (Routledge: London, 2007), pp. 71–74.

[15] Ibid, p. 71.

Authors	Classification criteria adopted
Till (2004)	Types of missions (functions) Range / geographical reach Professional qualifications and skills State of preparation Afloat support Versatility Assimilation of new technologies
Barber et Sipos (2004)	Types of missions Range Degree of autonomy when conducting projection operation
Haydon (2007)	Foreign policy interests determining the missions assigned to the navy

In sum, naval scholars have mainly established their classification (and their ranking) according to the types of missions that the navies can fulfil: global projection, regional projection, offshore defence, coastal defence, police operations, and symbolic presence. The hierarchies obtained are thus based on functional ranks. To define to which rank a navy belongs, various quantitative and qualitative criteria have been employed (as summarised in Table 3.1), but the main emphasis is put on the order of battle, the geographical reach and the type of missions. As Till noted, what is important is where a navy can sail, what it can do once arrived and for how long.

Ranking Navies: Criteria and Indicators[16]

Building on that literature review, one can devise five main classification criteria, which, used in conjunction with one another, help in the discussion of the hierarchy of naval forces and the representation of small navies. The first ranking criterion employed in the literature is the order of battle, that is the number of vessels in service and their tonnage and type. (indeed, a navy possessing many light ships does not have the same capabilities as a navy possessing fewer ships of higher tonnage such as aircraft carriers.) Anyway, this is a purely quantitative criterion that does not correspond to the very reality; indeed, a very strong navy on paper (number and types of vessels) but operating out-of-age and/or lightly armed ships is 'large' only by name. Having that in mind, one can complement the purely quantitative indicators with an indicator that better takes into account the reality: the fire power and the state of modernity and technological sophistication of vessels and equipment (intrinsic material qualities). Hence, the criterion of the order of battle becomes less quantitative and thus more pertinent (order of effect). For example, regardless of the numerically favourable balance of power that the

---

[16] See note 5.

Soviet Navy had in the 1970s and1980s (notably with attack submarines), based on qualitative criteria, the US Navy was always considered by almost all authors as dominant, not only globally, but also in the field of submarine warfare, despite the overwhelming Soviet numerical superiority in certain areas.

A quantitatively powerful and modern navy may not be able to fulfil a range of diversified missions (full spectrum), and may actually be one-dimensional, because the quantity, power and modernity criteria do not take into account the degree of versatility of the fleet as such. Till has thus emphasised the necessity to take into account the diversity of the forces so as to identify a navy's ability to conduct the widest possible range of missions. A versatile (and flexible) navy would 'ideally' possess the following components: strategic deterrent forces (SSBNs); expeditionary and projection forces (SSNs, aircraft carriers, principal surface ships, and amphibious ships); surveillance and protection of Sea Lines of Communication (SLOCs) forces (light frigates, anti-submarine units, and maritime patrol aircraft), coastal forces (corvettes and patrol boats); police and constabulary forces; and finally logistics and support forces. The existence of specialised and autonomous forces (such as coastguards) can also increase the versatility of naval forces while allowing the purely military components to concentrate on combat missions. In other words, the more balanced the fleet is the more versatile it is. However, with limited resources compromises are essential, even among the most powerful navies such as the US Navy that has to 'balance between capabilities, capacity, and fiscal reality' when calculating the size of the force, and rely upon liberal concepts such as the 'freedom-loving nation's' 1,000-ship Navy to 'police the maritime commons'.[17]

Some of the prominent naval missions (notably expeditionary warfare and peacekeeping) require blue-water projection capabilities, that is to say the capability of operating far away from home for as long as possible. To account for this, one needs to look at the reach and sustainability criteria, i.e. the range of the fleet and its capacity for sustained operations. Indeed, a navy that possesses some major surface ships but without appropriate logistical means (support ships, forward bases) and without appropriate anti-aircraft protection and anti-missile defence (theatre missile defence, carrier aviation), will not be able to conduct a sustained expeditionary operation in hostile territory, and thus cannot be considered as a true 'global' navy. It is also important to take into account not only the logistical means of support but also the general support to the fleet. Thus, one has to take into account more general indicators demonstrating the intrinsic power of states, such as naval industry, overall economic performance of the country, and so on.

Global navies are expected to possess the capabilities to conduct sustained and diverse operations far away from home autonomously (away from any coalition). However, a growing number of so-called 'medium' or even 'small' navies possess the capabilities to operate within coalitions (interoperability), often

---

[17] Admiral Michael Mullen, 'What I Believe: Eight Tenets That Guide My Vision for the 21st Century Navy', *US Naval Institute Proceedings*, 132/1 (2006), online version.

under the auspices of international organisations such as the UN, NATO or the EU. For them, what is important (or feasible) is not to operate autonomously, but to perform well within a multinational naval framework. As their resources are finite, this may require a high degree of specialisation. This trend among 'small' navies fit, well with the above-mentioned US concept of a '1,000-ship navy' or global maritime partnership.

A number of adjustment criteria also need to be taken into consideration. Sailors' training, professional qualifications and moral conditions, as well as countries' overall economic performance are additional qualitative indicators that can marginally modify the ranking of navies. Finally, classifying navies requires taking account of the relationship between the means and the objectives: in fact, a regional navy, whose means coincide with the objectives that the government has assigned to it, such as coastal defence, may be very effective in achieving its mission if its degree of specialisation is great, even if it cannot claim to be an oceanic navy. In this case, it is the adequacy between the means/capabilities and the (assigned) objectives/missions that will reassess the classification of navies, although this latter type of hierarchy can be highly subjective, as it may be difficult to sort out which limitations are voluntary and which ones are resulting from the country's overall economic performance and resources.

Table 3.2: Ranking Criteria and Indicators

Criteria	Indicators
Order of battle	Number of vessels Tonnage and types of ships
Order of effect	Power of weaponry State of modernity
Versatility/flexibility	Types and diversity of missions
Range/sustainability	Geographical reach Capacity for sustained operations Logistics and afloat support
Autonomy and cooperation / interoperability	Capacity to operate autonomously Capacity to operate within a coalition
Other qualitative and political adjustment variables	Professional qualifications Sailors' moral dispositions Correlation between means and objectives Voluntary limitations

As summarised in Table 3.2, one can sort out six interrelated sets of criteria (each one linked to a certain number of indicators) to classify navies: the order of battle (or, in other words, the number and types of forces); the order of effect (i.e. power of weaponry and state of modernity of the fleet); the versatility (these three first criteria allow assessing the types of mission a navy can conduct); the capacity to operate far away and on a sustained basis (reach and sustainability); the capacity to operate autonomously or in cooperation, as well as various adjustment variables, such as the quality of training, sailors' moral dispositions, voluntary limitations, and the correlation between the available means and the assigned objectives. Using those criteria, one can propose the following ranking of navies:

Rank 1:

Symbolic navies   As in Morris's study, these are navies that cannot fulfil any mission properly, including policing territorial waters. Their role is thus symbolic and not operational. To attain this rank it is enough to possess an established organisational structure. This differentiates this rank from non-state actors possessing some naval assets (pirates, terrorists, smugglers) that could be attributed rank 0, although their means may often exceed those possessed by rank 1 navies; some of them even possess some sort of formal organisation.

Rank 2:

Navies able to conduct police and constabulary operations in their territorial waters (and sometimes in their EEZs), and to contribute to coastal defence (mainly in cooperation with allies), but cannot participate in projection operations.   To attain this rank, a navy should possess a number of patrol boats adapted to the geographical area to police. The more extensive this area is and the more its strategic depth increases, the more demanding qualitative material needs are. Due to the proliferation of criminal actors at sea, and due to the considerable resources at their disposal (such as fast boats, sometimes armed), attaining rank 2 requires a significant effort compared to a rank 1 navy. That said, repelling a military attack would require a cooperative response (e.g. in the framework of NATO). It must be noted that some NATO or EU rank 2 navies have managed to participate in 'out-of-area' operations, but with a very limited and highly specialised contribution.

Rank 3:

Navies able, in addition to conducting police and constabulary operations, to perform coastal defence autonomously, and to participate, within coalitions, in limited projection operations.   To attain this rank, it is necessary to go beyond policing duties and enter the field of combat operations. Indeed, a rank 3 navy should be able to conduct operations whose combat intensity is relatively high. Furthermore, it is necessary to have the capacity to fully integrate within multinational (coalition) forces, even with a limited contribution, so as to participate in projection operations. The leap in qualitative terms and versatility between rank 2 and rank 3 is very significant.

Rank 4:

Navies able, in addition to conducting police and constabulary operations and to performing coastal defence autonomously, to conduct limited projection operations autonomously, and to participate, within coalitions, in high intensity projection operations. To separate a rank 4 from a rank 3 navy the most relevant criteria concerns the projection capabilities (range, sustainability, autonomy). Indeed, the main difference between these two ranks comes from rank 4 navies' capacity to actively participate in various projection operations, including high intensity ones.

Rank 5:

Navies able, in addition to conducting police and constabulary operation and to performing coastal defence autonomously, to conduct projection operations autonomously, and to participate in high intensity multinational projection operations assuming the role of leading partner. Rank 5 navies assume a leadership role over lower rank navies. The versatility of forces and the number of ships at their disposal play an important role. In addition, modern weapons systems are also crucial; rank 5 navies need to quickly assimilate new technologies (such as Network-Centric Warfare) and routinely use them, so as to keep their pioneering role.

Rank 6:

Navies able to perform any type of missions that could be assigned to them, to operate on a sustained basis all over the world and without any outside help. This rank somewhat constitutes the 'ideal' situation aimed at by naval planners. However, the operational maintenance of such a navy necessitates a continuous effort, which requires priority investments by the government, including in the field of new technologies. Obviously, only navies of economically very wealthy states may have the potential to reach rank 6.

Rankings and the Representation of 'Small' Navies

The literature review, the subsequent analysis of the classification criteria and the establishment of a theoretical hierarchy show that the ranking process is more complex than simply differentiating a 'small' navy from a 'large' one. However, in discourses, the complexity of the reality is often reduced to binary identities and oppositions, such as 'blue-water navies' versus 'non blue-water navies', all the more since the main ranking criteria are related to the diversity of the missions and the hierarchies are mostly functional. Consequently, navies able to fulfil the objectives assigned to them by their government such as policing territorial waters and the adjacent EEZs as well as coastal defence (e.g. rank 3 navies) are still systematically represented as 'inferior' on a scale ranging from 'small' to 'global'.

When it comes to categorisation and ranking, more than the navies' capabilities in absolute terms, 'what is [...] important is the position of each navy relative to the others'.[18] Ranking is a process of 'othering' and it substantially contributes to the construction of states' international reputation. Since navies have traditionally been an indicator of states' power, they contribute to their prestige.[19] Ranking has important consequences in terms of categorising navies and more importantly their states: 'simply put, there is a general correlation between ranking of a nation's navy and a nation's status in the international system'.[20] The idea that the international order is highly hierarchical is widely accepted, and the ranking of navies contributes to reinforce this belief. Kearsley explains that ranking navies combines the desire 'by both authors and practitioners of naval power alike to compare and contrast navies on a global scale with the desire of obtaining a linear list that reflects an international maritime pecking order'.[21]

Through the ranking process, 'one' reality is constructed, i.e. a 'global' navy (ranks 5–6) is 'superior' compared to a 'small' navy (e.g. ranks 1–2 or even rank 3) because the 'ideal' situation (towards which it is 'normal' to tend) is to possess projection capabilities. The consequence of this construction is that a 'small' navy's natural path seems to follow a linear evolution towards more projection capabilities, be it autonomously or in coalition through interoperability and specialisation (as shown in Figure 3.1).

There is no doubt that for a variety of strategic reasons certain 'small' navies, e.g. in East and Southeast Asia, may need to grow, as they are facing emerging threats (regional competitors, non-state actors, etc.). As for Western navies, the incentive comes from the emphasis put on projection operations since the end of the Cold War as a way to contribute to the stability of the liberal international order. This chapter does not contest either navies' right to 'grow' or the rationality behind that. However, it highlights that so-called 'small' navies are systematically represented as 'inferior' and that the alternative to this 'inferiority' consists in following a linear evolution towards more projection capabilities. Consequently, the very ranking process contributes to the widespread rhetoric about power projection, as discussed below.

---

[18] Aaron P. Jackson, 'Keystone Doctrine Development in Five Commonwealth Navies: A Comparative Perspective', *Papers in Australian Maritime Affairs*, 33 (2010): p. 12.

[19] Till, op.cit., p.116.

[20] Captain (N) Laurence M. Hickey, 'Enhancing the Naval Mandate for Law Enforcement: Hot Pursuit or Hot Potato?', *Canadian Military Journal*, 7/1 (2006): p. 46.

[21] Harold J. Kearsley, *Maritime Power and the Twenty-First Century* (Dartmouth Publishing Co. Ltd.: Aldershot, 1992), p. 175, quoted in Lindberg, *Geographical Impact*, p. 32.

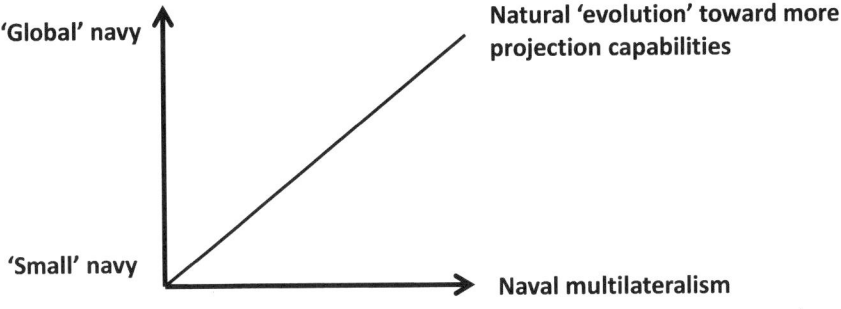

Figure 3.1   'Small' navies' natural 'evolution'

Small Navies and the Projection Discourse

Framed within the realist approach to International Relations, the concept of security that prevailed during the Cold War was centred on states' survival, territorial defence and national security. Western navies were integrated within the Euro–Atlantic system of defence, and in case of war, they would have contributed to the war effort by performing logistical tasks and defending Europe's maritime approaches as well as the Euro–Atlantic SLOCs, i.e. to secure the command of the Atlantic. Apart from the US Navy, and to a lesser extent the British and the French navies, the other European navies were reduced to territorial defence and regional escort/ASW roles (e.g. Spain) or specialised roles within NATO (e.g. Belgium with minesweeping).

The end of the Cold War and the vanishing of the Soviet threat opened up the door to a rapid expansion of the security agenda. A wide range of risks and threats, including non-military ones like economic threats, human rights violations, civil unrest, migrations, environmental degradations, and transnational criminality are now included in the agenda.[22] Non-state actors (such as terrorists, pirates and smugglers) have become prominent as sources of threats. In this context, Western armed forces are increasingly engaged abroad in various types of projection operations, ranging from high intensity military campaigns (such as the 2011 Libya campaign) to counter-piracy operations (such as EU operation Atalanta at the Horn of Africa) to counter-immigration police operations far away from home.

This evolution is linked to an influential discourse on the projection of security. This discourse proposes that security should systematically be projected beyond one's own boundaries.[23] The key idea is the need to tackle the risks and threats

---

[22]   On the expansion of the security agenda see Keith Krause and Michael C. Williams, 'Broadening the Agenda of Security Studies: Politics and Methods', *Mershon International Studies Review*, 40/2 (1996), pp. 229–254.

[23]   Germond, 'The European Union at the Horn of Africa'.

as far away as possible, at the source, and as soon as possible. Projection is not restricted to military interventions but also has a non-military dimension (such as counter-immigration, counter-trafficking, etc.). This rhetoric can be found in almost every security policy documents released by Western states, the EU and NATO in the past decade and a half.[24] The dominant discourse on the projection of security is backed by a geopolitical sub-discourse, based on simple geo-societal representations, such as 'us-stable-safe' versus 'them-unstable-dangerous', which also normalises the idea that the security (of the 'us') will be obtained by intervening (projection of security) in the 'them' territory, i.e. beyond one's own boundaries/territorial waters. In other words, one's own security depends on the ability of the 'us' to influence the 'them'.

This dominant discourse has influenced the formulation of naval missions in the post-Cold War era. Western navies' focus is clearly put on projection operations, which requires some sort of power and forces projection capabilities. In the 21st century, Western navies are expected to be able to contribute to the general effort aiming at projecting security as far away as possible beyond their own boundaries. Even police operations at sea take place far beyond states' territorial waters; for example, EU co-financed and coordinated counter-immigration police operations have taken place as far away as the coast of Senegal. In other words, the role of navies has evolved from defensive and regional escort duties to projection activities, including expeditionary warfare, counter-terrorism, counter-piracy, and counter-immigration. Since those types of operations are increasingly internationally integrated, operating within coalitions is becoming crucial for Western navies. This has been acknowledged by the highest ranked Western navies (i.e. ranks 6, 5 and 4), such as the British, French, Italian, German, and US navies.[25] States that

---

[24] See for example Ministry of Defence, *Defence White Paper: Delivering Security in a Changing World*, presented to Parliament by the Secretary of State for Defence by Command of her Majesty (Crown TSO: London, December 2003), pp. 4, 7; Ministerio de Defensa, *Revisión Estratégica de la Defensa* (Secretaria General Técnica: Madrid, May 2003), pp. 49–50 (English version: pp. 47–48); Federal Ministry of Defence, *White Paper 2006 on German Security Policy and the Future of the Bundeswehr* (Berlin, 2006), pp. 21–22; EU, *A Secure Europe in a Better World: European Security Strategy* (Brussels, 2003); NATO, 'The Alliance's Strategic Concept', approved by the Heads of State and Government participating in the meeting of the North Atlantic Council in Washington, DC, 23–24 April 1999, *Press release*, NAC-S(99)65, 24 April 1999, §20. For a longer discussion of this trend, see Basil Germond, 'Venus Has Learned Geopolitics: The European Union's Frontier and Transatlantic Relations', in Jussi Hanhimäki, Georges-Henri Soutou and Basil Germond (eds), *The Routledge Handbook of Transatlantic Security* (Routledge: London and New York, 2010), pp. 206–217.

[25] See Admiralty Board, Future Navy – Operational Concept (Admiralty Board: London, 2001), NAVB/P(01)13, pp. 3–5; Assemblée nationale, Avis n°1867 sur le projet de loi de finance pour 2005 (Commission de la défense nationale et des forces armées: Paris, 2004), p. 15; Marina Militare Italiana, Rapporto 2003 (Ministero della Difesa: Roma, 2004), see 'Introduzione'; Inspekteur der Marine, Transformation – Marine Auf

possess limited naval resources (ranks 2 and 3 navies) often stick to a rhetoric that represents their navy as fully able to operate autonomously when it comes to the defence of national interest and integrity as illustrated by Portugal and Finland:

> In order to autonomously face purely military missions, the Navy has a high-readiness task-force, able to depart from Lisbon and project force in areas where the national interest is at risk.[26]

> The Commander of the Navy leads the Navy under the Chief of Defence and is responsible for the maintenance and development of the capability of maritime defence as well as for maritime surveillance, securing territorial integrity and safeguarding vital sea lines of communication in accordance with the mission statement of the Defence Forces.[27]

When it comes to projection operations, the rhetoric is different, with a strong emphasis put on multinational operations and multilateral frameworks. For example, Norway has stressed that 'multinational solutions will become increasingly important as a strategy for the further development of Norway's Armed Forces'[28] and non-NATO Finland reassessed the importance of participating in multilateral operations and announced that its navy's contribution to international crisis management will increase.[29]

As long as a 'small' navy can operate within a larger coalition it transcends its initial ('inferior') status and 'evolve' closer to the 'ideal' situation (i.e. a global projection navy). In this case, the status of 'small navies' ceases to be negative. Consequently, multinational naval operations are positively represented by 'small' navies. In Sweden, it is implicitly recognised that multinational naval operations are necessary to ensure the state's national interests:

> The navy should be able to participate in marine operations together with other countries, in Sweden and within and outside our region. Through them, Sweden

---

Kurs! (Bundesmarine: Bonn, 2004), p. 3; Inspekteur der Marine, Zielvereinbarung für die Deutsche Marine (Bundesmarine: Bonn, 2003); US Navy, Marine Corps and Coast Guard, Naval Operations Concept 2010: Implementing The Maritime Strategy, available at http://1.usa.gov/18jWk3o, pp. 28–29.

[26] Portuguese Navy, *Military defence and support to foreign policy*, Brochure, available at http://bit.ly/1hArXJb, p.2.

[27] The Finnish Defence Forces, 'Facts about National Defence' (Public Information Division of Defence Command: Helsinki, 2008), p.21.

[28] Forsvarsdepartementet, The Further Modernisation of the Norwegian Armed Forces 2005–2008, Proposition to Parliament No. 42 (Oslo: 2004), pp. 7–8.

[29] Government report, *Finnish Security and Defence Policy 2004* (Helsinki, 2004), VNS 6/2004 vp, p. 125.

will be able to effectively contribute to the protection of shipping and other maritime activities.[30]

However, multinational naval operations are not only seen as a way to overcome resource limitations but also as a way to learn from others. For example, the advantage of operating alongside a senior partner has become a leitmotiv of the Republic of Singapore Navy:

> We find a lot of value from learning from others and as a small navy, we can learn a lot from the U.S. Navy". [...] "Ultimately we are all Sailors and operate at sea so there are many similarities; just the scope of operations is different.[31]

Being able to operate within a coalition becomes an objective as such against which performances can be evaluated. In Ireland, the key performance indicators (KPI) to monitor Irish armed forces' achievements against the 2011–2014 Strategy Statement include:

> Flexible and adaptive conventional land, sea and air military capabilities, capable of operating jointly and interoperable with like-minded states.[32]

For some navies (mainly of rank 2), specialisation is the only way to contribute to larger coalitions, such as for Estonia and Lithuania:

> Navy keeps its focus on mine countermeasures capabilities. The Navy will continue to develop mine clearance capabilities that are necessary for participating in international operations and for guaranteeing host nation support.[33]

---

[30] Regeringskansliet / Ministry of Defence Sweden, 'A functional defence: Government Bill on the future focus of defence', Fact sheet summarising Bill 2008/09:140 (Stockholm, 2009), p. 2.

[31] Major Choo Wai Kit, RSN, quoted in Mass Communication Specialist 2nd Class Juan Pinalez, 'Republic of Singapore Navy Sailors Visit George Washington', 15 October 2011, Commander US Pacific Fleet, available at http://www.cpf.navy.mil/news.aspx/000673.

[32] Department of Defence and Defence Forces, *Strategy Statement 2011–2014* (Station Road, Newbridge, Co. Kildare, 2011), p. 33.

[33] Eesti Kaitsevägi/Estonian Defence Forces, 'Estonian Long Term Defence Development Plan 2009–2018' (Public Affairs Department of the Ministry of Defence: Tallinn, 2009), p. 10.

Having become a member of NATO, Lithuania specialises in the area of MCM and develops appropriate capabilities that will be a part of NATO's MCM force.[34]

Those navies may specialise at the expense of other coastal defence capabilities, but are confident they can rely upon NATO in case of an attack.

In sum, naval multilateralism is a sub-discourse within the discourse on power projection. The role of navies is clearly defined: projection. Those which cannot do it autonomously (for reason of limited resources) have only one option left, i.e. integrating within coalitions. Representing 'small navies' as 'inferior' contributes to this dominant discourse on the projection of security, as it gives the impression that there are only two options left: either to reproduce the structure and capabilities of the larger navies, which possess projection capabilities, or to find 'salvation' in multilateral naval cooperation.

Conclusion: The Dilemma of Small Navies

Some navies are objectively small, because their resources are restricted, due either to their state's limited economic performance and wealth or to their government's 'low-profile' defence strategy and policies. However this chapter has shown that in the collective imagery 'small' navies are represented and constructed as opposed to 'large' navies which possess the capabilities to project power and forces beyond their own territorial waters (binary identities). In the literature, navies are ranked using two main recurring criteria, i.e. the reach and projection capabilities. Thus, the resulting naval hierarchies are principally functional (symbolic, constabulary, coastal defence, or projection navies). These hierarchies are widely used outside academia, including naval establishments and defence ministries.

Navies which do not have projection capabilities tend to be represented, constructed and considered not only as 'small' but also as 'inferior' on a scale ranging from local to global navies. In other words, the linear evolution and the goal towards which each navy should tend is normalised through a dominant discourse on the projection of security. Although navies contribute to various non-projection missions, the analysis of the discourse on naval missions has identified the following rhetoric: 'so as to contribute to the security and stability of the liberal international order, Western navies should be able to project security beyond their territorial waters'. In a not-so-distant past, the nobility of the art of war at sea was characterised by the battle between two fleets on the high seas, i.e. *guerre d'escadre*, while all other roles (including expeditionary warfare) were considered as inferior. Today, the 'noble' role consists in projecting power, forces and, in general, security overseas, whereas coastal defence and police tasks are regarded

---

[34] *Ministry of National Defence*, 'White Paper: Lithuanian Defence Policy' (Ministry of National Defence: Vilnius, 2006), UDK 355(474.5) Vh-05, p. 43.

as less prestigious, which further contributes to the construction of 'small navies' as 'inferior'.

So-called 'small navies' have the possibility to overcome their 'inferiority' if they manage to integrate within multilateral naval frameworks and coalitions, as this allows them to contribute, even modestly, to the general effort consisting in projecting security and securing the liberal international order. In the 21st century, what matters for Western navies is the order of effect, not the order of battle.[35] In other words, through multinational naval cooperation the emphasis is put on the collective final cause rather than on individual material considerations, which fits well with the Liberal conception of international relations.

In sum, the criteria used to categorise 'small' navies as well as the 'options' available for those which aspire to become 'medium' or at least to surmount their 'inferior' status contribute to the dominant discourse on the projection of security. In turn such a discourse normalises, legitimises and reinforces certain practices such as multinational naval operations aimed at influencing events ashore in a bid to stabilise the liberal international order.

---

[35] Julian Lindley-French and Wouter van Straten, 'Exploiting the Value of Small Navies: The Experience of the Royal Netherlands Navy', *The RUSI Journal*, 153/6 (2008), p. 67.

Chapter 4
Transforming Small Navies by Systematic Innovation: A Framework for Productivity, Efficiency and Effectiveness

Michael Mulqueen and Terry Warburton

In December 2012 *The Economist* marked the end of a grim year with a warning from its columnist Schumpeter that 'the age of austerity' showed no sign of waning: 'It is going too far to say that austerity is turning out not to be an age but an aeon. But it would make sense for business and governments in the West to start acting as if that might be the case'.[1] Forgiving a little journalistic polemic Schumpeter's identification of four interlocking lessons from the rubble of broken business models and failing government policies over the four previous years is not without some applicability to the organisational modelling of small navies to be attempted in this chapter: The first of these lessons – to look to emerging markets for inspiration – translates simply as asking and supplying the user of the product or service concerned what s/he finds useful and affordable. Unilever, a global name in established consumer markets, is held up by Schumpeter as having turned a challenging time into a profitable one. Using consumers as its product advisors and problem solvers has led it to provide smaller packs of detergent to cash-strapped Spaniards and shrunken packages of potatoes to the 'new poor' of Greece. The second lesson is to stop aiming 'middle class product and service delivery' at a market which has become poorer: 'Many companies continue to (do so). But their numbers are shrinking as the marginalised is going mainstream'.[2] The third and fourth lessons can be summarised as follows: a market of poorer consumers is a strong market for cheaply priced goods and technology allows lower cost suppliers to provide unusually capable service and product delivery. The article notes that in the United States the White House's Office of Social Innovation has examined grassroots innovators from emerging markets and points to the value of dealing with scarcity as an opportunity.

---

[1] The Economist. 'Gold-hunting in a frugal age'. *The Economist*, December 2012: p. 62.

[2] The Economist, Gold-hunting, p. 62.

Companies that adopt models of systematic innovation report sustained gains in productivity, efficiency and effectiveness.[3] This chapter contends that systematic innovation can provide similar benefits to small navies, provided such navies can adjust their formal and informal structures to enable innovation throughout the organisation. It is important to note at the outset that innovation has become something of a catchphrase in political and popular discourse. The term 'systematic innovation' is used here to describe an approach to organisational management, derived from industrial economics, which promotes user, lead user and open-source problem-solving models. It is associated, in particular, with the work of Eric von Hippel.[4] Systematic innovation is further adapted here for the purpose of it being a conceptual framework that innovation-focused small navies can use to expand their military capabilities and/or expand their activities to support economic growth, scientific enquiry and social development including education. Specific focus here is on military and economic growth. It will be argued, economically, that by adopting systematic innovation, a small navy can move from being a net consumer of state resources to a producer or enabler of wealth in the interests of the state and citizens it serves. A focus on the contribution that small navies can make economically appears particularly apt in the wake of the financial crises faced by many states since 2008.

In particular we point to the utility of users, lead users and open-source innovation networks. Users are consumers of naval services who, through their use of these services, recognise how they might be improved and, frequently, develop an innovative solution. Lead users are a particular group of consumers who recognise the need for improvement especially early. By harnessing users and lead users small navies can unlock otherwise absent expertise and pursue adaptive solutions that germinate outside of familiar organisational boundaries. In addition, a small navy can act as a solution seeker in open-source innovation networks established to address a problem, military or economic. A hallmark of open-source networks is that they greatly expand the intellectual gene pool that can be applied to a problem.[5] Such gene pools, which may include users and lead users, can be enabled by systematic innovation techniques to provide unusually efficient, effective and productive outcomes. The chapter contends that by enhancing network performance, open-source innovation provides an important component in a framework that unfamiliar partners brought together in multi-agency networks to tackle complex security threats can use to more coherently

---

[3] Michael Mulqueen and Terry Warburton, 'Breaking with tradition: Remodelling naval strategic thinking and outcomes using an open innovation approach,' *Administration* 60, 4 (2013): p. 89.

[4] Eric von Hippel, *Democratizing innovation* (Cambridge MA: MIT Press, 2007a); Eric von Hippel, 'Horizontal innovation networks – by and for users.' Industrial and Corporate Change 16, 2 (2007b): pp. 298–315; Eric von Hippel, *The sources of innovation* (Oxford: Oxford University Press, 1995).

[5] von Hippel, *Democratizing Innovation,* op.cit.

and fruitfully collaborate. Such networks can take various forms, address diverse challenges, from piracy to economic collapse, and incorporate actors both within and clearly distinct from military form, shape and function.

Overall, the authors argue that systematic innovation, through user, lead user and open source innovation networks, provides to small navies a coherent framework to more closely align their mission, strategy and operational achievements to needs and skills in civil society while enhancing military capability. The navy can, thus, become more clearly a relevant standing capacity of its state and society. Broadening organisational function in the manner mapped out here carries the risk that the ability to undertake critical military tasks will be weakened. But the authors posit that careful rollout of systematic innovation can enhance military effectiveness. Indeed, by stimulating invention of low cost naval technologies, systematic innovation is already providing to small, low budget navies access to net-centric capabilities that were previously out of reach.

Chiefly economic reasons provide justification both for the argument being mounted here and its timing. Other important reasons of national security also pertain. These can be summarised as (1) a mismatch between the costs of maintaining naval power and the austerity implied in the economic policies of many Western states since 2010, (2) the particular vulnerabilities of small navies – by dint of their smallness – to economic uncertainty, (3) unintended or undesirable national security consequences that may arise from these vulnerabilities and (4) fractured decision making in defence organisations facing severe financial pressures.

In the aftermath of economic crisis governments must carefully profile expenditure cuts so that they achieve economic recovery goals while minimising public dismay. If they fail and further economic calamity results the public bind to the state may come under significant pressure and instability in national security will be a distinct possibility.[6] As Buzan and Wæver suggest, the prominence of national security on the policy agenda will be a function of perceptions concerning nearness of threat.[7] This resonates with the difficult spending choices facing governments pursuing policies of austerity: do we risk social insecurity on our doorstep by making cuts to healthcare and education or do we trim back on expensive ships used to contain threats far out to sea? The cost to Britain of the Royal Navy's six Type 45 destroyers, £6.5 billion, is worth noting here.[8] Many

---

[6] Dick K. Nanto, *Economics and National Security: Issues and Implications for U.S. Policy*. CRS Report for Congress (Washington DC: Congressional Research Service, 2011); Barry Buzan, *People, States and Fear: An Agenda for International Security Studies in the Post-Cold War Era* (Hemel Hempstead: Harvester Wheatsheaf, 1991); Michael Mulqueen, *Re-evaluating Irish national security: affordable threats?* (Manchester: Manchester University Press, 2009).

[7] Barry Buzan and Ole Wæver, *Regions and Powers* (Cambridge: Cambridge University Press, 2003).

[8] Douglas Fraser, 'Jobs for the Clyde Boys', 19 March 2013, accessed 31 March 2013. http://bbc.in/18yP3HM.

navies, including those of global or near-global repute such as the Royal Navy, have experienced severe outcomes of expenditure cuts in this context. These cuts have manifested in substantial fleet, administrative, personnel and operational profile reductions.⁹ Fuel starvation is another outcome and a particularly difficult one for naval managers to counter because it plays also to the very real problem of reducing the substantial carbon footprint of diesel-fuelled fleets. A more extreme outcome – scrapping a navy or placing it into abeyance – is not inconceivable and, indeed, has recent historical precedence. The Irish Navy was at one point in 1970 reduced in operational capacity to one officer with one pistol aboard a fisheries research vessel.¹⁰ Twenty nine years later the Irish government considered transforming its navy into an unarmed coastguard.¹¹ All of this occurred many years before the collapse of the Irish economy between 2008 and 2011 and concomitant threat to the entire Eurozone economy.

Small navies are vulnerable to policies of austerity in particular ways. Many do not possess a supply chain large enough to create noticeably significant economic growth at the national level, even if direct and indirect employment arising from fleet procurement, maintenance and other activities are of considerable value to the port cities concerned. Large navies can point to large contract shipbuilding (i.e. US$500m+) and other port industrial activity as measures of impact necessary for the turnaround of the regional or even national economy. Even so, as noted above, this is no immunity to cuts. But cuts are, perhaps, less likely to threaten existentially the organisation itself. Taking the example of Ireland's navy, the loss of a single ship would reduce the state's flotilla by fully one eighth. By reducing operational capacity to an even greater degree, the loss would raise doubts over the ability of the service to contribute to Irish/EU defence in meaningful ways. However, an environment of austerity would appear to be the one in which naval planners are destined to operate in during the second decade of the twenty-first century:

> European defense spending, which decreased steadily after the end of the Cold War, began shrinking at an accelerated pace in the aftermath of the global economic crisis of 2008 ... (T)otal defense spending of the 37 countries studied in this report decreased from 263 to 220 billion euros between 2001 and 2011, with more than half of these reductions occurring after 2008. This decline in available resources constitutes the chief challenge for European defense. A

---

⁹ Nick Hopkins, www.guardian.co.uk, 8 May 2012, accessed 16 March 2013. http://bit.ly/Jap6IBl.

¹⁰ Padhraic Ó Confhaola, *The Naval Forces of the Irish State, 1922–1977* (PhD thesis, National University of Ireland, Maynooth, 2009).

¹¹ Marese McDonagh, 'Uproar after Smith denies axe for Navy and Air Corps', 10 August 1999, accessed 16 March 2013. http://bit.ly/1jI1eKd

reversal of this trend in the coming years is unlikely given European political and socioeconomic realities.[12]

The drive towards austerity policies in many states carries with it a heightened risk of unintended and undesirable consequences for national security. From a naval perspective, a false economy would occur if cuts to operational effectiveness ended up increasing the costs to states arising from criminality and security threats routed through the maritime domain.[13] The capacity of states to contain societal instability brought about by economic hardship and sharp increases in the long term unemployment rate will be limited where naval austerity hinders economic recovery. In this regard, there is mounting evidence linking the resources of the maritime domain to significant and sustainable economic growth.[14] Such growth would be undermined where, for example, the decision to deploy wealth creating, ocean-deployed assets, such as wave energy farms turned on investor confidence in the security of waters.[15] Of course, it may be argued that austerity has little to do with the core problem which is that small navies, because they are small, may not be able to provide the scale of security necessary for an investment climate at sea. However, as this and the following chapter argue, systematic innovation is a route to technology that can act as a force multiplier, can be used to 'de-conflict' decision-making between services, and can facilitate networked, better value naval actions. More broadly small navies, which adapt to incorporate systematic innovation, can be reconfigured from being expensive standing assets that consume national income to being actively engaged generators of national wealth.

In addition, loss of equipment and/or service personnel to budgetary trimming can conceivably have a disproportionate impact on small navies. In small navies, equipment – notably ships – tends to be used to perform multiple tasks and, thus, may be spread thin. Furthermore, responsibility for major naval business areas will frequently rest with a small cohort of personnel, or even with an individual. Hence, operational inefficiencies can occur in areas ranging from administrative support through to gunnery and intelligence analysis expertise at sea. This is to set aside the question of expenditure on previous training, which, when transferred ashore, would be of limited economic potential to the state.

It is also reasonable to suggest that the organisational scramble for shrinking budgets in many states is impacting on decision making coherence in some small

---

[12] David J Berteau, Guy Ben-Ari, Joachim Hofbauer, Priscilla Hermann, and Sneha Raghavan, *European Defense Trends 2012: Budgets, Regulatory Frameworks and the Industrial Base* (Washington DC: Center for Strategic & International Studies, 2012).

[13] Mulqueen and Warburton, 'Breaking with Tradition'.

[14] Valerie Cummins, 'Opportunity in the face of adversity: The potential role of the military in contributing to Ireland's economic recovery with a focus on the Irish Naval Service.' *Defence Forces Review* (2011 pp.: 7–12; IMERC, Irish Maritime Energy Resource Cluster Strategy 2011–2016 (Cork: IMERC, 2011).

[15] Mulqueen and Warburton, 'Breaking with Tradition'.

navies.[16] For small navies operating to modest, shared (i.e. inter-service) defence budgets while facing imminent fleet replacement or major maintenance costs, the challenge is especially onerous. Recent historical evidence exists of the quite extraordinary impact financial preservation imperatives can have on cohesive security decision-making; after the September 11 attack, one EU island-state undertook a high-level review of its national security policy but did not directly consult with its navy.[17] This problem corresponds with that of institutional 'safe path following' to be discussed further below.[18]

The chapter will proceed in accordance with the following structure: Firstly, it will attempt to identify where systematic innovation, as a conceptual framework for small navies to become generators of economic growth, can correspond with the corpus of literature on military organisational development. In this regard, the authors focus, in particular, on ideas of the postmodern military associated with Hables Gray, Metz, Micewski, Moskos, and Williams, among others.[19] Secondly it will consider how systematic innovation in practice might be applied without diminution of the small navy's capacity to fulfil familiar military roles. At issue here also will be the 'stickiness' of 'safe path following' and other features of historical institutionalism in organisational settings, which might hinder moves towards formal and informal structures for innovation.[20] Thirdly, it will treat in some detail ways and means to undertake systematic innovation in small naval contexts. This discussion will focus especially on the potency of users, lead users and open source innovation networks. The chapter will then proceed to its

---

[16] Author's interview

[17] Mulqueen, *Irish National Security*.

[18] Mulqueen, *Irish National Security*; Theda Skocpol and Paul Pierson, 'Historical institutionalism in contemporary political science' in *Political science: State of the discipline*, ed. Ira Katznelson and Helen Milner (New York and London: W.W. Norton & Co, 2002) pp. 693–721; Jesper P. Olsen and James P. March, 'Institutional Perspectives on Political Institutions,' *Governance: An International Journal of Policy and Administration* 9, 3 (1996): pp. 247–64.

[19] Chris Hables Gray, *Postmodern War: the new politics of conflict* (New York: The Guildford Press, 1997); Steven Metz, *Armed Conflict in the 21st Century: The Information Revolution and Post-Modern Warfare* (Carlisle, Penn: Strategic Studies Institute, US Army War College, 2000); Edwin R. Micewski, 'Leadership responsibility in postmodern armed forces,' *Civil-Military Aspects of Military Ethics* (Volume 2): (Military) *Leadership and Responsibility in the Postmodern Age*, eds. Edwin R. Micewski and Dietmar Pfarr (Vienna: National Defense Academy, 2005) pp. 5–12; Charles C. Moskos, *The Postmodern Military: Armed forces after the Cold War*, eds. Charles C. Moskos, John Allen Williams, and David R. Segal (New York: Oxford University Press, 1999); John Allen Williams, 'The Postmodern Military Reconsidered,' *The Postmodern Military: Armed forces after the Cold War*, eds. John Allen Williams, David R Segal Charles C Moskos, (New York: Oxford University Press, 1999) pp. 265–88.

[20] Mulqueen, *Irish National Security*; Hall and Taylor, *Three New Institutionalisms*; Skocpol and Pierson, *Historical Institutionalism*.

conceptual conclusions and, thus, lead to Mark Mellett's analysis of systematic innovation in practice in Ireland's Naval Service.

Locating Systematic Innovation

Innovation is very often stimulated by the innovator's dissatisfaction with that which is current. Innovators bring forth and apply existing or new ideas, techniques, or technologies in unimagined or unfamiliar ways. Adherents of systematic innovation reject explanations of innovation as something in the 'nature' of certain people. Instead anyone can be an innovator and innovation can take numerous forms.[21] Consequently, systematic innovation scholars focus on mapping the sources of innovation and, in the fashion of applied research, on delivering practical steps that better enable innovators to unsettle assumptions.[22] Systematic innovation is therefore a quest to stimulate and accelerate innovation among the many rather than the few. From this point a parallel can be drawn with military scholars who have endeavoured to incorporate aspects of the postmodern research agenda into strategic studies since the end of the Cold War. Postmodern scholarship seeks to destabilise settled, widely accepted and, thus, power laden knowledge. It is rooted in twentieth century scientific debates on the nature of enquiry and rejection of the positivistic insistence on settled, observable knowledge.[23] According to Agger, 'positivism suggests that one can perceive the world without making assumptions about the nature of the phenomena under investigation; hence people are taught to accept the world "as it is", thus unthinkingly perpetuating it'.[24] Blind acceptance is anathematic to innovation. Mapped onto the strategic studies agenda postmodernism has resulted in conceptualisations of military force, structure and threat noticeably different from those that came to be familiar during the twentieth century. For example, Moskos et al envisage military organisations that undertake unprecedented roles, are androgynous in make-up and ethos, and have a greater

---

[21] von Hippel, *Democratizing Innovation*.
[22] von Hippel, *Democratizing Innovation; The sources of innovation*; Mulqueen and Warburton, 'Breaking with Tradition'.
[23] Richard Devetak, 'Postmodernism', *Theories of international relations*, eds. Andrew Linklater, Richard Devetak, Matt Paterson, Jacqui True Scott Burchill (Hampshire and London: Macmillan, 1996) pp. 179–209; Jean Francis Lyotard, *The postmodern condition: A report on knowledge* (Manchester: Manchester University Press, 1984); Steve Smith, 'Reflective and constructive approaches', *The globalisation of world politics*, eds. John Baylis and Steve Smith (Oxford: Oxford University Press, 2001) pp. 224–51; Stephen Strasser, *Understanding and explanation: Basic ideas concerning the humanity of the human sciences* (Pittsburgh: Duquesne University Press, 1985).
[24] Agger, Ben. 'Critical theory, poststructuralism, postmodernism: Their sociological relevance.' *Annual Review of Sociology* 17 (1991): p. 109.

permeability with civilian society.²⁵ Micewski imagines a greater place for civilian business models, such as contracting out functions and restructuring hierarchies.²⁶ Metz is also concerned at the prevailing wisdom for fixed hierarchies and divisions of labour:

> The trend in the commercial world has been toward a blurring between management and staff. If this is extrapolated to the military, it might be necessary to consider whether the division of a service into enlisted personnel and commissioned officers makes sense in the 21st century. In addition, the organisation of militaries into land, sea and air services needs to be assessed.²⁷

Singer, from an internet technologist's perspective, predicts an acceleration of the impact that television coverage had on domestic political opinion in the United States during the Vietnam War. The defining 'warrior ethos' will erode. Laws and codes of war are being left behind by technology and will need to be overhauled in part or fundamentally as a result of it.²⁸ The means of attack and response may or may not involve the use of violence. In this regard, Metz points to non-traditional, networked enemies and multidimensional asymmetry.²⁹ In this vein can be located a fast growing concern with Big Data and its usage as well as with the vulnerability of cyber networks, including those governing critical state and corporate infrastructures.³⁰

Till has done some useful exploratory work on the application of postmodernism in the maritime domain in the context of his much broader analyses of seapower.³¹ Nevertheless the absence of scholarly treatments is noticeable and surprising given the many innovations associated with the exercise of naval power at sea, from the bridge to the galley.³² It may be that this reflects caution on the part of practitioners to move away from safe, established pathways that reflect and

---

[25] Moskos et al, *The Postmodern Military*.

[26] Micewski, 'Leadership'.

[27] Metz, *Armed Conflict*.

[28] P.W. Singer, *Wired for War: The robotics revolution and conflict in the 21st century* (New York: Penguin, 2009).

[29] Metz, *Armed Conflict*.

[30] Richard A. Clarke and Robert K. Knake, *Cyber Security: The next threat to national security and what to do about it*, (New York: Ecco, 2010); Jason Andress and Steve Winterfeld, *Cyber Warfare: Techniques, Tactics and Tools for Security Practitioners* (Waltham, MA: Syngress, 2011); Bruce Waterfield, 'Activist accused of waging net war from bunker', *The Sydney Morning Herald*, 30 March 2013.

[31] Geoffrey Till, *Seapower: A guide for the twenty first century*, 3rd edn. (New York: Routledge, 2013).

[32] Jeremy Black, *Naval Power: A History of Warfare and the Sea from 1500* (Hampshire: Palgrave Macmillan, 2009).

reproduce a 'sealed-in' military culture.[33] The discussion now turns to the impact that systematic innovation may have on military coherence in small navies and that which institutional path following in small navies can have on their innovation.

Systematic Innovation and Its Implications for the Military Role

The intention of the chapter is to provide a conceptual framework that innovation-focussed small navies can use to expand their military capabilities and/or their activities to support economic growth, scientific enquiry and social development including education. Specific focus here is on military and economic growth. It is argued that by adopting systematic innovation models, a small navy can accelerate latent and active innovation. It can, thus, be better positioned to move from being a net consumer of state resources to a producer or enabler of wealth in the interests of the state and citizens it serves. The importance of so doing is clear in the context of the difficult economic circumstances facing many states in the second decade of the twenty first century; these circumstances pose a threat to the operations and even the viability of small navies.

A survey of the literature indicates correspondence between the dissatisfaction with established knowledge and practice that gives rise to innovation and postmodern military thinking. Since the end of the Cold War postmodern scholars have sought to unsettle established, hegemonic wisdom about what it is military force can and should do. Yet this movement does not appear to have impacted significantly on naval scholarship and practice. Notwithstanding a noticeable awakening to the importance of constabulary and maritime security operations a focus on blue water and Mahanian traditions remain highly influential.[34] In this regard it is important that the framework can help conceptually address the trade-off between a small navy acting adaptively to impact on domestic economic growth through innovation and its capacity to conduct core naval activities. The framework connects with broadened sectoral security through the means by which security is identified in five sectors – military, political, ecological, societal and economic – each of which interconnects with the other.[35] This interconnectivity implies the risk of spillover from one sector to another when an existential crisis occurs. For example, systemic economic meltdown – long argued as a necessary risk if the competitive winner-loser cycle of capitalism is to function – can

---

[33] Frank Ledwidge, *Losing Small Wars: British Military Failure in Iraq and Afghanistan* (Yale: Yale University Press, 2011).

[34] Alfred T. Mahan, *The influence of sea power upon history: 1660–1783*, 5th edn. (New York: Dover Publications, 1987); UK Ministry of Defence. 'Innovative ways sought to improve the security of maritime operations – 28 January 2013', www.gov.uk, accessed 1 April 2013. http://bit.ly/18yQJBb

[35] Barry Buzan, Ole Wæver, and Jaap de Wilde, *Security: A New Framework for Analysis* (Boulder, CO.: Lynne Rienner, 1998).

trigger political and social crises and, perhaps, violent, military reaction. It flows from this that economic malfunction of a scale sufficient to threaten existential consequences within a state should be something with which military organisations are concerned.[36] This is not to say that the military response need necessarily be a violent one. Rather, as we have argued elsewhere, it can at least in part be about re-orientating standing military assets, including naval ships and personnel, to contain the likely causes of conflict. As the next chapter will demonstrate this has led one small navy, Ireland's, to spearhead a collaborative research cluster that is focussed on achieving significant employment and GDP growth in the maritime domain.

In theory, systematic innovation should, therefore, better equip small naval managers to achieve state investment in military capabilities when corresponding military threats are considered to be low or when public expenditure is in decline. By defining the enemy in economic terms – and so by broadening assumptions about what constitutes an enemy for a military force – naval organisations can, as they always do, set about creating lines of defence and offence and arguing for resources accordingly. The end state for such modelling is not decisive victory over an opponent but curtailment of a threat through enabling innovative activity that generates economic growth.

However, naval mangers thinking perceptively about innovation need to factor in and, where possible, manage the legacy of previously dominant wisdom concerning the role, function and purpose of the navy. Alteration in formal and informal structures to facilitate systematic innovation may appear within a small navy or to its sister military organisations of state a significant and even threatening move away from that which the navy was established to achieve. An important consideration in this regard is competition between and within military services, each hungry to leverage the greatest share of available resources.[37] A deliberately innovative small navy by making itself more relevant to state and citizenry concerns may be perceived among its armed forces family to be undermining the position of air and land power.

In terms of the conceptual framework this problematic can be usefully thought about from the standpoint of historical institutionalism, an approach associated with the identification of certain features of institutionalisation, most notably path dependencies and critical junctures. Path dependencies can be defined in terms of organisational reliance on familiar routines and practices of appropriate behaviour in order to survive (e.g. how to deal with financial cutbacks). Hence, path following may well have merit some of the time. However, self-reinforcing or positive feedback processes in the organisation can unduly bolster path dependency. Established paths are shot through with power relationships that privilege some interests and ignore others.[38] Institutions are, in the main, the results

---

[36] Mulqueen and Warburton, 'Breaking with Tradition'.
[37] Mulqueen, *Irish National Security*
[38] Mulqueen, *Irish National Security*

of gradual evolution as a consequence of path dependency.[39] While historical institutionalism therefore assumes incremental change as the norm, it can also account for occasional moments of significant transformation, known as critical junctures.[40] Events external to existing institutions occur at a particular time and order of sequence to trigger a reaction which may ultimately result in moves to a new trajectory or pathway.[41] The sequence and timing of economic collapse in many states since 2008 may provide the environment for change. Organisational adaptation to systematic innovation may be one resulting trajectory. Tempering the likelihood of such fundamental changes are positive feedback mechanisms that support the recurrence of a predominant pattern. Hence, the process is frequently characterised by a powerful inertial 'stickiness'.[42] Separating critical moments, which prompt only evolution, from critical junctures which activate organic change, is a fundamental point of consideration for small navy leaders seeking to bring their organisation in new directions. The chapter argues only that systematic innovation can benefit small navies where such navies adapt their formal and informal rules governed practices. Where they do, open source innovation techniques, in particular, can help to de-conflict decision making. With this note of caution in place the remainder of the chapter will set out in some detail the principal models of systematic innovation before deriving its conclusions.

Systematic Innovation for Small Navies

We contend that for small navies it is possible to move beyond the frequently nebulous use of the term 'innovation' in popular and political discourse and instead pursue innovation as a systematic approach to making gains of efficiency, effectiveness and productivity. The framework proposed is intended to facilitate organisational transformation whereby small navies can, with conceptual coherence, reimagine the limitations of their roles at sea and ashore, better adapt to the prevailing threat environment and seize opportunities that may rest outside familiar notions of what navies should and should not do. Economically, by becoming the solution seekers to corporate entrepreneurship, such navies can move from being net resource users to wealth enablers for the states and societies they serve. Small naval assets, including ships and people, can be deployed to assist entrepreneurs undertake activities including pre-market product development and proof of concept trials. Naval personnel can up-skill to facilitate and generate inward and outward enterprise. Fixed assets and personnel can be put to work collaboratively in funded research. In terms of militarily specific gains the small

---

[39] Skocpol and Pierson, p. 709
[40] Simon Bulmer and Martin Burch, 'Organizing for Europe: Whitehall, The British State and European Union,' *Public Administration 76* (1998): pp. 621–608.
[41] Mulqueen, *Irish National Security*
[42] Skocpol and Pierson, *Historical Institutionalism*, pp.701–2

navy can champion invention and product development from new entrants outside of the established (and expensive) defence sector and, therefore, increase potential access to new technologies at lower cost. A secondary but critically important potential advantage is enhanced political and social relevance of the small navy; this takes on currency when governments decide the direction and scale of public sector cuts. Below, three features of systematic innovation are proposed as a framework that small navies can pursue.

As von Hippel notes, the processes of innovation are often misunderstood. We have become accustomed to think of innovation as something that takes place in the research and development (R&D) departments of large corporations or in laboratories. But the sources of innovation vary greatly.[43] The first important source of innovation is user innovation. Users can be defined as consumers who might suggest or develop innovations that are need-prompted or created by technique-refining through use, or as practitioners who use a product or artefact and change or adapt in in some way to better increase its use value to them.[44] User innovation occurs frequently.[45] The self-reliance required of them at sea and their interaction with a range of non-military 'consumers' at sea and ashore would suggest that navies can be managed as fruitful spaces for user innovation. Specific examples of this will be discussed in the next chapter. But for now it is worth briefly considering the Irish navy's use of user innovation to address the carbon footprint of its flotilla's diesel engines. The process has resulted in trials of a kite sail for powering naval ships at slow speed when loitering on patrol offshore. The concept has been developed whereby the kites hold sensors for environmental-monitoring, direction-finding, thermal imaging and night vision. The project envisages Ireland's modestly funded small navy being able to access low-cost/high-utility situational awareness and networking to a capacity commensurate with prohibitively expensive satellite based technologies. A successful outcome would create a market for the producer and, for the navy, an affordable force multiplier in the maritime security role with parallel operability in Search and Rescue (SAR), fisheries protection and other eco-focused tasks.

Lead users constitute the second major source of innovation. According to von Hippel, 'Lead users experience needs that will become general in a marketplace, but experience them months or years earlier than the majority of the target market…They are typically ahead of the entire adoption curve in that they experience needs before *any* responsive commercial products exist – and therefore often develop their own solutions'.[46] A useful example is provided by an Irish naval officer who, while at sea, began to consider how a ships hoist used for launching Rigid Inflatable Boats (RIB) might be applied to limit dangers he had observed in boarding wind turbines at sea. The result – a new form of hoist –generated

---

[43] von Hippel, *Sources of Innovation*.
[44] Mulqueen and Warburton, 'Breaking with Tradition'.
[45] von Hippel, *Democratizing Innovation*.
[46] von Hippel, *Horizontal Innovation*.

potential commercial and naval service value as well as the obvious benefit of saving lives.

Open source innovation, which is the third source of innovation suggested for the framework, is named as such because an inventor or solver of an innovation challenge – the source of the innovation – is independent of the seeker of that invention or innovation.[47] Open source innovation has its roots in the early days of computer programming when university-based developers shared solutions in collegiate ways.[48] Many 'seeker and solver' networks are being established in this way to increase the problem solving gene pool that can be applied to a challenge. The potential for intellectual refreshment in this strategy is clear when considered against the backdrop of a 'sealed in' military culture and safe pathways turned inward for preservation of traditions, budgets and standing. Nevertheless, as discussed below, successful calls for solutions are defined by precise guidance regarding what is sought and the structures of project governance. In the corporate sphere Proctor and Gamble, which markets a 'stable of brands' of which twenty-three turn in excess of $1 billion a year each, have created the online Connect and Develop system on which Proctor and Gamble specify challenges and those able to provide solutions can respond.[49] We suggest that small navies undertaking this process will tend to become more open to change in respect of role, working practices, enabling systems and incentive structures for problem solvers, who may not have formal employment ties to the navy. Correspondingly, they will take a much broader view of who innovators are and how to harness their potential and value, as necessary.

For small navies this has resonance both in terms of their involvement in projects of economic growth and in more traditional security-related activities. In terms of the latter it is again worth noting a trend towards the establishment by states of networks comprising diverse actors to tackle complex networked security problems. Radicalisation provides one ready example: Experts in policing, defence (including naval defence) and intelligence are being brought into problem solving groups alongside religious leaders, educationalists, social workers and so on. To work effectively such networks must navigate through the legislative, procedural codified and cultural frameworks within which each actor operates and so overcome contradictions of approach that may be exposed when actors gather around the table. Open source innovation provides a basis for dynamic interplay, whereby network actors may be solution seekers for one challenge but problem solvers for another; in this way the limitations implied in organisational silos can be relaxed and decision making de-conflicted in favour of shared intellectual capital. It is interesting how corporations have done this for business gains despite the constraints implied in high value commercial secrecy.

---

[47] Mulqueen and Warburton, 'Breaking with Tradition'.
[48] von Hippel, *Sources of Innovation*.
[49] BBC Radio 4, 'In Business', London: BBC Radio 4, 11 October 2007.

Research on systematic innovation in the corporate sphere has focussed on the ways and means of innovation among groups seeking to collaborate as users, lead users or by means of open source networking. Churchill, Sonnack and von Hippel have developed guidelines on how to find lead users, on lead-user group operations and practices, and on how to identify important emerging market or sector needs. They have also formulated a workshop-based method for generating solutions.[50] There is also an emerging body of work on toolkits, or design interfaces, which enable trial and error experimentation and allow the customer to take an active part in product development.[51] From a service delivery perspective it is noteworthy that equipping users with toolkits for customisation has resulted in increased user satisfaction (Franke and von Hippel 2003).[52]

Similarly, the underpinning key concepts and mechanisms for applying open-source principles have been developed. Proctor and Gamble's 'Connect and Develop' system, noted above, is one successful example. A number of 'go-between' organisations have been established to facilitate open source innovation between companies that have problems requiring solutions and the solvers able to provide them. Some examples are www.innocentive.com, www.ninesigma.com, www.yet2.com and www.yourencore.com. Randolph H. Pherson, Katherine Hibbs Pherson, Richards J. Heuer and Sarah Miller Beebe – from the perspective of structured analytic techniques – have developed a series of step-by-step methods of de-conflicting decision making that appear readily applicable to specifying the challenges and selecting the solutions of networked innovation in maritime security contexts (Pherson and Hibbs Pherson 2012, Heuer and Pherson 2010, Miller Beebe and Pherson 2012).[53]

Conclusion

Facing many small navies in the second decade of the twenty-first century is an operational environment largely defined by the swingeing financial cuts being

---

[50] Joan Churchill, Mary Sonnack and Eric von Hippel, *Lead user project handbook: A practical guide for lead user project teams* (Cambridge MA: MIT Press, 2009).

[51] Nikolaus Franke and Frank Piller, 'Value creation by toolkits for user innovation and design: the case of the watch market,' *Journal of Product Innovation* 21, 6 (2004): pp. 401–15.

[52] Nickolaus Franke and Eric von Hippel, 'Satisfying heterogeneous user needs via innovation toolkits: The case of Apache security software,' *Research Policy* 32 (2003): pp. 1199–215.

[53] Sarah Miller Beebe and Randolph H. Pherson, *Cases in Intelligence Analysis: Structured Analytic Techniques in Action* (Washington DC: CQ Press, 2012); Randolph H. Pherson and Katherine Hibbs Pherson, *Critical Thinking for Strategic Intelligence*, Washington DC: CQ Press, 2012; Richards J. Heuer and Randolph H. Pherson, *Structured Analytic Techniques for Intelligence Analysis* (Washington DC: CQ Press, 2010).

forced upon them and the citizens they serve by governments challenged by the lingering after effects of economic collapse. Relevance in the minds of the public who pay for them is a currency that is rising in value at a time when decisions are being made for cuts and the debate focuses mainly on the scale and direction that cuts will take. Staying relevant by demonstrating the ability to help tackle the most serious threats facing their countries suggests many small navies should be closely considering ways to impact positively on domestic economic gain. The chapter suggests a framework that small navy managers can use to position their organisation for this purpose and, furthermore, to more clearly align it with society through supporting activities of science, industry and social good especially in hard-pressed times.

Like the corpus of postmodern military thought systematic innovation relates to a rejection of settled norms about the limits of what navies can or should do. Systematic innovation involves the application of new or existing ideas, techniques, products and services to unfamiliar problems and in novel ways. Unlike the broader postmodern agenda in social sciences the framework proposed here assumes that some generalisable statements can be made about small navies, notably their inability to absorb severe financial cutbacks and the unintended but serious consequences that may arise for national security as a result: It is not entirely unreasonable to suggest that some small navies could disappear altogether and others be so denuded of capacity that they are operationally incapable of interdicting clear and present threats and preventing potential ones. The framework, thus, claims interplay between structure (i.e. common features of small navies) and agent, at which level it is possible to reimagine the role, shape and function of navies in ways that defeat fixed traditions in favour of competing understandings of possibilities.[54]

The application of the framework is centred on the adoption of user, lead user and open source innovation techniques. It rests on the assumption that small navies will adjust their formal and informal rules governed practices to successfully implement innovation. The benefits of so doing should include the small navy as a more significant actor in the economic growth of its state and gains in military operational capabilities through, for example, development of technologies normally beyond reach by reason of cost. By adopting systematic innovation small navies can awaken latent innovation within the organisation, expand their problem-solving gene pool beyond it, de-conflict networked decision making and, through careful management of the process, grow in adaptive capacity. Nevertheless the authors do not underestimate the potency of institutionalised path following within the naval organisation and would caution small naval leaders thinking perceptively about innovation to consider the management of change attendant to it. Navies can be very traditional places.

---

[54] Anthony Giddens, *The Constitution of Society: Outline of the theory of structuration* (Cambridge: Polity, 1984).

Further development work in theory and particularly in practice operationally, in a range of new contexts, will further extend knowledge and understanding of this important field. The next chapter – Mark Mellett's analysis of introducing innovation into Ireland's small navy – takes that developmental work a stage further.

Chapter 5

Adaptive Dynamic Capabilities and Innovation: The Key for Small Navies Protecting National Interests at and from the Sea

Mark Mellett

With over 70 per cent of the earth's surface covered by water the attainment of an ecosystem-based ocean governance regime is a *sine qua non* for the sustainable development of the marine. Institutionalising such a regime will increasingly become a challenge. This is not just because of the relative size of the marine and its resources but is also linked to a simple reality that in a world of increasing scarcity, more and more market activities will have a maritime dimension. At sea there is no supranational governing authority; accordingly for states with large maritime jurisdictions the opportunities associated with exclusive sovereign rights will also bring a governance obligation wherever a state desires to exercise its jurisdiction. The institutional arrangements associated with governance at sea are complex. They require cross-cutting structures within government, where policy is formulated, the market which seeks to provide goods and services, and civil society who underpin the legitimacy of the sovereign rights vested in the state while desiring socially inclusive growth. Ecosystem-based ocean governance requires that the institutional arrangements between government, market and civil society should be defined by norms and principles which include *inter alia* sustainability, ecosystem approach, adaptation, stewardship, precautionary approach, subsidiarity and transparency. Critical also are good science and an appropriate integrated security and compliance regime. Small navies play a critical role as sovereign instruments of state in the attainment of ecosystem-based ocean governance while protecting national interests at and from the sea. Increasingly, however, it is clear that in a world of growing complexity new institutional arrangements and the systematic, rational, embracing of open and ecosystem-centric innovation are essential for the post-modern era.

Institutional arrangements that underpin Ocean Governance are sandwiched between two conflicting principles, *mare liberum*, or freedom of the seas and *mare clausum*, enclosure of the sea. Grotius, in 1609, declared that 'the sea is one of those things that cannot become private property... no part can be considered as the territory of any people whatsoever'. By the late 1900s, however, in the words of the

Chairman of the United Nations Law of the Sea (UNCLOS) drafting committee, Alan Beesley, 'the law of the sea was in a state of disorder bordering on chaos'. It is against the backdrop of these two principles that navies, coastguards and other state agencies must act as instruments of state policy in the waters where states have jurisdiction or an interest.

Between 2006 and 2009 Ireland made three submissions to the United Nations Commission on the Limits of the Continental Shelf (CLCS).

Through these submissions, including one joint submission, Ireland claims jurisdiction over the extended Continental Shelf which in some instances is up to 1200 kilometres from the baseline. This is far beyond the States Exclusive Economic Zone (EEZ). Ireland now claims jurisdiction over almost twice the seabed area it claimed at the time of the last White Paper on Defence in 2000. The area is almost 1,000,000 square kilometres or almost three times the size of Germany. With the largest sea area to land ratio in the North West European Union, it is somewhat of a surprise that Ireland still only receives 1.2 per cent of its GDP from the maritime sector. The fact that the UK receives 5 per cent, Belgium 8 per cent, Denmark 11 per cent and Norway 20 per cent from their maritime sectors point to the potential open to Ireland.

This potential can only be fully realised in a sustainable manner, however, if the market opportunities are understood, government policy is appropriate and civil society is engaged and, where necessary, enabled. Understanding Ireland's relationship with the sea will challenge the best of political and social scientists not to mention economists. Notwithstanding this, one critical piece of data can be traced back to the Treaty of Independence, Article 6 of which provided that until Ireland had the capacity to provide for her own coastal defence it would be provided by 'His Imperial Majesty's forces.' So, as the institutions of the Irish State stood up in the aftermath of independence, few looked to the sea and so it is that a sense of sea-blindness was institutionalised. This characterised Ireland's relationship with the sea for many decades and helps explain why Ireland has the smallest navy along the Euro–Atlantic rim. In recent years, however, there has been a new awakening to the interlinkage between Ireland's maritime wealth and national interests. In 2012 the Irish Government launched its Integrated Marine Plan with the aim of underpinning appropriate policy, stimulating market interest and engaging with civil society. It set as a modest target the doubling of the GDP contribution from the marine by 2030. More recent policy and strategy initiatives by the Irish Government included the adoption of maritime security and surveillance as one of the State's policy themes during the 2013 presidency and the launch of the Atlantic Strategy action plan.

In 2013 the Irish Government published a Green Paper on Defence inviting submissions that would help inform the formulation of a Defence White Paper in 2014.

The governance challenges and opportunities associated with Ireland's maritime jurisdiction are multifaceted. Ireland is geostrategically located on the western frontier of Europe and provides an interesting case study in the context of the development of a small navy in a postmodern era. The State straddles some of the world's busiest air and sea lines of communications (SLOCS) between Europe and North America. Indeed it is not surprising that Churchill described the Ports of Cork, Berehaven and Lough Swilly as 'the sentinel towers to the western approaches' of Europe. Critical infrastructure such as high speed fibre optic cables linking North America make landfall in Ireland or follow the Irish seabed towards the UK and European mainland. This infrastructure helps power the combined economies of Europe and North America. It is also infrastructure which has played a pivotal role in ensuring nine of the ten top global ICT companies have located in Ireland. Into the future the strategic advantage of access to the time series data in these cables could serve to advantage financial decision takers poised in Ireland to exploit the fractional time difference of these data in Ireland vis-à-vis London/Frankfurt and New York.

With one of the richest fisheries resources in the world the level of fishing activity remains high. It can be argued that the fishery resource within the Irish Exclusive Economic Zone (EEZ) in the first instance belongs to the Irish people. However, agreed institutional arrangements under the Common Fisheries Policy (CFP) and enabled by an exclusive competence in the European Union allow for a transfer of the property rights relating to a portion of these fish to other actors.

This property rights transfer only occurs however if the fish are caught in accordance with the CFP. There are varying statistics relating to the level of fraudulent fishing activity occurring, with some suggesting it may be between 15 per cent and 20 per cent while others indicate that they may in some instances be much higher.

Estimates vary regarding the true potential value of the yet to be found hydrocarbon and mineral resources over which Ireland has exclusive sovereign rights. Extrapolating on the work of Lorna Siggins and using current day prices and the expansion of jurisdiction suggest that oil and gas reserves may have a future value of between one and two trillion euro. Bad actors also use the oceans. Some have established trade routes with, for example, quantities of cocaine being routed from South America through the Caribbean onwards through Irish jurisdiction, while cannabis from North Africa also transits the area. Statistics of the Maritime Analysis Operations Centre Narcotics (MAOC-N) suggest that over 70 per cent of the seizures of cocaine and cannabis have been transported on small fishing and sailing vessels. Statistics also suggest that European consumption of cocaine, primarily routing from South America, has doubled in the period 1998–2008.

Historically illegal arms shipments have also been shipped through Irish jurisdiction, some intercepted, some not, some meant for Ireland some en route to other jurisdictions. Other terrorist-linked events include the loss of the Air India Flight 182 south-west of Ireland. The Irish jurisdiction also encompasses some of the world's premier wave resources. While presenting a huge opportunity for the development of a renewable industry, in the context of defence operations the energy translates into a hostile sea for the Defence Forces and the patrol vessels of the Irish Navy. This imposes a significant penalty for the delivery of defence and security services. In 2000 the largest wave ever measured by scientific instrument at 29.1 metres was recorded off the west coast of Ireland.

Increasingly there is a growing recognition of the vulnerability of ecosystem services and non-market value of the marine and its function as the earth's principal regulating biosphere. The ocean is both the world's largest CO_2 sink and also the earth's greatest regulating biosphere. The rise in ocean acidification as a result of anthropogenic activity is leading to CO_2 saturation of the ocean and a reduction in biodiversity undermining the ability of the sea to absorb further CO_2. This is having a profound effect on vulnerable marine ecosystems and into the future could threaten the survival of vertebrates in the ocean. At a macro level the impact of climate change as well as triggering more severe weather events, particularly at sea, will also impact on food and water security. Looking forward to the next 40 years, the most significant population increases will take place in the areas where natural resources and the infrastructure of modernity is already the scarcest.

Ninety-five per cent of human population growth is occurring in countries already struggling with poverty, illiteracy and civil unrest. This will continue to force migration and increase demand for food and water. It is also likely to trigger more complex humanitarian crises. These are contingencies for which First World states must prepare, forcing greater cross-cutting in government between the agents of responding states and greater internal and external state policy coherency. In the context of ocean governance there are growing trends in piracy with the Mallaca Straits, Horn of Africa (HOA) and the Gulf of Guinea (GOG) areas of concern. As an open economy in which 97 per cent of Irish trade by volume and 90 per cent by value travels by sea it is in Ireland's national interest that appropriate governance regimes to protect sea lines of communications are institutionalised. As remarked by Sir Julian Corbett 'It is commerce and finance which now more than ever control or check the foreign policy of nations'. Sovereignty tensions at sea in Asia and elsewhere signal challenges for the future as competition for resources becomes keener and the desire for greater enclosure comes to the fore.

While there will always be a requirement for presence at sea, for small navies it is increasingly apparent that the effectiveness of deployed assets is directly linked to an enhanced understanding of activity at sea. Externally a number of policy initiatives have been helpful in this regard. European Union regional initiatives have been helping shape the agenda in areas such as information sharing and cooperation. The drive towards a common information sharing environment (CISE) has at its core a philosophy of a 'need to share' information. Improvements in maritime domain awareness are being achieved through greater regional and sub-regional cooperation. Initiatives such as the European Defence Agency (EDA) MARSUR project are helping to institutionalise platforms that facilitate greater local cooperation. The Atlantic Strategy has sought to achieve better policy and strategy coherence between the five Atlantic states of France, Ireland, Portugal, Spain and the United Kingdom. The strategy seeks to build regional engagement along five themes: ecosystem approach, reduction of carbon footprint, sustainable exploitation of the seafloor, responding to threats and emergencies and promoting socially inclusive growth. In support of the Atlantic Strategy, as one of its EU

Presidency initiatives, Ireland is currently leading an initiative between the five Atlantic navies. This aims to create a framework for cooperation centred primarily on areas such as combined naval activities, enhanced information exchange and research development technology and innovation. Since the foundation of the Irish Navy this initiative reflects the most ambitious government policy recognition of the importance of collaboration between navies.

However, the freedom afforded by Government for bottom up and local transformation is of most significance in the context of the development of the Irish Navy in recent years. To best understand how this transformation has been institutionalised it is of value to look first at the evolution of the Irish Navy. The Irish Navy was founded just after World War II and until recent years developed mainly in isolation and with the minimal of engagement with other navies. In the period between 1990 and 2004 the evolution of the Irish Navy was as an initially inwardly innovative Service with its post-modern approach stemming from a series of reviews of the Defence Forces. In the 1998 Price Waterhouse study of the Air Corps and the Naval Service, a fleet of eight offshore patrol vessels was recommended for the navy as a capability profile suited to just one 'minimalist scenario' relating to the State's national interests. With the study guiding the navy down a service-delivery path, triggers for a post-modern approach were contained in passages such as: 'The challenge which must be faced, therefore, is to get the Naval Service ... to operate to standards of cost, efficiency and value for money closer to those which would apply in the civilian world'.

Many of the report's recommendations, including a commitment to the provision of a modern eight-ship flotilla and a process of continuous investment and vessel replacement, were codified into Irish defence policy. The Naval Service Value for Money Implementation Plan facilitated the attainment of a policy strategy match. Established as the principal seagoing agency of the State, the navy was tasked with delivering to the maximum all of the government's requirements in the maritime domain. By shaping its operational capability, the navy institutionalised the agility to 'swing' from one service to another or, in many cases, simultaneously delivered a variety of services through what it described as 'multitasking'. Capacity for concurrent multiple activities serves as a key institutional strength for innovation network participation. Through restructuring, the navy increased patrol days by over 50 per cent. These patrol days served as inputs to navy activities across the four programmes of the Defence Forces:

Programme 1 – contingent capability;
Programme 2 – on-island security and support to other agencies;
Programme 3 – international peace and security;
Programme 4 – defence policy, military advice and corporate services.

An in-depth discussion on post-modernism is beyond the scope of this chapter. However, in order to set a context for what is to follow the fundamental explanation that underpins post-modernist thinking is one of no pre-suppositions. In a postmodern setting Moskos et al suggest that the military will need to be more multi-purpose in mission, increasingly androgynous in make up and ethos, and with a greater permeability with civilian society. This facilitates the concept of the individual, actively in dialogue, rather than the individual as the end of a conduit of 'influence'. It is in the context of post-modernism that Micewski et al introduce a market dimension suggesting that the military will need to consider practices that echo civilian business models. The restructuring of the internal naval hierarchies facilitated internal cross-cutting arrangements which were complemented through the formalisation of external institutional arrangements with stakeholders. These arrangements were codified through nearly twenty service delivery protocols with underpinning formal and informal service level agreements (SLAs). These served as seeds for the evolution of the move from an inward innovative approach to a more open innovation culture. Through SLAs the nature of Irish Defence Forces and in particular naval operations was evolving in a balance between the requirements of government and civil society and the capability of the navy in a manner similar to that envisaged in von Clausewitz's trinity. In summarising his political framework for the study of war, von Clausewitz developed his 'Amazing Trinity' (*eine wundeliche Dreifaltigkeit*): the government; the people; the commander and his army.

> 'These three tendencies are like three different codes of law, deep rooted in their subject and yet variable in their relationship to one another ... Our task, therefore, is to develop a theory that maintains a balance between these three tendencies, like an object suspended between three magnets'.

The ethos of service delivery in the navy had as its focus the requirements of government and civil society as the consumers of services, rather than just focusing on the navy as a producer of services.

With the navy very much positioned within the Defence Forces as the servant of government and civil society the navy's strategic approach to achieve its mission was built around a campaign plan operating along three lines of development/training, support and operations. In its planning process the Irish navy concluded that its strategic centre of gravity is adequate, integrated resources and systems, while its strategic end-state is to protect and further Ireland's interests at and from the sea. Effort is coordinated using a modified Kaplan and Norton balanced scorecard approach with four perspectives: resources, development, innovation and performance (see Table 1).

The modified Balanced Scorecard acts as a strategic performance management framework that helps command within the Naval Service monitor its performance and manage the execution of its strategy. Performance indicators for each perspective facilitate the maintenance of balance, thereby ensuring a comprehensive and integrated approach to mission attainment.

Table 5.1 Perspectives of Irish Naval Service's campaign plan

Perspective	Description	Driver
Resource	To manage the procurement and maintenance of resources required to meet the mission.	Justify
Development	To develop resources in order to meet the mission.	Add value
Innovation	To sense and explore, seize and exploit ideas that enhance attainment of the mission.	Game Change
Performance	To monitor, review and manage Naval Service performance in fulfilling the mission.	Transform

From the perspective of its strategy the Irish Navy has looked at how adaptive dynamic capabilities can be institutionalised within the organisation. There is a broad consensus that 'dynamic capabilities' contrast with ordinary or operational capabilities by being concerned with change.[1] Dynamic capabilities are defined as the ability to integrate, build and reconfigure internal and external competencies to address rapidly changing environments.[2] In short 'dynamic capabilities' govern the rate of change of ordinary capabilities and it is the notion of dynamism which is vital for a resilient strategy in a complex world. This enables the transformation required by government for a changing operational environment. It necessitates a responsive culture shift, enabling the seizing of 'fleeting objectives', recognising that opportunities come to pass not to pause. This resonates with the principles of von Clausewitz such as the ability to act quickly with audacity while retaining a capacity for prudence.[3] Building on the notion of 'dynamic capabilities' which is suggestive of the operational level and the ability to exploit a changing environment is the need to consider how 'dynamic capabilities' can be institutionalised into the organisation at not just the strategic level but also at the operational and tactical levels thereby equipping it better to sense and explore the environment. O'Reilly and Tushman refer to a review of a number of studies relating to 'dynamic capabilities' noting that several explicitly acknowledge the linkage between dynamic capabilities and organisational adaptation.[4] Looking at adaptation from the perspective of institutions Gupta et al note that '...institutions

---

[1] Winter, S., Understanding Dynamic Capabilities. *Strategic Management Journal*, Vol. 24, No 10, Special Issue: Why Is There a Resource Based View? Toward a Theory of Competitive Heterogeneity (October 2003), pp. 991–995.

[2] Teece, D.J., Pisano, G. and Shuen, A. Dynamic capabilities and strategic management. *Strategic Management Journal* 18(7), p.516. (1997).

[3] Aron, R., Tenenbaum, S., (1972) Reason, passion, and power in the thought of Clausewitz. *Social Research* Vol.39, No. 4 (Winter 1972). pp. 599–621.

[4] O'Reilly, C., Tushman, M., Ambidexterity as a dynamic capability: Resolving the innovator's dilemma, *Research in Organizational Behavior*, Vol. 28: pp.185-206. (Elsevier 2008).

that promote adaptive capacity are those institutions that (1) encourage the involvement of a variety of perspectives, actors and solutions; (2) enable social actors to continuously learn and improve their institutions; (3) allow and motivate social actors to adjust their behaviour; (4) can mobilize leadership qualities; (5) can mobilize resources for implementing adaptation measures; and (6) support principles of fair governance'.[5]. Providing for adaptation, which is often linked with resilience, and accepting 'adaptive dynamic capabilities' facilitates the crafting of a more embracing strategy. Such a strategy exploits the present, catering for those repeatable routines and competencies that are associated with routine service provision, while simultaneously looking to the future by exploring and exploiting opportunities for evolving technologies and future services. In arguing for a strategy characterised by 'adaptive dynamic capabilities' provision is made for an understanding that while we may not be always able to choose outcomes we have nonetheless created these outcomes.[6] By accepting Stacey's argument that organisations are complex responsive processes of relating, in which outcomes emerge in the interplay of everyone's plans and intentions we can more easily appreciate the significance of adaptation.[7] Incorporating adaptation through the concept of 'adaptive dynamic capabilities' as a strategy for a post-modern setting will provide the agility to exploit favourable and mitigate unfavourable outcomes, unexpected as they may be. While the Naval Service has clearly demonstrated a progressive agility to incorporate change by institutionalising adaptive dynamic capabilities, there are certain external drivers over which it has had little control. In recent years the most critical is the impact of the economic recession on the provision of resources and the capability profile to deliver defence, security and government services.

With the expansion of Ireland's maritime jurisdiction following the lodging of claims over the State's extended continental shelf with the United Nations CLCS a new paradigm has begun to emerge. The contribution to GDP from the marine sector in Ireland is probably the lowest of the Euro–Atlantic rim countries and yet the resource potential is extraordinary. Creating the conditions for the necessary investment to more fully realise the potential from our ocean wealth requires appropriate ocean governance structures, including security. The provision of an appropriate integrated defence, security and compliance regime for this area clearly has resource implications. Six of the eight ships of current fleet of the Naval Service have reached or passed their thirty-year notional life as described

---

[5] Gupta, J., Termeer, C., Klostermann, J., Meijerink, S., van den Brink, M., Jong, P., Nooteboom, S., Bergsma, E., (2010) The Adaptive Capacity Wheel: a method to assess the inherent characteristics of institutions to enable the adaptive capacity of society *Environmental Science & Policy* 13 no. 6:459-471 (2010)

[6] Stacey, R., *Complexity and Organizational Reality, Uncertainty and the need to rethink management after the collapse of investment capitalism.* 2nd Edition. (Routledge: New York 2010). p.xi

[7] Ibid.

in current policy. Orders for two replacement ships were placed in 2009 with an option for a follow on order. It is clear that Ireland's State security is inextricably linked with its maritime security. Providing appropriate resources is of course inextricably linked with Ireland's economic security. In short if the provision of an appropriate level of capability is threatened because of the economic security situation then it can be deduced that the economic deficit itself is an enemy. In his Treatise on War, Clausewitz theorises that out of the dominant characteristics of the enemy 'a certain centre of gravity develops ... on which everything depends. That is the point against which all our energies should be directed;.[8] Where tax receipts remain less than government spending it is reasonable to conclude that the centre of gravity is 'unemployment'. The emergence of a new paradigm should not be a surprise. This paradigm is nested in the innovation policy being driven by the Minister for Defence and his Department and in turn operationalised by the Defence Forces Chief of Staff's transformation agenda. The leadership of both the Minister for Defence and the Chief of Staff demand that the Defence Organisation should not look at itself as separate from other sectors of the Public Service or indeed the institutions of the State in the context of utilisation of resources. Calaprice has quoted Einstein as saying that 'The significant problems we face cannot be solved by the same level of thinking that created them'.[9] Challenging the public sector not just to look at the quality of its services but also to look at a broader role in terms of governance opens interesting possibilities. For the Naval Service the policy and transformation agenda require it to examine how it can enhance its relevance, become more useable and improve its capacity to adapt. In short, how can it change from being a consumer of resources to a producer of resources and an enabler of enterprise and wealth? In short the Defence Force is asking the question how does it institutionalise an understanding that rather than being seen as a cost centre it is seen as an investment centre with the potential in certain instances to be a profit centre.

While the 'Amazing Trinity' has long been used to examine the nature of war, it is suggested that it can also help with the development of this interesting new paradigm for defence strategy in a postmodern setting. It is in the context of postmodernism that Micewski et al introduce a market dimension suggesting that the military will need to consider practices that echo civilian business models, such as contracting out functions and restructuring their hierarchies.[10] Against the backdrop of von Clausewitz and postmodernism it is also interesting to

---

[8] von Clausewitz, C., *On War*. Translated and edited by Sir Michael Howard and Peter Paret. (Princeton, NJ: Princeton University Press, 1976).

[9] Calaprice, A., ed.. *The Expanded Quotable Einstein*.2nd edn (Princeton: Princeton University Press 2000).

[10] Micewski, E., Leadership responsibility in postmodern armed forces. In *Civil-Military Aspects of Military Ethics (Volume 2): Military Leadership and Responsibility in the Postmodern Age*, Edwin R and Dietmar Pfarr, 5–12, (Vienna: National Defense Academy 2005)

look at governance from the perspective of the three mechanisms by which the processes of governance can be expressed: the marketplace, the government, and the institutions and arrangements of civil society.[11] From the perspective of von Clausewitz's 'Amazing Trinity' this raises an observable gap in that a 'market' perspective is not visibly catered for. Linking our discussion to the von Clausewitz 'Trinity' facilitates a refinement by including a market perspective which allows for the interplay between the military, government, society and the market to be considered. Such a paradigm specifically permits addressing important perspectives such as military resources and outsourcing, the threat to sovereignty from economic collapse and the role of the military in innovation and enterprise. The various interactions are depicted in Figure 5.1. It is argued that developing an approach centred on adaptive dynamic capabilities in the context of these four tendencies allows us to further the work of von Clausewitz thereby facilitating a more robust strategy for a post-modern setting.

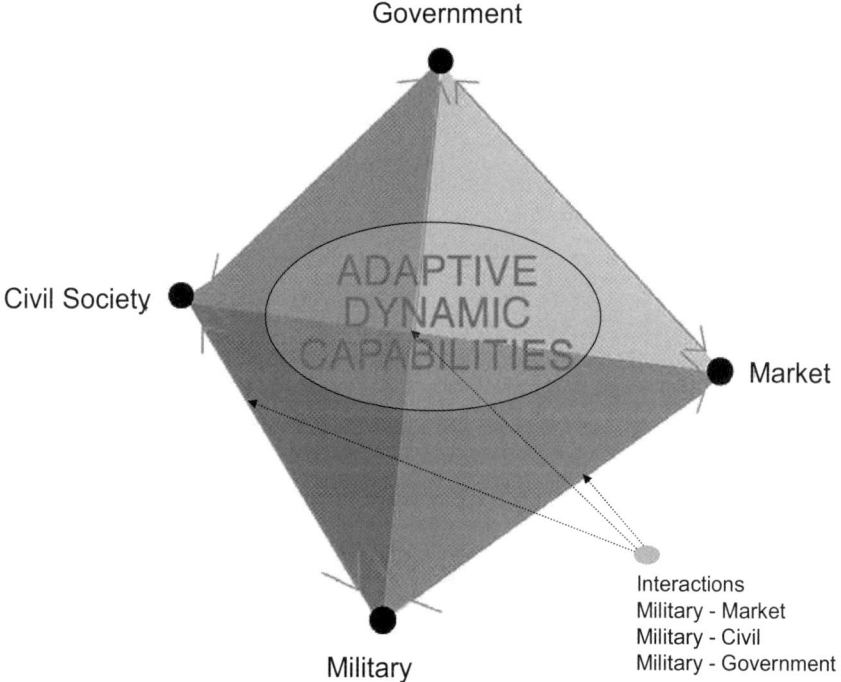

Figure 5.1   The von Clausewitz Trilogy with Market Perspective

---

[11]   Olsen, S., Sutinen, J., Juda, L., Hennessey, M., Grigalunas, T., *A Handbook On Governance and Socioeconomics of Large Marine Ecosystems*, (Coastal Resources Centre, University of Rhode Island 2006).

At the strategic level in Defence, the establishment of a Defence Enterprise Committee provides a framework for the Defence Organisation to institutionalise the relationship with the market. At the level of the navy developing the competencies and ensuring that mindsets are appropriately sensitised for the move from inward to open innovation required an institutionalised reflective capacity across the hierarchy of the organisation. This is in keeping with the philosophy of Moskos et al who argue that the post-modern soldier must be a warrior, a diplomat and a scholar, thereby setting the scene for greater coherency for a military contribution to grand strategy. An early innovation partnership led to the location of University College Cork's (UCC) Coastal Marine Research Centre to the Irish Naval Base at Haulbowline, thereby helping to formalise the navy's relationship with UCC. Another agreement on foot of a government decision led to the establishment of the National Maritime College of Ireland (NMCI), a constituent college of Cork Institute of Technology (CIT), with the navy as an educational partner adding significantly to the enhancement of reputation and institutional knowledge. As an institution the NMCI also added to the enhancement of the warrior skills required by the sailor of today. In the context of scholarly development the NMCI and the extended campus of CIT contributed, in a significant manner, to reinforcing the institutional capacity of the Irish Navy to generate knowledge. It did this by facilitating the establishment of educational and work-based learning (WBL) programmes incorporating recognition of prior learning (RPL), a model that has now been institutionalised across the Defence Forces. Consequent on these networks, virtually all commissioned and non-commissioned personnel within the Defence Forces can attain higher-certificate or degree level accreditation. In some cases WBL Masters level and professional PhD, have been institutionalised. This framework facilitated the development of an innovative culture grounded on innovation for the many. In terms of planning, decisive points relating to the creation, facilitation and application of knowledge in the lines of operation support the Irish Navy's goal to become a 'smart navy' and a knowledge institution, with knowledge creation a feature of every sailor's job description. From an innovation perspective the NMCI acted as a 'game changing' platform for the inculcation of innovation within the Naval Service. It is however the challenge of dealing with complexity that has brought about a culture shift and prompting some of the most radical thinking within the Naval Service.

Within the Naval Service it is recognised that there is a new environment that strategic leaders are increasingly calling a 'VUCA' environment. Coined in the late 1990's, VUCA is a military-derived acronym which stands for volatility, uncertainty, complexity, and ambiguity.[12] One key consideration serves to illustrate the VUCA environment. The ability to make decisions in any organisation is directly linked to the quality, timeliness and relevance of the data that underpin the information available to the decision taker. In 2013 it is estimated that there are

---

[12] Richard, J., *The Learning Army, Approaching the 21st Century as a Learning Organisation.* 1997 http://1.usa.gov/192sP0K (accessed 29 May 2013).

approximately 3.8 zeta bytes of data in the world. Such an overwhelming amount of data is driving a world of science and enterprise focused on big data, analytics, algorithms and prediction. It is however also forcing a reality that no organisation or institution has the capacity alone to turn data into information, then into intelligence which in turn drives the knowledge required to underpin wisdom. The complexity associated with such large amounts of data require that there is a need to rethink the traditional mindset of 'need to know' and adopt a mindset of a 'need to share'. This philosophical change is what underpins the Common Information Sharing Environment philosophy (CISE). When it is considered that by 2020 estimates suggest that there will be 40 zeta bytes of data in the world the problem becomes clearer. Increasingly it is being recognised, that those in business, public sector and militaries that do not address the issue of managing data will be blinded by a blizzard of data. There is also a growing risk of liability in cases of poor data management where there is a failure to act on data that are available in the organisation. This point is recognised in the Irish Government's Public Service Reform Plan 2014-2016 which highlights the data as one of four key themes and promises a new Government ICT Strategy in 2014. For the Naval Service it is increasingly apparent that to gain power there is a need to cede power by acknowledging that no institution or organisation, indeed no state, will have all the answers in a VUCA world. To deal with such complexity it is argued there is a requirement to create new partnership arrangements through diverse and multidisciplinary networks. The realisation of using complexity to deal with complexity is the underlying philosophy within the Naval Service which is helping it evolve from an open innovation to an ecosystem-centric innovation institution. A key enabler to this is the development of the post-modern sailor whose skills development as a warrior is fundamental to the delivery of core defence and security services. However, the development of the sailor's scholarly skills facilitates the inculcation of a broader understanding of policy, market and civil society issues and serves as a hedge for complexity. It offers the potential for the individual to move more freely in the worlds of research and entrepreneurship. It also serves to reinforce the individual's confidence in his/her own competence. Finally it enhances the capacity of the individual to refine his/her diplomatic skills which are essential not just in terms of the core business of the Service but also in the context of innovation. Whether it be open innovation or ecosystem-centric innovation the key to building strong innovation networks and partnerships is building strong relationships. Strong relationships are built on principles such as trust, reciprocity, collaboration and communications, the key to which is diplomacy.

 The development of a platform through which to institutionalise an ecosystem centric innovation culture and deal with the VUCA environment evolved initially in a piecemeal and informal manner. Developing a research capacity in the NMCI served as a focal point to advance the dialogue between UCC's Coastal Marine Research Centre, CIT and the Naval Service. Over a five-year period the institutional arrangements between the three partners became stronger with the establishment of the Irish Maritime and Energy Resource Cluster (IMERC).

The establishment of IMERC was achieved through an agreement between the Flag Officer Commanding the Irish Naval Service and the Presidents of UCC and CIT. This agreement was institutionalised by the Minister for Defence and the COS. In 2011 the Taoiseach (Irish Prime Minister) launched the IMERC strategy bringing significant political support from a number of government departments, including Defence, Education, Energy, Enterprise, Marine and Transport. The cluster has continued to grow in strength attracting enterprise and creating jobs. It has also facilitated the creation of the Halpin Research Centre in NMCI, a portal through which most naval research is being channelled and the sixteen million euro Beaufort laboratory which will be the world's largest wave energy research facility. The current master planning and foresight exercise aims to target thousands of jobs directly or indirectly linked to the cluster by 2025. A twenty-five million euro Science Foundation Ireland Award made after a competitive process will see over forty companies clustering around the growing numbers of indigenous small and medium enterprises and the five foreign direct investment (FDI) companies which have already incorporated into Ireland as part of the IMERC. From the perspective of the Naval Service the IMERC platform has already contributed directly to significant savings in maintenance and energy spending as a direct result of co-created innovative strategies. Capability is being improved through the development of bespoke technology and renewable energy technologies which could greatly enhance ship-borne surveillance systems while further reducing fuel bills. The approach is designed firstly to ensure that the knowledge that naval personnel gain contributes to RDI and enhanced technology within the Defence Forces thereby improving Defence Forces capability. Secondly, it aims to ensure that naval personnel are poised to contribute to Ireland's economic growth particularly in the maritime space using their enhanced skills and maritime corporate knowledge. This helps ensure the Naval Service contributes to Ireland's smart economy and enhances enterprise in SMEs.[13] Thirdly, it provides for potentially low-cost RDI solutions for the Irish Naval Service and wider Defence Forces problems. It is facilitating the examination of capability development which allows failing in the lab rather than in the field. Fourthly, from the perspective of inward direct investment, the unique partnership is seen by Ireland's Industrial Development Authority as helping to make the State an attractive prospect for 'clean tech' industries. Fifthly, as a provider of security architecture, as well as a developer of security and technology architecture in, inter alia, maritime energy, shipping, transport and recreation-related areas, naval innovation partnerships send a powerful signal to potential investors. Finally, the approach has the effects-based outcome of creating jobs, thereby attacking the economic deficit.

The diversity of the networks that the navy and its partners have established has served as a catalyst for the adjustment of organisational behaviour and rule-governed practices. The result has been that newer forms of innovative practices

---

[13] Department of the Taoiseach. *Building Ireland's smart economy: A framework for sustainable economic renewal*. (Dublin: The Stationery Office 2008).

now associated with open innovation are being created. While maintaining a balance with the resource, development and performance perspectives, the Irish Navy has taken a transformational interpretation of innovation in the application of its campaign plan. Through the adoption of innovation networks, the Irish Navy has embarked on internal and external processes aimed at sensing, exploring and seizing opportunities. Through the creation of innovation partnerships, seized opportunities are being exploited with a view to maximising enterprise, technology and job creation while always maintaining a link with the core services of the navy. In the final analysis we live in an age of uncertainty where complexity can only be handled by complexity. For the Defence Forces and the Naval Service embracing innovation at all levels is rational and systematic. Using adaptive dynamic capabilities in the context of ecosystem centric open innovation is providing a powerful strategy for operations in the VUCA environment. It is also underpinning the COS transformation agenda enhancing the Defence Forces, including the navy's, relevance to government and society while protecting national interests internationally, at and from the sea and on island.

Chapter 6

Small Navies in Asia: The Strategic Rationale for Growth

Michael McDevitt

Introduction

This paper explores the strategic rationale and budgetary arguments that justify the on-going modernisation and expansion of the South Korean, Vietnamese, and Australian navies. At first blush it is the People Liberation Army Navy (PLAN) that provides the incentive. The story is more complex. It turns out it would be wrong to portray China as the single factor at play in each of the countries because their geostrategic situation is different, in turn this determines threat perceptions, which drive investment decisions. That said, it would also be a mistake not to recognise that China's naval modernisation is also a factor in each case.

The Evolving Strategic Setting: China Moves to Sea

The maritime balance of power in East Asia began to change about 16 years ago when China had the political motivation and the economic resources to address what has been a historic strategic weakness – its vulnerability to military intervention from the sea. The political motivation for Beijing was provided by fears that newly democratic Taiwan was moving toward de jure independence and the PLA, short of nuclear escalation, was essentially powerless to prevent it, particularly if the United States elected to militarily support Taiwan.[1]

History is also a factor. China's 'Century of Humiliation' started in in the mid-19th century with its defeat in the Opium War by the British who came from the sea. Over the decades China was repeatedly humiliated by foreign powers that exploited China's weakness along its maritime approaches. A reading of US Seventh Fleet operations in the Taiwan Straits during the 1950s, when multicarrier

---

[1] While Taiwan is a priority for campaign planning and the PLA's most likely contingency, it would be a mistake to consider Taiwan as the only reason that the PLA is modernising. See *China's Revolution in Doctrinal Affairs: Emerging Trends in the Operational Art of the PLA*, Conference Report, ed. James Mulvenon and David Finkelstein, (Washington DC, 2005), p. 12.

Task Forces operated with impunity, overflying Chinese coastal cities, is a more modern reminder of Beijing's incapacity regarding its seaward approaches.[2]

China is moving its defence perimeter hundreds of miles to sea for several reasons. First, if China chooses to solve the issue of reunification with Taiwan through force of arms it will be accomplished through a joint air and maritime campaign. Second, including Taiwan, almost all of China's unresolved security issues are maritime in nature and are within the so-called first island chain.[3] Third, its economic development depends upon imports and of raw materials and exports of finished goods that travel mainly by sea, and, fourth, and perhaps most importantly, the fact that China's economic centre of gravity is located along its Eastern seaboard and is vulnerable to an attack from the sea.

By moving its defences far to sea, it is making the security situation of the countries like South Korea, Japan and Vietnam that live in the shadow of China worse. It is creating what political scientists call a 'security dilemma' – one country's defence become so effective its neighbours fear for their own security.

The Chinese have coined a term to describe what they are trying to achieve militarily: PLA strategists refer to it as 'counter intervention operations'.[4] In practical terms, this refers to the knitting together of a large submarine force, land-based aircraft carrying anti-ship cruise missiles, and in the near future, ballistic missiles that have the ability to hit moving ships. These capabilities all depend on a very effective ocean surveillance system that can detect and accurately locate approaching naval forces.

Whether one call's the PLA's emerging capability anti-access/area denial (A2/AD) as the Pentagon does, or 'counter invention operations', the desired strategic outcome is the same – keep US naval and air forces as far away from China as possible. The strategic implication of this for those of China's neighbours who depend upon the US to underwrite their security raises a serious question: will the United States *be able* to support us in a show down with China?

What about Asian Nations that Do Not Live in the Shadow of China?

Many Asian countries, such as Australia, are not directly impacted by China's counter intervention concept because they are effectively out of range. They are

---

[2] Edward J. Marolda, *Ready Seapower: A History of the US Seventh Fleet*, Naval History and Heritage Command, Department of the Navy, (Washington DC, 2012), pp. 40–52.

[3] The first island chain starts with the Japanese archipelago, continues southwest through the Ryukyu Islands and Taiwan and then continues south through the Philippines. It is the eastern boundary of China's three 'near seas'; the Yellow, East China and South China Seas.

[4] Mark Stokes, 'China's Quest for Joint Aerospace power: Concepts and Future Aspirations,' in *The Chinese Air Force: Evolving Concepts, Roles, and Capabilities*, ed. R. Hallion, R. Cliff and P. Saunders, (Center for Study of Chinese Military Affairs, Institute for National Strategic Studies, National Defense University, Washington DC), p. 38.

outside of China's defence arc. What does command the attention of countries like Australia are the long term implications of missions that the PLA Navy is now beginning to perform that are not directly related to the territorial defence of China and its possessions.[5] The best way to characterise these new (for China) missions is 'peacetime' operations. The 2009 PLA Defence White Paper elected to use the awkward circumlocution 'Military Operations Other Than War' (MOOTW).[6] In a nutshell, this new concept generates a requirement for the PLA Navy to be able to operate globally because China's global economic interests have created global political interests.

The PLA in general and the PLA Navy in particular are now expected to support UN-sanctioned missions such as counter piracy, respond to situations where PRC citizens are in jeopardy or require evacuation, protect sea lines of communication, respond to natural disasters, and if necessary demonstrate PRC resolve in support of embattled friends in Africa and along the South Asia littoral. As China's global interests have expanded over the last decade the PLA Navy, unique among the PRC's military services, is now deeply involved in integrating distant, prolonged peacetime operations as part of its core mission set.

These new PLA Navy missions require a different mix of naval capabilities than the wartime counter intervention operation. During wartime the surface ship component of the PLA Navy is much less important than its submarine force and land-based naval aviation arm which play important 'counter intervention' roles. However, during peacetime missions the surface force assumes pride of place. The mission requires a new mix: surface ship requirements that are better suited for distant seas operations, than the PLA Navy surface force of the 1990's. The MOOTW mission set values capabilities such as multi product logistics ships, amphibious ships with helicopter facilities, more destroyers with better endurance, helicopter hangers and large flight decks, and capable medium to long range air defences. Such missions have almost certainly created the basic rationale behind the PLAN's decision to build a modest aircraft carrier force in order to provide air cover for distant naval operations.[7] The aircraft carrier will also provide the PLAN with a credible power projection capability. For countries like Australia, it is not difficult for them to imagine that in a decade or so PLAN carrier task groups routinely operating in Southeast Asia and the Indian Ocean.

It is important to note that after over four years of uninterrupted anti-piracy operations in the Arabian Sea the PLA Navy has learned how best to deploy and

---

[5] See Michael McDevitt and Frederic Vellucci, 'The Evolution of the People's Liberation Army Navy: the Twin missions of area-denial and peacetime operations,' in G. Till and P. C. Bratton (ed.), *Sea Power and the Asia-Pacific: The Triumph of Neptune?* (Routledge:Abingdon, Oxon, 2012).

[6] *China's National Defense in 2008*, Information Office of the State Council of the People's Republic of China, January 2009, p. 12.

[7] Li, Nan and Christopher Weuve, 'China's Aircraft Carrier Ambitions: An Update,' *Naval War College Review*, Winter 2010, p. 15. http://bit.ly/1gemYuk

sustain surface combatants, amphibious ships, and support ships on distant stations for long periods of time; over nine months in some cases. They are learning quickly because the anti-piracy patrols are a real world 'battle-laboratory' for the PLAN, providing it an opportunity to observe the day-to-day operations of most of the world's great navies and absorb best practices for its own use.[8]

The Case of South Korea

The Republic of Korea (ROK) has become a de facto maritime nation in the decades since the end of the Korean War. Its economy, politics and entire web of relationships are across the sea. But, since that war ended with an armistice, the threat of another North Korean attack still looms. The inherent maritime orientation of South Korea has only slowly been translated into naval power because of the threat posed by the North Korean Army, now backed with nuclear weapons. Of necessity, the South Korea army and air force received a great deal of the defence budget, while the ROK Navy focused on littoral missions that could deal with North Korean attempts to either delay reinforcements form the United States or insert North Korean special forces into South Korea.

The Modern ROK Navy

The official strategic vision for a new regional ROK Navy was outlined in March 2001 when President Kim Dae-jung said in a speech, 'We will soon have a strategic mobile fleet that *protects state interests in the five big oceans and plays a role of keeping peace in the world [emphasis added].*'[9] Importantly for the ROK Navy, this speech was made when the perception of North Korea as a threat was very low because of what was known as the 'sunshine policy'.[10] The concept of a South Korean ocean-going navy had been percolating for several years within

---

[8] Michael McDevitt, 'PLA Naval exercises with International Partners', in R. Kamphausen, D. Lai, T. Tanner (ed.), *Learning by Doing: The PLA Trains at Home and Abroad*, (Strategic Studies Institute, US Army War College, Carlisle, Pa 2012), p 102.

[9] President Kim Dae-jung's speech before graduating midshipmen, Korea Naval Academy, Chinhae. Cited in http://bit.ly/19yRfPG

[10] The Sunshine Policy was South Korea's policy towards North Korea from 1998 until 2008. It was conceived by South Korean President Kim Dae Jung in the hope that the two Koreas could achieve a relationship of 'peaceful coexistence'. The policy resulted in greater political contact between the two States and some historic moments in inter-Korean relations, including two Korean summit meetings in Pyongyang (June 2000 and October 2007) and brief meetings of family members separated by the Korean War. In 2000, Kim Dae Jung was awarded the Nobel Peace Prize, for his efforts to achieve lasting peace in Korea.

the senior leadership of the ROK Navy, and the reduced threat perception made it possible for more money to be allocated to the navy.[11]

The ROKN's evolution from a small force primarily dedicated to protecting the nation's territorial waters and islands to a force that also has regional ambitions, started in the early 1990s with the decision to create a submarine force. Three small coastal 150-ton submarines were procured from Germany. Three Type 209 submarines built in Germany followed these boats, and they, in turn, were followed by Korean-built boats. Today, 15 years later, the ROK Navy has ten Type 209 submarines and is building three new, bigger, and more capable, Type 214 boats. The first of these, with Air Independent Propulsion, was launched in June 2006.

The surface force generally followed the same template, but all of the ships were built in Korea; while the sophisticated combat systems came from abroad. In the late 1990s, the three ship KDX I (3,200-ton) destroyer class was followed by six KDX II (5,000-ton) destroyers. Today, the ROKN has built three world-class AEGIS equipped destroyers: the KDX III class. At 11,000 tons full load, these are largest AEGIS equipped destroyers in the world.[12]

The vision of a 'five ocean or blue water navy' suffered a political blow because the investigation into the *Cheonan* sinking[13] by a North Korean mini-submarine found that the ROK Navy had not focused enough on dealing with North Korea. As a result, in September 2010, the ROKN CNO issued a statement that said; 'A consensus has been built among Navy leaders that it is time to put an emphasis on deterring North Korean maritime provocations rather than developing our blue-water capability.'[14]

The ROKN shifted focus to littoral war fighting, concentrating on the North Korean submarine threat. Pyongyang's inventory of midget submarines (40 small 300 tonners, and 10 minis) is challenging. One of the most embarrassing features of post-sinking investigation was the finding that ASW readiness for ships operating in the Yellow (West) Sea was neglected because of the ROK Navy assumption that the Yellow Sea was too shallow for effective submarine operations.[15]

The mission set aimed at North Korea was recently expanded to encompass taking the lead in "sea control" around the peninsula shortly before North Korea's

---

[11] See the official ROK Navy website at: www.navy.mil.kr/about/oceannavy_5jsp

[12] The US Navy's Flight IIA DDG -51 class full load displacement is 9,200 tons.

[13] The ROK navy corvette, *ROKS Cheonan*, broke in two and sank on 26 March 2010 because of an underwater explosion. A subsequent investigation determined that it was destroyed by a torpedo, which exploded under its keel, which was fired by a North Korean midget submarine. Both halves of *Cheonon* were subsequently salvaged and are on display at ROK Navy 2nd Fleet headquarters. This author has visited the site.

[14] Jung Sung-ki, 'Navy to focus on littoral warfare,' *Korea Times*, 9 September 2010, http://bit.ly/19Zvh7E

[15] Park Chang Kwon, 'The Long Term Impacts of Cheonan Sinking on the Alliance Naval Concepts and Operations' a paper prepared for the 5th Annual KIMS-CNA Conference 1–2 December 2011. In author's possession.

third nuclear test on 13 February, 2013 and the subsequent wave of unprecedented warlike rhetoric raised tensions in Korea. The current ROK Navy CNO publically called for a 'strategic manoeuvre fleet' saying:

> The Navy will go beyond the current maritime operations concept under which it relies on the US Navy and plays a role only support ground operations …it is illogical for it to passively operate…and we will seek to change the current paradigm by swiftly securing maritime superiority and projecting naval power toward strategic targets.[16]

Justifying a Blue Water Navy

Sea lane security   South Korea – as a rising power with maritime interests that at times conflict with China's – has a powerful incentive to develop blue water naval capabilities regardless of what China does. It is dependent upon international trade, which creates an imperative to protect its sea-lanes of communication (SLOCs) with significant naval capabilities. The best example of ROK concerns with sea lanes is the active participation of the navy in the anti-piracy operations in the Gulf of Aden where they are currently deployed with Combined Task Force (CTF 151). The anti-piracy mission has provided the ROK Navy with its first out of area mission in its history.

Maritime Disputes with China

China and South Korea have disputes stemming from overlapping EEZs in the Yellow Sea which lead to disputes over sovereignty and fishing rights. Both China and South Korea claim the submerged Ie Do Reef/Suyan Rock, which is located closer to South Korea in its EEZ, but it is also within China's claimed EEZ. South Korea has raised China's ire by building a maritime research laboratory on the reef. China responded by increasing its patrols in the area. In addition, as fishery stocks in the Yellow Sea are depleted through overfishing and pollution, Chinese fishermen are venturing into South Korean waters more frequently. South Korea has called on China to respect the median line between the two countries in the Yellow Sea and restrict fishing in these waters until they can arrive at a permanent settlement. The 2011 stabbing to death of a South Korean coast guardsman by Chinese fishermen represented the nadir of multiple incidents involving South Korean Coast Guard attempts to intercept Chinese fishing.[17]

---

[16]   Song Sang-ho,'Navy pushes blue-water operations', *The Korea Herald*, 7 February, 2013.
[17]   Terence Roehrig, 'South Korea-China maritime disputes: toward a solution', *East Asia Forum*, 27 November, 2012 http://bit.ly/18DUQ2m

Hedging against Japan

Exploring the poisonous history between Japan and Korea is beyond the scope of this paper. But the latest major disruption of relations between these two US allies over the issue of Dokdo/Takeshima is important because it relates to the rationale behind navy building in South Korea.

The rocky outcrop, known as Dokdo in South Korea and Takeshima in Japan, is considered by both countries part of their own respective territories, and the dispute over them has been an on-going spoiler in bilateral relations. The ROK government unilaterally occupied them in 1954, and since that time have been under the administrative control of Korea. The ROK government maintains a small Coast Guard detachment on the island.

There is an emotional element based on historical memory to the 'Dokdo' issue for South Korean's. This nationalist narrative claims losing Dokdo in 1905 was the preliminary step leading to the legitimisation of Japanese colonial rule. According to some analysts Koreans think that as long as they have effective jurisdiction, there's no point taking the risk that they may lose the islands by taking the case to the International Court of Justice as Tokyo has proposed several times. They also argue that referral of the case to the ICJ appears to concede that Japanese claims to the islands are valid.[18] To emphasise the issue of historic memory it is worth noting that the largest ship in the ROK Navy, its 14,000 ton LPD, capable of embarking 750 ROK Marines, is named *Dokdo*.

Summary Thoughts on the South Korean Case.

The rationale for a ROK blue water navy rests on the complex mix of necessity; because South Korea is a maritime nation, a desire for South Korea to be recognised as a responsible global stakeholder; something an open ocean force provides, the need to deal with North Korean maritime threats, and the perceived requirement to have a naval hedge against both China and Japan.

Whether the Republic of Korea will ever be able a commission a navy capable of satisfying this ambitious set of missions remains to be seen, but they are off to a good start. In addition to impressive capabilities, the ROK Navy has over four years' worth of anti-piracy deployment experience, that is informing and accelerating the evolution of the ROK Navy from purely a coastal defence focus on the North Korean Navy, to one that can operate throughout the Indo-Pacific region. It has most of the high end capabilities found in Japan's MSDF, and for all practical purposes it is already a smaller version of that neighbouring fleet.

---

[18]   Mark Selden, 'Small Islets, Enduring Conflict: Dokdo, Korea-Japan Colonial Legacy and the United States,' *The Asia-Pacific Journal: Japan Focus*, http://www.japanfocus.org/-Mark-Selden/3520

The Case of Vietnam

According to the Stockholm International Peace Research Institute (SIPRI), Southeast Asia's defence spending has grown by 42 per cent in real terms over the years between 2002 and 2011. Vietnam has been one of the leading contributors to this dramatic increase in regional defence spending. Vietnam is buying capabilities, mainly from Russia, that will contribute to its ability to defend its EEZ and disputed claims in the South China Sea. In early 2011, the 11th National Congress of the Vietnam Communist Party declared that the modernisation of Vietnam's armed forces and defence industry is one of five key tasks to be accomplished in the next five years (2011–15). According to General Phung Quang Thanh, Minister of National Defence, priority would be assigned to modernising the navy, air force, air defence, and electronic and technical reconnaissance.[19]

Vietnam is focused on weapons that will improve its sea denial capabilities within 200 nautical miles of its coast.[20] Hanoi has not issued a maritime strategy, but it did publish a *Defence White Paper* in 2009, in which the navy's responsibility was described as strictly managing and controlling 'the waters and islands in the East Sea under Vietnam's sovereignty' to include maintaining maritime security, sovereignty and sovereign rights, jurisdiction, and national interests at sea. This *White Paper* drew on a 2007 resolution by the fourth plenum of the Communist Party of Vietnam (CPV) Central Committee, mandating development of a comprehensive national 'Maritime Strategy towards the Year 2020', to fully integrate economic development and maritime national defence measures.

---

[19] Carl Thayer, 'The Tyranny of Geography: Vietnamese Strategies to Constrain China in the South China Sea', *Contemporary Southeast Asia: A Journal of International and Strategic Affairs*, Vol. 33, No3, December 2011, pp. 348–369.

[20] The concepts of sea control and sea denial date back to the writings of Alfred Thayer Mahan and his near-contemporary Julian Corbett, and stem from notions of 'command of the sea'. A search of their writings will yield often-contradictory definitions of these terms. My understanding is that 'sea control' means having the capability to prevent an enemy from using some segment of maritime geography for as long as one wishes. In other words, one party can use the sea at its pleasure while an opponent cannot. *This is hard to accomplish in practice unless one also controls the air above the water in question.* 'Sea denial'" on the other hand, means temporary control of an area of water. Implicit is the idea that control will be contested and that neither side has complete freedom to use the sea as it wishes. Many books talk about and around this topic. For the best-extended discussion, see Colin S. Grey, *The Leverage of Sea Power: The Strategic Advantages of Navies in War* (New York: The Free Press, a division of Macmillan, Inc., 1992), 19, 274.

Vietnam's Strategic Motivation[21]

Vietnam remains deeply distrustful of China as a result of their long history of conflict, and most recently the 1979 Chinese 'lesson teaching' invasion. They have, however, nominally resolved both land border and maritime border in the Gulf of Tonkin with China. That is not the case in the South China Sea; where both claim sovereignty over all of the Paracel and Spratly Islands groups.

China has possession of the Paracels, after having militarily seized the westernmost islets in the group from South Vietnam in 1974, and then defeating a Vietnamese Navy surveillance mission to the islands in 1979. Since that time Vietnam has not militarily challenged Chinese possession of the Parcaels. Vietnam's basic approach to the South China Sea is informed by its long history of dealing with China – the need to carefully manage the overall Vietnam–Chinese relationship.[22] So while Hanoi accuses China of threatening behaviour, 'bullying' its neighbours, and unjustifiably 'showing groundless demands against international law',[23] there is still a regular procession of high-level visits to Beijing by Vietnamese party and state officials.

Diplomatically, attempting to get China to actually conclude a binding code of conduct for behaviour in the South China Sea remains a Vietnamese objective.[24] But Hanoi is not relying on diplomacy alone. Vietnam is strengthening its maritime security posture. Hanoi in the past decade has moved to establish closer relationships with non-regional powers, particularly the United States and India.[25] In addition to seeking powerful friends, Vietnam has been making serious investments in its own maritime capabilities. The most newsworthy has been the six Kilo class submarines ordered from Russia in 2009, the first of which arrived in Cam Ranh Bay on January 3, 2014.[26]. Professor Carl Thayer, a veteran specialist

---

[21] This section is drawn from Lewis Stern and Michael McDevitt, 'Vietnam and the South China Sea', in M. McDevitt (ed.), *The Long Littoral Project: the South China Sea: A Maritime Perspective on Indo-Pacific Security*, (CNA 2013), pp. 61–72. www.cna.org

[22] Ibid, p. 79.

[23] Viet Long, 'China's Strategy of Widening Disputed Areas in East Sea', *Quan Doi Nhan Dan Online (Hanoi)* 18 June 2011, in OSC-SEP20110708178001

[24] Stern,' Vietnam and South China Sea'. p.82.

[25] For instance, see Juan Pinalez, 'Vietnam Representatives Visit USS George Washington', *Navy News Service*, NNS110309-12 (9 March 2011), http://1.usa.gov/19EeWdk; Patrick Barta, 'U.S., Vietnam in Exercises Amid Tensions With China', *Wall Street Journal* (16 July 2011), http://on.wsj.com/18DVBbE; and 'India, Vietnam: Testing China's Patience', *IRGA* (26 September 2011), http://bit.ly/1cpqlvV; and Donald Kirk, 'Seoul and Hanoi Eye a Glowing Partnership', *Asia Times Online* (10 November 2011), http://bit.ly/1c6rdaI

[26] Want China Times, "Vietnam Receives its first Russian Kilo-class submarine," http://www.wantchinatimes.com/news-subclass-cnt.aspx?id=20140106000034&cid=1101

on the Vietnamese military at Australia's Defence Force Academy, said Vietnam was seeking a credible deterrent against China.[27]

It is not just submarines; Vietnam has ordered four Russian built Gepard class corvettes. The first two, fitted for attacking surface ships are already in commission, the second two, still building, will be optimised for anti-submarine warfare. Vietnam is also license producing at least ten 550 ton fast attack craft that are fitted with anti-ship cruise missiles. When combined with the so-called Bastion Coastal Defence System, also from Russia, which consists of truck mounted anti-ship cruise missiles, along with its 20 odd Su-27/30 aircraft that are capable of maritime strike, and the announced purchased of four very modern Dutch corvettes of the SIGMA class, Vietnam is putting in place a modest but capable off-shore naval force.

Summary Thoughts on the Case of Vietnam

Knitting all these off-the-shelf purchases together into an integrated force, with effective surveillance and command and control is still to be accomplished, but Hanoi's intent is clear. There is little question that it is Chinese naval capability that is the focus of these procurements. It is investing significant resources to make certain it can defend its maritime claims, and avoid a replay of the 1988 South Johnston Reef clash with the PLA Navy in which it had two landing craft sunk, a third badly damaged and 64 men killed.

The Case of Australia

In May 2009 Australia issued a Defence White Paper that said Australia's most basic strategic interest remained the defence of Australia against direct armed attack, including armed attacks by other states. It also stated as a strategic priority the security, stability and cohesion of Australia's immediate neighbourhood. Finally, it emphasised that Australia has an enduring strategic interest in the stability of the wider Asia–Pacific region, from North Asia to the Indian Ocean – the so called Indo–Pacific.

As an island nation, that is heavily dependent on trade it is no surprise that the 2009 Defence White Paper laid out a vision for a strengthened Australian military built around a more capable navy. It outlined an ambitious program of capability enhancements for the Navy, including twelve future submarines, three Air Warfare Destroyers (AWDs), two landing helicopter dock amphibious ships (LHDs), replacement frigates, and for the Australian Air Force, the Joint Strike Fighter.

As it turned out, the ink was scarcely dry on the White Paper when the Government began slashing defence, calling into question this ambitious

---

[27] Thayer quoted in Greg Torode, 'Vietnam buys submarines to counter China', *South China Morning Post*, (17 December, 2009), http://bit.ly/1bRJZPk

programme. The reason for this about face, according to a Senior Analysts at the Australian Strategy Policy Institute (ASPI) is:

> It is not that Australia has suddenly felt more secure. If anything, events in the region have elevated fears that the rise of China will upset the strategic stability upon which Australia's prosperity is built. Nor is there any sense that Australia can relax because the United States has reasserted its commitment to the Asia-Pacific. Rather the recent retrenchment in Australian defense spending is largely the result of domestic politics. The Australian polity has an acute aversion to deficits and debt.[28]

As a result both major political parties in Australia are in a race to return the budget to surplus and pay down the debt as quickly as possible. As a result, virtually all the navy modernisation plans have been stretched out, but a reading of Defence Minister Smith's speech at the Lowy Institute in August 2012 implies that the major elements of the ambitious naval modernisation plan will not be cancelled out right.[29]

Naval Ambitions – Surface Ships

Australia has turned to Spain for two of its most ambitious new ship classes, the Air Warfare Destroyer (AWD) to be known as the *Hobart* class, and its two large amphibious ships (LHD's) the future *Canberra* class.

The AWD is based on the Spanish Navy's *Alavaro de Bazan;* an AEGIS combat systems equipped frigate (at 6,400 tons this is a large frigate). They are being constructed in Australia based on the Spanish design. When these three AWDs finally deliver over this decade, Australia will join Japan and South Korea as the only navies in the Indo-Pacific region with the AEGIS air defence system.

The Indian Navy currently has a monopoly on aircraft carriers in the Indian Ocean region. How long that monopoly remains depends upon current Australian plans to purchase two new 27,000 ton LHDs. The model is Spain's LHD *Juan Carlos I,* which has a ski-jump bow so it can launch Harrier STOVL tactical fighters. Thus the Australian LHDs will be big enough to carry a small detachment of Harriers and act as a mini-carrier as US LHDs currently do.

If Australia actually executes its procurement plans and launches these ships it is not likely that it would attempt creating an air wing from what would be very old rehabilitated Harriers. More likely, *if it elects to take tactical aircraft to sea at all,* in the *Canberra* class, the world's most technically advanced STOVL, the

---

[28] Mark Thompson, 'Confusion Down Under: Australia and the US Pivot to Asia,' East-West Center, Asia-Pacific Bulletin, No 180, 18 September 2012 www.EastWestCenter.org/APB

[29] Steven Smith, Minister for Defence – Speech to the Lowy Institute on the 2013 Defence White Paper, http://bit.ly/1ibqSIM

F-35B, would be the only option. Australia is already planning to buy the Air Force variant of the F-35, and should the STOVL F-35B survive development rigors, this will be an expensive but attractive option.[30]

Naval Ambitions – Submarines

Perhaps the most ambitious element of Australia's naval modernisation program is the plan to replace its six Collins class boats with 12 large conventionally powered 'next generation submarines'. This is challenging because Australia has had a terrible experience with its Collins class, its first indigenously built submarines. These boats been plagued with design and reliability problems from the outset, as a former Commanding Officer of two of them makes clear in newspaper *The Australian:*

> 'I don't believe the Collins-class are sustainable in the long term and many of the expensive upgrade plans which have been proposed would be throwing good money after bad .... Over the last two years, I believe these problems have become worse... Throughout my command of both *Collins* and *Waller*, full capability was never available and frequently over 50 per cent of the identified defects were awaiting stores... *Collins* has consistently been let down by some fundamental design flaws, leading to poor reliability and inconsistent performance. The constant stream of defects and operation control limitations makes getting to sea difficult, staying at sea harder and fighting the enemy a luxury only available once the first two have been overcome."[31]

The cost estimates for the new class of some 36 billion Australian dollars has caused plans for the new class to slip to the back burner, with some estimates suggesting the first new submarine will not deliver until 2030. The reality is that the Australian navy is going to have to live with the Collins class for some time longer.[32]

---

[30] The F-35B could have a significant impact strategic impact on Asian navies. It could bring top-tier naval TACAIR capability back within reach of many nations who are friends or allies of the United States. Not only those already operating STOVL ships such as India, but also to those who may not have seen the point of building vessels that could only launch AV-8s. If the F-35B proves itself on US ships, it is foreseeable that many other countries will reconsider carriers or TACAIR capable amphibious ships as part of their fleets. I suspect both the Japanese with its 18,000 to *Hyuga* class 'helicopter destroyer' and the South Koreans with its similar sized *Dokdo* class LPH would be interested in a proven variant of the F-35B.

[31] Cameron Stewart, 'Obsolete Collins fleet a lost cause,' *The Australian* 21 April, 2012, http://bit.ly/IfkfVu

[32] 'Defence cuts threaten Australian subs,' *UPI.com*, 7 March 2013, http://bit.ly/1emR9OM

Summary Thoughts on the Case of Australia

The Australian Navy has long been known for its professionalism and competence. Despite its modest size (12 major surface combatants, 6 conventionally-powered submarines, a few helicopters, two amphibious ships, two replenishment ships, and small MPA [RAAF] forces) over the past decade it has been a regular participant in operation in and around the Persian Gulf.

Its force structure is ageing, and if Australia is serious about its desire to protect its seaward approaches to the north and west it will need to accomplish the modernisation programme spelled out in its last Defence White Paper. This programme will also provide the needed hedge against the slowly developing emerging power-projection capability of the PLA Navy. While China and Australia have strong commercial and trade connections, Australia, any more than any other country in Asia, does not want to be vulnerable to any coercive behaviour from China. A sea denial capability base on submarines, land-based aircraft, (and perhaps in the future sea-based aviation), and surveillance of its maritime approaches is the best way to prevent that from happening.

Conclusion

Building and maintaining navies is expensive. Because the cost is so high, the strategic rationale for a naval force has to be well thought out and be compelling to decision makers. It also means that the countries must have some degree of economic vibrancy. With one exception, in Asia it is the army not the navy, that is the predominate service; therefore the strategic rationale for investing in a navy also has to be able to survive inter-service completion for funds. As a result when looking at modernisation plans of the small navies of Asia each case is unique; geo-strategic circumstances, threat perceptions, dependence on maritime commerce, national ambitions and financial resources are all different.

South Korea, for example, is for all practical purposes a maritime nation. Its export driven economy depends on maritime commerce to connect it to the globalised world, its entire web of political relationships is effectively across a sea. It is building a modestly sized multi-mission navy to deal with its land-based northern 'cousin', as well operate throughout the Indo–Pacific region. The strategic rationale that has underwritten this effort is a combination of North Korean belligerency, lingering antipathy toward Japan, latent worries about China, and a politically shared vision that South Korea has a responsibility to play a role as a global 'responsible stakeholder'.

The case of Vietnam is less complex. Vietnam's economic growth over the past decade has provided the means for Vietnam to seriously focus, for really the first time in its history, on its maritime domain – specifically the South China Sea. Both China and Vietnam claim all the islands, features, and shoals in the South China Sea. China seized the Vietnam-occupied portion of Paracel Island archipelago in 1974 – an action still disputed by Hanoi, and in a clash in the Spratly Islands in 1988 that killed a lot of Vietnamese sailors and soldiers. In order to better protect itself and its holdings in the Spratly Islands from a growing Chinese maritime capability, Vietnam is expanding its maritime forces and is creating its own 'mini-area denial capability' consisting of submarines, small surface combatants and land-based aircraft all armed with anti-ship cruise missiles.

The case of Australia reflects the ambivalence many Asian countries feel regarding China's long-term behaviour toward its neighbours. Some in Australia are increasingly concerned about the growth of Chinese power and the related relative decline in US power in East Asia. This issue has triggered a major debate in Australia over whether it would be more strategically sensible to begin to balance its relations between Beijing and Washington.[33] In the meantime it is politically fixated on balancing its budget, which is apparently more politically important than hedging against an assertive China. As a result it has stretched out the funding for a future naval and air force that can defend the maritime approaches to Australia from maritime power projection.

---

[33] See for example, Hugh White, *The China Choice: Why America Should Share Power*, (Black Inc: Melbourne Australia 2012).

Chapter 7
The Republic of Korea Navy – A 'Big' Small Navy

Ian Bowers

Introduction

A product of the division of the Korean Peninsula and the geo-strategic conundrum that followed, the Republic of Korea Navy (ROKN) has for the majority of its existence been an adjunct force to its larger service rival, the Republic of Korea Army. Defined by the limited threat posed by the naval forces of North Korea, the ROKN has been confined to a defensive littoral role, charged with ensuring that North Korea could not violate South Korean maritime territory or use the sea as an arena for preemptive attack. This focus on deterrence and territorial protection in combination with an overall narrowness of security perceptions on the part of the South Korean leadership left the ROKN, despite its relatively large size, as a small navy. Its mission set and capabilities were limited and it possessed no real power projection or regional operational capabilities. This began to change, however, in the 1990s when changes in the South Korean government and its view of Korean security provided the navy with the opportunity to expand and modernise not only its platforms but its mission set also. Its goal was to transition from a limited small navy to a medium force that could operate on a regional level performing blue-water operations while at the same time maintaining its traditional deterrent function in South Korean waters. However, despite some initial successes, the realities of the security situation on the Korean peninsula, the need for sustained political support, and the constraints of budgetary allocations have made attaining this goal difficult. What this chapter aims to do is first explain the nature of the ROKN modernisation programme and second, demonstrate the various internal and external factors that have driven or constrained ROKN development, showing that the transition from a small to a medium or large navy only can only occur when all of these influences are aligned in support of such a goal.

Background of the ROKN

At the end of the Korean War, South Korea was in a state of economic and social chaos and as a result became almost wholly reliant on the US for both its security and economic prosperity. This reliance was underwritten by the granting of large amounts of commercial and military aid and institutionalised with the signing of the Mutual Defence Treaty which came into force in 1954. This treaty and its attached minutes would set the tone for South Korean military development and its operational posture for years to come as it granted the US command over all branches of the South Korean military and as a consequence of South Korean economic and industrial weakness put the US in control over South Korean procurement and defence development.[1] Such control had a significant initial influence over the ROKN as it was viewed by the US as being somewhat extraneous to requirements given the limited capabilities of North Korea's navy and the overwhelming dominance of land power on the peninsula. This reflected the US's view of South Korean military development being conducted solely with peninsular security in mind. It is clear that following the Korean War the US directed South Korean forces towards ensuring security against further aggression from the North and limited them to this task maintaining that regional anti-communist efforts were not to be part of South Korea's force development efforts. In part this was to done to reduce the defence burden of keeping large numbers of US troops on the peninsula, but was also a response to fears that South Korea might reignite the war or destabilise the delicate security balance in the region.[2] As a consequence of these factors the ROKN was provided with limited equipment, most of which was of WWII vintage, and was mandated with ensuring that North Korea did not violate South Korean maritime territory and protecting South Korean fishing rights. The resultant weakness in the ROKN ensured that that it would not have any significant offensive or power projection capability and would be confined to deterrence and local security operations only.

This limited mission set would continue despite the South Korean military gaining greater operational independence in the 1970s and 1980s and the ROKN gaining in size and power over this period. The underlying cause of this was the continued threat posed by North Korea. In an operational environment that was dominated by the land, the ROKN was always going to struggle to gain any parity in resources with the other branches of the South Korean military.[3] Indeed the operations the ROKN conducted were aimed at extending the strategy of deterrence into the maritime theatre and much of their focus was based on ensuring that South Korea could maintain watch over North Korea's seas and could prevent incursion into South Korean waters or infiltrations by land. The

---

[1] Second Progress Report by the Operations Coordinating Board to the National Security Council on NSC 170/1: United States Objectives and Courses of Action with Respect to Korea, 29 December 1954 in *Foreign Relations of the United States, 1952–54, V XV, Korea Part 2*. (Washington DC: 1984), pp. 1943–1956.

[2] Memorandum of Discussion at the 208th Meeting of the National Security Council, 29 July 1954, *FRUS, 1952–54, V. XV, Korea Part 2*, p.1854.

[3] The ROKN's share of the defence budget is traditionally the lowest of the three services and between 1974 and 1992 it received between 15.8 per cent and 21per cent of the overall allocation

inherent weaknesses of the ROKN were also enforced by necessities of future war planning and the dominance of the army within the corridors of power in Seoul. On the first point, the ROKN in a time of war was to become subordinate to the superior forces of the USN which would arrive en masse to conduct offensive operations thus large amounts of power projection capability were not needed. On the second point, following the end of the war, with some minor exceptions South Korea was governed by a series of military dictatorships which were dominated by army personnel. As such the ROKN was marginalised in the decision-making process and, while they did undergo substantial build-ups in firepower, platform numbers and capabilities in the period leading up to the 1990s, the reality of their operations remained the same. South Korean security under these military dictatorships was seen within the limited framework of the peninsula and as such, despite maintaining a relatively large number of platforms, the ROKN was limited by the overarching need to ensure peninsular security and an inability to look towards maritime operations on a wider regional level.[4]

This reality was reflected in the various procurement programmes that the ROKN undertook in a 30-year period between the early 1970s and 1990s. This force improvement effort was part of a wider ROK military programme aimed at developing specific technologies to allow for a more independent defence posture and a reduction in South Korea's reliance on the US military and industry for its defence needs.[5] Between 1974 and 1995, the ROKN's capabilities saw substantial improvement growing from a force of approximately 20,000 men to one that was over 45,000 strong (not including the Marine Corps). Its platform numbers also increased, going from 63 surface platforms (including patrol craft) and 80 assorted landing craft to a force with 40 destroyers and frigates, 122 patrol and coastal vessels, 51 landing and amphibious craft with submarines, modern frigates and logistic support ships on order.[6]

However, this impressive increase in men and equipment does not reveal the full picture. An important part of these developments was the use of suppliers other than the US and the increasing indigenous capability to build and construct their own patrol boats, corvettes and frigates, albeit armed with European and US weapons systems. It is also essential to understand that despite these improvements and the deployment of heavy destroyers of the *Gearing* and *Sumner* Class, the operational focus was very much maintained on North Korea. In this period the North Korean Navy also underwent significant force improvement efforts, launching new classes of missile-armed fast attack craft, high speed amphibious

---

[4] ROKN Headquarters, *Navy Vision 2020* <해군 비전 2020> (Gyeryon-dae, 1999), p. 80.

[5] This force improvement programme was known as Yulgok and lasted between 1974 and 1992.

[6] International Institute of Strategic Studies, *The Military Balance 1975–1976* (London, 1975), p.56. International Institute of Strategic Studies, *The Military Balance 1995–1996* (London, 1995), pp. 185–186.

ships and submarines. As a result much of what the ROKN did was in direct response to these developments.

Indeed in looking at this period the attempts of the ROKN to purchase submarines are indicative of the influence the North Korean Navy had over its operations. The ROKN's pursuit of submarines was first broached in 1975 by then South Korean President Park Chung-hee who felt that the ROKN needed subsurface capabilities to counter those of North Korea whose own submarines were being supplied by Russian and China. The initial request for assistance was made to the US who was reluctant to help feeling that ASW work could be better conducted by surface platforms rather than submarines.[7] While the US pressured the ROK into dropping this request, it resurfaced in the 1980s and with a greater independent economic capability the ROK was able to pursue European submarine manufacturers, resulting in the signing of an agreement in 1987 with German company HDW for 9 Type 209 submarines.[8] What this episode demonstrates is not only a gradual reduction in US influence over South Korean procurement but the absolute emphasis in countering the developments made by North Korea. Despite what were significant upgrades in capabilities the narrow focus of the South Korean defence establishment limited the ROKN's ability to look beyond littoral operations around the Korean peninsula.

The Beginning of Change: Internal Developments

The strictures placed on the ROKN began to be lifted following the advent of full democracy in South Korea. The election of Kim Young-sam in 1993 altered the make-up of government as his administration sought to tackle the dominance of the South Korean army which had permeated all levels of governance and to bring corruption, which had become rampant in the military, under his predecessors, under control. What this meant for the ROKN was that army dominance over all levels of policy was broken and that a new foreign and security direction under this government would give them a wider role in South Korean defence. What followed was a broader foreign policy which looked toward embracing globalisation and meeting the realities of operating within the post-Cold War world.[9] One essential

---

[7] Memorandum of Conversation, 27 August 1975. Retrieved from http://1.usa.gov/17VN0CG

[8] Chung, Eui-sung, *Ultramodern Conventional Submarine KSX As a Leverage for the Future Defense of the Korean Peninsula*, (Seoul, 2007), pp. 141–142.

[9] Moon, Chung-in, 'South Korea Recasting Security Paradigms' in Muthiah Alagappa (ed.), *Asian Security Practice: Material and Ideational Influences*, (Stanford: 1998). pp. 264–287. This move to embrace globalisation was named *segyehwa* and called for the political, economic and social embrace of the outside world. See: Samuel S. Kim. 'Korea and Globalization segyewha A Framework for Analysis', In Samuel S. Kim (ed.) *Korea's Globalization* (Cambridge, 2000), pp.1–28.

part of this new policy was the widening of South Korea's definition of its own security, while previously seen in a relatively one-dimensional manner, namely peninsular security and the maintenance of deterrence, a more comprehensive view was beginning to take hold with policy documents looking toward future threats and the prospect of a modern, economically strong South Korea positioning herself as a responsible and independent actor within a potentially unstable but increasingly prosperous Asia.

While Kim Young-sam initiated this switch, it was his two successors, Kim Dae-jung and Roh Moo-hyun who provided the ROKN with the opportunity to truly look away from the limitations of the maritime environment of the Korean Peninsula. The key reason for this was the adoption of the Sunshine policy, which was a step change in how the South would deal with North Korea. Essentially, using diplomacy and economic incentives both Presidents looked to normalise relations with North Korea while at the same time increase South Korean involvement in regional and global matters. Indeed the defence policies of Roh very much looked towards the future, in that he attempted to create a leaner more modern South Korean military, one that was much less reliant on the US and focused on developing a military in line with South Korea's regional ambitions. This policy was formalised in 'Defence Reform 2020' which built on the developments of previous defence reform initiatives and signalled the move from a military which was bound to the paradigm of US dependence and the North–South confrontation to one which was ready to embrace the new security environment, advances in technology and meet the needs of a modern middle power.

What these developments in foreign and defence policy meant for the ROKN was that with many of the previous constraints such as army intransigence and US reluctance removed, for the first time there was an internal political environment in which non-traditional threats and a wider regional role was appreciated and built upon. Indeed in 1995 The ROKN Chief of Naval Operations; Adm. An Byeong-tae proposed to President Kim Young-sam that the Navy should be able to develop a blue water capability to meet not only South Korea's future security needs but also match the wider vision of the president's foreign and defence policies. Thus it was at this time that the ROKN was granted permission to pursue a construction and force modernisation effort that would not only be able to maintain watch over the North but react on a regional basis to threats and be suitable to represent South Korea on a global stage with a navy befitting a middle power. With successive administrations a policy of naval expansion in terms of missions and reach and modernisation in terms of platforms and weapons systems was supported both as an individual effort to only develop the ROKN and as a wider effort to develop the South Korean military in to a modern independent and forward looking force. As such naval modernisation which is a long term project gained support from successive administrations, such modernisation was different to that of the 1970s and 1980s as for the first time operations outside of the littoral became a component of future force improvement plans.

The Implementation of a Regional Policy

The move towards creating a more advanced naval capability had been in the minds of ROKN planners for some time before the 1990s as they looked upon the maritime environment in East Asia and recognised the potential dangers of ignoring the developments around them and focusing purely on the threat from North Korea. Thus in 1993 when Kim Young-sam came to power a clear opportunity arose for the ROKN to put forward ambitious plans for naval development and place them within the context of the political and foreign policies of the administration. The plan presented by the ROKN to Kim Young-sam was based on constructing a fleet strong enough to represent the interests of South Korea in a regional setting from the peninsula to the Straits of Malacca. A fleet which would be able to match the greater powers of Japan, China and the US and would be representative of South Korea as a prosperous middle power in Asia.[10]

Initially the force modernisation plan was set out in a 1998 document called 'Navy Vision 2020' and was then modified in a further policy document published in 2008 named 'Navy Vision 2030'. Both plans set a force improvement goal of a navy that would be based around the concept of mobile fleets which would be similar in make up if somewhat smaller to the carrier groups of the USN and which would be able to respond to emergencies both around the peninsula and in the wider region. These fleets would be equipped with advanced technology and would take advantage of the RMA. In doing so there would be a focus on network-centric warfare, effects based operations and interoperability between the ROKN, other navies and other branches of the South Korean military.

Navy Vision 2020 set out a more benign environment on the peninsula and much of what was written was predicated on unification and the subsequent reduction in the need for South Korean land forces. With such a change the document set out the future role of the ROKN as being the primary defender of Korean security through protecting its maritime interests against regional instability by utilising asymmetric warfare as a force multiplier against its stronger regional neighbours. The document stated that the ROKN was a vehicle for the protection of national prosperity through protecting its maritime interests in terms of SLOC protection and defending the country's maritime territory. These concepts while not revolutionary in the wider sense of the naval roles of the major powers such as the US, the UK and Russia or Japan was a major change in operational thinking for the ROKN given its previous focus on littoral operations and deterrence.

The proposals were modified somewhat in 2008 when 'Navy Vision 2030' was published. The most significant difference between the two publications was that the latter was not predicated on the unification of Korea, but stated that it was likely that South-North relations would improve over this period.[11] While again being

---

[10] Author conducted interview with Adm. An Byeong-tae.
[11] ROKN Headquarters, *Navy Vision 2030* <해군 비전 2030> Gyeryon-dae: 2008), p. 8.

optimistic, this is a sign of the importance of the inter-Korean relationship and the security situation on the peninsula to the development of the ROKN. Without stable relations or even unification, it would be difficult for the ROKN to develop into a significant regional navy while it was forced to maintain operations against the North and compete for funding against the strategically essential army and air force.

Navy Vision 2030's concept for the ROKN's future role has some similarities to the one described above, with a focus on the development of advanced naval power and asymmetric capabilities in order to ensure deterrence and protect South Korea's territory.[12] It centres on the development of sea control and power projection capabilities which would allow the ROKN to secure victory in a time of war. This was to be achieved through having a mobile fleet capacity which would be capable of strategic and envelopment operations within a multi-dimensional battle space. Power projection, a major theme in the document was to be utilised to attack the enemy's rear and the ROKN was to be able to independently protect the country's SLOC in a time of war.[13] Alongside these roles Navy Vision 2030 acknowledged to a greater extent the increasing global interests in of the ROK and the role of the navy in protecting them.[14] This would include its civilian maritime operations on a regional and even global basis, protecting the country's maritime jurisdiction and performing operations commensurate with Korea's middle power status such as PKO and humanitarian operations and multi-lateral cooperation exercises.[15]

How these goals would be met in terms of force structure and developmental direction did not change significantly over the two documents. The major difference being the acknowledgement in Navy Vision 2030, that the ROKN would need to maintain its deterrence capabilities against North Korea and as such the force structure would have to reflect the need for a concentrated littoral operations capability. The force structure goal that was forwarded in both documents surrounded the concept of a mobile fleet which would have modern C4I capabilities.

Translating these visions of the future of the ROKN into reality has been a complex process, which began well before 1995. Importantly, the drive for an advanced naval capability has been characterised by a multi-faceted force improvement effort, which has looked to add new capabilities and reinforce existing ones through domestic platform development and the addition of both indigenously designed and imported weapons systems. And while the future force plans may have been predicated on reduced tensions on the peninsula, what the ROKN has attempted to do is develop a force structure that has blue-water regional operations as an integral element but would allow the ROKN a

---

[12] Ibid. 15.
[13] Ibid.
[14] Ibid. 16
[15] Ibid.

qualitatively superior if numerically smaller force than that of the North. As such it is imperative to recognise that the force improvement project has so far attempted to balance the current need for more advanced littoral capabilities and the desire to strike out in regional operations.

In examining the force development programme itself, the size and nature of the undertaking becomes clear and reflects the difficulty the ROKN has had in developing the mixture of small and large platforms required for both littoral and regional operations. The priority in the initial part of the force development plan was to construct submarines and heavy surface forces and to some extent the development of the lighter units such as frigates and patrol boats was sacrificed due to economic defence procurement pressures. However as will be seen the political and operational requirements for these littoral platforms has in recent years hindered the development of larger blue-water vessels.[16]

The surface aspect of the improvement program drew on the KDX program which was initially conceived in 1981.[17] This was a program to construct 3 new classes of surface combatant designed to replace the aging existing surface fleet. The first class, the KDX-I (*KWANGAETTO DAEWANG CLASS*) of 3,855 tons was first laid down after significant delays in 1995.[18] Armed with modern ASW, AAW and ASUW weapons with helicopter carrying capability and an advanced combat system, this ship was a major step forward in combat capability. The design delays meant that only three were built, as priority was given to the construction of the KDX-II (*CHUNGMUGONG YI-SUNSHIN CLASS*) a larger and more capable ship which was approved in 1996, as such it should be seen as the first vessel constructed within the guidelines set out by Adm. An a year previously. At 5,500 tons and carrying an array of advanced weaponry, its major development in terms of force improvement was its area air defence capability. Six of this class were built, the first being laid down in 2001. The culmination of the KDX programme was the KDX-III (SEJONG DAEWANG CLASS) equipped with the AEGIS system, cruise missiles and long range air defence capability, they are true multi-purpose vessels capable of operating in a high threat environment and possessing strong C4I capabilities. While more were planned, due to their high cost only three of these ships were built with the first being commissioned in 2008. What the KDX programme provided was the ability to upgrade existing capabilities and procure new ones. The KDX-II and III met many of the requirements set out above, capable of 3 dimensional operations; these modern vessels form the bulk of the ROKN's ocean capability and meet the need for both flexibility and mobility.

In addition to the KDX program the ROKN commissioned an LPD in 2007. Named the *DOKDO* after the ideationally important island, it was classified with

---

[16] The Chosun Ilbo (2007) *Navy to Build up Strategic Fleet with Six Aegis War Ships*. Retrieved from http://bit.ly/1fG3Jwq

[17] From this point the author will refer to all ships by the KDX designation.

[18] Stephen Saunders, *Jane's Fighting Ships*, (Jane's Information Group: Surrey, 2010). p. 465.

some pride as the largest vessel of its type in Asia. With a 19,000 ton full load displacement and capable of carrying a large number of troops and tanks with 10 helicopters, this ship was major leap in the ROKN's amphibious and air capability. Planned as a three ship class, only one has been built with the second having a tentative date of 2018–2019, however no firm announcement of procurement plans has been made. Originally designed to be the flag ship of the strategic mobile groups, this ship is underpowered and with only one in its class has now been assigned to an amphibious flotilla. Despite these problems, the *DOKDO* is capable of performing humanitarian and PKO missions on the international stage and providing amphibious and air support to operations regionally and in the littoral.

Alongside these vessels, the ROKN is building up to 20 new frigates (FFX/ *ULSAN CLASS*), up to 40 new patrol boats (PKX/*GUMDOKSURI CLASS*) and a new LST variant which is planned to be operational between 2014–2018.[19] All of these ships are direct replacements or additions to existing capabilities and demonstrate the size of the construction project the ROKN is undertaking. While these ships offer high technology combat potential they are not specifically aimed at ocean going capability but fall into the category of replacing existing platforms and upgrading existing missions. Thus they are aimed at deterrence, anti-North Korean operations both in peace and wartime, the protection of South Korea's EEZ and an increased amphibious capability, something which would be vital considering South Korea's goal of reducing reliance on the US and its military.

The submarine development program of the ROKN is similar to the KDX programme in that it was designed to be a tiered build of capabilities culminating in an indigenously designed 3000 ton submarine. The project began with the ordering of the Type 209 submarines, 1 of which was built in Europe and the remainder in South Korea using kits supplied by Germany.[20] Before the last in this class was completed there was a recognition by the ROKN of the limitations of the Type 209 in terms of their undersea duration, as a result, the second phase of the submarine project was initiated with the ordering of 9 Type 214 submarines from HDW, these would again be built in Korea using components assembled in Germany.[21] The Type 214/KSS-II (*SOHN WONIL* CLASS) are equipped with AIP providing much greater endurance, more advance sensors and have the ability to launch Harpoon or similar missiles from their torpedo tubes.[22] The KSS-III, a 3000 ton submarine, designed and constructed in South Korea is still in its infancy and after numerous

---

[19] Eleanor Keymer, *Jane's World Navies Issue Five May 2010* (Jane's Information Group:, Surrey 2010), p. 278.

[20] Ibid p.460.

[21] Information from Military Data – Submarines (in Korean) www.navy.mil.kr (retrieved 18 January 2012)

[22] It is reported that the AIP systems allows the Type 214 to remain submerged for up to three weeks. Korean manufacturers are to have improved the performance of the Type 214 but there are no verifiable details, additionally Korean media have reported that the ROK have found several problems with the Type 214 design including excessive vibration.

delays the first of the class is expected to launch in 2022. Equipped with a VLS and cruise missiles, this submarine when operational will be a large step up for the ROKN providing them with covert strike and power projection capability.

With the addition of these new platforms the basic force structure of the ROKN is based upon three Fleet Commands each of which is responsible for a set geographic location around the peninsula. Set up in 1986 the three Fleet Commands are the basis of the ROKN's deterrence mission. Under the overall control of Naval Operations Command but individually responsible for the defence of specific geographic locations around the peninsula they primarily consist of 1 destroyer per fleet (at this time 1 KDX-I per fleet) which act as the flag ship and a number of frigate and patrol boats.[23] As such they are assigned with deterrence and incursion prevention in wartime and being the initial line of defence in any war time assault scenario. Additionally, they protect the South's EEZ and outlying islands, an important role considering their disputed status, the issue of resource protection and the emotive issue of Dokdo's sovereignty.

Alongside the Fleet Commands and directly under Naval Operations Command are a number of disparate units responsible for specialist missions, such as amphibious operations, large surface operations and the navy's submarine and aviation elements.[24] It is here where the mobile fleet concept first proposed in 1995 is now based. Created in 2010 and designated as the 7th Mobile Flotilla, the new unit is now made up of two squadrons each led by one AEGIS KDX-III and supported by three KDX-II destroyers, suggesting that the AEGIS ships will act as the command platform around which the other ships will operate.[25] Additionally other units such as submarines and amphibious assets will be added when needed. This unit meets many of the requirements set out in 1995; although smaller than originally planned it reflects the drive for flexibility and mobility.[26] Able to respond to emergencies on both sides of the peninsula and regionally, it demonstrates the compromise between ocean operations and homeland defence. The flotilla is currently based at Chinhae and Busan, but will move to a new naval base on the Island of Jeju. When this base is completed, it will allow the 7th mobile fleet easier access to South Korea's SLOC and to the disputed regions of the NLL, Dokdo and Ieodo.

What is essential to recognise is that these changes have provided the ROKN with a regional operating capability and much greater range of war fighting options.

---

[23] Ministry of National Defense, *Defense White Paper 2006,* (Seoul, 2006) p. 53.

[24] Ibid.

[25] Republic of Korea Navy, *Construction of the 7th Flotilla one step closer* <해군 제기동전단 창설, 뭄 한절음더> (Seoul, 2010), Republic of Korea Navy News Release. Retrieved from www.navy.mil.kr

[26] Although the original plan is unavailable, it seems that it called for three fleets each based around an aircraft carrier and supported by numerous types of smaller vessels, including screening ships, support ships and submarines. Author interview with Adm. An Byeong-tae & Republic of Korea Navy Headquarters, *Navy,* pp. 113–115.

The addition of the KDX-II and KDX-III vessels allow for area air-defence, strike and power projection and essentially multi-functional vessels which have a role both in blue-water operations and in the littoral around the Korean peninsula. This evidenced by the rotating deployment of one KDX-II ship to the Gulf of Aden on anti-piracy missions and the use of the remaining large surface platforms on training exercises around the peninsula focused on potential North Korean scenarios. Additionally, the main role of the KDX-III with its AEGIS system has been to track North Korean missile launches and act as command and control platform for ROKN at heightened tension. This shows that the ROKN never ignored the need for maintaining deterrence but recognised the utility of a mixture of light and heavy multi-functional modern warships which would have efficacy both on the open ocean and in the environment surrounding the peninsula.

Hindrances on Force Development

The difficulties the ROKN faces in maintaining its drive for a regional capability are manifest and replicate in reverse the multitude of factors that worked in their favour in the 1990s and 2000s. The two most important hindrances have been shifting political winds in Seoul and the ever unpredictable threat from North Korea.

In 2008, Lee Myung-bak was elected president of South Korea. Coming from the political party opposite that of his predecessors, he came into power with an agenda that sought to reverse many of the changes in defence and foreign policy that Roh Moo-hyun had introduced. Central to this reversal was the aim of resetting the US alliance and moving closer to Washington, in addition he sought to refocus the military away from the future threats paradigm for force modernisation and focus on the threat posed by North Korea. This placed significant pressure on the ROKN and while many of their ongoing projects were not cancelled most were delayed or scaled back on his taking office as budgetary concerns curtailed the ambitious force development plans initiated by his predecessors.[27] This point serves to emphasise the reliance the ROKN has had on political support and that long term force improvement requires it.

While adjustments to domestic policy were ongoing in March 2010 North Korea sank the ROKN vessel *Cheonan* near the Northern Limit Line killing 46 South Korean sailors. Following the sinking the ROKN came under severe criticism for ignoring the threat from the North and focusing too much on building a regional fleet capacity. Much of this criticism was unfair given that much of what the ROKN had constructed was multi-functional and was nearly always constructed with a North Korea scenario in mind. However following the sinking, the ROKN briefly dropped all public language relating to blue-water operations and development and

---

[27] Lee Seo-hang, Issue of Oceanic Navy and Complement of Naval Force after Warship *Cheonan* Incident, *A Sejong Commentary* No.181 (Seoul, 2010).

subsequent to this the government focused on increasing production of platforms aimed at improving the ROKN's capabilities to combat the threat to the Northern Limit Line and counter future North Korea Asymmetric attacks.

Additionally the Lee government published a defence reform plan known as Defence Reform 307.[28] This plan formalised the policy of future defence modernisation focusing on North Korea and espoused the under-explained yet important concept of proactive deterrence. This is an aggressive build-up of forces aimed at countering any threats that North Korea might pose with overwhelming force.[29] As a result recent procurement programmes have focused on weapons systems that would counter perceived North Korean advantages. For the ROKN this has resulted in the acceleration of construction of the *Incheon* frigates and *Yoon-young-ha* patrol boats, vessels which are designed for warfare in the littoral and in the case of the frigates more advanced ASW capabilities. While the ROKN has plans to construct up to 15 new destroyers only 3 have been officially approved and given the competition for funding and the need to maintain construction of the other vessels such ambitions will prove difficult to realise.[30] Thus it clear that despite many of the assets developed in previous years being multifunctional, the description 'blue water' is damaging in a political environment where local defence is key. For the ROKN as a small navy to advance into regional operations, sustained consistent political support and relative stability on the peninsula is absolutely essential. Without these two factors the ROKN will remain to a large extent limited to littoral, deterrent operations.

Conclusion

The fate of the ROKN rests very much in the politics of South Korea and the actions of North Korea. For much of its history the ROKN has been defined by the strengths or weaknesses of the North Korean Navy and as the threat developed the ROKN likewise expanded in firepower and platform numbers, but its mission did not change. It remained a small navy, given that it was tasked with maintaining watch over the littoral and had little or no responsibilities in terms of offensive operations or wider regional missions. The changes in government, ending of military rule and subsequent reassessment of the North–South paradigm and South Korea's future security needs provided the opportunity for the ROKN to modernise its forces and widen its mission set. Sometimes this has been misconstrued as developmental effort that ignored the littoral for blue-water operations however as has been shown the ROKN attempted and in many ways succeeded in creating

---

[28] This plan is also known as Defence Reform 11–30.

[29] For a full assessment of this plan see: Bruce Klingner, South Korea: *Taking the Right Steps Towards Defence Reform* (The Heritage Foundation: Washington DC).

[30] The three new destroyers will be equipped with Aegis and are scheduled for launch between 2023 and 2027.

a balanced modernisation programme. This was hampered by budgetary realities and with a political shift to the right combined with the actions of North Korea, the ROKN once again has been forced to forgo its wider ambitions and focus the majority of its efforts towards North Korea. Despite gaining strike and some power projection capabilities, the limitations in its forces and the lack of political support means that the ROKN remains a 'big' small navy.

Plate 1 Port side view of the Norwegian guided missile patrol craft *Skjold* (P 690) underway. The craft is painted in a splinter camouflage scheme. Craft such as these, designed to deny sea control within coastal waters, reflect a well-established task for many small navies. (US Navy Photo by Don Montgomery)

Plate 2 An example of more recent preoccupations is provided here as the crew of Royal Norwegian Coast Guard patrol boat KV *Tor* (W334) simulates being a skiff taken over by pirates as Royal Norwegian Marinejaggers use rigid hull inflatable boats and a helicopter to storm the skiff and regain control. (US Navy photo by Mass Communication Specialist 1st Class Peter D. Lawlor)

Plate 3   The crisis management team aboard the Republic of Singapore Navy Formidable-class multi-role frigate RSS *Supreme* (FFG 73) directs firefighters from the machinery control room as part of a shipboard fire-fighting exercise during multi-national Rim of the Pacific (RIMPAC) exercises in 2010. (US Navy Photo provided by Singapore Navy)

Plate 4   The Republic of Singapore Navy frigate RSS *Supreme* (FFG 73), leads the USS *Chung-Hoon* (DDG 93), the RSS *Vigour* (FFG 92), and RSS *Stalwart* (FFG 72) in a formation during Cooperation Afloat Readiness and Training (CARAT) exercises off Singapore in 2011. CARAT is a series of bilateral exercises held annually in Southeast Asia to strengthen relationships and enhance force readiness. (US Navy photo by Mass Communication Specialist 3rd Class Andrew Ryan Smith)

Plate 5   The Republic of Korea Navy destroyer *Munmu the Great* (DDH-976) moves into formation during a trilateral exercise with US Navy and Japan Maritime Self Defense Force ships in the East China Sea in June 2012. The exercise is designed to improve interoperability and readiness among the three navies. (US Navy photo)

Plate 6   The South Korean Navy submarine *Nae Dyong* (SS 069) underway during multinational Rim of the Pacific (RIMPAC) exercises in 2012. Twenty-two nations, forty-two ships, six submarines, more than 200 aircraft and 25,000 personnel were scheduled to participate in the biennial exercise, RIMPAC is the world's largest international maritime exercise. (US Navy photo provided by Japan Maritime Self-Defense Force)

Plate 7　　Small craft suspected to be from the Islamic Republic of Iran Revolutionary Guard Navy, manoeuvre aggressively in close proximity of US Navy vessels in the Strait of Hormuz in 2008. Vessels such as these offer one way for a small navy to harass its larger counterparts and can contribute to a multi-faceted anti-access strategy. (US Navy photo)

Plate 8　　In 2008 Somali pirates in small boats hijacked the MV *Faina*, a Belize-flagged ship carrying a cargo of Ukrainian T-72 tanks and related equipment. The ship was forced to proceed to an anchorage off the Somali Coast and was released after a ransom was paid. Sometimes the absence of an effective small navy can have serious consequences. (US Navy photo)

Plate 9　　　The Armed Forces of Malta counter-piracy vessel protection detachment demonstrates aerial boarding procedures during Eurasia Partnership Capstone (EPC) in 2011. Participants for EPC 2011 included approximately 100 representatives from Azerbaijan, Bulgaria, Georgia, Greece, Malta, Romania, Ukraine and the United States, who focused on strengthening maritime relationships between Eurasian nations. (US. Navy photo by Mass Communication Specialist 3rd Class Caitlin Conroy)

Plate 10　　The Offshore Patrol Vessel HSwMS *Carlskrona* (P04) of the Royal Swedish Navy which operated as HQ ship for EU NAVFOR in 2010. Converted from a minelayer in 2002, the *Carlskrona* reflects the changes in Swedish naval policy since the end of the Cold War. (EU NAVFOR image)

Plate 11   Personnel from the Belgian Navy Ship *Godetia* (A960) provide weapons familiarisation training to sailors from the Cameroon Navy at Douala (Cameroon) as part of a five-day port visit to kick off the European Africa Partnership Station (APS) West engagement. (US Navy photo by Mass Communication Specialist 1st Class Gary Keen)

Plate 12   The Royal Danish Navy frigate HDMS *Iver Huitfeldt* (F361) underway in the Arabian Sea in January 2013. *Iver Huitfeldt* was assigned to Commander, NATO Task Force 508 supporting Operation Ocean Shield, maritime interception operations and counter-piracy missions in the region. (US Navy photo by Mass Communication Specialist 2nd Class Deven B. King)

Plate 13   Officers from the Vietnamese People's Navy on USS *Chafee* (DDG 90) learn search and rescue plotting techniques during the annual Naval Exchange Activity between Vietnam and the US. The event, held annually since 2010, promotes cooperation and understanding between US and Vietnamese Navy participants. (US Navy photo by Mass Communication Specialist 2nd Class Joy Kirch-Kelling)

Plate 14   Chilean fast attack craft *Teniente Serrano* (LM 38), *Teniente Orella* (LM 37) and *Teniente Uribe* (LM 39), and patrol craft *Guadiamarina Riquelme* (LM 36) proceed in formation of the coast of Iquique. Vessels such as these are typical amongst many small navies. (US Navy photo by Mass Communication Specialist 1st Class Darryl Wood)

Plate 15 The L.É. *Niamh* (P52) leads four other Irish patrol vessels during annual exercises. *Niamh* is one of two *Róisín*-class large patrol vessels that were built for the Irish Naval Service in Appledore (UK) in the late 1990s/early 2000s, based on a design adapted from the Mauritanian Vigilant class. (Image provided by Irish Naval Service)

Plate 16 L.É. *Emer* (P21) is one of three Irish offshore patrol vessels built in the now defunct Verlome yard in Cork in the 1970s and early 1980s, procured with the assistance of funding from the European Union. After decades of service in rough seas these ships are at the end of their useful lives and *Emer* is due to be replaced by one of two new OPVs currently under construction for the Irish Naval Service in the UK. (Image provided by Irish Naval Service)

Chapter 8
'Best Little Navy in Southeast Asia': The Case of the Republic of Singapore Navy

Swee Lean Collin Koh

Introduction

During an interview with the Straits Times in 1992, then chief of the Republic of Singapore Navy (RSN) Commodore Teo Chee Hean envisaged that the navy aspired to become the 'Best Little Navy in the World'.[1] Seven years later, American defence analysts rated the RSN as the 'Number 1 naval force in the region, way ahead of larger and more mature Southeast Asian fleets'.[2] This accolade apparently continues to stick, as naval expert Eric Grove described the RSN's impressive ability to project force into distant waters despite its small physical size.[3] Today small navies no longer merely reside in the shadow of the navies of major powers, since they have demonstrated their ability to contribute meaningfully to international security, the Finnish and Swedish participation in European Union Naval Force's Operation Atalanta off the Somali coast being one such instance. It is worthwhile to examine small navies and their contributions to international security. This chapter hopes to draw useful lessons for small navies from what could possibly be touted 'Best Little Navy in Southeast Asia'. It argues that, with deft use of technology, human capital and diplomacy, the RSN is capable of transcending its physical limitation to contribute meaningfully to regional and international security. However, practical and geopolitical constraints could potentially limit its degree of freedom in force structure development and even peacetime activities.

Some Caveats

An attempt to benchmark the RSN with other 'small navies', in order to draw precise comparisons, could present conceptual difficulties. Therefore, the first caveat in order is that this chapter does not attempt to prescribe an absolute

---

[1] Felix Soh, 'Course set for the Best Little Navy in the World', *Straits Times*, 5 May 1992.
[2] Felix Soh, 'S'pore navy is No 1', *Straits Times*, 11 June 1999.
[3] Eric Grove, 'The Ranking of Smaller Navies Revisited', see Chapter One.

definition of 'small navy' while acknowledging that the term implies some limitations in physical size, capabilities, functions and geographical reach vis-à-vis large and medium-sized navies. In any case, overlaps in the above mentioned criteria make such absolutist categorisation difficult. The Royal New Zealand Navy, for example, fits most of the criteria as a small navy, yet it is still capable of projecting limited force in the Asia–Pacific region, including the Southern Ocean. With no more than 4,500 active personnel in service and a ship strength hovering at approximately 30 hulls, the RSN is regarded as a small navy. This is probably where the contrast ends, for the ability of the RSN to project force over considerable distance is another matter altogether. The second caveat in order is that this chapter does not aim to provide a monotonous survey of the RSN's evolution, for this has been dealt with in earlier works.[4] It also will not delve too deeply into the policy discourse, but will provide a broad sweep of the strategic thinking behind the RSN's force structure and activities. The functional aspects of RSN in terms of force structure and activities constitute the focus of this chapter.

Strategic Thinking behind Singapore's Naval Policy

To date, there is no official document that could coherently elucidate Singapore's naval thinking. The 40th Anniversary Commemorative Book, *Onwards and Upwards*, published in 2007 could be best described as a 'coffee table book' instead of a naval policy document.[5] So far, only a single defence white paper, *Defending Singapore in the 21st Century*, has been published, in 2000.[6] However, these two publications are short on the details of the underlying strategic thinking of Singapore's defence and naval planners, though they provide some insightful information. To piece the disparate pieces together, the author relies on the few, albeit limited, official publications but also inferences from a range of open-source public statements, speeches, interviews and press releases available. The basic starting point is to delve into Singapore's foreign policy thinking. After all, the navy constitutes a fungible instrument of a country's foreign policy. There is no reason to believe that the RSN is any exception. Since gaining independence in 1965, Singapore has consistently practised five principles for its foreign policy,

---

    [4] For the historical and contemporary evolution of the RSN's organisation, policies, force structure and operations read for instance a chapter on the RSN in James Goldrick and Jack McCaffrie, *Navies of South-East Asia: A comparative study* (London and New York: Routledge, 2013), 136–53; and Swee Lean Collin Koh, 'Seeking Balance: Force Projection, Confidence Building and the Republic of Singapore Navy', *Naval War College Review*, Vol. 65, No. 1 (Winter 2012), pp. 75–92.
    [5] Republic of Singapore Navy, *Onwards and Upwards – Celebrating 40 Years of the Navy* (Singapore: SNP International, 2007). http://bit.ly/18scIPE (accessed 18 June 2012)
    [6] Ministry of Defence, Singapore, *Defending Singapore in the 21st Century* (Singapore: January 2000).

namely: good neighbour policy; relevance and usefulness; sense of community; multilateralism; as well as deterrence and defence.[7] The RSN's roles in securing Singapore's national interests reflect these principles.

These principles reflect the innermost beliefs and perceptions of Singapore's policymakers. Firstly, Singapore's small physical size, which consequently means a lack of strategic depth, underlies her geostrategic vulnerability. The island city-state's leaders did not fail to pay particular attention to the Iraqi invasion of Kuwait in 1990 to stress the reality that interstate aggression, particularly by the strong against the weak, is not a thing of the past.[8] From the maritime geostrategic perspective, Singapore is considered also a 'geographically disadvantaged country'[9] since she is practically boxed in on all sides by much larger neighbours – chiefly Indonesia and Malaysia – on which she depends for goodwill to ensure unimpeded access to the vital sea lines of communication (SLOCs) – in particular those plying the Straits of Malacca and Singapore and the South China Sea – the key to Singapore's national survival and prosperity. Until recently, Singapore's relations with Indonesia and Malaysia could be deemed troubled at best due to historical animosities and a myriad of contemporary issues related to water supply, illegal sand trade and territorial claims. It therefore remains imperative for Singapore to maintain a good neighbour policy in order to maintain cordial relations with her neighbours.

Secondly, history deeply influences Singapore's security psyche. The fall of Singapore, then under British colonial rule, back in 1942 to Japanese occupation highlighted the need for self-reliance in deterrence and defence against potential

---

[7] See for instance, Speech by Mr Lim Hng Kiang, Minister for National Development and Second Minister for Foreign Affairs, on 'The Challenges to Small Nations' Foreign Policies' at the Ministry of National Development (MND) Auditorium on Saturday, 29 July 1995 at 3.00PM, Ministry of Foreign Affairs, Singapore.

[8] 'Fall of Kuwait "shows S'pore has right defence policy",' *Straits Times*, 12 August 1990. In 2008, in reference to the Russian invasion of Georgia, then Singapore Defence Minister Teo Chee Hean wrote: 'The threat of military adventurism and foreign interference is not a thing of the past, as recent events have demonstrated. Can we defend ourselves if attacked? Better still, can we prevent ourselves from being attacked and deter foreign intervention, so that we do not suffer the same fate like Kuwait back in1991 or like Lebanon?' See Teo Chee Hean, 'Total Defence for Singapore,' *Military Technology*, Vol. 32, Issue 2 (2008), p. 14. Read also Speech by Minister for Defence Dr Ng Eng Hen at the Committee of Supply Debate 2012, Ministry of Defence, Singapore, 6 March 2012. http://bit.ly/IkLKgR (accessed 29 November 2013)

[9] Theoretically, Singapore possesses 150 kilometres of coastline and three nautical miles of territorial waters, even though the country's foreign affairs ministry has since 1980 claimed up to twelve nautical miles of territorial waters and an exclusive economic zone – a claim which Singapore repeated after winning sovereignty over Pedra Branca, a rocky outcrop with Malaysia in the easternmost outlet of the Straits of Johor into the South China Sea in 2008. 'MFA Spokesman's Comments on an Exclusive Economic Zone around Pedra Branca,' Ministry of Foreign Affairs, Singapore, 25 July 2008.

aggressors. However, Singapore's defence policy is more than just deterrence and defence. The complex array of traditional and non-traditional security challenges in the Asia-Pacific region carries transnational spill-over effects, considering the close geographical proximity between the countries. As such, interstate cooperation is perceived as the most effective approach in dealing with those challenges.[10] As is characteristic of most small states, Singapore also places tremendous emphasis on international law and institutions as the fundamental basis of such cooperation. The most immediate institution Singapore normally turns to is the Association of Southeast Asian Nations (ASEAN), a regional grouping which was founded by Singapore together with her four neighbours – Indonesia, Malaysia, The Philippines and Thailand in 1967. Despite her largely metropolitan outlook, it is interesting to note that a significant portion of security cooperation embarked upon by Singapore is found at the intra–ASEAN level. Sense of community, particularly at the ASEAN level, and multilateralism is reflected in the RSN activities to date.

Finally, as a veteran Singaporean diplomat once pointed out: 'either you're at the table or on the menu,'[11] it is perceived by Singapore to be important, notwithstanding her physical limitations, to create niche spaces where security cooperation is concerned to highlight her usefulness and relevance to regional and international partners. In part, it has got to do with Singapore's perceived need to 'punch above its weight' but also, a necessity given the perceived transnational ramifications to her national security stemming from distant threats.[12] However, despite the RSN's recent forays into distant, 'out-of-area' operations, its primary security preoccupation remains in the immediate region. It merely expands the spectrum of plausible missions the RSN has to undertake, ranging from conventional warfighting to constabulary operations against non-state threats. Therefore, the RSN is primarily tasked for seaward defence and protection of

---

[10] This has been the recurring theme of Singapore's security policy discourse, particularly since the turn of the century. Read for instance Dr Ng Eng Hen, Minister for Defence of Singapore, 'Emerging Risks to Global and Asia-Pacific Security,' *Military Technology*, Vol. 37, Issue 3 (2013), p. 27; Dzirhan Mahadzir, 'Interview: Ng Eng Hen, Singaporean Minister of Defence,' *Jane's Defence Weekly*, 31 January 2012; and an article by former Defence Minister Teo Chee Hean, 'Meeting the Challenges of Singapore Defence,' *Military Technology*, Vol. 34, Issue 2 (2010), pp. 16–18.

[11] Speech by Senior Minister Professor S Jayakumar at the S Rajaratnam Lecture at Shangri-La Hotel on Wednesday 19 May 2010, Ministry of Foreign Affairs, Singapore. http://bit.ly/1gilsY4 (accessed 18 June 2012)

[12] For instance, then Defence Minister Teo Chee Hean remarked in 2005: 'It's important that Singapore is contributing to the reconstruction of Iraq. What happens in this part of the world has an impact on Singapore's security and also our economic stability.' See 'Minister visits RSN ship deployed to Gulf,' Ministry of Defence, Singapore, 25 February 2005. http://bit.ly/1cQRNmn (accessed 29 November 2013)

SLOCs while participation in international operations, no doubt an important facet underpinning this full-spectrum concept, remains a secondary focus.[13]

As the following discussion will demonstrate, the RSN force structure and activities represent an attempt to balance between pragmatism and geopolitical sensitivities and they reflect Singapore's foreign policy principles.

Technology and Geopolitics in the RSN Force Structure Developments

The RSN has traditionally had to face resource and manpower constraints even in the rosiest times of increased defence budget appropriations. Declining fertility rates look set to see little improvement over time (see Figure 8.1), which would have an adverse impact on overall RSN manning levels. Land-space represents another concern. To offset these limitations, the RSN leverages on technology as a force multiplier while ensuring that overall operational effectiveness is not compromised. For example, through extensive shipboard automation the *Endurance*-class landing platform docks (LPDs)[14] are manned by a crew of 65 as opposed to 130 on board the old *County*-class landing ship tanks (LSTs) which it replaced in the early 2000s. The Changi Naval Base in particular is a notable example. Compared to the old Pulau Brani naval base which it replaced, the new base made extensive use of energy-efficient solutions and information technology to reduce expenses and manpower needs.[15] Notwithstanding the consistent defence spending, given competition for funds to implement diverse components of the Singapore Armed Forces (SAF) transformation program the RSN also faces the need for cost-savings. In the area of procurement, while technological force multipliers are essential for such a small navy as the RSN, a multi-pronged strategy is adopted to not only maximise the defence dollar but optimise capabilities according to its needs. This comprises not just the purchase of new equipment from abroad, but also the upgrading of existing capabilities and if foreign solutions are found wanting, the RSN would turn to indigenous solutions instead.[16] Even in

---

[13]   Then Defence Minister Teo Chee Hean remarked to the press in 2010 that the Singapore Armed Forces' preoccupation remains with national defence and security. 'S'pore committed to playing its part in international security operations,' *Channel NewsAsia*, 30 September 2010.

[14]   The locally-designed LPDs, classified as LSTs in RSN service, are more than twice the displacement of the Second World War-vintage LSTs.

[15]   Speech by Chief of Navy, Rear-Admiral Ronnie Tay, at the Opening Ceremony of Changi Naval Base, Ministry of Defence, Singapore, 21 May 2004. (url no longer available)

[16]   Yet given its limited size and resources, a former RSN chief pointed out in 2007, the navy could not engage in whole-spectrum research and development and has to judiciously adopt, adapt and, in selected areas, develop technologies relevant to not just the RSN but the SAF as a whole. 'Republic of Singapore Navy: Chief of Navy Rear Admiral Ronnie Tay,' *Jane's Defence Weekly*, 26 April 2007. In addition, the RSN is known to 'recycle' items

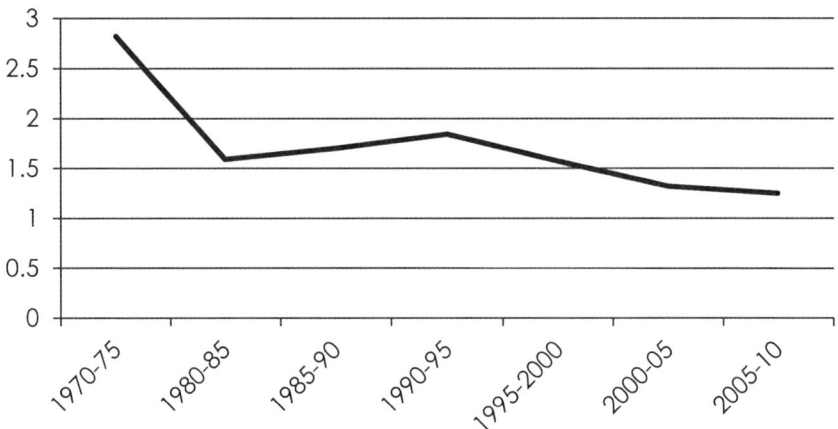

Figure 8.1   Singapore's Total Fertility Rate per Woman

Source: United Nations, Department of Economic and Social Affairs, Population Division, World Population Prospects: The 2010 Revision, Volume 1. Comprehensive Tables (United Nations, New York and Geneva, 2011)

routine operations and maintenance, the RSN turns to innovative technological solutions, such as indigenous development of new, tropical climate-optimised ship paint schemes for RSN ships.[17] Besides technological solutions, the RSN also attempted to compensate for manpower and resource constraints through human resource management approaches such as maximising its limited human capital pool by expanding personnel contributions at all levels.[18] To maximise synergy amongst its elements and their overall potential capacity, the RSN also embarked on force restructuring. For example, in 2006 two separate squadrons – the 191 Squadron that operated the LPDs, and the 195 Squadron that operated the smaller

for use, such as for instance equipping the new frigates with Harpoon ASCM launchers removed from the missile craft which they replaced.

[17] The new paint scheme led to cost-savings of over S$20 million per year, while condition and structural monitoring technologies on board RSN ships added millions of dollars' worth of annual maintenance savings. Speech by Chief of Navy, RADM Lui Tuck Yew at the Opening of the Naval Platform Technology Seminar 2001 at Singapore Expo Centre, Ministry of Defence, Singapore, 10 May 2001. http://bit.ly/1fYD6D4 (accessed 29 November 2013)

[18] For example, the RSN has implemented initiatives to expand the job scope of its warrant officers and specialist (a non-commissioned officer equivalent) corps, such as deploying senior warrant officers as combat information centre supervisors – an appointment traditionally held by commissioned officers. Speech by Dr Ng Eng Hen, Minister for Manpower and Second Minister for Defence, for the Launching Ceremony of RSS Supreme, Ministry of Defence, Singapore, 9 May 2006. http://bit.ly/1dKPvdB (accessed 29 November 2013)

landing craft – were merged into a single, new 191 Squadron. In 2009, the old Coastal Command was merged within a newly established Maritime Security Task Force that is capable of coordinating the efforts of all services of the SAF while facilitating closely with the other civilian agencies, primarily the Police Coast Guard and the Maritime Port Authority of Singapore.

In the foreseeable future, the RSN, like its sister services in the SAF, would continue to leverage on technology as a force multiplier to offset its resource and manpower constraints. Such a plan has already been set in motion since the early 2000s, under the 'One SAF' concept, which envisages an integrated and full-spectrum capable SAF which could transcend its manpower and resource limitations yet at the same time, through the 'sum of all parts' achieve maximum potential in terms of firepower and force projection.[19] By that extension, the RSN plays a critical role with its balanced force of anti-air, anti-surface, anti-submarine, aerial maritime surveillance, sub-surface and sealift capabilities – all melded into a coherent, synergistic web of diverse SAF capabilities via Singapore's equivalent of the network-centric operations concept known as Integrated Knowledge Command and Control (IKC2). RSN's centrepiece contribution to IKC2 is none other than the six *Formidable*-class stealth frigates which, in the words of a former RSN chief, serve as the 'key nodes in the IKC2 network of a third-generation SAF'.[20] The RSN's part of IKC2 appears to be a concerted effort over the past decade. In addition to the new frigates, the RSN has also modernised existing warships and inducted unmanned technologies to orient its forces towards fulfilling the IKC2-based 'One SAF' concept. Being arguably the best-equipped navy in Southeast Asia, the RSN runs the potential risk of being perceived as upsetting the regional naval balance as seen in its induction of LPD-type amphibious landing ships when its neighbouring counterparts were then still operating mainly vintage landing ships, as well as being the first regional navy to introduce submarines with air-independent propulsion. Singapore's defence policymakers appear keenly aware of this and as far as the modernisation of the SAF on the whole is concerned,

---

[19] According to then Singapore Chief of Defence Force Lieutenant General Neo Kian Hong in 2012, the notion of 'One SAF' is to ensure a more integrated SAF, using all services' capabilities for all different types of missions, be they conventional or non-conventional. See 'Briefing: Punching above its weight,' *Jane's Defence Weekly*, 9 February 2012.

[20] With a sophisticated command, control and communication suite on board, the 3200-ton frigates probably serve as 'flotilla leaders' coordinating the actions of other RSN surface and sub-surface units with support from the air force. In addition, the frigates with their long-range multi-function radars and Aster anti-missile missiles are incorporated as part of the SAF's Networked Air Defence, extending the umbrella further ashore. 'Interview: Rear-Admiral Chew Men Leong, Chief of Navy, Republic of Singapore Navy,' *Jane's Navy International*, 23 April 2009; see also Speech by Mr Teo Chee Hean, Minister for Defence, at the Commissioning Ceremony of RSS Intrepid, RSS Steadfast and RSS Tenacious, Ministry of Defence, Singapore, 5 February 2008. http://bit.ly/1fYDu4y (accessed 29 November 2013)

strived not to 'rock the boat' on regional stability judging from a consistent trend observed in Singapore's policy discourse in this regard.[21]

Therefore, while technology forms the central philosophy of the RSN's force structure development due to its manpower and resource constraints, it has to temper with geopolitical sensitivities in its procurement processes. Perhaps other than budgetary considerations, the RSN has apparently eschewed certain capabilities which could be deemed as destabilising.[22] The first is a supersonic anti-ship cruise missile (ASCM) capability. So far no such capability has been procured by the RSN even though her neighbours had already acquired supersonic ASCMs, an observation quite uncharacteristic of Singapore, which has always perceived a need to maintain a military technological edge over her neighbours.[23] Another weapon is a land-attack cruise missile (LACM) capability. The RSN's frigates – perhaps the most ideal launch platform – were not equipped with the LACM despite the recent proliferation of navalised LACM capabilities amongst some Asia-Pacific navies.[24] The *Archer*-class (ex-Swedish *Västergotland*) conventionally-powered

---

[21] Then Singapore Defence Minister Yeo Ning Hong best summed this up in May 1991: 'We have no enemy. We threaten nobody. To threaten anybody is to create instability that we have so assiduously worked to prevent. But by appropriate investment in defence, we ensure that nobody threatens us and destabilises our economic growth.' See 'Investment in defence small price to pay to protect assets: Dr Yeo', *Straits Times*, 26 May 1991. In 1997, then deputy secretary of policy at Singapore's Ministry of Defence Chua Siew San as saying: 'As we build up our capability we don't want people to get the wrong idea'. Robert Karniol, 'Country briefing: Singapore – Diplomacy teams up with deterrence', *Jane's Defence Weekly*, 20 April 1997. Incumbent Defence Minister Ng Eng Hen stressed in 2012 that 'it is certainly not our intention to precipitate any arms race'. 'Briefing: Punching above its weight,' *Jane's Defence Weekly*, 9 February 2012.

[22] Weapons that can be deemed destabilising have some or all of these characteristics—that they decrease warning time, give one country 'breakthrough' capabilities, lead to a broadening of target sets, permit no effective countermeasures, give one side better information concerning another's military preparations, and create hostility; David Mussington and John Sislin, 'Defining Destabilising Arms Acquisitions,' *Jane's Intelligence Review 17*, No. 2 (February 1995), pp. 88–90.

[23] The RSN once mulled the possibility of acquiring a supersonic ASCM to equip the frigates, perhaps inspired by her neighbours back in the early 2000s. However, there were apparently concerns about its feasibility given the heavy sea traffic and therefore cluttered surface background, which could pose dangers for such a weapon to hit an innocent ship instead of a legitimate target. Since then, nothing was heard about the RSN intending to procure a supersonic ASCM capability, even after the Indonesian Navy successfully tested the Russian-supplied Yakhont missile in April 2011. Keynote Address by Mr Peter Ho, Permanent Secretary (Defence), at the Naval Platform Technology Seminar 2003, held at Singapore Exposition Conference Hall, Ministry of Defence, Singapore, 11 November 2003. http://bit.ly/1hsDKcm (accessed 29 November 2013)

[24] Some of the MBDA Sylver vertical-launch system (VLS) modules on board the frigates are reportedly the 'longer' A50 variant which is designed to fire the long-range Aster-30 area air defence missile. 'Singapore Navy passes milestone en route to area

submarines are not equipped with any submerge-launched standoff weapon such as ASCM or LACM, even though the Royal Malaysian Navy's *Scorpene*-class submarines are armed with submerge-launched SM-39 Exocet ASCM. Another area that is visibly missing in the case of the RSN, which has acquired bluewater-capable assets to date, is afloat combat support in the form of a replenishment vessel, which was reportedly considered in 2001 but shelved in order to focus funds on the frigate programme, yet nothing has been heard of since.[25] In summary, these observations appear to reflect Singapore's attempt to balance between operational requirements while paying due attention to geopolitical sensitivities. The RSN has for decades been embarking on a consistent process of gradual and judicious force structure development, akin to a form of unilateral naval arms control.

Practical and Geopolitical Challenges in the RSN's 'Outward' Orientation

Diplomacy forms a facet of Singapore's defence policy, as reflective in the RSN's activities undertaken to date. The geographical scope of commitment is generally also a function of the ability of the RSN to project force further out beyond the immediate Southeast Asia. As Figure 8.2 shows, most security cooperation that includes those involving the RSN was confined to Southeast Asia up to the 1980s, and in the 1990s broadened to include cooperation with security partners in the wider Asia-Pacific. At least up to 2010, the 'outward' orientation of Singapore's security cooperation had been evident. It was only in the recent couple of years that Singapore and her ASEAN partners began to ramp up security cooperation. On the whole, over the past decades, much of Singapore's security cooperation has been wide-ranging, and as Figure 8.3 shows, demonstrates a clear inclination towards multilateral as opposed to bilateral initiatives it was used to having in the earlier decades. This trend could be explained by the scourge of transnational, non-traditional security challenges since the early 2000s, which spurred deeper forms of security cooperation. The RSN is much involved in regional security cooperation due to the predominant maritime nature of Asia's littoral geography. In addition, the RSN represents the foremost military instrument for Singapore's forays into international security operations in distant regions.

---

defence capability,' *Jane's Navy International*, 16 April 2008. However, this same VLS could have been capable of launching LACMs.

[25] 'Singapore Naval Programs Could Face Problems,' *Defense Daily International*, 18 May 2001. Even more notable was that Singapore Technologies Marine in recent years unveiled a roll-on, roll-off/passenger–type, multipurpose support ship targeted for export. Among the roles envisaged for this interesting vessel is underway fleet replenishment, implying that Singapore possesses the capability to build such a ship for the RSN in the near future if the program is ever revived. 'Singapore Launched Fleet Support Vessel,' *Kuala Lumpur Security Review*, 8 June 2009, www.klsreview.com/ (accessed on 18 June 2012) (website no longer active).

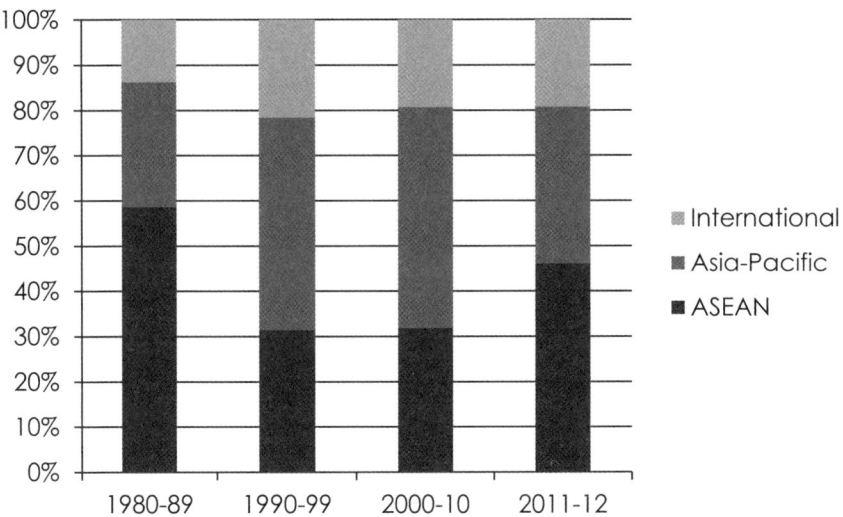

Figure 8.2   Geographical Spread of Singapore's External Security Cooperation

Source: Author's database tapping on diverse sources.

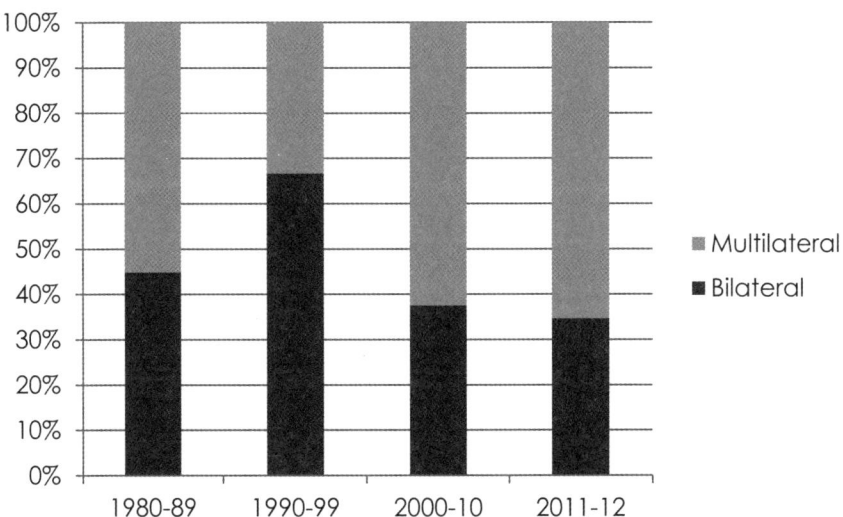

Figure 8.3   Scope of Singapore's External Security Cooperation

Source: Author's database tapping on diverse sources.

The usual set of existing and new bilateral and multilateral security cooperation aside, the RSN has stood at the forefront of positing Singapore as the regional hub of maritime security cooperation. To date, it hosted a number of 'breakthrough' activities, for instance the inaugural Asia-Pacific multilateral submarine rescue Exercise Pacific Reach in 2000, inaugural Western Pacific Naval Symposium (WPNS) Multilateral Tactical Training Centre Exercise in 2001, inaugural WPNS Multilateral Sea Exercise in 2005, the 17th Proliferation Security Initiative Exercise Deep Sabre (the first such exercise in Southeast Asia) in 2005, and inaugural ASEAN Regional Forum Maritime Security Shore Exercise in 2007. Besides hosting these activities, the RSN is also pivotal in positing Singapore as a small country capable of providing niche contributions to regional and international maritime security. For instance, in 2009 the Changi Command and Control Centre (or Changi C2 Centre) was established and made available as a regional centre for collaboration in maritime security and other areas via the constituent Multinational Operations and Exercise Centre and Information Fusion Centre.[26] Beyond the region, aided by its possession of bluewater-capable assets, the RSN was able to project limited force since 2004 into distant areas in support of international security operations, in some cases providing niche capabilities and even taking on command responsibilities, such as that of Combined Task Force 151 tasked with securing the SLOCs of Gulf of Aden against Somali pirates – the first in 2010 and the third time in 2013. Notwithstanding these achievements to date, the RSN does face practical and geopolitical limitations to its force projection ability and contributions to regional and international security, as illustrated in the two case studies below.

Malacca Strait Patrols, 2004 onwards

With an average of 60,000 ships passing through each year, the Malacca Strait is one of the busiest waterways in the world. Its security is critical to the economic well-being of Asia, particularly so for energy-hungry economic giants of Northeast Asia, which rely heavily on Middle-Eastern petroleum supplies. With such strategic and economic importance attached to it, the scourge of piracy and armed robbery plaguing the strait since the late 1990s garnered immense international attention. The US Government in 2004 was said to be misreported by the press as having the intent to deploy marines to help police the Malacca Strait under the Regional Maritime Security Initiative (RMSI).[27] What happened thereafter was nothing short of controversial. Of the three Malacca Strait littoral states –

---

[26] Speech by Mr Teo Chee Hean, Minister of Defence, at Ground-Breaking Ceremony of the Changi Command and Control Centre, 27 March 2007, 4.00PM at Changi Naval Training Base, Ministry of Defence, Singapore. http://bit.ly/1bDem1e (accessed 29 November 2013)

[27] William Choong, 'US – It's not for us to police Malacca Straits,' *Straits Times*, 6 June 2004.

Indonesia, Malaysia and Singapore – the latter was the first to endorse the idea of international policing efforts to safeguard safety and security of navigation in the waterway.[28] This would not have been surprising, given that Singapore had always emphasised multilateral, collective security approaches and she regards piracy and armed robbery in the Strait as not just the problem of the littoral states but that of the international community as well.[29] However, the governments of Indonesia and Malaysia were also quick to oppose RMSI[30], thus putting Singapore in an awkward position that risked discord with her immediate neighbours. Apparently not wanting to project the wrong impression of disharmony amongst ASEAN member states – which could have dealt a serious blow to the credibility of the regional grouping – the Singapore Government later changed tune, agreeing with Indonesia and Malaysia on the primary responsibility of the straits littoral states to ensure security of the waterway even if it insisted that international efforts involving all stakeholders remain necessary.[31] Moreover, even though Singapore preferred joint patrols as a more decisive modality for the trilateral Malacca Strait Patrols (MSP), she deferred to the decision made by Indonesia and Malaysia to downgrade original intentions to conduct trilateral joint patrols to just coordinated patrols instead.[32]

The MSP was officially launched in July 2004, and it later expanded to include an aerial maritime surveillance component dubbed 'Eyes-in-the-Skies' in 2005, incorporated information exchange provisions and was also joined by Thailand in 2008. In 2006, the Lloyd's Joint War Committee delisted the Malacca Strait from the 'High-risk war zone' category, a feat which was attributed by the straits littoral

---

[28] 'Singapore confirms talks with US over troops in Malacca Straits,' *Agence France Presse*, 5 April 2004; see also 'Singapore seeks joint patrols of Malacca Straits, involving Japan,' *BBC Monitoring Asia Pacific*, 20 May 2004.

[29] Then Singapore Defence Minister Teo Chee Hean even questioned the ability of the Southeast Asian littoral states bordering the Malacca Strait to police the waterway. See 'Littoral states 'cannot protect Malacca Strait',' *Lloyd's List*, 27 April 2004.

[30] Kuala Lumpur and Jakarta deemed the matter as a national sovereignty issue, though they did not dismiss external help outright, only that this would have to be approved by the Malacca Strait littoral states. 'Malaysia doesn't want outside help to patrol Malacca Straits, minister says,' *Associated Press Newswires*, 8 April 2004. See also 'RI Navy rejects US presence in Malacca Straits,' *LKBN ANTARA*, 27 October 2005.

[31] Donald Urquhart, 'S'pore welcomes joint patrol proposal,' *The Shipping Times*, 21 June 2004.

[32] Under a joint patrol format, the patrol forces of the three Malacca Strait littoral states would have the right of 'hot pursuit' of seaborne criminals across national maritime boundaries. Coordinated patrols essentially excluded that provision, thus confining respective forces within their own waters. Marcus Hand, 'Indonesia, Malaysia pull back from joint patrols of Malacca Strait,' *Lloyd's List*, 5 July 2004. Nonetheless, recognising the limited effectiveness of such coordinated patrols, the three countries later inked the Terms of References and Standard Operating Procedures for the MSP to incorporate 'hot pursuit'. 'Military chiefs sign key pact on Strait of Malacca,' *The Jakarta Post*, 22 April 2006.

states to the MSP.[33] MSP had been a watershed in the history of intra-ASEAN security cooperation, for the first time demonstrating that ASEAN countries could collectively address a common security problem without external direct intervention. The outcome also constituted a political victory of sorts for ASEAN, by demonstrating that ASEAN is not a 'talk shop' – a criticism commonly directed at the regional grouping. However, this probably came at a price for the navies of the Malacca Strait littoral states, perhaps more so in the case of Indonesia.[34] The RSN emerged in a far better shape compared to its experience back in 1975–1980 because it was better prepared for such a contingency. However, the RSN's fleet of 11 *Fearless*-class patrol vessels were probably also strained in trying to fulfil Singapore's responsibilities for the Malacca Strait but also in other waters, in particular those surrounding the disputed islet of Pedra Branca. Since 2004, these patrol vessels were apparently placed under increased operational tempo which shortened their useful service lifespans, as evident in the recent reports of RSN plans to replace them with eight new patrol vessels beginning in 2016.[35]

International Security Operations since 2004

The SAF was no stranger to international security operations ever since it took part in United Nations peacekeeping operations in 1989. The RSN for instance supported the Australian-led Intervention Forces in East Timor in 1999. However, in distant waters beyond the immediate region, the RSN saw no action until 2004, when the *Endurance*-class LPD was deployed under Operation Blue Orchid to the North Arabian Gulf in support of UN-mandated multinational efforts to assist in Iraq's post-war reconstruction. This unprecedented deployment gave RSN personnel rare real operational experience and helped elevate the international profile of both the navy and Singapore. Strategically, it also constituted a major

---

[33] 'Maritime piracy declining in Malacca Straits – Malaysian daily,' *BBC Monitoring Asia Pacific*, 19 August 2009.

[34] The over-stretched Indonesian Navy, with a vast maritime geographical area to police, had to divert more assets to the Malacca Strait, thus leaving other parts of the archipelago under-policed. The recent incidents involving asylum-seeking boatpeople in the Sunda Strait bordering Australia could be one such indication.

[35] 'MINDEF signs contract with ST Engineering to construct naval vessels,' *Channel NewsAsia*, 30 January 2013. The official reason for replacing the patrol vessels was because they had neared the end of their 20-year life cycle. This development seemed unusual since the patrol vessels were commissioned in the mid-1990s and should have been slated for service life extension upgrades in 2015–20, going by the patterns observed in the missile gunboats (commissioned in the 1970s, upgraded in the 1990s and decommissioned in 2009) and corvettes (first units commissioned in 1990, upgraded in 2009–10). This could have meant that the patrol vessels were subjected to higher-than-usual operational tempos which shortened their useful lifespan thus making upgrades uneconomical. However, the reason for replacement might also be due to the RSN's quest for a larger, more flexible and capable platform capable of modular functionalities.

political feat by demonstrating Singapore's ability to 'punch above its weight' by contributing meaningfully to international security. The RSN embarked upon further distant deployments afterwards. In 2009, the RSN launched Operation Blue Sapphire, participating in multinational counter-piracy efforts in the Gulf of Aden under the CTF151 banner. The LPDs were the workhorses of the Singapore's new international security contributions because, until the arrival of the frigates, they were the RSN's only bluewater-capable platforms available for prolonged 'out-of-the-area' missions.

This appeared to be the case because in September 2012 a *Formidable*-class frigate was deployed to the Gulf of Aden instead. Official pronouncements were that as many RSN units as possible ought to receive the opportunity to gain operational exposure. It would seem that stress has crept into the LPD force after sustained high operational tempo since 2004.[36] The LPD could have been the most ideal platform in terms of on-board space and endurance compared to the frigate because the latter was designed with a capacity of 70 crew members on board. For the purpose of Operation Blue Sapphire, however, it had to deploy with a crew of 145. As such, on-board living space had to be maximised in order to cram double the original crew size into the frigate, with potential habitability problems in the long run. The anticipated strain on machines and men could have spawned questions about the RSN's long-term sustainability in participating in such missions – notwithstanding the political and operational benefits. This was evident when the Singapore Government announced in September 2012 its plan to review future commitments to Operation Blue Sapphire.[37]

---

[36] In the same year when one LPD was deployed to the North Arabian Gulf to aid in Iraq's post-war reconstruction efforts, in December 2004 all three remaining LPDs were devoted to Operation Flying Eagle – the SAF's humanitarian and disaster relief effort for Indonesia's Aceh Province which was afflicted by the Indian Ocean tsunami. This was followed by subsequent years' rotations to the Middle East, including Operation Blue Sapphire in 2009, not to forget also that the LPD is the workhorse for the RSN's midshipmen training deployments to distant areas. All these meant that all four LPDs were considerably overworked and required a period of 'downtime' to consolidate maintenance efforts and crew training.

[37] During his visit on board the frigate RSS *Intrepid* on duty in the Gulf of Aden, Defence Minister Ng remarked that 'At least for this deployment, we will continue; whether there is a subsequent one or more deployments, we will see how it is.' He added that a military response to piracy cannot be the 'sole or dominant response', calling it 'doesn't make sense cost-wise, capability-wise.' Jermyn Chow, 'Singapore will reassess Gulf of Aden involvement,' *Straits Times*, 28 September 2012. Singapore's uncertainty with regard to its commitment to Operation Blue Sapphire stood in contrast with the commitment of its coalition partners, such as the EU Naval Force and NATO which had extended their commitments to the Gulf of Aden patrols to December 2014.

'Best Little Navy in Southeast Asia' Then and Now ... How about the Future?

This chapter highlights some of the practical and geopolitical challenges the RSN confronts in its force developments and cooperation with external partners, as highlighted in the case of the MSP and Operation Blue Sapphire. Some of these constraints are probably not unique only to the RSN, especially in the case of enduring physical constraints most small navies face vis-à-vis the major navies, particularly the ability to project force into distant waters over sustained durations. Notwithstanding these limitations, the RSN demonstrated the ability to punch above its weight, through deft utilisation of technology, human capital and diplomacy, as well as selective contributions to niche areas of multilateral security. For a small navy which has existed for less than half a century and the odds it faces, the feats accomplished to date are admirable, though clearly there are limitations to how much the RSN could achieve. A continued healthy economic growth would ensure sustained long-term, concerted strategy in procurement process, allowing the RSN to gradually overcome some of its physical limitations. However, in the foreseeable future, the RSN would continue to face geopolitical constraints to its development process. On an optimistic note, gradual improvement of interstate trust and mutual confidence in Southeast Asia and beyond in the wider Asia–Pacific, as well as a growing recognition of the need for greater cooperation than competition, could open new avenues for the RSN in surmounting some of those geopolitical constraints to its force development and scope of external activities. Its present strategy of balancing pragmatism and geopolitical sensitivities would continue to serve the RSN well into a future, positing it as a noteworthy example of a small navy capable of transcending its physical limitations to contribute meaningfully to regional and international security.

Chapter 9
Small Navies and Border and Immigration Control: Frontex Operations in the Mediterranean

Giampiero Giacomello and Chiara Ruffa

In recent years, a growing number of navy units have been deployed at sea in humanitarian support operations, such as the NATO intervention in Libya and Sudan, anti-piracy operations in the Indian Ocean and border control interventions in the Mediterranean Sea. These operations share two important characteristics: they appear quite removed from what is traditionally intended as 'sea power' and small navies usually contribute to these interventions. This chapter focuses on border control activities in the Mediterranean Sea. It compares maritime operations launched by France, Italy and Spain within the Frontex framework, the EU agency dealing with border control.

These operations have been variously labelled as ineffective.[1] In 2011, at least 1,500 persons lost their lives when trying to cross the Mediterranean Sea. According to several international organisations and human rights organisations and the ICRC (International Committee of the Red Cross), these tragedies could have been avoided.[2] The casualty figures are even higher for 2010, 2009 and 2008.[3] What explains this ineffectiveness? Is there any element on the tactical–operational side that could explain part of this humanitarian disaster?

Our chapter focuses on tactical and operational aspects of the conduct of border control and search and rescue operations and we trace how these impact the targeted people, the migrants trying to get from Northern Africa to Europe. Navy forces and coastguards from different EU countries seem to understand their role differently and implement a common mandate in different ways. Furthermore, in each country the law enforcement authorities in charge vary. This chapter explores underlying logic, mandates, rules of engagement and coordination of different

---

[1] Human Rights Watch, The EU's Dirty Hands. Frontex Involvement in Ill-Treatment of Migrant Detainees in Greece, *Human Rights Watch*, September 2011; Frontex: Human Rights Responsibilities, *Parliamentary Assembly of the Council of Europe*, 25 April 2013, http://bit.ly/18965Mq (accessed 12 May 2013)

[2] http://bit.ly/1bYjJ66

[3] *ICRC annual report 2012*: http://bit.ly/1b0Q3r7 (accessed 23 May 2013) http://bit.ly/Iud4bK (accessed 23 May 2013)

European navies in their effort of managing migration flows in the Mediterranean. It is based on preliminary empirical work on navy officers from different countries conducted between 2011 and 2012.

One caveat is necessary. By most measures the navies examined here, those of France, Italy and Spain, are by no means 'small' but rather medium-size. Yet, the bulk of Frontex operations are carried out by small navies, including those of Ireland, Cyprus, Greece and Malta, together with medium-size navies.[4] Frontex coordinates the activities of numerous navies, many of which are small, and this research focuses on coordination issues that apply to the same extent to both small and medium-sized navies. To date our research has not focused specifically on the smaller contributors. Nevertheless, we believe that most dynamics outlined in this chapter are equally relevant to small and medium-sized navies. In addition to this, the comparability between such navies holds true because our analysis focuses on only a (relatively) small portion of those navies, that is, the part that is earmarked for Search and Rescue operations. More specifically in the case of Italy we considered the 'Guardia Costiera' (much like the US Coast Guard, although its Italian counterpart is a branch of the Navy), while France deploys the 'Gendarmerie Maritime' and Spain the 'Guardia Civil'. These forces are supported by the customs or border police and, clearly, also by their respective navies. But the role of the latter is more on logistics, training and administration than on actual operations. Hence, when we consider these specialised sections of those national navies, we are really focusing on small navies within the wider institutions, making the overall size of the Italian, French and Spanish navies of little immediate relevance.

It seems clear that small and medium-sized navies are being increasingly employed in a number of operations that appear quite removed from what is traditionally intended as 'sea power': from humanitarian support to the NATO intervention in Libya and Sudan, to anti-piracy operations in the Indian Ocean and border control in the Mediterranean. 'Border control' and humanitarian support – while not brand new activities per se – seem to be attributing a new role to navies. Border control at sea can hardly be separated from the humanitarian mission of helping people in distress. If a group of people approaching the maritime frontier of a country is on board a vessel in distress and these people are in need of help, border control patrols have to intervene and provide assistance. The law of the sea is clear on the matter. If the patrol is from the Navy or a law enforcement body of a democratic country, the intervention is unavoidable because the country it belongs to is bound by international human rights covenants and treaties. The patrol is also obliged to provide support because some of the individuals in difficulties may actually be refugees or asylum-seekers. A small group of European navies – notably Southern European – have been more and more occupied in this humanitarian

---

[4] For a list of all contributing countries see http://bit.ly/1cyK9x7 (accessed 26 May 2013). The bulk of the contributing navies are from small countries.

capacity, trying to provide help to the so-called 'boat people',[5] while, at the same time, still being responsible for the border security of their countries.

The broad issue of illegal immigration is not only relevant for the discipline of European studies, but also for mainstream International Relations and security studies more specifically. From a policy perspective, this could shed light on how to make Frontex and small navies more effective and more aware of the complex institutional, organisational and intercultural dynamics at play. In particular, in this chapter, we would like to put border control operations into perspective, looking at dynamics at play at sea.

Albeit challenged, the link, or even the 'nexus' between migration and (national) security is well established.[6] This chapter is a simple 'probe' into this nexus, but from a viewpoint that has remained, thus far, quite unexplored. The chapter is organised as follows. First, we discuss international laws regulating maritime operations. We present the role played by Frontex, the European border control agency and we briefly illustrate some of the organisational problems it faces by outlining two specific operations as examples.Finally, we present a preliminary empirical study of the way in which Italy, France and Spain deal with maritime border control and rescue operations.

International Norms on Migration and Small Navies

International migration has put conventional norms regulating rescue of human beings at risk at sea under increasing pressure. In 2006, for example, Fiona Adamson studied the impact that international migration flows may have on states' core national security interests.[7] In particular, she identified three dimensions of national security affected by international migration: state capacity and autonomy, the balance of power, and the nature of violent conflict. Adamson concluded that migration management presented a far greater security challenge to weak and failing states than to advanced post-industrial ones. However, liberal democracies, like the ones we consider in this chapter, seem engrossed by the effects that

---

[5] The term 'boat people' was coined to identify South Vietnamese people who, after the collapse of their country, between 1976 and 1979 tried to escape from the re-unified Republic of Vietnam by boat.

[6] See for example, Nana K. Poku and David T. Graham (eds) *Redefining Security: Population Movements and National Security*, (Westport, CT and London: Praeger, 1998), Thomas Faist, 'The Migration-Security Nexus.: International Migration and Security before and after 9/11', *Willy Brandt Series of Working Papers in International Migration and Ethnic Relations* 4/03, School of International Migration and Ethnic Relations, Malmö University, 2004 and Fiona B. Adamson, 'Crossing Borders: International Migration and National Security', *International Security*, Vol. 31, No. 1, Summer 2006, pp. 165–199.

[7] Adamson, F; (2006) 'Crossing Borders: International Migration and National Security'. *International Security*, 31 (1) pp. 165–199.

'unchecked' masses of immigrants may have on the state's capacity and autonomy, to the point of adopting 'illiberal' measures.

In the late 1990s, Christian Joppke noted that states' capacity of controlling unwanted migration was in decline.[8] Joppke's argument has been also embraced by Adamson et al, who dedicated a whole issue of the *Journal of Ethnic and Migration Studies* to the 'the limits of the liberal state'. In the introduction to the special issue, Adamson et al underlined the use of liberal norms by states for exclusionary purposes and the possible emergence of an 'illiberal liberalism'. Andreas too argues that illicit globalisation, of which illegal immigration is on the most relevant components, is the 'poster child' for arguments that states are losing control, but that the state may even exploit such illicit globalisation, including hopeless migrants.[9]

It is not, or rather, not only, the executive branch and political leadership that are highly concerned with seemingly unstoppable migration flows, but, even more so, societies and voters themselves. Rudolph observed that while sovereignty is willingly ceded by states for economic gain from greater trade and/or capital mobility, public concern over the social, political, and economic effects of high levels of international migration indicate a strong, and sometimes unquestionable, propensity for the maintenance of sovereignty over access to social and political community.[10] As Rudolph correctly concludes, in the public's eyes borders still serve the important symbolic function of preserving stable conceptions of national identity, which still represent the cornerstone of the nation-state.[11] Given these conditions, it would be quite inexplicable if national armed forces – navies in our specific case – were not fully employed.

The well-known characteristics of the sea environment – its emptiness, vastness and featureless-ness – have always had a profound impact on the type of activities that can be undertaken at sea. Furthermore, because such an environment is fundamentally not human-friendly, people going to sea have felt a strong commitment to helping other fellow mariners in distraught conditions. Such a common and persistent behaviour has then been formalised and codified in the customs of the law of the sea to the point that the obligation to help is now enshrined in customary international law. Even in combat conditions, those rules tend to be followed.[12] As Klepp notes, 'irregular migration routes across the

---

[8] Christian Joppke, 'Why Liberal States Accept Unwanted Immigration', *World Politics* 50(2), 1998, pp. 266–93 (reprinted in: Andrew Geddes, ed. *International Migration*. London: SAGE, 2011).

[9] Peter Andreas, Illicit Globalization: Myths, Misconceptions, and Historical Lessons, *Political Science Quarterly* 126(3) (Fall 2011): pp. 403–425.

[10] Christopher Rudolph (2005), Sovereignty and Territorial Borders in a Global Age. *International Studies Review*, 7: 1–20. doi:10.1111/j.1521-9488.2005.00455.x

[11] Rudolph, Sovereignty and Territorial Borders in a Global Age.

[12] Natalino Ronzitti (2006) *Diritto Internazionale dei Conflitti Armati*, Terza Edizione, Torino: Giappichelli)pp. 266–68.

Mediterranean Sea from the African continent to Europe were closed by military control'.[13] This measure is certainly not new for the Mediterranean. Apart from during actual wars, for over two centuries the anciently called Barbary Coast states – Morocco, Algeria, Tunisia and Libya – lived and prospered on piracy for wealth and slaves. The Mediterranean Sea then continued to be an area of intense military traffic and, at times, confrontation, until the end of the Cold War. With the end of the Cold War, the Mediterranean became a physical obstacle that all aspiring immigrants from Northern and sub-Saharan Africa had to overcome in order to reach Europe's shores. While illegal immigrants caught at the EU Eastern border in the open plain can be easily stopped and even sent back if it is possible to assess quickly that they are not refugees, migrants stopped at sea, and almost always in not sea-worthy vessels, add to their status of immigrants or asylum seekers that of 'persons in distress at sea'.

For the safety of people at sea, the International Convention for the Safety of Life at Sea (SOLAS), adopted in November 1974, states that ships are obliged to go to the assistance of vessels in distress. Following that, the International Convention on Maritime Search and Rescue (SAR) was adopted at a conference in Hamburg in 1979. Before SAR, there was no international system for standardised search and rescue operations. Currently SAR guarantees that 'no matter where an accident occurs, the rescue of persons in distress at sea will be co-ordinated by an SAR organisation and, when necessary, by co-operation between neighbouring SAR organisations'.[14] Following the adoption of the SAR Convention, the Maritime Safety Committee of the International Maritime Organisation (IMO) divided the world's oceans into 13 search and rescue areas. The countries in each of these areas then are responsible for search and rescue 'regions', where Maritime Rescue Coordination Centres (MRCC) are located. Relevant for this chapter is the 'Mediterranean Search and Rescue Area'.[15]

Both SOLAS and SAR were further revised in 2004, making even more pressing the obligation for rescuing people 'in distress at sea', thus requiring that those rescued should be quickly taken to a 'place of safety'. Guidance on what constitutes a 'place of safety' is indicated in the IMO guidelines. More specifically, a place of safety is a location where rescue operations are considered to terminate, and where:

---

[13]   Silja Klepp 'A Contested Asylum System: The European Union between Refugee Protection and Border Control in the Mediterranean Sea', *European Journal of Migration and Law* 12 (2010) 1–21:1)

[14]   *International Maritime Organization (IMO)*, 'International Convention on Maritime Search and Rescue' (SAR), adopted 7 April 1979, available from http://bit.ly/Isqd6g, (accessed 13 March 2012).

[15]   See Neptune, 'Mediterranean Rescue Areas', available from http://bit.ly/197mKju (accessed 14 March 2012) or IMO, 'Global Maritime Search and Rescue Areas', available from http://bit.ly/1glc0TU (accessed 14 March 2012).

1. the survivors' safety or life is no longer threatened;
2. basic human needs (such as food, shelter and medical needs) can be met;
3. and transportation arrangements can be made for the survivors' next or final destination.[16]

Assistance to 'persons in distress at sea' can be further complicated if all, or some, of the people being rescued claim asylum. At that point, the shipmaster, regardless of whether he or she is a navy officer or a civilian captain, is obliged, in addition to alerting the closest RCC (Rescue Coordination Centre) and the UNHCR (United Nations High Commissioner for Refugees), not to ask for disembarkation of the rescued individual in the country of origin or from which they fled, 'nor to share personal information regarding the asylum-seekers with the authorities of that country, or with others who might convey this information to those authorities'.[17]

The Mediterranean SAR works according to the same logic. All areas of responsibility of the main EU member-states that are the focus of our research, namely Spain, France and Italy, are somehow 'shadowed' by the SAR zones of all the North African countries, that is, Egypt, Libya, Tunisia (provisional), Algeria and Morocco. Italy's most Southern SAR zone is actually 'shadowed' twice, by Libya and then Malta. This situation has some important consequences, the most important of which would be that, in principle, SAR responsibilities should primarily rest with the North African countries' emergency services. Even if border control authorities in those countries, unofficially, did not stop would-be migrants from leaving Northern African shores, once the migrants were on board and afloat, the SAR system would apply.

Long-standing customs and maritime tradition clearly state that shipmasters have an obligation to provide assistance to those in distress at sea, regardless to their nationality, status or the circumstances in which they are found. These conditions, of course, prevent the shipmaster or the commanding officer of a military vessel from questioning the legality or ultimate goal of what these people were doing. Hence, if groups of migrants are intercepted by any ship or military vessel, whether they are in international or national waters, they have the right to be helped and be brought to safety on the land. Once the migrants are landed, they have to be properly fed and dressed and then identified. Even if they do not claim asylum-seeker status, which would further extend the period of staying in the country, the whole process takes a long time. The treatment of these people once they arrive in the respective EU countries is outside the scope of this chapter.

---

[16] IMO et al. 2006: p. 6
[17] IMO et al 2006: p. 10

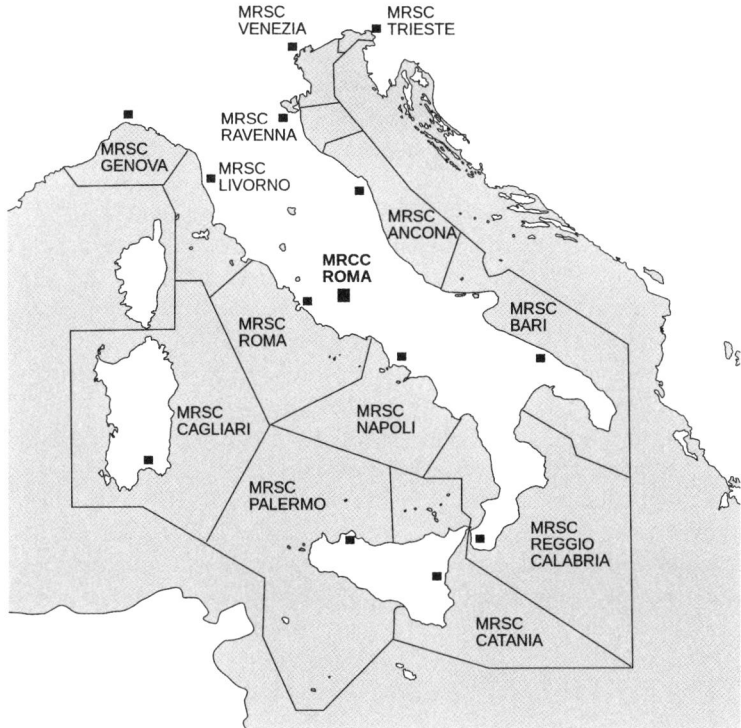

Figure 9.1   SAR Areas in the Mediterranean . [Wikicommons: http://en.wikipedia.org/wiki/File:Area_SAR_IT.svg]

Frontex and Its Organisational Problems: Implications for Small Navies

While rescue at sea is a well-established norm for navies, border protection against illegal immigration has become new and increasingly important. Navies and other national and international actors are tasked with border protection against an increasing flow of migrants. Frontex was created in 2004 as the border control agency of the European Union. Its core goal is to coordinate the action of its member states at its border, either sea or land borders. Since its inception in 2004 Frontex has been at the forefront of the policy debate. Many human rights organisations have denounced and criticised Frontex behaviour.[18] In the past ten years, a growing number of migrants have died trying to reach Europe by crossing the Atlantic or the Mediterranean. While data on the matter is still largely anecdotal, Human Rights Watch, for instance, has denounced human rights violations perpetrated by Member

---

[18]   *Human Rights Watch*, September 2011 Also, for this reason, Frontex has recently announced closer collaboration with UNHCR and it has committed itself at deploying at least one human rights expert for every operation.

States and Frontex when dealing with migrants.[19] But at a closer look, Frontex has a very limited set of things it can do.

First, by mandate its operational activity is limited to 'the coordination of specific joint operations of Member States' border-guard authorities'. Frontex neither replaces national border-guard services, nor does it have independent executive powers. For its operations it remains largely dependent on Member States' technical and human resources. Recital 4 of its founding regulation emphasises that '[t]he responsibility for the control and surveillance of external borders lies with the Member States'. Second, Frontex coordinates joint patrols on the High Seas and in the territorial waters of third countries from which irregular migrant boats depart. By doing so, it has become increasingly more difficult for asylum seekers to reach EU territory. Third, extra-territorial patrols are problematic per se because of a number of legal questions, because of the simultaneous application of the law of the sea, the international rules on search and rescue as well as refugee law and a lack of a common interpretation of these rules.

While it is the main focus for European studies scholars, the actual implementation of the mandate by Frontex has been largely overlooked. Maritime border control and its related activities are being implemented by member states. Yet, 'a closer look at the Agency's tasks reveals that its powers are limited and that the responsibility for operational activity at sea continues to lie largely with the Member States. The EU should speak out against Member States' practices that are in breach of international refugee law and use Frontex as a tool to increase the awareness of protection issues amongst national border-guard authorities'.[20] A Frontex official has defended the position of his agency underlining that:

> Frontex activities are supplementary to those undertaken by the Member States. Frontex does not have any monopoly on border protection and is not omnipotent. It is a coordinator of the operational cooperation in which the Member States show their volition. If some of our critics think it is not enough they should fix their eyes on decision-takers, as Frontex only executes its duties described in the Regulation 2007/2004.[21]

Frontex has been heavily criticised by Member States for its unclear mandate. Paraphrasing Rijpma, 'Frontex has been successful at blame shifting of the member states'.[22] Also 'blame shifting is one possible reason to explain the delegation of

---

[19] Estimates are based on reports in the media; see, for instance, http://fortresseurope.blogspot.com

[20] J.J. Rijpma, (2010) Frontex: Successful Blame Shifting of the Member States? *Analysis of the Real Insituto El Cano* (69)

[21] Frontex Regulation 2007/2004

[22] Rijpma, 'Frontex: Successful Blame Shifting of the Member States?' * ARI 69/2010 A Frontex: Successful Blame Shifting of the Member States? (ARI): 1

authority to an agency'.[23] Frontex was not only intended to restore the public's trust, it also allowed the Commission and the Member States to shift the blame for human suffering and the loss of life that coincide with ever more desperate attempts to evade stricter border controls. In addition, a failure to curb irregular migration would reflect badly on the Agency rather than the Community institutions or the Member States themselves. It is important to realise that Frontex's role is limited to providing support and expertise to the Member States.

Frontex is a relatively weak actor. This is not at all to justify Frontex's mistakes, of which there have been several. Among others: it is an instrument of an essentially flawed EU migration and asylum policy; by reinforcing the management of external borders, it is making it much more difficult for people in difficulty to reach Europe; the Agency reinforces a securitised perception of what is essentially a humanitarian problem through 'its one-sided mandate, the background of most of its staff in national law-enforcement agencies and its military-style operations'.[24] However, as Rijpma has suggested,

> by turning a blind eye to the practices of its Member States which prevent people from leaving certain third countries, the EU allows the right to seek asylum to be emasculated, either because asylum seekers cannot leave their country or because they are forced to stay in a third country that cannot adequately process their request or may refoule them.[25]

EU studies scholars tend to depict Frontex as 'the outcome of a "re-balancing" of powers between the Member States, the Council and the Commission following the communitarisation of the policy on external borders after the Treaty of Amsterdam, constituting an important shift from the intergovernmental coordination of operational activity under the Council to a more Community-based approach'.[26]

However, the need to provide humanitarian support has been framed as a humanitarian emergency and 'the authorities' apparent incapacity to deal with this situation has eroded the authority of Member States' governments and the Commission'. In any case, Member States are in no way prevented from patrolling their waters independently or in cooperation with other Member States or third countries, where this is complementary to the activities of the Agency. Article 3 of the Frontex Regulation determines that the Agency shall 'evaluate, approve and coordinate' Member States' proposals for joint operations and 'may itself, and in agreement with the Member State(s) launch initiatives for joint operations'. In theory, an independent risk-assessment should be at the basis of the Agency activity. However, Frontex has responded timely to Member States' request for assistance.

---

[23] Paul Magnette, *Citizenship: The History of an Idea.* Essex: ECPR Press, 2005: 6
[24] Rijpma, 'Frontex: Successful Blame Shifting of the Member States?'
[25] Ibid.
[26] Ibid.

Once a decision to implement a joint operation has been taken an operational plan is drafted in close consultation with the participating Member States. This plan forms the blueprint for the operation and contains important information such as timing, modus operandi, operational area, communication channels, available technical means and human resources as well as a detailed budget. In the case of sea operations, an International Coordination Centre (ICC) is established in the host Member State which provides the coordinator in charge of the centre. The ICC coordinator is also the Head of the Joint Coordinating Board (JCB), consisting of representatives of the participating Member States (National Officers) and Frontex experts, including a risk analyst. The command and control of the participating assets remains in national hands, through the National Officers, who have the possibility of consulting with their superiors before giving orders. The ICC coordinator implements the decisions related to operational activities taken by the JCB. The tactical command remains under the authority of each specific asset, or as directed by national authorities.

The presence of Member States' ships participating in joint operations in the territorial waters of third countries normally has its legal basis in bilateral agreements between a Member State, usually the host Member State, and the third country in question. The involvement of Frontex arguably has its legal basis in a broad interpretation of Article 12 of the Schengen External Borders Code which states that the purpose of border surveillance is to prevent unauthorised border crossings, in combination with Article 14 of the Frontex Regulation that says that the Agency has the task of facilitating the cooperation between Member States and third countries. Often, the bilateral agreements allowing for extra-territorial patrols are not agreements under public international law. Rather they are non-binding Memoranda of Understanding between Ministries of the Interior. This means that they escape parliamentary scrutiny in the Member States.

Frontex has never publicly endorsed a practice of diverting ships at sea, even if this might be due to the legal uncertainty regarding this practice rather than to a more principled position on the matter. Although in strictly legal terms national border guards are just as much bound by the Schengen Borders Code and fundamental rights as Frontex, a Community body can be expected to have a greater awareness of the applicable Community rules and be more sensitive to questions of protection. 'The Agency could and indeed should play a role in improving national border-guard sensitivity towards protection issues and improve awareness of these services' obligations under Community and international law' (Rjipma). Frontex has recently concluded working arrangements with the UNHCR and the IMO. There is a UNHCR liaison officer in Warsaw. Although the Agency is very hesitant to give a larger role to the UNHCR in its operational activities, UNHCR is now being involved in the Agency's training routines. Cooperation with the yet-to-be established Asylum Support Office and the European Fundamental Rights Agency would allow further progress to be made.

Scholars have shown that Frontex's mandate is relatively limited. Our empirical research will explore variations across member states. Variations lie in the way each Member State manages pre-existing organisational differences in the way border control is structured and organised but also in the way each Member State is managing the current emergencies at the border. Frontex plays a 'successful blame shifting role of the Member States'. In all our three cases, public opinion at the specific moments in time has blamed Frontex for not being a successful agent.

In March 2012, a new flow of migrants started crossing through the Mediterranean towards the Italian island of Lampedusa, a trend that increased with improving weather conditions.[27] It soon became apparent that there was insufficient coordination between the various agencies responsible for policing these waters. Two inflatable boats were rescued by the 'Guardia di Finanza' (Italian financial police) while drifting away. When the Guardia di Finanza entered one of the boats, five people had already died and 300 others were provided shelter or hospitalised. The 'Marina Militare' – the Italian Navy – had identified another inflatable boat but its helicopters were unable to locate it.[28] Many different state agencies – ranging from the police, to the navy to the financial police – were in charge of these rescue and border control operations. Observers said that this contributed to the confusion.[29]

An earlier example, from March 2011, revealed similar problems albeit in a different operational context. While the NATO intervention in Libya, UNIFIED PROTECTOR, was ongoing 72 people (50 men, 20 women and 2 babies) left the shore of Libya in a rigid hull inflatable boat without much food, water and little petrol. After 18 hours, the captain of the boat called a priest he knew in Italy and he sent a distress alert. The Italian Maritime Rescue Coordination Centre (MRCC) was immediately informed, located the boat and sent messages to all ships around to look for the boat.

A few hours later, after the distress signal, a helicopter hovered over the boat and provided water and biscuits also indicating they would come back. After about ten days, some of the migrants noticed personnel on a warship looking at them with binoculars and taking photos but without providing any help. Those were later identified to be either a Spanish ship under NATO command (*Mendez Nunez*) or the Italian vessel ITS *Borsini*. Despite the proliferation of NATO warships and naval helicopters in the seas between Sicily and Libya the boat was not rescued and eventually washed up on the Lybian shore after 15 days at sea. Only 9 people of the 72 survived.[30] In the next section, we will compare the organisation and training of three navies in the Mediterranean to explain why they act the way they do and if procedures and activities could be (or should be) done differently.

---

[27] http://bit.ly/1glcw4i (accessed 17 March 2012)

[28] 'Frontex: Human Rights Responsibilities', *Parliamentary Assembly, Council of Europe*, 8 April 2013, Doc. 13161 http://bit.ly/1cPdCmm (accessed 24 May 2013)

[29] 'Frontex: Human Rights Responsibilities', *Parliamentary Assembly, Council of Europe*, 8 April 2013, Doc. 13161 http://bit.ly/1cPdCmm(accessed 24 May 2013)

[30] 'Frontex: Human Rights Responsibilities', *Parliamentary Assembly, Council of Europe*, 8 April 2013, Doc. 13161 http://bit.ly/1cPdCmm (accessed 24 May 2013)

Old Wine in New Bottles? A Comparative Exploratory Study

This chapter presents preliminary finding, and formulate, hypothesis on potential frictions we could find in the field when it comes to Frontex implementation. We conducted exploratory research on secondary sources and explorative interviews with officials and navy officers for Italy, France and Spain. It brings to the front the role of small navies Frontex has conducted a well-defined number of maritime operations in the Mediterranean: Italy and Spain have played leading roles, while France has only played so far an auxiliary role. Table 9.1 summarises the operations in which these three countries have been involved.

Table 9.1   Frontex operations 2004–2013

	Year	Number of days	Host member state	Operational area
Hera	2006	126	Spain	Canary Islands/ Atlantic
Agios	2006	62	Spain	Western Mediterranean Sea
Nautilus	2006	11	Malta	Central Mediterranean Sea
Poseidon	2006	11	Greece	Aegean Sea/ Eastern Med.
Hera	2007	285	Spain	Western Mediterranean Sea
Minerva	2007	30	Spain	Western Mediterranean Sea
Indalo	2007	22	Spain	Western Mediterranean Sea
Hermes	2007	22	Italy	Central Mediterranean Sea
Nautilus	2007	69	Malta/Italy (Lampedusa)	Central Mediterranean Sea

	Year	Number of days	Host member state	Operational area
Poseidon	2007	60	Greece	Aegean Sea/ Eastern Med.
Zeus	2007	16	Spain, Belgium, Romania, Germany, Poland, Portugal, Latvia, Italy, Netherlands, Sweden, Greece	?
Hera	2008	406	Spain	Canary Islands/ Atlantic
Minerva	2008	33	Spain	Western Mediterranean Sea
EPN-Indalo	2008	22	Spain	Western Mediterranean Sea
EPN-Hermes	2008	64	Italy	Central Mediterranean Sea
Nautilus	2008	152	Malta/Italy (Lampedusa)	Central Mediterranean Sea
Poseidon	2008	292	Greece	Aegean Sea/ Eastern Med.
EPN-Euxine	2008	31	Romania	Black Sea
EPN-Heras	2009	381	Spain	Canary Islands/ Atlantic
EPN-Alpha Reinforcement	2009	30	Portugal	
EPN-Minerva	2009	39	Spain	Western Mediterranean Sea

	Year	Number of days	Host member state	Operational area
EPN-Indalo		50	Spain	Western Mediterranean Sea
EPN-Hermes		184	Italy	Central Mediterranean Sea
EPN-Nautilus		172	Malta	Ce
Poseidon		381	Greece	Aegean Sea/ Eastern Med.

The three countries differ in the kind of operations they have been involved in but also in the agencies that are tasked with the actual implementation of the operations. Table 9.1 summarises these differences, on which we elaborate in the remainder of this section.

Italy[31]

Italy's geographical position and its 'easy' access in the middle of the Mediterranean makes its case relevant to the study. Furthermore, cooperation between Italy and Qaddafi's Libya and the informal operational methods carried out in the Mediterranean Sea have acted as a trailblazer of the overall EU refugee policy.[32] Some of these practices could determine profound changes in the legal basis and the formal regulations of the European refugee regime so that the principle of non-refoulement might first be undermined and then abolished in this process.

Italy has three different agencies tasked with its coastal defence and maritime border control: the Navy is responsible for long-range sea patrol, the Coast Guard for maritime traffic control and SAR operations and the *Guardia di Finanza*[33] (GdF – financial police) for customs control within territorial waters. Italy's Coast Guard (CG) is part of the Italian Navy with a specific focus on the 'civilian' use of the waters surrounding Italy. In fact, the guidelines and operational directives for the CG currently come from the Ministry of Transportation and Infrastructure, not

---

[31] This section is based on interviews to Navy officers conducted by our graduate student research assistant, Giovanni Battista, between November 2011 and March 2012. We would like to express our gratitude and appreciation for Giovanni's work and dedication.

[32] Klepp, 'A Contested Asylum System', 2010

[33] The *Guardia di Finanza* is a law enforcement branch that specialises in border control and financial and economic crimes. It is equivalent, to some extent, to the US IRS as it is under control of the Department of the Treasury.

the Ministry of Defence. The National Responsible Authority for Maritime SAR is indeed the 'Ministero dei Transporti e Infrastructure', 'Comando Generale del Corpo delle Capitanerie di Porto' – 'Guardia Costiera' (Minister of Transportation and Infrastructures, general Command and Port Authority, Coast Guard). The main Italian MRCC is in Rome and 13 other centres cover the whole of Italy's coast.[34]

Navy vessels assigned to the Coast Guard for sea patrol are under the 'Comando delle Forze di Pattugliamento Costiero' (COMFORPAT – Command of Coastal Patrolling Forces). These Coastal Patrolling Forces belong to the NUMC (Nuove Unità Minori Combattenti) type, of stealth design and equally capable of operating in high seas or near the coast. The Navy ordered two new vessels, NUPA ('Nuove Unità da Pattugliamento d'Altura') type, which should join the NUMC in the near future for more specific high-seas patrol. The crews on these ships come from different Navy specialisms, including helicopter pilots and the San Marco Marine Brigade. Their main areas of operations are, currently, the Southern Mediterranean and the Sicily Channel (between Sicily and Tunisia), outside the national waters. In these areas lay some of the most trafficked 'rotte della speranza' (literally routes for hope), that is the routes taken by boats of migrants leaving African shores for Europe. Operational guidelines for the Coast Guard mandate that, if there is a request by anyone (civilian merchant ships or other seafarer observers) for intervention classified under SAR, naval units intervene according to standardised search and rescue procedures, otherwise, national identification protocols are followed.

On COMFORPAT units it is the Commandant, supported by other specialised officers such as the 'LegAd', the legal advisor, who decides, on a case by case basis, what type of intervention is best to guarantee the safety both of the persons in distress and of his crew. Overall, dedication to the mission and training levels within the whole crew are considered to be high level. For scouting and observation the vessels are equipped with helicopters, which are being upgraded from the older AB212 to the new NH-90. In addition, located at NATO Sigonella base, there is the 41st 'Stormo Antisommergibili' (anti-sub squadron), with nine Breguet Br.1150 Atlantic planes for Maritime Patrol Aircraft (MPA), which assist COMFORPAT with long-range surveillance and observation. Furthermore, the Br.1150, with a crew of 13, who are mixed Navy and Air Force personnel, can drop emergency packages as well as inflatable rafts to seafarers in need of assistance.

The *Guardia di Finanza* operates in national waters as well as in the 'contiguous zone', namely that area within 24 miles of the coast. In this area, given that the GdF is tasked with border and immigration control, when units from other law enforcement agencies, such as the national police or the *Carabinieri* or even Navy vessels are involved, coordination as well as command and control are exercised by the GdF. SAR or national identification procedures are the same as the Navy

---

[34] These are: Genoa (1), Livorno (2), Rome (3), Naples (4), Reggio Calabria (5), Bari (6), Ancona (7), Ravenna (8), Venice (9), Trieste (10), Catania (11), Palermo (12), Cagliari (13), Pescara (14).

operating outside the 'contiguous zone'. The *Guardia di Finanza* is also the link between FRONTEX and Italy's government and law enforcement agencies that operate in border and immigration control functions.

France

France has been mainly involved in Frontex operations with an auxiliary role. Since the creation of Frontex in 2004, France has not taken the lead in any maritime operation. However, its contribution and its support to Frontex are strong. France has taken part in all Frontex maritime operations with a supporting role by sending troops and financial support. While French politicians perceive its supporting role in other neighbouring countries serves also to control immigration into France, public opinion is more divided. Former French Prime Minister, Francois Fillon, declared to the European Commission President Barroso that 'it would be more clever if the European mission of Frontex could repatriate to Tunisia migrants that are intercepted rather than bringing them in Lampedusa, as it does now'.[35] Of course, this raises the question of whether these migrants coming from Tunisia may need to be given asylum, which would potentially put Member States in a position of potentially violating human rights.

France and Italy parallel their position very much. In this respect, they both seem to frame Frontex as a scapegoat, while their public opinion seems to be much more critical towards them in general. 'There is no rule that provides for the reception and free movement on European territory of illegal economic migrants. A large portion of the Tunisian migrants who have arrived in Italy, are not destined, as some suggest, to be resettled in different European countries, they are destined to return to their country.' Italian Foreign Minister Franco Frattini praised Fillon's proposal.

In France, three different sub-state agencies are in charge of implementing maritime rescue and border control operations: the Navy, the National Police, Customs and the Gendarmerie Maritime. The Gendarmerie Maritime – a peculiar French institution unheard of in common law systems – frames its involvement as a result of the new flow of migrants. As the organisation states: 'in the Mediterranean, the intensification of illegal migration flows via sea directed towards the northern shore of the Mediterranean has led EU member states to strengthen their cooperation. Coordinated by the agency Frontex, this consists of launching joint maritime operations in support of countries most affected by the migration pressure (Spain, Greece and Italy).'[36] 'The diversity of missions means employees require to have a double culture: at the same time gendarme and sailor, the maritime gendarmerie has to have a solid training in both domains.'[37]

---

[35] http://bit.ly/IudQpe (accessed 10 May 2013)

[36] Website of the French Navy - Marine Militaire http://bit.ly/1cPdXFF (accessed 17 March 2012)

[37] http://bit.ly/1dD91su (accessed 1 May 2013)

The French Navy is involved as well. 'The national navy locates itself at the heart of the maritime rescue mechanism and more than a quarter of its operational activities, its buildings and ships are dedicated to that.'[38] As in the Italian case, the division of labour between the Navy is responsible for long-range sea patrol, the Maritime Gendarmerie for maritime traffic control and SAR operations and the Customs police for customs control within territorial waters. The role of the French National Police is one of coordination among these several actors. So far, France has always contributed to Maritime Operations with personnel from each of these agencies . It remains to be seen how this would play out in the case of France leading its own operations.

Spain

Spain has taken the lead in a number of operations, such as Operation Indalo, among others. Spain has so far greatly stimulated international participation in its mission. However, its leading role is always very clear. For instance, when a Dutch ship was implementing a Frontex operation in high seas in front of the Spanish border the Guardia Civil was coordinating the operation from the HQ.[39] The Guardia Civil is the agency primarily involved in coordinating other agencies, namely the National Police and to a larger extent the Armada, the Spanish Navy. The Spanish Navy, thanks to its means, experience, legal competencies and knowledge of the maritime domain, is a key actor in Maritime Security operations at national level. The Spanish Navy permanently deploys ships in maritime surveillance tasks to maintain awareness of what is happening at sea, thus preventing risks and – if necessary – responding to threats. Different Spanish departments, both military and civilian, have responsibilities on Maritime Security-related activities and therefore, in order to ensure the effectiveness of these operations the Spanish Navy has signed several cooperation agreements.

'The Spanish Navy – along with other Constabulary and Customs departments – collaborates in the seizure of drugs coming from the other side of the Atlantic. The Navy also participates alongside the Civil Guard and other agencies in maritime monitoring activities to stop the mafias involved in the illegal traffic of migrants.' According to Royal Decree 194/2010 of 26 February, crew members of Spanish Navy ships are considered as law enforcement authorities when performing Surveillance and Maritime Security missions in accordance with their legal mandate and other international legislation. The most important agreements in this area between the Ministry of Defence and the Spanish Navy with other departments are: Inter-departmental agreement between the Ministry of Defence and the Ministry for Public Works (Port Authority) for information exchange, to fight drug trafficking, on Collaboration and Coordination between the Spanish Navy and the Civil Guard in the maritime domain.

[38] http://bit.ly/1cPdXFF (accessed 1 May 2013)
[39] www.armada.mde.es, (accessed 28 March 2012)

Conclusions

International migration, as Anderson argued, has moved to the top of the international security agenda, due in part to concerns that migration flows provide conduits for the spread of international terrorism. Even though this concern has been proved rather flimsy, it is undeniable that illegal immigration runs high on the list of what worries the Europeans. Southern Europeans, Greeks, Spanish, Italian and the French (although to a lesser extent) and others are, at times, convinced that their countries will be overwhelmed by illegal migrants from Africa who leave from the shores of Northern Africa. As Frontex coordinates EU Member States carrying out border controls not only in their territorial waters, but also on the high seas and within the territorial waters of third countries, the role of the EU agency has become increasingly important and highly visible to the European public.

This chapter should be considered a probe into a field of research that has been somehow overlooked in the past, but it is far from limited to the Mediterranean.[40] Our analysis points at severe coordination problems among states and within states tasked with border control in the Mediterranean. Most factors hindering coordination are located at either the domestic or the cross-national level. First, the process of 'buck-passing' – the responsibility of not managing illegal immigration – is not only a dynamic occurring at the European institutional level, as highlighted by existing literature. Also, bureaucratic institutions within each state are unclear as to what are tasks and responsibilities and on how to share them. Overall small navies together with other law-enforcement agencies such as the police or the budget police need more and better guidelines for effective border control operations and humanitarian rescue. Second, coordination problems arise cross-nationally, particularly when rubber dinghies get close to the border of Search and Rescue Areas.

While indeed most humanitarian disasters seem to have occurred in the Northern African Search and Rescue Areas, according to international legal provisions, Southern European small navies have the responsibility in trying to avoid humanitarian disasters also in areas that are not strictly speaking under their responsibility. Enhancing cross-national and subnational coordination together with transparency and accountability would be a good strategy to enhance border control in the Mediterranean Sea.

---

[40] See for instance Matt Siegel, 'Ship of Asylum Seekers Capsizes off the Coast of Java', *The New York Times* (global edition), 28 June 2012, 3.

Chapter 10

Small Navies in the Black Sea: A Case Study of Romania's Maritime Power

Deborah Sanders

Situated on the western part of the Black Sea, with a littoral coastline of 244 km, Romania has important economic and security interests in the Black Sea. It has a large commercial port, Constanta, ambitious plans to diversify its energy dependence and to develop and exploit its underwater energy sources and important riverine interests where the Danube crosses its territory and joins the Black Sea. For Romania, maritime power, the ability to use the maritime domain, has also been an important means of demonstrating its support for key allies and commitment to alliances, in particular the US and NATO. In order to protect and advance these maritime interests, and use the maritime domain to achieve key foreign policy goals, Romania, in common with many of the other newly independent states of Eastern Europe and the former Soviet Union, has attempted to build a small professional navy. Using Romania as a case study this chapter will examine the challenges of building a small effective and efficient navy. It will argue that Romania's maritime power has been adversely shaped and affected by the immense challenges of building a stable democratic state over the last two decades. Domestic political challenges including a significant delay in implementing military reform due to political instability and an economic crisis have had a profound effect on both the quantitative elements of Romania's maritime power; that is the means or resources Romania has to use the maritime domain as well as its capacity to use them; the qualitative elements of maritime power including military professionalism, morale and training. Recent challenges such as the global economic crisis in 2008 and ongoing political instability have also had an impact on Romania's maritime power. As maritime power is ultimately the attempt to use the maritime domain to achieve a desired political effect, Romania's relations with other littoral states and key players in the Black Sea, such as the US, have also played a role in shaping the effectiveness of its small navy. This chapter argues that Romania's relationship with two Black Sea littoral states, Russia and Ukraine, and one key player in the region, the US, play an important role in shaping the ability of its small navy to use the maritime domain. Maritime training exercises with the US as well as Romania's active participation in regional maritime security operations have enhanced the professionalism of its maritime service personnel and their ability to use the maritime domain. However, poor relations with both Russia and Ukraine, in particular maritime disputes with

Kyiv, continue to negatively shape the parameters of Romania's maritime power. In addition, Romania's close relationship with the US and its recent decision to host elements of the US missile defence shield, is also likely to impact negatively on relations between Bucharest and Moscow.

Romania's Interests in the Black Sea

Romania has important economic and security interests in the Black Sea. At a recent meeting of Black Sea Economic Cooperation (BSEC) the Romanian President highlighted the importance of Black Sea cooperation for the Romanian economy. He argued that cooperation was vital to overcome the current economic crisis, to stimulate prosperity, develop common infrastructure and to protect the Black Sea environment.[1] Romania's also has additional economic interests in the Black Sea: tourism. The Romanian President has recently highlighted the importance of developing and investing in Romania's tourist infrastructure as tourism is a key sector for future economic growth.[2] Romania's Black Sea coast is an important local and international tourist destination. Around 1.34 million tourists visited Romania in 2010 and this figure looks set to increase annually by 6.7 per cent.[3] In a discussion with the World Tourism Organisation Secretary General in Bucharest, the Romanian President highlighted the importance of developing Romania's ecological tourism in particular along the Black Sea.[4]

Romania also has important energy interests in the Black Sea: both in terms of diversifying its energy dependence and in developing and exploiting its underwater energy resources. In an attempt to diversify Romanian energy sources and increase the long term security of supply for European states, a Pan European Oil Pipeline (PEOP) project, has been proposed. This project would link the Romanian port of Constanta with Trieste in Italy and would make Romania a vital Black Sea energy transit state. The PEOP, with a proposed total length of 1,320 km, would join Romania, Serbia, Croatia, Slovenia and Italy and almost half of the pipeline would be built inside Romania.[5] Oil would be supplied from the Caspian to Georgia

---

[1] Traian Basescu 'Black Sea cooperation is extremely important for Romanian economy', *Hurriyet Daily News*, 26 June 2012.

[2] Traian Basescu, 'Tourism could be one of Romania's advantages in economic growth', Permanent mission of Romania to the United Nations. *AGERPES*.

[3] 'Romania a golden opportunity', Our World, *USA Today*, Thursday 22 September 2011.

[4] Basescu, 'Tourism could be one of Romania's advantages in economic growth', Permanent mission of Romania to the United Nations. http://bit.ly/1fjNz9o accessed 11 December 2013

[5] Srkjan Mihajlovic, General Manager of TRANSNAFTA, 'Overview of the Pan European Oil Pipeline (PEOP) pipeline', at the 2nd Oil Forum of the Energy Community, 8–9 November 2010, Belgrade Serbia.

and shipped across the Black Sea to Constanta. This proposed pipeline would generate significant revenue for the Romanian Government, allow the government to diversify its imports, distribute energy throughout the country and create new jobs.[6] In addition, plans to transport liquefied Azerbaijan gas from Georgia across the Black Sea to Constanta have also increased Romanian interests and potential influence in the Black Sea. The Azerbaijan–Georgia–Romania interconnector is a key priority for the Romanian Government as it would further establish Constanta as a major port in the Black Sea. This project could also reinforce Romania's role as a key European energy transit state as supplies could be made available to Romania's neighbours.

Romania also has additional energy interests in the Black Sea as natural gas deposits have been found in its exclusive economic zone. In late 2011 the Romanian Government awarded a number of contracts for the exploration of offshore gas 170 km off the Romanian coast. In February 2012 Romania's first deep water exploration well discovered significant amounts of natural gas.[7] After a visit to the deep water well, the Romanian President highlighted the importance of this discovery for the Romanian economy. He stated that exploitation could begin in 2015 and that gas deposits could 'create a chance at total energy independence' for Romania.[8] The President has also referred to these gas deposits as a 'substantial resource in the Black Sea' that would not only enable the Romanian economy to grow and develop but also create the potential for Romania to be an exporter of natural gas.[9]

Romania also has important riverine interests that link with, but extend beyond, the Black Sea. The Danube is Romania's most important river, not only for transportation but also for the production of hydroelectric and nuclear power. Romania has two hydroelectric power plants on the Danube at the Iron Gate and two nuclear power plants in Cernavoda in south-east Romania.[10] The Danube, classified as an international waterway, crosses Europe from west to east from its source in Germany's Black Forest to the Black Sea in Romania. The Danube is an important water route for domestic Romanian shipping and international trade. It is navigable for river vessels along its entire Romanian course and for sea-going

---

[6] Vlad Popovici, 'The Hidden Benefits of Southeast European Pipeline Politics', *Balkanalysis.com*, 21 September 2010. http://bit.ly/19hkEl0

[7] Alexandru Camburu, 'Petrom and Exxon discover natural gas in Romania's Black Sea', *Business & Macroeconomy*, 4 February 2012.

[8] 'Romanian President: Black Sea Deep-water well may produce by 2015', *Natural Gas Europe*, 6 March 2012.

[9] 'Romania looks to natural gas to fuel energy needs', *Natural Gas Europe*, 10 March 2012.

[10] Mirel Bran, 'Persistent drought in Romania threatens Danube's power', *The Guardian Weekly*, 13 December 2011.

ships as far as the port of Braila.[11] In recognition of the economic importance of this 2,850 km river, which crosses Germany, Austria, Slovakia, Hungary, Croatia, Serbia, Bulgaria and Romania, former communist President Ceausescu built a canal from the port of Cernavoda to Constanta to shorten the trade route by 400 km.[12] The 64 km Danube–Black Sea Canal which became operational in 1984 was the costliest engineering project in Romania's history. The economic importance of the Danube to the Romanian economy was seen most clearly after the NATO bombing campaign against Serbia in 1999. Romania suffered substantial economic losses when the Danube was closed to commercial traffic because of NATO's destruction of bridges. Total net losses to the Romanian economy ran to hundreds of millions of dollars.[13] Romania's riverine interests, however, have been recently challenged by the increase in Danube piracy, which is a growing concern for regional shipping. Piracy had increased noticeably along the 240–350 km stretch of the Danube's Romanian waterways.[14] In February 2012 a Ukrainian Danube shipping company which uses the route complained to the Romanian river police that one of its tugs had been robbed after being boarded.[15]

Building a Small Navy

Romania's ability to use the maritime domain to protect and advance these interests was, however, in the early years of independence, adversely affected by the challenges of military reform after the revolution. Throughout the 1990s, Romania struggled with military reform and this had an adverse effect on its military and by extension its ability to build a small professional navy. In common with other post-communist militaries, military reform in Romania was hampered by a lack of resources and civilian expertise, oversized and inefficient structures and obsolete military equipment.[16] In the early years after the revolution, the Romanian Government focused on depoliticising, downsizing and restructuring the military

---

[11] Nicolas Spulber, 'The Danube-Black Sea Canal and the Russian Control over the Danube', *Economic Geography*, 30/3 July 1954, pp. 236–245.

[12] David Turnock, 'The Danube-Black Sea Canal and its impact on Southern Romania', *GeoJournal* 12/1, 1996, pp. 65–79.

[13] Daniel N. Nelson, 'Romanian Security', in Henry F. Carey, *Romania since 1991 Politics, Economic and Society*, Oxford: Lexington Books , 2000 pp. 461–483.

[14] Antonios Kalmoukis, 'Piracy in European Waters – A Novelty?', *Dalimbassieris Maritime*, 8 February 2012, http://bit.ly/IFk9am

[15] 'Danube piracy a growing concern for regional shipping', *Maritime Bulletin*, 20 January 2012.

[16] Larry Watts, 'Romanian Public Attitudes to Defence and Security Sector Reform', p. 270.

and consolidating civilian control and had some early success.[17] Between 1990 and 2000 the Romanian Armed Forces (RAF) was reduced from 320,000 personnel to 180,000 and by 2002 further reduced to 129,000.[18] The immense challenges of building a 'NATO-like military' led, however, to a widening gap between stated military goals and implementation.[19] By 1997 Romania's military reform, the building of a small navy, had lost both momentum and focus due to the challenges of economic transformation and domestic political instability.

Military reform was hampered by the lack of economic reform and restructuring in Romania. Romania's transition from communism proved to be painfully slow in the economic realm.[20] In the early years after the revolution, the Romanian Government failed to carry out institutional reforms and depoliticise the economy.[21] The Romanian state bank also issued significant unsecured loans to clients with political influence and state companies. As a result the Romanian banking authorities revealed that between 1992 and 2004 over 4 billion dollars in non performing credits were lost to the state.[22] In light of the absence of structural reforms, international creditors were unwilling to provide economic assistance and in 1996 the IMF withheld the final tranche of a standby agreement.[23] In a sign of the poor state of Romania's public finances, the newly elected President, Emil Constantinescu, was forced to borrow money to pay public officials in December 1996.[24] Between 1997 and 1999 the Romanian economy shrank and by 1999 defence spending had, for the first time, dipped below the crucial two per cent level.[25] In 2000, in an evaluation of the readiness of the RAF, the Minister of Defence and the Chief of the General Staff concluded that, due to resource constraints, the military remained unprepared and poorly trained. In particular, the navy had received only 15 per cent of the fuel it required for operations and 70 per cent of air force pilots were not operational because of a lack of flying time.[26]

---

[17] Marian Zulean, 'Professionalisation of the Romanian Armed Forces', in Antony Forster, Timothy Edmunds and Andrew Cottey, *The Challenge of Military Reform in Postcommunist Europe*, Basingstoke: Palgrave Macmillan 2002 pp. 115–133.

[18] General Mihail Popescu, 'Military Interoperability with NATO', in Larry L. Watts (ed) *Romanian Military Reform and NATO Integration*, (The Centre for Romanian Studies, UK, 2002), pp. 151–167.

[19] Larry L. Watts, 'Introduction the Convergence of Reform and Integration', in Watts *Romanian Military Reform and NATO Integration*, pp. 9–20.

[20] Tom Gallagher, *Modern Romania*, New York: New York University Press, 2008.

[21] Ibid. p.114.

[22] Ibid. p.117.

[23] Ibid. p.132.

[24] Ibid. p.148.

[25] Larry L. Watts, Democratic Civil Control of the Military in Romania: An Assessment as of October 2001, *Conflict Studies Research Centre*, December 2001, p. 15.

[26] Zulean, 'Professionalisation of the Romanian Armed Forces', p.124.

Political infighting and instability also delayed Romania's military reform and the building of a small navy in the 1990s. The 1996 victory of the pro-democratic opposition ushered in a period of coalition politics that was characterised by inefficient and ineffective government exacerbated by political divisions and dissent.[27] Governmental effectiveness was crippled by the 'algorithm principle', in which appointments were made on the electoral strength of the ruling parties rather than on competencies. As a result, ministers and deputy ministers were rotated and failed to build up expertise in a particular department. Between 1996 and 2000 four different ministers served as Minister of Health while the Minister of Finance had thirteen different deputies.[28] The effectiveness of the coalition government was further undermined by disagreements between the upper and lower chambers which slowed down the lawmaking process and the rejection of legislation by parliamentary committees.[29] An attempt to revive the coalition by reshuffling the government failed in light of growing dissent within the coalition.[30] As a result of coalition bickering between 1996 and 2000 Romania had three Prime Ministers which also hampered the introduction of necessary economic and military reforms.[31]

As coalition infighting increased amongst the parties elected in 1996, political partisanship also began to replace military professionalism as the criteria for military postings to the Ministry of Defence and the Romanian General Staff, hampering the building of a professional small navy. The increasing politicisation of military appointees was seen in 1997 when the highly qualified Chief of Staff, General Dumitru Cioflina was replaced by General Constantin Degeratua, who, breaking with tradition, had not commanded an independent fighting unit. The politicisation of the military continued throughout the late 1990s as President Constantinescu continued, even in the face of radical military downsizing, to promote a number of senior military officers to command positions. Despite plans to release 5,600 majors, 3,800 lieutenant colonels and 1,670 colonels in 2000,

---

[27] Gallagher, *Modern Romania*, p.144.

[28] Lavinia Stan, 'Romania: in the Shadow of the past', in Sabrina P. Ramet, *Central and South East European Politics since 1989*, Cambridge: Cambridge University Press, 2010 pp. 379–400.

[29] The coalition government was formed by the CDR, the Democratic Convention of Romania, together with the UDMR, Democratic Union of Magyars in Romania, and the Social Democratic Union, which included the Democratic Party (Romania's former FSN, National Salvation Front party).

[30] Gallagher, *Modern Romania*, p.168-169

[31] Watts, *Democratic Civil Control of the Military in Romania: An Assessment as of October 2001*, p. 20. In 1996 former trade union leader and Bucharest Mayor Victor Ciorbea was forced to resign and was replaced by academic Radu Vasile, who lost his party support in late 1999 and was replaced by economist Mugur Isarescu, the National bank governor.

President Constantinescu promoted almost two hundred colonels and generals.[32] These political appointments undermined morale, discipline and the readiness of the RAF.[33]

Romanian military reform was, however, put firmly back on track in 2001 and this created the necessary conditions for the construction of a small effective navy. The introduction of the Membership Action Plan at the NATO Summit in Washington, as a tool to support countries seeking to join NATO, combined with a strong commitment from the newly elected President, Ion Iliescu and the Social Democratic Party, to joining NATO in 2004, led to more focused, systematic and effective military reform, including the building of a small navy. During the 1990s the Romanian navy had been significantly downsized and by 2002 a large proportion of its ships had reached their decommissioning dates. In light of the urgent need to modernise its fleet and ensure NATO interoperability, the Romanian Government purchased two second hand multi-role Type 22 Frigates from the British Royal Navy in 2004. The acquisition of these frigates was seen by the Romanian government as an important part of the naval modernisation process providing the Romanian navy with modern ships and more advanced capabilities able to participate in NATO missions and operations. As a result of this modernisation the Romanian navy has just over 7,000 personnel and principal platforms include three frigates, four corvettes, 16 patrol vessels and five mine warfare vessels.[34] The Romanian navy also has a Kilo class submarine the SSK *Delfinul* which is used as a training ship and is currently inactive. Although the reactivation of this modern submarine has remained a priority for the Romanian navy, it has yet to receive the necessary funding and it is unclear what role it would play in advancing Romanian interests in the Black Sea.[35] The Romanian navy also has some limited sea lift capabilities. These include two ferry boats, one roll-on roll-off ship and various cargo ships.

Reforms introduced by the Romanian Government in light of the desire to join NATO also had a profound impact on the building of a professional small navy. In 2001 the government introduced a new integrated system of management for defence acquisitions in which acquisitions and procurement were not only directly linked to military missions for the first time, but also established clear single service lines of responsibility. The new system identifies and establishes the requirements for new military assets based on missions and security threats, the priorities for acquiring these systems and provides logistic support over the entire life of a new weapon system up until its retirement from service and disposal of

---

[32] Ibid. p.18.

[33] Ibid. p. 24.

[34] European Defence Information, Romania, armedforces.co.uk, http://bit.ly/1aYnsnm

[35] 'Romania's submarine forces', *Jane's Underwater Warfare systems*, 12 May 2011.

redundant systems and equipment.[36] The Romanian Government has recognised that the absence of such planning and control of redundant systems can be an unnecessary drain on defence budgets.[37]

A number of reforms introduced, in light of Romania's desire to join NATO, have also significantly improved military morale and increased military, including naval, professionalism. In particular, the introduction of a personnel policy and career management system has rehabilitated the military career, increased transparency and ensured equal opportunity for all military personnel seeking promotion.[38] Prior to 2001 the Romanian military lacked a set of coherent principles laying out the career evolution of military personnel and a model for determining what functions would be performed at what rank. This lack of a clear and coherent human resources and management system led to structural and functional deficiencies in the management of the officer corps and a decline in the value of military careers.[39] In order to further improve military professionalism, Romania has introduced a military career guide, optimised the role of the independent military selection committee, defined posts according to military rank and implemented a system of personnel data management.[40] Professionalisation of the military has also been increased by the reorganisation of Romania's military education system.[41] The professionalism of the Romanian armed forces has been increased further by the decision to end conscription in 2007 and develop fully professional standing forces. In recognition of the importance of developing a professional navy, conscripts were phased out in the maritime component in 2005.

The professionalism of Romania's navy has also been enhanced by its active participation in training exercises with other NATO members. The US in particular has invested heavily in developing the qualitative aspects of Romania's military power. Since 1993 more than a thousand exchanges and training programmes

---

[36] Georghe Matache, 'The New Procurement Concept, in Watts, *Romanian Military Reform and NATO Integration*, pp 135–150.

[37] Ibid. p.138.

[38] George Christian Major and Sebastian Huluban, 'From Hardware to Software Reforms in Romania's Civil-Military Relations', *Baltic Defence Review*, 8/2 2002. pp. 103–123.

[39] ' Gheorghe Cristian Maior, 'Personnel Management and Reconversion, in Watts, *Romanian Military Reform and NATO Integration* pp. 57–81; Constantin Gheorghe, 'Force Restructuring, in *Romanian Military Reform and NATO Integration*, pp. 121–134; also see 'Romanian Defence, 2004–2009, Five years of NATO membership', Romanian Ministry of National Defence, p.27

[40] Romanian Defence, 2004–2009, Five years of NATO membership', *Romanian Ministry of National Defence*, p.27.

[41] 'The US presence in Romania' Fact Sheet – US Department of Defense Presence in Romania. http://1.usa.gov/1b1tMcJ

have taken place between US and Romanian forces.⁴² The US has a number of programmes which have improved the qualitative aspects of Romania's maritime power by developing in particular the skills of its marines and its small maritime-air component. In May 2010 the US marines and sailors of scout platoon, Headquarters and Service Company, 1st Tank Battalion visited Romania to train and advise on how to provide humanitarian support while promoting regional stability and conducting other theatre-level security cooperation activities. During this visit, Romanian marines and soldiers participated in a number of exercises including the development of combat marksmanship, convoy operations and patrolling techniques.⁴³ In July 2011, under the auspices of the Summer Storm Amphibious Bilateral Exercise 11, US marines and sailors, with Echo Company, also conducted a five-day training exercise with Romanian Marines from the 307th Marine Infantry Battalion. This exercise not only increases the interoperability of Romanian and US forces, but also allowed the Romanian marines to develop their ability to conduct military operations in urban terrain.⁴⁴ Less than a month later the Romanian navy's air arm conducted two days of training with the US Navy assault ship the USS *Whidbey Island*. During this exercise Romania's three Puma helicopters operated by the Black Sea Knights squadron practised deck landings aboard the US platform.⁴⁵

The Romanian navy's participation in training exercises and maritime security operations has increased Romania's interoperability and compatibility with NATO and EU allies and Black Sea states and, moreover, provides the navy with the experience necessary to develop a professional force. The Romanian navies' participation in NATO's counter-terrorism operations in the Mediterranean, Operation Active Endeavour, has increased its professionalism, readiness and interoperability with NATO allies. Since 2005 Romania's frigates, *King Ferdinand* and *Regina Maria*, have both carried out maritime security operations in the Mediterranean including deterring and disrupting maritime terrorist operations, escorting maritime platforms and naval diplomacy.⁴⁶ In 2011 the Romania navy also participated in NATO's arms embargo operations off the Libyan coast. The frigate, *King Ferdinand*, was activated in March 2011 to impose the embargo and

---

⁴² Cpl. R. Logan Kyle, 'Marines, Romanian troops put rounds down range in combat marksmanship course', 28 May 2010, http://bit.ly/IuzZ6U

⁴³ Cpl. Dwight A. Henderson, 'American, Romanian Marines Conduct Bilateral MOUT training, 11 August 2011, http://bit.ly/IuzYjg

⁴⁴ 'Romania's nascent naval helicopter force trains with US navy', *Jane's Navy International*, 4 August 2011.

⁴⁵ This point is made by Larry L Watts, 'The Transformation of Romanian Civil-Military Relations: Enabling Force Projection', *European Security*, 14/1 2005, pp. 95–114.

⁴⁶ Romanian Defence, 2004–2009, Five Years of NATO Membership, *Romanian Ministry of National Defence*, p.24

was engaged in escort, interdiction, surveillance and air control missions.[47] At a ceremony, before the launch of the frigate for operations off Libya, the Minister of Defence, Gabriel Oprea, highlighted how Romania's participation in this operation had significantly increased the standard of training for the crew.[48]

Ambitious plans to further transform the Romanian military and augment its maritime power are, however, likely to be affected by the ongoing political instability and the economic crisis that hit Romania in 2008.[49] Future ambitious, and ultimately costly, plans to improve Romania's maritime power announced by the Minister of Defence include a new surveillance system connected to NATO commands and the acquisition of new capabilities including mine hunters, corvettes and a logistic ship.[50] However, the economic crisis and the inability and, at least initially, the unwillingness of the government to implement necessary economic reforms could impact negatively on these procurement programmes. The effects of the global economic crisis hit Romania in 2009. After almost ten years of rapid growth. Romania's export market collapsed as a result of decreased demand from other EU members and as interest rates remained high domestic consumer demand also fell rapidly. High spending in the years leading up to the economic crisis had also left Romania with a large public debt.[51] The cycle of elections that followed from 2007–2009, including European parliamentary elections, Romanian local and parliamentary elections and Romanian Presidential elections, not only distracted policy makers from the crisis, but, also led to a lax attitude to financial matters. As a result Romania entered the economic crisis unprepared, and, after almost a year of internal political strife amongst the coalition members, economic reforms were not implemented. In March 2009, after the Romanian economy contracted for the first time in nine years, the Romanian Government asked the International Monetary Fund, the European Commission and the World Bank for a loan of almost 20 billion Euros.[52] However, in September 2009 the coalition made up of the Democratic Liberal Party, the Conservative Party and the Social Democratic Party collapsed and the remaining minority government, led by Prime Minister Emil Boc, was removed in a vote of no confidence. After the collapse

---

[47] 'Romania's participation with forces in NATO operation to enforce arms embargo against Libya', *Ministry of National Defence*, Information and Public Relations Directorate.

[48] 'Ceremony is held as Regele Ferdinand frigate leaves on mission', Romanian National News Agency *AGERPRES*, Permanent Mission of Romania to the United Nations, http://mpnewyork.mae.ro/en/romania-news/524.

[49] Romanian Defence, 2004–2009, Five Years of NATO Membership, *Ministry of National Defence*.

[50] Sorin Frunzaxverde, 'Strategic defence in Romania', *Defence Management Journal*, issue 36, http://bit.ly/197N0dy

[51] Romania, Project on Democratic Transitions, 31 May 2012, http://www.democratictransitions.net/Romania.

[52] Laura Stefan, Dan Tapalaga, Sorin Ionita, 'Romania', *Nations in Transit*, Washington: Freedom House 2010

of the coalition government, Romania entered a political and administrative stalemate in which the minority caretaker government was unable to make the difficult decisions demanded by the economic crisis.[53] In light of the absence of a government during the winter of 2009 and the failure to implement reforms, the IMF blocked the delivery of the third and fourth instalments of the IMF loan. Throughout 2010 and 2011, the Romanian Government struggled with recession and austerity.[54] Although the government introduced a tough austerity plan in 2010, and made progress in restoring Romania's macroeconomic balance, by the first quarter of 2012 the economy had officially entered recession.[55]

Further economic progress is, however, likely to be undermined by the ongoing political crisis in Romania. In 2012 the Romanian President, Traian Basescu, was suspended from office by the country's parliament after a number of disagreements with the Prime Minister, Victor Ponta, of the Social Democratic Party. In light of this ongoing political crisis, and public protests at the introduction of tough austerity measures, the Romanian government will struggle to implement controversial economic reforms agreed to under the IMF's economic assistance programme. Economic uncertainty and the ongoing political instability are likely to have a negative effect on Romania's ambitious maritime procurement plans. Plans to cut its budget deficit to 1.9 per cent of GDP from 4.4 per cent in 2011 could impact negatively on military modernisation and future military procurement.[56]

Relations with Other Littoral States and Key Players in the Black Sea

The effectiveness of Romania's small navy is also shaped and affected by relations with two Black Sea neighbours, Ukraine and Russia, and relations with a key player in the region, the US. Romania's ability to use the maritime domain has been directly affected by two maritime disputes with its neighbour Ukraine. The first dispute has been over the status of Snake Island and the subsequent delimitation of maritime borders in the Black Sea between Romanian and Ukraine. This dispute was resolved in 2009 in Romania's favour and, while Romania received almost 80 per cent of the disputed maritime domain in the Black Sea increasing its continental shelf in a region rich in oil and gas reserves, the outcome has done little

---

[53] Laura Stefan, Sorin Ionita, 'Romania', *Nations in Transit*, Washington: Freedom House 2011

[54] 'Romania's economy: Buckle up, A tight budget and a credit squeeze will make 2012 a tough year', *The Economist*, 10 December 2011.

[55] 'Romania to slash public sector spending for IMF deal', *Jane's Intelligence Weekly*, 7 May 2010; Romania's political crisis', *STRATFOR Global intelligence*, July 6 2012.

[56] 'Next! A country where governments have the longevity of mayflies', *The Economist*, 5 May 2012.

to improve already strained and difficult relations with Ukraine.⁵⁷ An additional maritime dispute between Romania and Ukraine has also damaged relations and threatens Romania's control of the lower Danube and by extension its maritime power and influence in the Black Sea. In 2004 the Ukrainian Government began developing the Danube–Black Sea deep-water navigation route in the Ukrainian part of the Danube Delta on the Bystroye Canal.⁵⁸ The aim of this project, which links the Danube's Kilia arm to the Black Sea, is to increase the volume of goods transported via Ukrainian ports on the Danube. The Ukrainian project, which claims to offer a higher capacity, two-way traffic and lower fees for ships, represents a direct challenge to Romania's monopoly of goods transported on the Danube Delta and an economic threat to Romania's canal built further upstream which links the Danube to the Black Sea.⁵⁹ Estimates suggest that Romania could lose up to $1.5 million annually as international shipping could use the alternative cheaper Ukrainian route to the Sulina branch of the Danube River Delta.⁶⁰ As a result of allegations by Bucharest that Ukraine's canal was threatening the unique ecosystem of the Danube Delta, further development of the Bystroye Canal by Ukraine has been blocked until 2014. However, this issue is far from resolved as the Ukrainian Government is keen to develop its maritime presence in the Danube Delta. In light of this current maritime dispute as well as historical tensions over former Soviet borders, their respective treatment and recognition of minorities and disagreement over the future of the Moldovan enclave of Transnistria, relations between the two states have remained difficult and will continue to shape the ability of the Romanian navy to use the Black Sea.⁶¹

Strained relations with the Russian Federation also shape and affect Romania's maritime power. Romania's foreign policy priorities for 2011 reveal the poor state of relations with Moscow. Its main priorities in regard to Russia were to 'overcome stagnation in relations with a view to gradually normalising and making them pragmatic and predictable'.⁶² Relations deteriorated in 2010 in light of the expulsion of a Romanian diplomat reportedly caught spying in Moscow and what were perceived by Russian politicians as insensitive statements made by the Romanian President, Traian Basescu, about the Second World War on

---

⁵⁷ 'Ukraine loses the dispute over Snake Island to Romania', *OSW Centre for Eastern Studies*, 3 February 2009.

⁵⁸ Tadeuz Wanski, 'Ukraine- Romania: a sustained deadlock', *OSW Centre for Eastern Studies*, 30 December 2011.

⁵⁹ Ibid.

⁶⁰ Michael Shafir, 'Analysis: Serpents Island, Bystraya Canal, and Ukrainian–Romanian Relations, *RFE/RL* 24 August 2004.

⁶¹ For a discussion of these areas of tension see, Wanski, 'Ukraine– Romania: a sustained deadlock'; Taras Kuzio, 'Romanian–Ukrainian Espionage scandal exacerbates already poor relations', *Eurasia Daily Monitor* 6/51 17 March 2009.

⁶² 'Priorities of Romanian Diplomacy in 2011', *Romania Ministry of Foreign Affairs*, www.mae.ro/en/node/2147

national TV.[63] Despite Russia's commitment to increasing cooperation, and, in particular, Russian investments in Romania, relations remain strained and difficult and are unlikely to improve in the short term.[64] Romania's relationship with Russia is shaped by their common history, competing priorities in the Black Sea and Romania's active engagement and prioritisation of relations with the US. Russian intervention in and geopolitical interests in what was to become Romania has a long history and has had a negative impact on relations between these two states. Russia's first contact with the Principality of Moldova and future Romanian space was in 1711 and by the end of the 18th Century Russia made clear its territorial ambitious in the region when it sought to occupy the northern part of Moldova (Bukovina).[65] Russia's territorial ambitions were realised in 1812 when Russia annexed the Eastern part of Moldova, the region between the Prut and Dniester known as Bessarabia.[66] In 1940 Moscow again advanced its territorial ambitions when Bessarabia, Northern Bukovina and Snake Island on the Black Sea, which had all belonged to the Kingdom of Romania, became part of the USSR. Relations between Russia and Romania have also been affected by their differing views on the future of the Black Sea region. The main areas of contention between Romania and Russia have been over the future of Moldova and the status of Transnistria, in particular the continued presence of Russian troops in this disputed enclave.[67] Romania has also been keen to advance its national interests in the Black Sea. Not only has Romania been promoting its own energy interests in the region, but it has also directly encouraged and supported both European and US engagement in the Black Sea, directly challenging Russia's interests in the region.

Romanian–Russian relations have also been affected by its strategic partnership with the US. Although Romania's foreign policy priorities since independence have been Euro–Atlantic integration, it has also become one of Washington's closest allies in Europe. After the terrorist attacks on the US on 11 September 2001, the Romanian Government made clear its readiness to assist the US in countering the terrorist threat when it agreed that US troops could use Romanian territory in the event of a conflict with Iraq.[68] In a sign of Romania's commitment,

[63] Clive Leviev-Sawyer, 'Russia's message to Romania', *The Sofia Echo*, 20 August 2010; also see 'Romanian interested in constructive relations with Russia', *ITAR-TASS News Agency*, Moscow, 11 August 2011.

[64] 'Russia voices interest in closer cooperation with Romania', Statement by the Permanent mission of Romania to the UN, issued by the Romanian National News Agency: *AGERPRES*.

[65] Ionel Nicu Sava, 'Romania–Russian Relations in the context of Euro-Atlantic integration process', *Conflict Studies Research Centre*, September 2011.

[66] Ibid. p.3.

[67] 'Romania urges Moldova closer to NATO and Russia to withdraw troops from Transnistria', 10 October 2009, the Romanian news agency *Mediafax*.

[68] Tom Gallagher, *Romania and the European Union, How the weak vanquished the strong*, (Basingstoke: Palgrave Macmillan 2009) pp. 132–151.

in 2003, US soldiers used Romania's Mihail Kogalniceanu air base as a hub to send equipment and combat troops into Iraq during the early stages of the US-led invasion. Romania again demonstrated its firm commitment to Washington when Romanian troops were deployed to Iraq in support of US Operation Iraqi Freedom. More than 5,200 Romanian troops served in Iraq until they were finally withdrawn in 2009.[69] Romania's strategic partnership with the US was formalised in 2005 when US Secretary of State, Condaleeza Rice signed an accord with the Romanian Government establishing the first US military bases in a former Warsaw Pact country.[70] Under this agreement the US has use of four Romania military facilities: Mihail Kogalniceanu Air Base near the port of Constanta, Babadag and Cincu training areas and the firing ranges in Smardan.[71] These facilities as well as Constanta harbour have been used by the US for the movement of troops and equipment in transit between Iraq and Afghanistan.

The close strategic partnership between Bucharest and Washington also affects and shapes Romania's maritime power in the Black Sea. In September 2011 the Romanian Foreign Minister, Teodor Baconschi, signed an agreement with the US Secretary of State, Hillary Clinton, for the deployment of an American land-based Standard Missile Interceptor system in Romania.[72] This system which is expected to be deployed in 2015, will be located within the existing Romanian airbase at Deveselu, near Caracal, and will consist of a radar deckhouse, an associated Aegis command, control and communication suite, and a number of launch modules armed with Standard Missile Interceptors. This base will host elements of a wider US-led anti-missile defence shield set to cover Western Europe and parts of Eastern Europe, against long-range missiles from rogue states. Details of the agreement to host the interceptors suggest that Romanian maritime capabilities could be significantly augmented by the presence of US naval forces and capabilities at this site in Deveselu.[73] US Naval facilities in Deveselu will include an access control centre and support facilities for 250 personnel. There has also been considerable speculation that the US will also deploy the sea-based Aegis system on American guided missile cruisers and destroyers in the Black Sea to augment its land-based missile defence system.[74] In a traditional sense, Romania's

---

[69] Army Sgt Mark Miranda, Special to American Forces Press Service, 'Romanian Forces End Mission in Iraq', *American Forces Press Service*, US Department of Defence website, http://1.usa.gov/1bcYcFE

[70] 'Military Base in Romania approved', *Associated Press* 7 December 2005.

[71] 'US Military Engagements to Romania', Embassy of the United States Bucharest, Romania, 27 May 2008.

[72] Doug Richardson, 'Romania and Turkey agree to ABM deployments', *Jane's Missiles and Rockets,* 26 September 2011.

[73] For details of the two contracts see, 'Missile Defence Agency FY 2013 Military Construction, Defence Wide', http://1.usa.gov/1aYocZO

[74] Rick Rozoff, 'Romania: U.S. Escalates Missile Brinkmanship Against Russia', *Global Research,* 1 July 2012.

strategic partnership with the US, in particular the recent agreement to base BMD interceptors, will enhance Bucharest's maritime capabilities in the region. The permanent presence of a powerful ally on its territory as well as the deployment of US maritime platforms in the Black Sea would significantly enhance Romania's modest naval capabilities. However, Romania's enhanced military cooperation with Washington threatens to undermine relations with two of its most important Black Sea neighbours discussed earlier, Russia and Ukraine, which could impact negatively on the utility of Romania's maritime power.

Romania's already strained relations with Russia could be further complicated by its decision to host the US BMD system on its territory. Russia's opposition to the deployment of missile defence sites, initially planned for Poland and the Czech Republic, has strained Russia's relations with the US potentially putting Romania in a precarious and difficult position visà- vis its large Black Sea neighbour. In response to the announcement of the US missile defence site in Romania, the Russian Government has alleged that US action undermines strategic stability and Moscow clearly regards the US BMD system as a threat.[75] Russia remains wary of unilateral US missile defence plans in Europe, fearing that any system could be expanded to pose a threat to its own strategic nuclear forces.[76] Highlighting how this decision might impact on Romania, the Russian Ambassador to NATO, Dmitry Rogozin suggested that Bucharest's decision could lead to a serious regional problem.[77] Romania's decision to host elements of the US missile defence shield also risks antagonising already strained relations with Ukraine. Although Ukraine has not officially opposed the US–Romanian agreement, the Ukrainian Minister of Foreign Affairs, Kostyantyn Gryshchenko, has called for high-level consultations with Romania and the US on the deployment of the components of the missile shield in Romania.[78] In light of its non-aligned status, and poor relations with Bucharest, Kyiv is seeking assurances that the deployment will not harm its national security interests. The Ukrainian delegation to the Annual Session of the NATO Parliamentary Assembly held in Bucharest in 2011 highlighted Ukraine's concern that a military contingent in Deveselu would threaten the national security of neighbouring states and the Black Sea region as a whole.[79]

---

[75] Pavel Felgenhauer, 'Moscow sees military threats from all directions', *Eurasia Daily Monitor* 9/58, 22 March 2012.

[76] Ibid.

[77] Clive Leiev-Sawyer, 'Russia's message to Romania', *The Sofia Echo*, 20 August 2010.

[78] 'Ukraine calls for consultations with US over missile defence plans in Romania', *Jane's Intelligence Weekly*, 20 May 2011.

[79] 'Ukraine criticises US plans to deploy missiles in Romania', *Newslink Romania*, 11 October 2011.

Conclusion

With important security and energy interests in the Black Sea, Romania provides an interesting case study of the challenges of building a small professional navy. Early attempts to build a small navy were initially hampered by the delay in military reform due to political instability and the failure to reform and restructure the Romanian economy. As a result of these early challenges, Romania's maritime power was severely limited. It decommissioned many of its platforms and failed to modernise or procure new ships. In addition, naval professionalism was damaged by the lack of investment and neglect of the military and its increasing politicisations. More than ten years after the overthrow of communism, Romania did, however, finally begin to develop both the capacity and ability to use the maritime domain. In light of its desire to join NATO the Romanian government implemented a far-reaching programme of military reform that not only led to the procurement of a number of modern maritime platforms, but also the development of procedures to promote and develop naval professionalism. Naval professionalism has been further augmented by the Romanian navy's active participation in military training exercises and both regional and international maritime security operations. Ambitious future maritime procurement plans to increase the number of ships are, however, likely to be compromised by the current economic situation and ongoing political crisis in Romania.

Although Romania has made some progress in developing a small professional navy, its ability to use the maritime domain will continue to be affected by poor relations with two of the other littoral states, Ukraine and Russia. The ongoing dispute over the Ukrainian project to develop the Ukrainian part of the Danube Delta will continue to hamper the normalisation of relations with Kyiv and moreover, could threaten Romanian's riverine interests in the future. Strained relations with Moscow also negatively affect the context in which Romania uses its maritime power. Relations with Russia are unlikely to improve in the medium term. Outstanding areas of tension such as Moldova's potential membership of the EU, the status of Transnistria as well as the recent agreement by the Romanian Government to station elements of the US missile defence shield on its territory will limit the scope for improving future relations. Paradoxically while Romania's close relationship with the US has played an important role in facilitating the development of an effective small navy, it has done little to improve the context in which Romania uses that maritime power.

Chapter 11
A Small Navy in a Changing World: The Case of the Royal Swedish Navy[1]

Niklas Granholm

Introduction

There are some things you have to be a professional not to understand.

The sentence summarises a satirical short story written in 1912 by Swedish novelist Hjalmar Söderberg.[2] At a dinner party in Stockholm the guests discuss the difficult situation for the Royal Swedish Navy (RSwN). The storm clouds leading up to the First World War could be seen forming and Sweden found herself in between the great power-blocs of the day. Recent technological breakthroughs had produced the British Dreadnought class, followed by similar ship designs in other countries.[3] Should Sweden also acquire such ships, in spite of the staggering cost? Over brandy and cigars the dinner guests suggest a compromise: The navy will argue for what it thinks it can get funding for, rather than what it actually would like. Asking for something inadequate to the task while defending your professionalism is managed by referring to the 'special characteristics of the Baltic Sea', supposedly cancelling out the advantages of more capable ships of possible opponents. The hope is that when these ships have been built, the government will see reason and proper Dreadnoughts will be ordered.

A century later, Söderberg's satire is still valid. What today's defence planners would like they cannot get and convincing apprehensive politicians is an uphill

---

[1] Several colleagues, both active and retired, have given helpful comments and suggestions and provided information in writing this chapter. My warm thanks go to Dr. Peter Sigray FOI, Dr. Martin Lundmark FOI, Commodore Gustaf von Hofsten (RSwN ret.), Capt. Lars Wedin (RSwN ret.) and Johan Tunberger (the Royal Swedish Academy of War Sciences). The Royal Swedish Society of Naval Sciences generously contributed a grant from its funds, enabling me to take part in relevant conferences when beginning this analytical process. Any remaining weaknesses in the text are of course my own responsibility.

[2] Hjalmar Söderberg, 'Generalkonsulns F-båtsmiddag', in *Den talangfulla draken*, Stockholm, 1913.

[3] Kent Zetterberg in Johan Forslund (ed.). *Pansarbåtsinsamlingen 100 år.* Symposium fredagen 9 november 2012 (Stockholm 2012).

struggle. Much of the problems depicted by Söderberg describe the real-world issues of a planning equation that is almost never fully solved.

The situation in 1912 has some similarities with what the RSwN face today: convincing apprehensive politicians is difficult when cost estimates turn out to have been too optimistic, technological development and strategic change throws long-term planning into disarray. Times of austerity compound the problem further.

Aim

The aim of this chapter is to use analysis of modern seapower, combined with a short overview of Sweden's cold-war naval history, recent and current operational patterns as an empirical basis for discussion of future structures for the RSwN. In addition, observable geostrategic shifts are producing partly new circumstances. Changes to the military industrial base create new limits on what can possibly be produced nationally. Taken together, these changes today present the RSwN with a set of serious challenges. Lastly, an attempt is made to discuss what these changes could lead to by suggesting and discussing three alternative structures for the RSwN set against three types and areas of operations, within a time frame of five to ten years.

Seapower

The concept of seapower as a component of a nation's maritime strategy has been developed, discussed and analysed for many centuries.[4] Several contemporary analysts have applied the concepts to the modern world in order to forge recommendations for how seapower can be designed to achieve peace and prosperity at reasonable cost. Norman Friedman argues in his book 'Seapower as Strategy' that the enduring qualities of seapower as part of a national strategy offers attractive advantages for any nation that is so inclined.[5] Mobility, cost-effectiveness, inbuilt flexibility and the ability to effect a development without actually having to use force should make more nations avail themselves of seapower as a central component in national strategy. While Friedman writes from the great-power perspective of the United States, the arguments laid out are to an extent relevant also for a European power such as Sweden. In the situation after the end of the Cold War, navies designed for decisive oceanic battles are less

---

[4] Geoffrey Till refers to Mahan as the first to really talk about the concept of seapower. The role of the sea had of course been thought of and written about before, but Mahan was the first to popularise the concept. Geoffrey Till, *Seapower. A Guide for the Twenty-First Century*. (London: Frank Cass 2003),

[5] Norman Friedman, *Seapower as Strategy. Navies and National Interests*. pp. 226–232 (Annapolis: Naval Institute Press 2001).

relevant. Instead the long-term pattern seems to be a focus on limited wars and on the littorals. Much seems to point to the beginning of a new era in maritime security. Indications are that maritime strategies have to be thought of so that they better reflect this changed situation. Strategic choices have to be managed within a complicated national policy-making process, unique to each nation. One size does not fit all.

Geoffrey Till in 'Seapower – a Guide for the Twenty-First Century' helpfully defines seapower in terms of input and output.[6] On the input side are the resources required (navies, coastguards, civil maritime industries, the contribution of land and air forces where applicable) and their activities and operations. On the output side, seapower is about what it can achieve to influence the behaviour of others. This way of defining seapower has as its main advantage that it looks in terms of resources and actions: the means and its consequences, or put simply, the ends.

Till discusses the future of seapower by using three attributes of the sea as a basis: the sea as a resource base, as a medium for transportation, trade and exchange and as a medium of exchanging ideas.[7] Taken together, the attributes produce a global maritime system – the seas are all joined up and can produce benefits for all. But the system is vulnerable, and the role of navies is sometimes to guard the system from spoilers, prevent the spread of ideas and protect national sovereignty for reasons of international law, ideology or religion. A fourth attribute of the sea lies at the other end of the cooperation–conflict spectrum: the sea as an arena for dominion and sovereignty. In parts of the world, competition over what the sea can offer is intense. Till uses the example of the Asia–Pacific region where navies are being built up and the rivalries between regional nations is intense. The competition over resources in the sea (fisheries, oil, minerals etc), maritime crime (piracy, illegal fishing etc), resource degradation due to over-use, inadvertent or deliberate involvement in the conflicts of others and inter-state war in the maritime arena, are all examples of threats to the system. These are not limited to the Asia–Pacific region and could, if left unchecked, unfold into a threat to the global maritime system.

The future nature of seapower thus faces several changes, Till argues. Firstly, the relative importance of seapower will tend to rise as a function of increasing populations and demand for resources from the sea.[8] Secondly, attitudes to the sea will change. The relationship between the high seas and territorial waters is shifting, and the role of the high seas as traditionally belonging to no one is moving towards belonging to all. This is written into the United Nations Convention on the Law of the Sea (UNCLOS) but the process is by no means settled. Thirdly, the range of naval tasks is likely to broaden. The traditional role of navies are challenged and

---

[6] Till, *Seapower*. pp. 2–6.
[7] Till, *Seapower* .pp. 351–378.
[8] The role of the sea is also becoming the focus of extraction of energy by wind farms, wave-energy installations and sea-bed mining. Much of the information on the internet is dependent on transfer via sea-cables, all adding new importance to the role of the sea.

they will increasingly need to cooperate with non-military agencies, national and international, and engage in more 'soft' security tasks while retaining the capacity for high-end application of force. Fourthly, the focus on the littoral will remain. The end of the Cold War has changed strategic circumstances to the point where a blue-water conflict is seen as less likely. To effect developments on land from the littoral is seen as central.[9]

The Shadow of History: The Royal Swedish Navy in the Cold War[10]

For more than four decades the size, structure and development of the RSwN and the Coastal defence forces was mainly determined by the requirements of the Cold War.[11] The perceived existential threats to Sweden from the Soviet Union led over time to a defence force structure almost exclusively focused on an anti-invasion strategy.

In the Baltic Sea, the Second World War had led to the incorporation of the three Baltic States into the Soviet Union and the Cold War dividing line on the European mainland lay to the west of Sweden. Finland had survived as an independent nation, but paid a high price for her freedom.

At the end of the 1940s, it became clear that the Cold War had begun in earnest. Attempts at setting up a Nordic Defence League between Denmark, Norway and Sweden failed in 1948–49, and instead Denmark and Norway joined NATO, while Sweden developed an official declared policy of 'non-alignment in peacetime with the aim to neutrality in wartime'. With Finland's policy of cautious neutrality, this later came to be termed 'The Nordic Balance'.[12] This concept was not without

---

[9] Both Freedman and Till argue that the littoral focus will continue, and both in different ways also warn that this should not be taken as an eternal truth.

[10] The section on the RSwN in the Cold War is mainly based on Gustav von Hofsten & Frank Rosenius (eds.) *Kustflottan. De svenska sjöstridskrafterna under 1900-talet*, pp.129–195 (Stockholm 2009) and Sven Lagerberg Kustinvasion – Kustartilleri. Årsberättelse i Kungl. Krigsvetenskapsakademien avd. II den 17 februari 1959. (Stockholm 2003).

[11] The Royal Swedish Navy (*Kungliga Svenska Flottan*) consisted from 1902 of the Navy and the Coastal Artillery (*Kungliga Kustartilleriet*) which had been developed out of an earlier organisation tasked with defending the naval bases and major ports. Allan Cyrus, *Kungl Kustartilleriet 1902–1952. Vapenslagets historia utgiven av Kustartilleriinspektionen med anledning av Kungl Kustartilleriets femtioåriga tillvaro som självständigt vapenslag.* (Stockholm: Victor Petterssons Bokindustriaktiebolag 1952). Both the navy and the coastal defence forces trace their origins back to the 1520s when the Calmaric Union between Denmark, Norway and Sweden ended and the Swedish nation-state began to organise its armed forces in a more modern way. In 1522, the first ships, bought from the Hanseatic League, anchored in Stockholm which became the first main base of the RSwN. In the 1530s, the first modern coastal defence forces were organised to defend Stockholm.

[12] Edward L. Killhan, *The Nordic Way. A Path to Baltic Equilibrium.* pp. 2–7 (Washington DC: The Compass Press 1993).

flaws. If war had broken out in Fenno–Scandinavia neutrality would have failed, drawing the non-aligned Nordic countries (Sweden and Finland) into a Europe-wide war. It was highly unlikely that either of the countries would have sided with the Soviet Union. In Sweden, highly secret and extensive preparations were undertaken in case a Soviet attack would have drawn Sweden into the war. Much seems to point to the fact that the Swedish aspiration of neutrality was illusory, should the Cold War have turned 'hot', in spite of the officially declared policy.[13]

The gradual build-up in the Baltic region of Soviet air and naval assets led Swedish planners to reconsider the structure of the RSwN and coastal defence forces, as well as the overall defence structure. A landmark in this process was the Defence Bill of 1958 where trends of the post-World War II developments were addressed. The Korean War, the Prague Coup and the Hungarian uprising influenced the decisions made. Airpower had developed and large artillery ships had become redundant. Guided missiles and airpower changed the nature of naval engagements. The advent of nuclear weapons had also made large ships and troop concentrations vulnerable.[14] The Defence Bill of 1958 led to a shift in priorities between the three services: the defence budget was divided up so that the Army got one third, the Air Force one third, the RSwN one sixth and the final one sixth was used for joint purposes.[15]

Naval plan 60 (*Marinplan 60*) followed two years later where the long-term development of the RSwN was laid out. The Navy was to be structured towards a 'light-navy-concept' with fast attack-craft with torpedoes and guided missiles, submarines and defensive sea mines. Cruisers and destroyers were to be phased out, while escort ships for protection of commerce were to be retained.[16] Naval firepower was to be divided on to more and smaller hulls than previously and a class of command and control ship would be developed. The structure of the Coastal defence forces also progressed with the building of heavily fortified artillery batteries in the outermost archipelagos which had begun in the mid-1930s.[17] The concept for coastal defence

[13] Current studies of these plans and preparations add new dimensions to the understanding of Swedish strategy and war plans, and had implications for the structure of the RSwN, Coastal defence forces and Air force structures. For an overview of the subject matter of these secret policies, Robert Dalsjö, *Life-Line Lost. The Rise and fall of 'Neutral' Sweden's Secret Reserve Option of Wartime Help from the West*, (Stockholm: Santerus Academic Press 2006), Mikael Holmström, *Den Dolda Alliansen. Sveriges hemliga NATO-förbindelser* (Stockholm: Bokförlaget Atlantis 2011).

[14] Magnus Starck, Allmän sjökrigshistoria 1945–1965 (Stockholm: Marinlitteratur-föreningen/Bonniers 1975).

[15] In parallel with this, a programme for developing Swedish tactical nuclear weapons, initially seen as a stronger form of artillery, was pursued but was disbanded in the mid-1960s. Sweden signed the Non-Proliferation Treaty (NPT) in 1968, thus formally relinquishing nuclear weapons altogether.

[16] A decision not to build armoured battle-cruisers and instead replace them with three flotillas, based on one cruiser each had been made already in 1942. This can be seen as an early acknowledgement of the development of airpower.

[17] Urban Sobéus, *Havsbandslinjen i Stockholms skärgård 1933–1945* (Bohus 2000).

consisted of units with heavily fortified fixed position and mobile light and heavy artillery batteries, sea mines, guided missiles and coastal jaeger-battalions.[18] The entire coast and archipelago was covered, with emphasis placed on the naval base areas and archipelagos. The systems gradually became more modern. The nuclear dimension was taken into account in that entire naval bases, including repair yards, were built into fortified tunnels, and much of the coastal defence forces had access to fortified positions underground.

The basic concepts of the 1958 bill remained in effect until the end of the Cold War. However, the cost of maintenance and modernisation rose. A watershed for the RSwN was the Defence Bill of 1972, where the coastal defence force units maintained their number, while much of the RSwN's proposal to retain the anti-submarine warfare capability (ASW) intact and maintain the task of the defence of Sea Lines of Communications (SLoC) were disregarded by the government. Instead, the anti-invasion defence tasks were emphasised. This led to an increased focus on defensive sea-denial even closer to the Swedish coastline and in the archipelagos for the RSwN and more of an anti-invasion stance for the coastal defence forces. The long-term effects of this shift meant a gradual decline of know-how and capacity to conduct ASW and SLoC defence, leading to a near-exclusive focus on defensive sea-denial in an anti-invasion scenario in the Baltic Sea.[19]

The Defence Bill of 1972 was influenced by the strategic optimism of the 1970s with the ongoing diplomatic process that led up to the Helsinki accords in 1975. In effect it meant that détente was mortgaged in advance. In the early 1980s the Cold War again turned colder. One of the effects in the Nordic region was an increased number of submarine incursions into Swedish territorial waters. This had been part of the operational pattern for a long time, but a more assertive, even aggressive, tactic now became part of the picture.[20] The most visible of these was the 'Whiskey on the Rocks' crisis in October of 1981. A Soviet Whiskey-class submarine armed with nuclear torpedoes ran aground close to the naval base in *Karlskrona* in Southern Sweden. Arguably one of the most serious crises during the Cold War directly involving Sweden, the ability to credibly counter this and other ongoing incursions was questioned domestically and by other nations. Much of the operations and

---

[18] Håkan Söderlindh, Carl-Johan Engström, Bo Fahlander (eds.), *Kustförsvar. Från kustbefästningar till amfibiekår.* (Västervik 2002).

[19] To compensate for the removal of the task of SLoC-defence, substantial efforts were put into storage of critical primary goods (oil, grain, coal, salt etc) in underground caverns. A blockaded Sweden would still be able to function for many months.

[20] The writing on the submarine crisis is extensive. Per Andersson, *Vad gjorde de här? Personliga reflexioner om den främmande undervattensverksamheten.* (Tidskrift i Sjöväsendet 2010:3), Wilhelm Agrell, *Bakom ubåtskrisen. Militär verksamhet, krigsplanläggning och diplomati i östersjöområdet.* (Stockholm:Liber Förlag 1986), Bengt Gustafsson, *Sanningen om ubåtsfrågan. Ett försök till analys.* (Stockholm: Santérus 2010). Herman Fältström, Olof Santesson (eds.) *På spaning efter det okända. Bilder från det kalla krigets ubåtsjakt* (Stockholm:Försvarshögskolan 2010).

activities of the RSwN and the coastal defence forces was for the remainder of the 1980s centred on efforts to counter the submarine crisis. ASW close to shore and in the difficult waters of the archipelagos became paramount. The build-up of new ASW hunter-killer forces for this warlike task in peacetime was a tall order for the RSwN and the coastal defence forces. By the end of the 1980s, the process had produced a competent and increasingly effective capability for ASW in the Baltic.

The End of the Cold War – Strategic Change in the Nordic Region

With the fall of the Soviet Union in 1991, momentous change came to the Nordic region. The potential of an existential threat seemed to disappear. The three Baltic republics were once again free and independent. East Germany was integrated into the Federal Republic and democratic development could be seen in Poland. Finland could rid itself of the vestiges of the post-war era and attained more political leeway. It seemed that modernisation and democratisation of Russia could take place. Europe was seen as a continent and free and open conflict was a thing of the past. Sweden could join NATO's Partnership for Peace in 1994. Sweden became a member of the European Union in 1995, but remained outside the Euro zone.

This led to gradual changes of declared security policy, beginning in 1992. In its latest version, Swedish security policy doctrine has been expressed in the Solidarity Declaration of 2009 adopted by the Swedish Parliament.[21] The key notion is that military conflict in the Nordic region would not be limited to one country. Sweden would therefore not remain passive if a disaster or an attack should befall another EU-member state, Norway or Iceland. Sweden further expects these nations to act in a similar way if the same should happen to Sweden. Sweden should therefore be able to give and receive military support.

This process away from the Cold War declaratory stance can be described as Sweden's soft farewell to the neutrality policy of the Cold War.

Post-Cold War Retrenchments and Reform of the Swedish Armed Forces

Optimism of the early 1990s after the peaceful end of the Cold War led to substantial cutbacks for the whole of the armed forces. The burden of keeping a large military organisation sufficiently up-to-date had proved difficult and serious gaps were apparent. Awareness of this had been around for a long time, but the basic concept did not change until the Cold War ended. Military technology also evolved so that network-centric concepts for warfare led to changing views on future conflicts. In addition, the change in the concept of operations for international crisis-management operations, made these more demanding and riskier than before. While the existential

---

[21] *Ett användbart Försvar.* Government proposal 2008/2009:140. http://bit.ly/1kRuuM8

threats in the Nordic region melted away, peace-support and crisis-management operations of a more difficult nature presented itself, with UN-mandated intervention in the Balkan Wars in the first half of the 1990s a milestone.

For the RSwN and the coastal defence forces retrenchments meant that about 80 per cent of their wartime strength was disbanded. The anti-invasion tasks of the coastal defence forces were removed and the remainder was renamed the Amphibious Corps. An effort to emphasise quality and high-tech above quantity was made and much effort was put into incorporating network-centric concepts and technologies. In 2009 conscription in peacetime was disbanded and replaced with a system of contracted full-time or part-time sailors and soldiers.[22]

After these retrenchments, it is fair to say that the RSwN fits well into the bracket of small navies.

Table 11.1   The Royal Swedish Navy in 2009 as decided by the Defence Bill of 2009.

7 Corvettes	5 Visby-class, 2 Göteborg-class
7 Minehunters	5 Koster-class, 2 Spårö-class
4 Submarines	2 Gotland-class, 2 Södermanland-class
2 Support- and Patrol Ships	OPV HMS Carlskrona, Support ship HMS Trossö
1 Salvage and submarine rescue ship	HMS Belos
1 Signals intelligence ship	HMS Orion
2 Sail training schooners	HMS Gladan, HMS Falken
1 Amphibious battalion	Circa 150 combat boats of type Stridsbåt 90.
1 Base- and Support Battalion	
1 Naval Command- and Control Battalion	

Changes to the Defence Industrial Setup

The Cold War had also given Swedish security a strong focus on nationally developed high-tech and often bespoke solutions for defence systems and materiel. The origins of this policy can be found in the Second World War, when acquisition of weapon systems that Sweden lacked became nearly impossible. The model that gradually developed over the decades was based on close cooperation between

---

[22] That the process of dismantling the anti-invasion defence structure was not straightforward processes that led to structural imbalances is clear from recent analysis. Wilhelm Agrell, *Fredens illusioner. Det svenska nationella försvarets nedgång och fall 1988–2009* (Stockholm: Atlantis 2010*)*.

Swedish defence industry, the government and the Armed forces, producing several important systems (e.g. fighter planes, anti-tank weapons, armoured fighting vehicles and submarines) at reasonable cost. The relationship between these three over time developed into something of an iron triangle. However, by developing domestically, costs could be kept down and the systems could be made to fit the Swedish defence concept and open for the possibility of exports.

In the 1990s, much of the Swedish-owned defence industry was merged with, or sold to, foreign business interests. Much of the previously Swedish-owned defence industry is today Swedish-based but foreign owned. This in turn leads to strains on the traditional way of producing and procuring defence materiel. Agreements on 'seed-money' for the development of new ideas are harder to find and the consensus-oriented way of doing business is increasingly being questioned. While the defence-industrial setup has lost many of its preconditions, Sweden is in many ways a high-tech nation where technological know-how and a capability to produce defence materiel is still seen as important. In particular, SAAB with its long series of fighter planes retains a privileged position with close links to the government.[23] The Swedish defence industry's products apparently meet international demand, since defence exports from Sweden almost tripled from 2002 to 2011.

For the naval and marine industry sector, the two main developers of ships and submarines, *Karlskronavarvet* and *Kockums AB* respectively, are today foreign owned.[24] Especially in submarine development, the acquisition of *Kockums AB* by the German firm *HDW* in 1999, now controlled by *Thyssen Krupp Marine Systems*, has raised questions of the long-term future for the Swedish development of conventional submarines.

Changes to Operational Patterns – Increased Demand for the International Tasks and Missions

Optimistic views of the strategic changes in Europe in the 1990s led to a refocusing towards peace-support and crisis-management operations for the Swedish Armed Forces. The RSwN was initially not in demand for these tasks and instead the army developed this as its main task and expertise.

With the changing strategic setup in the Nordic region, the RSwN began mine-hunting operations in the waters of the again independent Baltic States in 1995. The three former Soviet Baltic republics had not taken part in the mine-clearing efforts

---

[23] Late in 2013, the Swedish government decided to buy 60 of the new E/F-version of the *Gripen* fighter, in spite of the fact that the C/D-versions already ordered from SAAB were yet to be delivered. While certainly an advanced fighter, it has raised serious questions of how this purchase will affect the rest of the Armed forces, including the Air Force itself, due to the cost of approximately €10.6 Bn.

[24] *Karlskronavarvet* was incorporated into *Kockums AB* in 1989.

that had been an ongoing task in Western Europe begun in 1945 and which are still ongoing to an extent. In the Baltic, between 40,000 to 50,000 sea mines remain unaccounted for. The total figure for dumped chemical munitions is about 40,000 tons.[25] These multinational mine-hunting operations have been a yearly recurrence since 1995 and have also contributed to building up naval know-how in the three Baltic States.[26] Around 1,000 mines and unexploded ordnance have been identified and cleared to date.

After the Israeli-Lebanese War in 2006, the RSwN contributed to the UN-mandated maritime peace-keeping operation in the eastern Mediterranean with two coastal corvettes. Operations in the Mediterranean marked a new phase for the RSwN, something it had not conducted in earnest since the Napoleonic Wars. From 2009, participation in anti-piracy operations off the Horn of Africa followed in the EU-led operation ATALANTA.[27]

A Swedish conventional submarine of the *Gotland*-class, developed for the complicated hydro-acoustic environment in the Baltic and fitted with air-independent propulsion (AIP), was leased, with Swedish crews, to the US Pacific Fleet to operate as a red-team for US carrier-groups for two years beginning in 2005.

The Amphibious Corps has done tours in Afghanistan, has deployed to Africa on peace-support missions and as embarked marines in several of the anti-piracy operations.

The exercise patterns have also developed so that multinational crisis-management exercises with NATO- and EU-countries as well as bilaterally now take place on a regular basis.

To summarise this narrative of the RSwN during and after the Cold War, some observations can be made. Firstly, the decades of the Cold War was far from a stable peace-time activity. Rather, the strategic crises that occurred and

---

[25] Around 175,000 mines have been dropped in the Baltic Sea and the Kattegat and Skagerrak on the west coast. The exact number of remaining mines is difficult to predict with accuracy due to time, oceanographic factors, weather conditions and construction. I am grateful to LtCdr Gunnar Möller, Head of the Mine Warfare Data Center (MWDC) of the Swedish Armed Forces, for providing me with this estimate. Regarding dumped chemical munitions, the HELCOM Final report from 1994, to be updated during 2013, is the authoritative source. Of the 40,000 tons dumped, 13,000 tons were actual chemical warfare agents. Helsinki Commission, the Ad Hoc Working Group on Dumped Chemical Munitions (HELCOM CHEMU). *Report on Chemical Munitions Dumped in the Baltic Sea*, Danish Environment Protection Agency. pp. 8–14 (Copenhagen 1994).

[26] These operations normally take place once a year on a rotating schedule between the Baltic nations: MCMOPEST, -LAT and -LIT, respectively.

[27] The Swedish Coastguard has also been part of operation ATALANTA. A maritime patrol aircraft (MPA) deployed to the Seychelles has made important contributions in building up a Recognised Maritime Picture (RMP) in the North western Indian Ocean. For a third time, the RSwN and Amphibious corps contributes to this operation, this time with an OPV, during the first half of 2013.

the technological developments affecting its long-term structure, at times placed the Navy and the coastal defence forces in demanding situations. The stakes were sometimes very high indeed. Secondly, the near exclusive focus on the anti-invasion tasks from the early 1970s and onwards opened up gaps in other areas, illustrated by the submarine crisis of the 1980s. More recently, the task of naval peace support operations and protection of commerce from piracy in new waters and in new coalitions, have presented themselves. Leasing out ships and crews to other nations and regular multinational exercises has also become part of the pattern. It is then somewhat of a paradox that while the number of units shrunk substantially in the 1990s, and a basic structure and rationale for operations in home waters for the territorial defence role remained, the demand has increasingly been for the 'away-game'. This illustrates a general inherent quality of navies: their in-built ability to provide their governments with a readily available and flexible asset, on call at short notice should the need arise. While the platforms and resources were often not designed for the task, the RSwN and coastal defence forces made use of what they had and tried to solve the tasks assigned to them. It also indicates that a navy designed for a narrow scope of tasks, can be caught on the back foot since the lead times for capability development are often long.

Changing Strategic Circumstances

The global strategic pattern is changing. Observable strategic trends range from the effects of climate change, the emerging great and medium-sized powers leading to a power shift from 'the West' to 'the East', a strong increase in sea-borne trade and technological developments leading to a virtual global interconnectedness. This spread of technology, resources and capabilities to new actors seems to accelerate a shift in power relationships in many parts of the world. Moreover, the factors under change are numerous and they develop according to their own inner logic and speed; yet are often intertwined. One result of this could be that long-standing notions of one single power attaining a globally dominating position are no longer possible.[28] As a result of their new wealth the emerging powers are now able to afford armed forces, chiefly airpower and navies. Particularly in the Far East, the armament programmes of China are one of the drivers of an arms race among her neighbours.[29] Recently, the United States has also declared a shift in her policies towards the western pacific region. With the end of the Iraq and Afghanistan interventions, coupled with long-term economic problems, there seems to be a shift away from a continental and towards more of a maritime emphasis in the overall military stance of the United States. How the effects of these policy shifts will play out is too early to determine, but the effects of them will in all likelihood

---

[28] This argument is developed by Zbigniew Brzezinski in *Strategic Vision. America and the Crisis of Global Power*, (New York, 2012).

[29] Geoffrey Till, *Asia's Naval Expansion. An Arms Race in the Making?* (London 2012).

be felt globally. One of the effects of the strategic shift is a focus on new military operational concepts enabled by new technologies. The Air-Sea Battle concept is now the focus of much of the debate and indicates that integrated systems of air and naval assets are emerging, altering the setup for how future conflicts might be fought.[30]

In the Nordic region, a more assertive Russia can be observed. An ambitious rearmament program runs in parallel with trends in a more authoritarian direction, where the rule of law is undermined and corruption is rampant.[31] Russia also attacked her neighbour Georgia in 2008 with military and naval forces. Clearly, inter-state war is not ruled out by Russia. While this does not automatically imply the risk of an armed attack against the Nordics, the Russian build-up of capabilities has to be taken into account when designing armed forces by neighbouring countries.

With the ice-melt in the Arctic – Sweden's northern neighbourhood – the region's changing geostrategic role has come into focus.[32] Fisheries, energy, minerals, overlapping territorial claims and not least shipping, are quickly changing the setup in this region. Coastguard tasks, nuclear strategic stability and ballistic missile defence are three security and military dimensions affecting the region. The Arctic's military strategic role is changing as a function of more human activity driven by the ice-melt in the Arctic Ocean.

The Nordic nations, members of or associated to the European Union, have also taken part in the multilateral arrangements to set up military crisis management units. These have not been deployed so far. Limits to the European security framework are apparent. EU–Europe does not yet seem to become a coherent actor in hard security, and further development of crisis management mechanisms have been put on hold. As a result of the euro-crisis, the armed forces of Europe now seem to be going through an uncoordinated process of retrenchments. In particular Great Britain and France, the two main European naval powers, are drawing down or are about to shrink their naval forces, resulting in less capacity for crisis management.

The above mentioned shift in focus of the United States will also be felt in the transatlantic region and Nordic regions. Fewer naval and military resources will be regularly deployed to the region, while more will gradually go to the Pacific region and the Middle East. A tacit assumption by the Nordics of a substantial US, British and French stabilising capability available in case of a serious crisis, is thereby tested.[33] The long-term effects could be that the Nordic region over time receives less attention in important western capitals. This in turn could lead to

---

[30] International Institute for Strategic Studies, *The Military Balance 2013*. (London 2013). pp. 30–31.

[31] Vendil, Carolina (ed.) (2012), *Russian Military Capability in a Ten-Year Perspective*.

[32] Smith, Laurence C. *(2010), The New North. The World in 2050*.

[33] Johan Tunberger and Jan Blomqvist, *Strategisk Vindkantring*, in Tommy Jeppsson (ed.) *För Sveriges säkerhet*. pp 45–82 (Stockholm 2012).

misunderstandings of the interests and intentions of important regional actors. A less stable and predictable region might result.

Moreover, the major western navies, and in particular the US Navy, have since the end of the Second World War acted as global guardians of the freedom of the seas. Will the US Navy and other western navies with current and projected available assets be able to uphold the freedom of the seas globally and over time given economic constraints and shifting priorities?

In addition, naval peace-support and constabulary operations in international frameworks are for nearly a decade a regular part of the operational pattern of the RSwN. This is a clear acknowledgement of the interests of Sweden as a heavily import- and export-dependent nation.

The global geostrategic and technological changes underway taken together indicate that there are several reasons why a rethink when designing seapower for a small nation such as Sweden is needed.

Designing Swedish Seapower

For a nation with a small navy and with vital interests in and of the sea in all of its aspects the developments described above are challenging. How should Sweden optimise her naval resources in today's dynamic world? Clearly, a great power perspective with a go-anywhere-do-anything-navy is neither relevant nor realistic. Norman Friedman, seeing the issues from a US perspective, warns of the risk of an overblown militarisation leading to resource competition as detrimental to societal values and economic development. Hence, a small navy is what Sweden can afford. This has to be part of the analysis along with the changing circumstances of the role of seapower according to both Friedman and Till. The tasks for a future RSwN will lie within the realm of providing better support for Swedish long-term interests while contributing to the preservation of a dynamic global maritime system in cooperation with others, as well as providing a component in defence of home waters. This leads to Swedish seapower designed not to force others into doing what it wants, but to prevent others from doing things to Sweden. By using all available naval and maritime resources in a more integrated manner than is the case today, a greater range of tasks can be conducted with better effect.[34] While Sweden possesses a range of qualified capabilities, defence industrial capacity,

---

[34] This is also the core argument in a recently published government committee analysing the organisation and use of Swedish maritime resources. The committee looked at the total naval and maritime resources, including the Swedish coastguard, which is unarmed in peacetime and is not part of the Swedish Armed Forces. While outside the scope of this analysis, the issues of naval and coast guard cooperation clearly deserves more attention. Jan Hyllander, *Maritim samverkan. Betänkande av maritimutredningen.* Statens offentliga utredningar, 2012:48 (Stockholm 2012).

population, know-how and tradition, there is no scope for any pretension of great-power ambitions.

With these factors in mind, an outline can be made. Firstly, no navy can disregard its home waters. In territorial waters and in the Swedish EEZ, a wide range of tasks must be possible: from surveillance, presence, coastguard and constabulary operations all the way up to and including high-end conflict.

Secondly, since 2006 constabulary operations away from home waters has been undertaken at regular intervals in multinational coalitions under an international mandate. This indicate that operating in an 'away-game' now has become a regular feature of the operational pattern for the RSwN and this seems likely to remain so. The contribution to international maritime security is, at least in part, an expression of enlightened self-interest of a nation highly dependent on the free and uninterrupted flow of sea-borne trade.

Lastly, the changes in the Arctic Ocean affect the geostrategic role of the region and are likely to affect the naval and maritime pattern there. While the High Arctic is still accessible only to ships designed specifically for arctic conditions, the North Atlantic – Sweden's northern and north western neighbourhood – is also likely to see more activity. While Sweden has no outstanding territorial claims in the Arctic Ocean, upholding good order at sea and contributing to maritime safety as well as freedom of navigation is a Swedish interest already today.

The three areas and types of operations – home waters, the away-game and the North Atlantic/Arctic – all present very different operational conditions where circumstances will vary over time. None of the three can be completely discounted. This generates a long-term problem for planners of the highest order: How should the RSwN then be structured to be able to accomplish these tasks?

Structuring the Royal Swedish Navy

To address the question of structure, three alternative structures for the RSwN are presented here. It would not be helpful to get into a detailed discussion of platforms in this context, at least not at the outset, since it would risk losing sight of the structural arguments. One structure would maintain the present size, numbers and tasks of the current RSwN, here called *Steady as she goes*. A second structure would have a near-exclusive focus on high-end operations in home waters, leaving the 'away-game' and constabulary operations to other nations: the *Ultra-light-navy*. A third structure would be one designed to address the three types of operations indicated above: the *Medium-light-navy*.

A Small Navy in a Changing World

The Matrix – Discussion of Structures versus Tasks

To discuss the three suggested areas and types of operations for them it is helpful to set the structures against the operations and areas. Conclusions can be drawn and indicate need for further analysis.

Table 11.2   Tasks versus structures

Areas and Operations vs. Structures	Home Waters	The 'Away-Game'	North Atlantic/ Arctic
Ultra-light-navy	- Useful in high-end operations inshore and in archipelagos. - Serious limits in constabulary ops and by adverse weather. - Small or no contribution to maritime security ops. - Difficult to maintain high-technological systems, limited capacity of re-roling due to small ships.	- No contribution with ships in maritime security operations. - Possible in riverine, inshore peace-support in nautically 'safe' waters. Transport to op. area needed. - Limited contribution to mine-hunting ops in the Baltic Sea.	- No capability.
Steady as she goes	- Contribution in high-end operations. - Limits in constabulary operations. - Contributes to maritime security ops, with limits in endurance. - Small numbers and sizes make some systems and know-how critically small to maintain and develop. - Little or no redundancy for contingencies. - Predictable for an opponent in high-end ops.	- Intermittent contribution to maritime security. - Maritime peace-support becomes an all-out effort.	- Some capability in ice-free waters, but limits due to small size of ships and adverse weather.
Medium-light-navy	- Contribution in high-end operations. - Near continuous contribution to maritime security ops. - Air-defence role possible. - Contribution to safety at sea. - Useful in naval diplomacy.	- Near continuous contribution to maritime security operations without leaving serious gaps in home waters. - A factor in naval diplomacy.	Capability in ice-free waters, some limits due to ice-conditions. - Adverse weather not a limiting factor.

The main advantage of the *Ultra-light-navy* is the focus on one main task: a high-end conflict in home waters. Patrol boats that make use of the archipelagos, guided missiles, mines and stealth would be central to the concept which focuses on Anti-surface Warfare (AsuW). The underwater dimension is based on fixed-position advanced mines and torpedoes. It makes it easy to communicate what is seen as important within the organisation and the choice of platforms and technologies is also made easier. A high niche expertise can be developed and cooperation or integration with amphibious defence forces can be achieved. The *Ultra-light-navy* is also cheaper and can hopefully be financed within today's limited defence economy. The structure has drawbacks, however. There would be no capacity for expeditionary tasks, the mine-hunting capacity would be called into question and the submarine arm could probably not be fitted into the structure. No contribution to constabulary operations at home or far away would be possible. The *Ultra-light-navy* would be able to play a role only in the most extreme scenario of a threat of a sea-borne invasion, but with little relevance in most other tasks. The structure lacks flexibility and provides little or no room for contingencies.

The *Steady-as-she-goes-navy* is today's RSwN. It can operate in Swedish home waters in most weather conditions, has a small but competent submarine arm, is able to conduct mine-hunting in the Baltic and has some capability for intermittent contribution to constabulary operations at home and far away. These operations have to be planned well in advance and have limited endurance, which indicates a lack of capability for contingencies. Know-how of amphibious operations and as embarked marines is maintained. Capacity in and know-how of Arctic conditions and ice-operations are limited. The structure can over time, but with limited endurance, manage the tasks in home waters. The limited number of platforms presents planners with difficult operational choices. To maintain the structure within today's defence economy will be difficult. Its future appears bleak in the medium to longer term since many system components will soon, or have already, reached a low or critical level. Professional naval planners describe the future in stark terms.[35] Serious questions are being raised on the viability of the new personnel system and the economics of the structure.[36] With current projections, it seems that systemic collapse threatens within three to five years.

---

[35] The situation is spelled out by Commander Evorn Mårtensson, RSwN, in a recent analysis. Today's naval structure cannot be maintained within the given economic limits, according to the author. *Vart är Marinen på väg? Behov av en ny plan. Tidskrift i Sjöväsendet* no.1/2013, pp. 38–48.

[36] In a report from November 2012, the National Audit Office criticises the readiness of the air force and navy. The readiness of the standing forces required according to decisions by the Swedish Parliament is not fully met. Vacancies in key competence areas are lacking which cannot easily be replaced by other personnel due to lack of redundancy and secondments to other parts of the armed forces. pp. 47–50. Jan Landahl, Thomas Dawidowski, *Bemanningen av marinens och flygvapnets stående insatsförband*. Riksrevisionens rapport 2012:18 (Stockholm 2012).

The *Medium-light-navy* assumes that the deficiencies in today's existing structure are remedied avoiding systemic collapse and two new capabilities are added. Firstly, to be able to better than today respond to contingencies and more or less continuously contribute to operations far away from home waters. Secondly, a capability to transport troops, materiel or other resources in response to contingencies in civil society by supporting other government agencies.

Comparison and Conclusions

A comparison between the three suggested structures provides several indications. While the present structure (*Steady-as-she-goes*), suffers from gaps and deficiencies, is not properly balanced and runs the risk of systemic collapse, it nevertheless provides choices for future development. To go towards the *Ultra-light* structure could solve the problem of keeping the structure affordable within the current fiscal limits. It would however, only be relevant in an unlikely anti-invasion scenario in the Baltic with an operational stance of inshore defensive-sea-denial. It would only be able to give a very slight contribution to maritime security in home waters at lower conflict levels. No capability for the away-game would remain.

The *Medium-light-navy* could go some way to solving the dilemma. Fixing the gaps of today to prevent systemic collapse and adding some capabilities would create a modicum of redundancy for military and civilian crisis management in the maritime arena. In addition it would be possible to give a more effective contribution to good order at sea in a world where western naval resources are shrinking. With the global geostrategic changes, this would be a security structure that better aligns Sweden's capabilities with her long-term interests in a fast-changing world.

Would a *Medium-light-navy* be affordable? Firstly, the outlined operational tasks would be manageable if procurement principles are formulated so that national champions are not automatically awarded contracts and less development is run directly by Swedish defence material agencies. This could open for a high-low mix of platforms. When not all systems are specified for high-end tasks, cost overruns would be less likely. Secondly, if platforms were procured out of series already developed, life-cycle costs could be kept at reasonable levels. Some systems would still have to be bespoke and state of the art while others could be given more of a general-purpose specification. The task of choosing these is clearly difficult, pointing to the need for further analysis. Thirdly, the added platforms suggested here would probably have to be bigger in size than today's platforms. It seems likely that this would make re-roling and modernisation of systems less costly over time – steel and space is cheap. Properly designed bigger platforms also provide for better sea-keeping abilities than smaller ones, enhancing operational choices and capabilities. Lastly, the wish of the Swedish government for more and better inter-agency cooperation between all Swedish maritime resources is clearly expressed. A medium-light structure of the RSwN able to carry out a broader range of tasks would be able to find its role in such a cooperative structure better than one with a narrow and near-exclusive high-end focus.

The net effect of the suggested *Medium-light-navy* would better align Swedish naval assets with her interests – a slightly altered input will provide a more relevant output, serving long-term national interest better than today in a rapidly changing world.

Chapter 12

The Strategic Value of Small Navies: The Strange Case of the Confederate Navy

Christopher Tuck

How valuable is a navy? The literature on contemporary maritime power focuses a great deal on the central contribution that navies make to the advancement of state interests in a globalised world. It would seem self-evident that a navy, even a small one, would be a valuable asset and that having a navy would certainly be better than not having one. Created from nothing in 1861, the Confederate States Navy (CSN) is widely regarded as a miracle of improvisation and a perfect example of just such a cost effective maritime instrument. However, attempts at a more systematic evaluation of the Confederate navy have often tended to be lost in the drama of the struggle itself. As a consequence, popular perception of the value of the CSN often focuses on its heroic performance in what is perceived as an unwinnable war. In this spirit Raimondo Luraghi asserts that the Confederate States Navy was 'conjured up from nothing to fight against the heaviest odds; facing in an unequal and awesome struggle an overpowering opponent; capable of defying it by performing heroic deeds that commanded respect even from the enemy; and overwhelmed in the end by the collapse of the very nation to which it belonged after a brave, ardent, and glorious life'.[1] Defined in this way, though, the value of the CSN was in its contribution to Confederate mythology rather than to the practical business of sustaining its physical survival. But is this a sufficient benchmark against which to judge the effectiveness of the Confederate States Navy and its consequent value to the state that created it?

Ultimately, this chapter argues that the value of small navies should not be judged in relation to the manner of their defeat, glorious or otherwise. In making this argument, this chapter examines the effectiveness of the Confederate Navy in a strategic sense: it looks at what objectives the CSN was set and whether its military activities achieved them successfully. Like other military instruments, the value of small navies should be judged against their performance as effective strategic tools – they exist to service goals set by the state. Even if a navy is a small one, this does not absolve it of a responsibility to meet as far it possibly can the roles and objectives allocated to it. Judged in this way, the Confederate

---

[1] Raimondo Luraghi, *A History of the Confederate Navy* (London: Chatham Publishing, 1996), p.10. See J. Thomas Scharf's, *History of the Confederate States Navy* (Avenel, NJ: Gramercy, 1996) for an extended expression of this viewpoint.

States Navy was, in the end, a valuable strategic tool for the Confederacy but its performance was problematic, especially in the early stages of the Civil War.

Indeed, the CSN provides something of a paradoxical case study on the value of small navies: it is, as the title of this chapter asserts, a 'strange case'. As this chapter will demonstrate, this paradox emerges from the fact that when the CSN was at its smallest physically, it was a 'big navy' in terms of its aspirations; equally, by the time it was physically a much larger navy, it had what might be regarded as a 'small navy' focus. The Confederate Navy was probably more effective in its latter incarnation than it was in the former.

Organisational and Operational Effectiveness

In the literature on the CSN, assessments of its effectiveness often coalesce consciously or unconsciously around two metrics. The first of these is the Confederate Navy's organisational effectiveness; that is, the extent to which the Navy was able to establish itself as a viable organisation. The second metric is the Confederate Navy's operational effectiveness: the military activities allocated to the CSN and the success with which it performed them. Each of these perspectives has merit.

Despite heavy obstacles, the CSN created an organisation that was able to put up a meaningful and spirited fight against the United States Navy (USN). Reflecting this perspective, a Confederate joint congressional committee noted in 1864 that: 'Taking into consideration the poverty of our means and the formidable power and boundless resources of our enemy, our people have no sufficient cause for shame and discouragement in the question of our navy.'[2] The poverty of Confederate means encompassed almost everything required to build a modern navy. In February 1861 the Confederate Navy consisted of ten vessels, none larger than a revenue cutter, mounting a total of 15 guns.[3] Yet the Confederate Secretary of the Navy, Stephen Mallory, had at his disposal only limited shipbuilding capabilities; there were chronic shortages in resources such as iron, tin, zinc, lead and seasoned timber; production facilities for iron-plate, marine steam engines, ordnance, rope and gunpowder were inadequate; the army took priority for manpower; and the navy's funding was restricted and often hand-to-mouth.[4] The formidable power and boundless resources of the Union navy were reflected in its meteoric growth: By December of 1862 the US Secretary of the Navy, Gideon Welles, could note that he had 'afloat or progressing to rapid completion' 427 vessels, and that his

---

[2] Joseph T. Durkin, *Confederate Navy Chief Stephen R. Mallory* (Tuscaloosa, AL: University of Alabama Press, 1954), p.295.

[3] William N. Still Jr, *Iron Afloat: The Story of the Confederate Armorclads* (Columbia, SC: University of South Carolina Press, 1988), p.7.

[4] For a discussion of Confederate difficulties see William N. Still, Jr, *Confederate Shipbuilding* (Columbia, SC: University of South Carolina Press, 1987).

organisation comprised more than 28,000 sailors and 12,000 mechanics and labourers.[5] Indeed, by the end of the war the Federal Navy comprised 670 ships and more than 50,000 personnel.[6] Despite these challenges, the CSN grew significantly in size and capability during the Civil War laying down or building 150 warships.[7] The Confederate Naval Department succeeded in creating shipyards, rolling mills, foundries, plants and works to provide for these ships. Moreover the Confederate Navy proved to be professional, dynamic and innovative, embracing such cutting-edge maritime technology as ironclads and mine warfare.[8]

Operationally, the CSN performed five general categories of activity during the Civil War: challenging the Union naval blockade; coast and harbour defence; commerce raiding; river defence; and blockade running. The Confederate Navy could count successes in all of these roles. For example, CSN ships engaged in several successful sorties against Union blockaders. On the 30–31 January 1863, the *CSS Chicora* and *CSS Palmetto State* sortied from Charleston and drove off the blockading forces, leading General P.G.T. Beauregard to declare that the Union blockade was over.[9] In relation to coast defence, such key ports as Charleston and Savannah were defended successfully from naval and amphibious assault and were taken finally only by Union land attack. CSN commerce raiding appeared wildly successful, ten raiders taking 245 Union prizes and precipitating a huge decline in the Union merchant fleet.[10] In river defence activities, the exploits of such ships as the *CSS Arkansas* on the Mississippi and the *CSS Virginia* on the James River both stymied major Union land assaults.[11] Finally, the CSN both provided support to civilian blockade runners and also ran its own: over the course

---

[5] Eric J. Graham, *Clydebuilt: The Blockade Runners, Cruisers and Armoured Rams of the American Civil War* (Edinburgh: Birlinn, 2006), p.19.

[6] Archer Jones, *Civil War Command and Strategy: The Process of Victory and Defeat* (New York, NY: The Free press, 1992), p.139.

[7] Jack Greene and Alessandro Massignani, *Ironclads at War: The Origin and Development of the Armored Warship, 1854–1891* (Conshohocken, PA: Combined Publishing, 1998),p. 46.

[8] For general coverage of the development and operations of the Confederate navy see R. Thomas Campbell, *Gray Thunder: Exploits of the Confederate States Navy* (Shippensburg, PA: Burd Street Press, 1996); for a discussion of CSN professional training see James Lee Conrad, *Rebel Reefers: The Organization and Midshipmen of the Confederate States Naval Academy* (Cambridge, MA: Da Capo Press, 2003).

[9] Greene and Massignani, pp.123–130.

[10] James Tertius deKay, *The Rebel Raiders: The Warship Alabama, British Treachery and the American Civil War* (Pimlico: London, 2003),pp. 230–232.

[11] See Rowena Reed, *Combined Operations in the Civil War* (Lincoln: University of Nebraska Press, 1993), pp.133–224.

of the war of the 1,300 attempts made to run the Union blockade 1,000 attempts were successful.[12]

However, neither an organisational nor an operational perspective provides a sufficient framework for assessing the CSN's effectiveness. Whilst Mallory certainly merits plaudits for creating a robust naval service, the existence of an organisation does not, in itself, make it effective. History is littered with carefully constructed military organisations that have not performed well – the Royal Navy during the American War of Independence would be a good example. Whilst focusing on the activities of the CSN moves us closer to a more robust assessment of its effectiveness, it is still an inadequate metric. Just as the mere existence of a military organisation does not guarantee its effectiveness, so history demonstrates that there is no automatic link between tactical and operational military success and success overall in war. Indeed, tactical and operational level military success may sometimes move one closer to defeat: the Japanese success in December 1941 at Pearl Harbor, for example, set Japan on the road towards a colossal strategic failure. Thus, a proper judgement on the effectiveness of the CSN needs to move beyond what the CSN was and what it did in a military sense and requires us to focus instead on what the intended effects were strategically.

Strategic Effectiveness

When we speak of the 'strategic effectiveness' of a small navy what is it that we mean? Strategy generally can be defined as the bridge between means and ends; in relation to the grand strategy of states, the ends are defined by policy and the means are those varied instruments available to governments to achieve them. More narrowly, military strategy can be defined as the use of military power for political purpose. Effective strategy, then, is strategy that disciplines military means to meet the intended political purpose.[13] Thus, one can distinguish between 'strategic effect' and 'strategic performance': all military activity has an effect, it is just that these effects may be negligible, or even negative, viewed from a political perspective. The effectiveness of a military organisation needs to be judged in relation to its strategic performance – not just that it has an effect, but that this effect moves the state closer to the attainment of its desired higher level political goals.[14] There can be a tendency to relieve small navies of the responsibility of effective strategic performance: since they are small, there can be an assumption that they are never likely to be more than an auxiliary element. That may often be true, but one of the things that define the nature of strategy is that it is non-linear:

---

[12] Stephen R. Wise, *Lifeline of the Confederacy: Blockade Running During the Civil War* (Columbia, CS: University of South Carolina Press, 1988), p.221.

[13] Colin S. Gray, *Modern Strategy* (Oxford: Oxford University Press, 1999), p.17.

[14] Colin S. Gray, *The Sheriff: America's Defense of the New World Order* (Lexington, KY: University Press of Kentucky, 2004), p.107.

there is no fixed relationship between military inputs and political outputs. Defeat may occur despite enormous military efforts; conversely, relatively small military inputs can have a significant impact on a state's ability to achieve its overall goals in a conflict.[15]

Thinking about the strategic performance of the Confederate Navy raises a first immediate question: does strategy matter? This may seem to be a perverse question, but in fact there is a body of the general literature on the Civil War that sees the outcome of the struggle between the Union and the Confederacy as fixed. In essence, such a view indicates that the material superiority of the Union ensured that the Confederacy was always going to lose. Shelby Foote asserted that the North 'fought the war with hand tied behind its back ... there was no way the South could have won'.[16] If one takes this view then strategy was irrelevant to the outcome of the Civil War: it did not matter decisively what either of belligerents did in relation to the use of their military power, the Confederacy was always likely to be ground down and crushed through attrition. On that basis, it might be possible to reach two contradictory conclusions regarding the effectiveness of the CSN depending upon the metrics that one uses. On the one hand, and working within the spirit of the 'Lost Cause' literature, one could conclude that, since the Confederacy was doomed to defeat, what mattered was the manner in which it lost: that it should fight a noble struggle that would sanctify the cause for which it was willing to be destroyed. This view was reflected in Edward A. Pollard's assertion in his 1866 history of the Civil War, entitled *The Lost Cause: A New Southern History of the War of the Confederates*, that: 'All that is left the South is "the war of ideas" ... the war has left the South its own memories, its own heroes, its own tears, its own dead.'[17] Here, the metric of CSN success is essentially intangible and associated with nobility, sacrifice, and a human struggle against the odds. Viewed in this way, the CSN's performance, for reasons already outlined, was a successful one: the CSN created a viable organisation, against the odds; it continued to contest the maritime aspects of the war right up to the death of the Confederacy; CSN victories buoyed morale in the South and dismayed the North; CSN officers such as Raphael Semmes became international heroes; it was a CSN ship, the *Shenandoah*, that was the last military unit of the Confederacy to surrender. On the other hand, if one focuses on the cost of the war, then the inevitability of the outcome of the conflict can lead one to argue that the efforts of CSN were an exercise in strategic failure. The material costs of the Civil War to the South were enormous: two-thirds of its assessed pre-war wealth destroyed; twenty per cent of the whites of military age killed (a proportion similar to that of Germany in the

---

[15] David Lonsdale, 'Strategy' in David Jordan et al, *Understanding Modern Warfare* (Cambridge: Cambridge University press, 2008), pp.32–33.

[16] John Griffin Jones, *Mississippi Writers Talking* (Jackson: University Press of Mississippi, 1982), p.66.

[17] Wolfgang Schivelbusch, *The Culture of Defeat: On National Trauma, Mourning, and Recovery* (New York: Metropolitan Books, 2003), p.59.

Second World War); the South remained under military occupation until 1877. Some insight into the longer-term human cost to the South is indicated by the fact that Mississippi's first post-war budget allocated a third of its total revenue to the purchase of prosthetics for injured ex-soldiers.[18] If defeat were inevitable then all that the CSN's efforts achieved was to ensure that it took longer for the Confederacy to lose: it drew out the conflict, compounding the costs, raising the consequences of defeat.

However, the notion that Confederate defeat was inevitable is not a unanimous one by any means in the Civil War literature. There is an alternative argument that Confederate defeat was a contingent outcome and that the relative strategic performance of both sides matters in explaining Confederate defeat: in other words, military activity does matter.[19] Thus, by the summer of 1864, Lincoln himself believed that his success in the election that year was unlikely: he had been warned in 1864 that his support was suffering a 'most alarming depression'; and by the summer he had his Cabinet sign blind a memo that stated 'it seems exceedingly probable that this Administration will not be re-elected'.[20] Such an outcome would likely have had profound consequences for the outcome of the conflict. In the event, the fall of Atlanta saved him, a point which suggests that the outcome of the Civil War was not preordained. If the answer to the question 'Does strategy matter?' is an affirmative one, then two other questions follow: what strategic objectives were set for the CSN in 1861; and, did these change? Using objectives as a metric allows us to reach the conclusion that the CSN's strategic performance was poor in the early stages of the war, but much improved later on.

The Strategic Performance of the Confederate Navy

Judged according to the assumptions of 1861, the CSN's performance in the Civil War was disappointing and was marked by some key failures. To understand this it is necessary to examine Mallory's view in 1861 of how the CSN would contribute to overall Confederate success. Central to Mallory's vision for the Confederate Navy was the role that ironclads would play in contesting Union sea control. At the outbreak of the war, the Union Navy was partially steam-driven but wholly composed of wooden ships. For Mallory, Confederate armoured ships would be a decisive instrument in ending the war, reflected in his assertion that: 'Such a vessel at this time could traverse the entire coast of the United States, prevent all

---

[18] Schivelbusch, p.38.

[19] See James M. McPherson, 'American Victory, American defeat,' in Gabor S. Boritt (ed.), *Why the Confederacy Lost* (Oxford: Oxford University Press, 1992), pp.17–42.

[20] Doris Kearns Goodwin, *Team of Rivals: The Political Genius of Abraham Lincoln* (London: Penguin, 2009), pp.646 and 648.

blockades, and encounter, with a fair prospect of success, their entire navy.'[21] Such ships would create a 'technical surprise' that would allow the CSA to seize the operational initiative from an opponent that clung to an obsolete heritage.[22] To put this another way, 'challenging the blockade' was not simply viewed as one of the roles that the CSN would perform during the war: Mallory believed that it would be the central war-winning role of the Confederate Navy. For example, Mallory saw the role of the ironclad *Virginia* not as one that would focus on the defence of the James River; rather, its overarching purpose was to exit the river, sail to New York City and burn it. Mallory surmised that the effects of this on Union morale and financial confidence would mean that: 'Peace would inevitably follow'.[23] As late as May 1862, Mallory continued to pin his hopes on the activity of ironclads, commenting: 'We look to *Virginia* alone'.[24] In many respects, then, the CSN at the outset of the Civil War had a 'big navy' mentality: its task was sea control and use of this sea control would enable the CSN to win the war for the Confederacy. As it transpired, Mallory's vision for the CSN could not be realised. One of the key difficulties, and one that was not unique to the Confederate Navy during the Civil War, was that the effects of technology as a force multiplier were overestimated. In this respect the Confederacy had three problems.

First, the CSN suffered in trying to innovate at the cutting edge of then extant technology. For example, many saw great possibilities in the prospects for submarines. One officer familiar with the submarine *CSS Hunley*'s early trials at Charleston commented that: 'I consider it a perfect success' and believed in relation to the Union fleet blockading Charleston that it was capable of 'destroying every ironclad the enemy has'.[25] But attempts by the CSN to make submarines an effective weapon ran into serious difficulties with propulsion, navigation, and endurance. In the end, the concept simply ran ahead of the available technology, producing intermittently successful but often terminally unreliable weapons: though becoming the first submarine to successfully sink a ship, the *Hunley* was so damaged that it sank.[26] The design of ironclads was also challenging. Perhaps the most powerful ironclad built by the CSN was the CSS *Tennessee*, but it embodied serious design faults including automatic gun shutters that tended to jam if hit as well as a steering and tiller mechanism which operated through ropes and chains

---

[21] Official Records of the Union and Confederate Navies in the War of Rebellion (ORN), Series II, Vol. 2, p.69.

[22] Luraghi, p.67.

[23] Durkin, p.195.

[24] Ibid., p.212.

[25] Mark K. Ragan, *Submarine Warfare in the Civil War* (Cambridge, MA: Da Capo, 2002), p.130.

[26] Spencer C. Tucker, *Blue and Gray Navies: The Civil War Afloat* (Annapolis, MD, Naval Institute Press, 2006), pp.264–267.

exposed to enemy fire.[27] Even ocean-going rams procured from the UK by the Confederacy proved problematic: having been compulsorily purchased by the British government after Union complaints and then taken into service by the Royal Navy, British naval officers believed that they were the 'weakest of our rams' and there were serious doubts about their ability to transit the Atlantic.[28] Problems in this respect afflicted both sides: Union submarines were no more effective than the Confederacy's[29] and Union ironclads also suffered significant design faults such as slow rate of fire, limited elevation in their armament, and vulnerability to plunging fire.[30] In consequence Union ironclads proved themselves a vulnerable technology: for example, the original Union ironclad, the *USS Monitor*, sank at sea; and in an attack on Charleston in 1863, five Union ironclads were wholly or partially disabled.[31] The difference was that the USN was not as reliant on technological reliability for success: it could substitute weight of numbers for performance.

Second, whilst the CSN may have performed miracles of improvisation to create a maritime infrastructure, that infrastructure was still not good enough to meet Mallory's aspirations. As early as 1861, Commodore Josiah Tattnall lamented that 'I have no fleet. Long before the Southern Confederacy has a fleet that can cope with the Stars and Stripes my bones will be white in the grave.'[32] Tattnall's frustrations were understandable. For example, in order to try and provide the enormous quantities of iron required to clad their armoured ships, the CSN was reduced to ripping up railroad tracks and rolling them into armour. In some cases, resort was made to the use of compacted cotton bales for armour to produce 'cotton clads'.[33] Pervasive shortages meant that time and time again it proved impossible to complete ironclads in time to meet key Union attacks: or, if they were completed, the compromises required to do so meant that the ships were defective. This problem was especially pernicious because the technological surprise posed by CSN ironclads would inevitably be short-lived: unless the Confederacy could use ironclads decisively in an offensive role, the Union would quickly be able to produce many more ironclads of their own. In early 1862, for example, the CSN had two ironclads at New Orleans, whereas the Union had none available in the Gulf region. But this potential advantage was negated by the fact that, of the two ironclads, one, the *Louisiana*, had engines so inadequate that she could only be used as a floating battery; and the second, the *Mississippi*, lacked

---

[27] R. Thomas Campbell, *Southern Thunder: Exploits of the Confederate States Navy* (Shippensburg, PA: Burd Street Press, 1996), pp.139–140.

[28] Richard I. Lester, *Confederate Purchasing and Finance in Great Britain* (Charlottesville, VA: University of Virginia press, 1975), pp.130–131.

[29] See Ragan, pp.84–92.

[30] Greene and Massignani, p.134.

[31] Ibid., p.142.

[32] Lester, p.90.

[33] Craig L. Symonds, *Lincoln and His Admirals* (Oxford: Oxford University Press, 2008), p.95.

guns, armour and engines.[34] At Mobile in 1863 attempts were made to construct four ironclads, but shortages meant that they had to be completed one at time. Of the four, the CSS *Nashville* was never completed, and two, the *Huntsville* and *Tuscaloosa*, had engines so poor that they could not even be deployed in Mobile Bay.[35] By the end of the war at least 10 CSN ironclads had been destroyed on the stocks, their completion prevented by critical shortages.[36]

Third, Mallory failed to recognise the full impact of the trade-offs associated with his ironclad concept. The weight of armour required to make his ships invulnerable to normal smoothbore artillery invariably had consequences for other aspects of the ship's performance. For example, the *Virginia* had a speed of only 5 knots and took 30–40 minutes and four miles to complete a 180 degree turn.[37] Vessels such as this were always likely to have poor sea-keeping qualities and to be confined, therefore, to rivers, harbours and estuaries. Compounding this problem was that the weight of armour often gave the ships much deeper drafts than anticipated, making operations in such waters problematic. The *Virginia*, for example, had a draft of 22 feet and had to be scuttled in May 1862 in response to the Union advance on Norfolk because the river escape routes were too shallow.[38] Similarly, at Savannah, the attempt by the ironclad CSS *Atlanta* to bring the blockading fleet to battle ended in June 1863 when it ran aground and was then battered by two Union monitors.[39]

In essence, whilst Mallory had in his mind the creation of a fleet of *La Gloire*-type ocean-going ironclads, the Confederacy could not produce ships that were more than coastal defence vessels.[40] The capacity of such ships in harbour defence was proven over the course of the war to be high; but their capacity for the primary role envisaged in 1861, that of breaking the blockade, was poor to non-existent. Mallory, for example, was euphoric after the *Virginia*'s showing in March 1862 in Hampton Roads and argued to its captain, Franklin Buchanan, that he should sail the *Virginia* to New York City and burn the port. Buchanan, though, refused, arguing that the *Virginia* was not able to do this: its poor sea-keeping qualities meant that it might sink on the way; its deep draft meant that it might not get into the harbour; and it might in any case succumb to Union attack in the attempt. Buchanan instead argued that the *Virginia* should be used for the defence of

---

[34] Chester G. Hearn, *The Capture of New Orleans, 1862* (Baton Rouge: Louisiana State University Press, 1995), pp.188 and 259.

[35] Craig L. Symonds, *The Civil War at Sea* (Santa Barbra, CA: ABC-Clio, 2009), p.150.

[36] Greene and Massignani, p.43.

[37] Tucker, p.155.

[38] Greene and Massignani, p.83

[39] Kevin Dougherty, *Strangling the Confederacy: Coastal Operations in the American Civil War* (Havertown, PA: Casemate Publishers, 2009). pp.132–133.

[40] Herman Hattaway and Archer Jones, *How the North Won: A Military History of the Civil War* (Urbana: University of Illinois Press, 1991), p.129.

Richmond.[41] Similarly, Beauregard's declaration in January 1863 that the sortie by *Chicora* and *Palmetto State* had broken the blockade at Charleston was simply not true. The two ironclads were too slow and too unseaworthy to pursue the Union blockaders into the open sea: thus, once the ironclads withdrew back to harbour, the blockade was simply re-applied.[42]

The primacy in early CSN strategy of breaking the blockade also had ramifications for assessing the impact of CSN commerce raiding and coastal defence. Mallory was clear that the purpose of commerce raiding was not simply to capture or destroy Union shipping; amongst other things, it was designed to undermine the Union blockade of Southern ports by drawing Union warships into a fruitless hunt for Confederate raiders across the world's oceans.[43] But the US Secretary of the Navy, Gideon Welles, rode out the storm of protest from Union maritime interests and continued to prioritise the blockade.[44] Early CSN efforts at coastal defence were also poor and the consequences of this were especially pernicious because they had a direct bearing on the Union's ability to strengthen the blockade. Thus, Port Royal, taken by the Union in November 1861, was used as a base of operations for ships blockading Charleston and Savannah. Fernandina, taken in March 1862, became an important base for Union blockade ships in the Gulf.[45]

Overall, the CSN did not achieve the early goals that it was set. Indeed, the failure of the CSN to live up to early expectations did not escape constituencies within the Confederacy. Mallory was investigated, though exonerated, by a joint Congressional committee after the scuttling of the *Virginia*.[46] The *Charleston Mercury*, a newspaper that was a recurrent critic of Mallory, argued that the Confederate Secretary of the Navy displayed 'superior feebleness'; another newspaper, the *Richmond Examiner*, lamented that the South's chances of a 'brilliant career in naval warfare' were lost to Mallory's incompetence.[47] In particular, there was great resentment at the perception that Confederate ironclads seemed doomed to be burnt or blown up by the CSN soon after completion. As the *Richmond Examiner* commented caustically: 'So long as Mallory reigns, all that he touches ... will explode or sink.'[48] In hindsight, some of the goals pursued by the CSN in the early stages of the war were unattainable. In particular, Mallory's faith in the decisive impact of 'next generation' naval technology as a force-multiplier

---

[41] Green and Massignani, pp.73–74.

[42] Bern Anderson, *By Sea and River: The Naval History of the Civil War* (New York: Da Capo, 1962), pp.160–161.

[43] J.W. Simson, *Naval Strategies of the Civil War: Confederate Innovation and Federal Opportunism* (Nashville, TN: Cumberland House, 2001), p.187.

[44] Peter Batty and Peter J. Parish, *The Divided Union: A Concise History of the American Civil War* (Stroud: The History Press, 2009), pp.151–152.

[45] Simson ,pp.70–74.

[46] Tucker, p.11.

[47] Durkin, p.192.

[48] Ibid., p.292.

proved wildly optimistic. Some, such as the drawing off of the blockaders to hunt down CSN raiders, might have been attainable. However, strategic performance is relative and the CSN failed to achieve some objectives simply because the USN generally was well handled during the war.[49] However, this story of failure does not capture adequately the full story of the CSN's strategic performance during the Civil War. Belligerents often find that the war that they fight is not the one that they expected. In consequence, just as the grand strategy of the Confederacy adjusted during the Civil War, so the objectives of the CSN also changed.

There was a general expectation at the start of the war that the conflict would be a short one,[50] and the strategy adopted by Mallory needs to be seen in this context. Suggestions have often been made as to alternative strategies that the Confederacy should have implemented. For example, in relation to cotton, the South imposed a de facto embargo early on in the war, because it was believed that this would force the Europeans into recognising the Confederacy and intervening in order to restore the supply of cotton. In retrospect, the belief in the power of 'King Cotton' was vastly over-estimated.[51] In retrospect, cotton might well have been better exported as early as possible in order to establish better credit for the Confederate government, or nationalised in order to bring it directly under the control of the government.[52] But such a view was as alien to the prevailing notion on both sides that the war would be short as the later introduction of conscription or taxing in kind. In part, this 'short war' expectation was driven by the prevailing conception of war at the time: the continued application of a 'Napoleonic paradigm' in which war would be decided through a decisive clash of both sides' main army. However, as one of the first examples of 'Industrialised People's War', embodying the material fruits of the industrial revolution and the political fruits of the French revolution, both belligerents had the capacity to mobilise ever-increasing proportions of the political, economic and social resources at their disposal, making a quick victory extremely problematic.[53] As the Civil War became progressively less limited, Confederate strategy focused increasingly on protraction and the wearing out of the Northern will to fight. The military manifestation of this was a move from a cordon strategy designed to meet Union attacks at the border to a focus on 'offensive defence' in which the Confederacy would engage some trading of space for time but would still place an emphasis on counter-attacks.[54] Increasingly, the purpose of such a strategy was to

---

[49] Dougherty, pp.182–197.
[50] Brian Holden Reid, *The American Civil War* (London: Cassell, 1999), pp.65–68.
[51] Tucker, pp.69–70.
[52] Lester, p.45.
[53] For a discussion of the American Civil War as 'industrialised people's war' see Stig Forster and Jorg Nagler, *On the Road to Total War: The American Civil War and the German Wars of Unification, 1861–1871* (Cambridge: Cambridge University Press, 1997).
[54] Gary W. Gallagher, *The Confederate War: How Popular Will, Nationalism, and Military Strategy Could Not Stave Off Defeat* (Cambridge, MA: Harvard University

wear out Union public support for the war, especially in the period leading up to the 1864 Presidential elections.[55]

This development was paralleled in the maritime sphere. By the spring and summer of 1862 it was clear to Mallory that the CSN's naval strategy was not working in the way that he had anticipated.[56] In this respect the CSN was having plenty of strategic effect, given the fear generated by CSN ironclads and the burgeoning list of Union merchant ships that had been sunk or captured; but it was poor in terms of strategic performance – this tactical and operational military activity was not producing the anticipated decisive impact against the Union. The blockade of the Confederacy was gradually strengthened, and Confederate ironclads proved unable to effect any decisive pressure on Federal control of the seas. In response, from 1862 the CSN's focus was on a less grandiose and more realistic contribution to the Confederacy's objective of wearing out the Union's willingness to continue the war. Seen in the context of a longer-term grand strategy of protraction, the CSN had significant value to the Confederacy, even if it remained a small navy.

In general, the role of the CSN changed from a concentration on the importance of independent, offensive operations focused on breaking the blockade, to a more integrated, defensive role focusing on wearing out the Union public's willingness to fight. The CSN, though larger physically than it had been at the outbreak of the war, shrank its ambitions and pursued activities more associated historically with small navies. Blockade running and coastal defence became the two pillars of this approach. Underwood notes that coastal defence became 'more important than breaking the blockade'.[57] Ironclads were an important part of this and an attempt was made to give all seaports a force of ironclad vessels. Thus, after the scuttling of the *Virginia*, for example, a new ironclad squadron was created on the James river, and this, plus shore batteries, river obstacles and torpedoes, kept the Union from advancing up the river for the duration of the war.[58] However, greater efforts were made to improve passive defences. This involved establishing defensive positions where possible outside of the reach of the guns of the USN; and also greater focus on passive defences such as obstructions, mines, and earth forts. Indeed, mines in the end were possibly the most effective of the CSN's defensive weapons. For example, the 100 mines deployed on the Roanoke River destroyed seven out of the twelve Union vessels sent there in the Union attempt

---

Press, 1997), p.115.

[55] Larry E. Nelson, *Bullets, Ballots, and Rhetoric: Confederate Policy for the United States Presidential Contest of 1864* (University of Alabama Press, 1980), p.27.

[56] Simson, p.123.

[57] Rodman L. Underwood, *Stephen Russell Mallory: A Biography of the Confederate Navy Secretary and United States Senator* (Jefferson, NC: McFarland and Company, 2005), p.96.

[58] Greene and Massignani, p.84.

on Fort Branch. Those deployed in Mobile harbour sank twelve USN ships.[59] Coastal defence also involved establishing effective shore batteries operated by trained crews. Heavy rifled guns were key; but other innovations included the use at Wilmington of a 'flying battery' of 2.75 inch artillery which could be deployed to cover grounded blockade runners.[60] These kinds of defences were successful in defeating the Union attack on Charleston in April 1863. The defences there comprised outer forts and batteries, and an inner layer of defences comprising more forts and batteries, obstructions, torpedoes, and two ironclads armed with spar torpedoes.[61] Blockade running was also crucial to extending the survival of the Confederacy, blockade runners bringing into the South some of the basic commodities required for the Confederacy to function: everything from food and clothing for the army through to paper upon which to print banknotes.[62] Wise comments that 'Without blockade running the nation's military would have been without proper supplies of arms, bullets, and powder'.[63] The crucial role of the CSN in support of blockade running was keeping the harbours open and, in the end, Charleston, Savannah, and Wilmington were taken by land, not sea.[64] Other activities also were not irrelevant to supporting protraction: CSN procurement activities in the United Kingdom created long running and often intense diplomatic problems in Anglo–US relations;[65] and the exploits of Confederate raiders such as the *Alabama* also helped sustain Confederate morale. Indeed, Mallory was well aware of the propaganda value of naval activity, noting in consequence to his officers that they should be sure that they aided in shedding 'the proper light' on the Southern cause.[66] Even the European-built ocean going ironclads, which, with the exception of the CSS *Stonewall*, never entered CSN service 'assumed in Southern eyes almost magical powers' and caused prolonged consternation in the North.[67]

In general, this defensive, supporting role focused on sea denial was broadly successful. Simson notes that: 'On the whole ... it must be said that Mallory's revised naval strategy worked.'[68] Luraghi agrees, arguing that in terms of protecting the rear of the Confederate army, of keeping control of ports for as long as possible and in allowing through crucial supplies, the CSN was 'very successful'.[69] But

[59] Durkin, pp.155 and 264.
[60] Greene and Massignani, p.185.
[61] Simson, p.133.
[62] Lester, pp.156–163.
[63] Wise, p.226.
[64] Underwood, p.96.
[65] See, for example, Amanda Foreman, *A World on Fire* (London: Allen Lane, 2010), pp.520–526.
[66] Durkin, pp.168–169.
[67] Batty and Parish, p.152.
[68] Simson, p.226.
[69] Ibid., p.229.

even in the more modest objective of political attrition, the CSN's achievements were somewhat mixed. Reflecting on the purpose of naval operations in 1864, Mallory asserted to Bulloch that: 'The simultaneous appearance of efficient cruisers on the New England coast and fishing banks, in the West Indies and South Atlantic, in the Pacific among the Whalemen, and in the East Indies, would have a decided tendency to turn the trading mind of New England to thoughts of peace. I am exceedingly anxious to do this.'[70] Commerce raiding was thus designed to put direct economic pressure on key mercantile interests in the North, undermining their support for the war and causing them to bring decisive pressure to bear on the Lincoln administration. Economically, however, the effects of commerce raiding were disappointing for the Confederacy: much of the Union shipping simply re-flagged itself and, overall, the Union economy boomed, reducing seriously the impact of CSN operations on the overall economic well-being of the Union.[71]

Arguments have been made by some that the CSN could have done things differently. For example, a scheme was mooted early on to buy ten ex-East India Company ships, a move which would have given the CSN an instant naval force. It was also argued by individuals such as Matthew Fontaine Maury that the CSN should focus on building a so-called 'Mosquito Fleet' of gunboats rather than focusing on ironclads. But the first was of questionable viability financially and the second proved manifestly inadequate in clashes in which such boats actually were used against the USN.[72] Perhaps the CSN should have placed more emphasis early on in developing torpedoes: P.G.T. Beauregard was certainly of this opinion and argued that a focus on torpedoes early on in the war would have rendered the blockade 'inefficient' and attempts by the Union to seize control of rivers 'next to impossible'.[73] But such a focus would have required remarkable prescience given at the Civil War's outset the experimental nature of the technology involved. Moreover, it would also have required at the start of the war a better appreciation of its likely longevity: but this appreciation was something which could only come about through experience.

Overall, the Confederacy survived long enough to create at least three points of crisis for the Union in the Civil War: in late summer 1862, with Lee and Bragg's moves into the Union; in mid-1863 in the period following the Union defeat at Chancellorsville; and in the summer of 1864 as the casualties mounted from Grant's campaigns in the East.[74] If the outcome of the Civil War was contingent, the CSN played its role in helping the Confederacy to place mounting political pressure on the Lincoln administration. If it was erroneous for Mallory to believe that the CSN could be independently decisive, the CSN could still be a valuable

[70] Larry E. Nelson, *Bullets, Ballots, and Rhetoric: Confederate Policy for the United States Presidential Contests of 1864* (University:University of Alabama Press, 1980), p.27.
[71] Batty and Parish, pp.151–152.
[72] Lester, p.91.
[73] Durkin, p.294.
[74] Gallagher, p.115.

tool, despite being so badly outnumbered by its adversary, as part of a more holistic grand strategy of attrition.

Conclusion

Virgil Carrington Jones argued that the Confederate navy was like a Greek tragedy: '[B]orn in adversity, nurtured on noble aspirations, and overwhelmed by irresistible odds.'[75] But judging the value overall of the CSN to the Confederacy requires moving beyond tales of individual heroism or remarkable organisational enterprise: the CSN has both of these in handfuls but they do not tell us much about the general effectiveness of the naval aspects of the Confederate struggle for independence. Overall, the CSN demonstrates three things as a small navy case study.

First, being a 'small navy' can sometimes be as much about aspirations as it is about size: the Confederate States Navy was a negligible force at its inception, yet its objectives, roles, and procurement were directed towards sea control and decisive battle against the Union Navy; Mallory believed that the CSN could single-handedly defeat the Union. By the time the CSN had grown to a respectable size, its activities were much more limited and it had embraced roles more associated with small navies, such as sea denial. Second, the fact that a navy is small does not relieve us of the responsibility of judging its value in relation to its strategic performance. Heroic exploits in the face of a much larger enemy make engaging history, and they may say much about the enterprise and sacrifice of individuals; however, they do not, of themselves, necessarily contribute to success overall in war. There is no automatic relationship between tactical military success and the attainment of strategic level political goals. Third, the strategic effectiveness of small navies cannot be judged in isolation of the strategic level of war generally. The fact that a navy is small does not mean that it cannot be effective; rather, it means that its potential contribution to the overall conduct and outcome of a war is likely to be closely tied to its contribution to other spheres: land operations; the diplomatic arena; the economic aspects of the war and so forth. Put simply, it is not the job of small navies to be defeated gloriously; instead, governments need to integrate the activities of navies, however small, into a coherent grand strategy because navies, even if heavily overmatched by their opponent, can still perform important functions in war.

---

[75] Quoted in Underwood, p.88.

Chapter 13

Learning to Be Small: The Experience of the British Pacific Fleet, 1944–45

Jon Robb-Webb

At first sight the Royal Navy is an unlikely candidate for inclusion in a volume dedicated to the exploration, examination and analysis of what is termed 'Small Navies'. However, as the conference that gave birth to this book discussed at some length, 'small' is purely a relative term, it has no absolute measuring scale of tonnage or hull numbers. Indeed as this chapter will demonstrate, not even a reduced list of capabilities is a prerequisite for categorising a Small Navy. Small is a comparison to something else, in this case the United States Navy (USN) during the last eighteen months of the Second World War in the Pacific. As such the British Pacific Fleet (BPF) can in some ways be regarded as a prime example of a Small Navy. In tonnage and hull numbers it was clearly very small in comparison. Probably much more importantly, it is an excellent example of how to not only become a Small Navy but also wield influence as one.

Lisle A. Rose, the eminent American naval historian, opens the third volume of his study on the rise of the USN with an apocryphal story about a grey spring morning in the Atlantic, south of Iceland, in 1943, when a line of new American destroyers meets the battered Royal Navy destroyer escort of a convoy. Washington had just announced that the USN had finally overtaken the RN in terms of tonnage and was now the largest Navy in the world. Immensely proud of this fact the commander of the US destroyers signals over to the British: 'Good morning. How is everything in the world's second largest navy?' In the finest traditions of crisp naval signals, back comes the reply: 'Fine. How's everything in the world's second best?'[1]

This anecdote illustrates two important issues. First, it is interesting that the exchange takes place in the Atlantic. Throughout the war the British dominated the Atlantic. In strategic priority, in the allocation of resources, and consequently in the nature of the war that was fought, the RN held the lead here. These USN destroyers may well have been brand new and luxuriously equipped in contrast to the British but they were in the minority, both for Washington's attention and stacked against everything the RN deployed.

---

[1] Lisle A Rose, *Power at Sea Vol. 3: A Violent Peace 1946–2006*, (Columbia:University of Missouri Press 2007) p. 1

The real, dramatic and irrefutable dominance of the USN at sea was actually, and unsurprisingly, to be found in the Pacific. As it was for the British in the Atlantic, so it was for the Americans with the Pacific. It was their casus belli, their strategic priority. It was there that the Chief of Naval Operations (Admiral Ernie King) deployed the USN's first team. It was the theatre where naval strategy dominated allied strategy, which in turn was dominated by the USN. Where the sheer scale of what American industrial power could put to sea was both unbelievable and unavoidable.

When the British returned to the theatre in the spring of 1945, they did so with effectively the most powerful surface fleet ever deployed by the RN.[2] Clearing the Mediterranean and the neutralisation of what remained of Germany's surface threat ahead of the Normandy landings had allowed the RN to deploy its major surface assets out to the Pacific. There was still a need for escort and support vessels in European waters, something that would indeed hamper British Pacific operations, but the freeing up of carriers, battleships, cruisers, and the like, allowed the Admiralty to dispatch a formidable fleet. It was however, completely and totally overshadowed by the USN.

The second issue is that the exchange casts an interesting light on the attitude of the RN in the face of this emerging leviathan. This is important because the attitude of all involved in the Pacific, from the heads of state, down through the Combined Chiefs of Staff, through the Admirals concerned, the fleet commanders, the ship captains, the liaison officers, to the ordinary sailor, was to be critical for the learning process that the RN underwent. Learning how to be small would be no easy task for a navy that had been dominate on the global stage for over a hundred years. Recognising, accepting and internalising such a profound change in status was to be one of the most significant aspects of the British Pacific Fleet experience. The six months that the BPF spent operating in the Central Pacific, alongside and then intimately with, though always under, the USN was to have long reaching consequences for both Navies.[3]

This learning process was one of the most important aspects of the British Pacific Fleet's experience and to be effective and profound there were certain conditions that had to be met. First the RN simply had to have presence in the theatre of operations. This was as much a political decision as it was related to military strategy. Secondly the Fleet would have to participate in the most advanced area of operations in the Pacific alongside the USN. These were operational and tactical

---

[2] H P Willmott described the BPF as the 'most powerful single strike force assembled by Britain in the course of the Second World War and, relative to its own time, was probably as powerful a force as any raised by the Royal Navy at any stage in its long history'. H.P.Willmott *Just Being There*, Paper presented to the Institute of Historical Research for the Julian Corbett Prize in Modern Naval History 1986 p. 2

[3] For a full exploration of how these six months impacted upon the post-War period see J Robb-Webb *The British Pacific Fleet Experience and Legacy 1944-50* (London: Ashgate 2013)

level decisions and rested in the main on the Fleet's capabilities and success in convincing the dominate partner of them.

Presence and participation were to be essential in the creation of a cadre within the RN that understood, first hand, the extent to which the USN in the Pacific was changing the character of naval warfare. Those that served in the BPF would share their personal experiences and the knowledge gained from adopting USN practices with the wider RN in the post-War period.

The omens were not good for the British Pacific Fleet when it was raised by splitting the Far East Fleet into the East Indies Fleet and the BPF with Admiral Sir Bruce Fraser hoisting his flag as C-in-C for the latter in October 1944. The Japanese had forced the RN out of the Pacific and back to Ceylon (Sri Lanka) two years earlier and there was no consensus at the grand strategic level of the Anglo-American alliance that a return was either needed or desirable. The British Prime Minister, Winston Churchill, initially took the view that his one available tool of strategic power, a RN commitment to the Far East, would better serve the country's interests by conducting an amphibious campaign to recapture lost imperial possessions: Burma, Malaysia and ultimately Hong Kong. In February 1944 the Prime Minister had supported a paper presented to the Chiefs of Staff that argued for a strategy which might well have been complementary to that pursued by the US but was certainly separate.[4]

This view was shared by the US Chief of Naval Operations, Admiral King. King had spent his professional career studying and planning for war across the Pacific against Japan and he wasn't very amenable to the idea of the British muscling in at the eleventh hour.

General Eisenhower is reputed to have said that the course of the war would have gone much more smoothly if someone had taken King outside and shot him. Churchill's Chief of Staff, General Ismay described him as

> Tough as old nails and carried himself as stiffly as a poker. He was stiff and stand-offish, almost to the point of rudeness. At the start, he was intolerant of all things British, especially the Royal Navy; but he was equally intolerant and suspicious of the American Army. War against Japan was the problem to which he had devoted the study of a lifetime, and he resented the idea of American resources being used for any other purpose than to destroy Japanese.[5]

Admiral Vian, who was to command the BPF's carriers wrote of King that,

> [His] attitude has sometimes been ascribed to Anglophobia. This is not altogether true. Certainly the Admiral's loyalty was given whole-heartedly to the Navy he served. It was a feeling which led him to look upon even the United

---

[4] UK National Archives (UKNA): CAB 80/79/114, COS (44) 114(0) 1 February 1944 'Overall Policy for the Defeat of Japan'.

[5] General Lord Ismay, *The Memoirs of Lord Ismay* (London: Heinemann 1960) p. 253.

States Army and Air Force as doubtful allies. It was perhaps engendered in some degree by jealousy of the Royal Navy, which for so long had dominated the oceans of the world.[6]

Churchill continued to press for a separate British strategy right up until a remarkable about face at the Octagon Conference in September 1944.[7]

Against this backdrop of strategic uncertainty and facing at best an ambiguous reception from the USN, the British Pacific Fleet would initially struggle to make their presence felt.

Presence and personal contact were essential ingredients in the BPF's recipe for success. From the outset of British planning it was those officers who had witnessed first-hand the nature of the war in the Pacific and the scale of American naval power that understood what would be required. 'The most striking feature to a new arrival in the Pacific area is the grand scale on which operations are carried out in the Central Pacific theatre.' The scale, for example, of American warships present for the Gilberts operation in 1943 was 'almost unbelievable to an officer who has seen most of the war from the Eastern Mediterranean.'[8]

The US Navy in the Pacific had developed a revolutionary style of naval warfare based around the fast carrier task force. Using an extended afloat logistics chain, these task forces were able to couple the strategic range of sea power with the tactical speed of response of air power to dominate the seas around their operational objectives.

Having witnessed the USN attack on Rabaul in November 1943, Cdr Smeeton, the RN liaison officer aboard the iconic USS *Essex,* identified a series of important developments in naval warfare which he believed provided lessons for the RN.[9] The raid was designed to cover the landings at Bougainville in the Solomon Islands. The raid began with massed strikes launched by the carriers USS *Saratoga* and *Princeton*. A second fast carrier task force consisting of USS *Essex, Bunker Hill* and *Independence* followed up the first. This in turn was followed by USN land-based bombers and finally by USAAF B-24 Liberator heavy bombers. Smeeton drew specific attention to the range at which the carriers launched; the suitability and the high number of aircraft deployed. Saturating the heavy defences at both the port and airfield installations was essential. This needed numbers, firepower and intensity which were in turn dependent on the operating tempo of the carrier's flight decks. This reduced casualties and cleared the way for land-based heavy

---

[6] Admiral of the Fleet Sir Philip Vian *Action This Day* (London: Frederick Muller Ltd 1960) pp.155

[7] See J Robb-Webb *Light Two Lanterns the British are Coming by Sea: Royal Navy Participation in the Pacific 1944–45* in G Kennedy [ed] *British Naval Strategy East of Suez, 1900–2000* (London: Frank Cass 2005)

[8] UKNA: ADM 199/1117 Observers with US Pacific Fleet 15/12/43

[9] UKNA: ADM 199/1523 Pacific Naval Operations 1944–1945 Observers with US Pacific Fleet report by Cmdr. R.M.Smeeton, 21/10/43-5/11/43 CV USS *Essex* para

bombers. These raids were rendered more effective through the use of an escort provided by the forward deployed carriers.[10] Integrating land and sea based air strikes to accomplish the mission of neutralising the Japanese threat from Rabaul to the amphibious landings.

The RN's Naval Air Observer with the US Pacific Fleet wrote to Admiral Boyd, Fifth Sea Lord [Air] at the beginning of March 1944:

> I think it is more than ever important for us to get as many carriers as we can into operation in this theatre as soon as they can be spared;. so that we can educate as many R.N. officers as possible in the conception of taking the war to the enemy by means of aircraft carriers; I may be wrong but I do not think the R.N. as a whole is sufficiently 'carrier minded', though we are probably a lot better than we were.

The RN had led the world in the development of the aircraft carrier during the first two decades of its existence. Then a combination of limited resources which discouraged investment in unproven technologies and inter-service rivalry over the control of air power at sea, which rapidly became about respective service strategy, stalled and then gave away this lead. As a consequence of this there was much that the Royal Navy needed to learn if it was to catch up with the USN in the Pacific.

The war in the Pacific was a different type of war from that which the Royal Navy had been fighting in the Atlantic and the Mediterranean. The simple facts of geography, the vast distances over which campaigns in the Pacific were fought, ensured that new methods of employing air power at sea were developed by the USN. Throughout the 1930s the USN had been wrestling with the strategic problem of war against Japan. In contrast to the British who possessed a network of naval shore establishments across the globe from which they could deploy naval power, the United States had been faced from the outset with the problem of projecting and sustaining naval power at huge distances from its shore base. Whereas in the European and Atlantic theatres the RN had carried out significant carrier-focused operations, such as the strike on Taranto or Operation Tungsten (the carrier strike on the Tirpitz), these were of limited duration and range. The RN carried out a detailed study of the 14 British carrier strikes conducted up to October 1944.[11] Of these, 11 were strikes on shipping and shore installations and three were minelaying. Their analysis identified that that on average the strikes were carried out by the equivalent of just under three [2.7] *Illustrious*-class fleet carriers, supported by one battleship, three cruisers and 10 destroyers. The operations lasted seven days and resulted in two strikes composed of 49 fighter aircraft and 37 bombers, dropping 23.5 tons of bombs. In addition some 70 per cent of the British carrier strikes were conducted within 60 miles of the coast, whereas the same percentage of USN *Essex* class carrier strikes in the Pacific took

---

[10] UKNA: ADM 199/1523 Pacific Naval Operations 1944–1945.

[11] UKNA: ADM 219/262 Analysis of British Carrier Strikes March 1945

place between 60 and 120 miles from land. The US also remained on station three or four times longer than the British and utilised on occasions some six times as many aircraft carriers.

All of this made it essential that the British understood American methods of utilising carriers, essential that they could demonstrate a capacity to match, in method if not quantity, the USN and essential that they convinced the Americans of their abilities.

As mentioned earlier, the negotiations at the grand strategic level between the Western Allies over British participation in the final stages of the war against Japan had not always been smooth. However, once the Prime Minister had changed his mind as to what form and where this commitment should be deployed agreement in principle was at least settled. Getting the required carrier presence in theatre was of course, only part of the difficulty for Admiral Fraser. Getting it accepted and utilised in the most advanced operations against Japan, where the RN would gain first-hand experience of this new way of naval warfare, was to be Fraser's most significant challenge.

Negotiations as to what, when, and importantly where the BPF were to operate, were long, often fractious when internal, sometimes heated between the allies, but always tortuous. Ernie King had reluctantly accepted the BPF on the condition that it be self-supporting, perhaps believing this was as good as no fleet. Admiral Nimitz was perhaps somewhat irked by the amount of time and attention needed to be paid to such a small military capability, if indeed it materialised at all.

Between October and December as the BPF was being assembled and worked up. Fraser struggled to establish shore-based facilities and logistic support. Fraser's dispatches to the Admiralty and increasingly frequent signals to Admiral Nimitz reveal much of his frustration at the complex chain of command within which he had to operate. A request for dockyard support or airfield capacity required political authorisation from not only the Australian authorities in Canberra, but also from London via the Admiralty to the Colonial Office and often Washington via Nimitz and King.

Fraser was also concurrently attempting to get agreement as to the Fleet's employment. This involved more negotiations with Nimitz and his staff. Nimitz appears to have initially viewed the imminent arrival in theatre of the Royal Navy as something of a mixed blessing at best and more often as an irritating inconvenience that took up far too much of the Admiral's time; certainly more than was warranted by their weight of force. Correspondence between Nimitz and Admiral King reveals, if not antagonism toward the British, then at least scepticism as to whether they make any meaningful contribution.[12] King had insisted upon the British being self-sufficient during negotiations with the Combined Chiefs of Staff and it was this point that he emphasised to Nimitz when the two met at the

---

[12] J Robb-Webb *Light Two Lanterns, the British are Coming by Sea: RN Participation in the Pacific 1944–45* in G Kennedy (ed.) British Naval Strategy *East of Suez*, 1900–2000 Influences and Actions, (London: Frank Cass, 2005)

end of November 1944 in San Francisco. King's memoirs claim that these doubts were not the result of any 'lack of good will' on the part of the RN but rather the question was one of actual capability. King's view was that although RN

> Ships had operated throughout the seven seas, they had never in modern times operated for long periods at such distance from any permanent established base, and so had not had the experience of replenishment at sea or of dealing with fleet material and supply so far from home. All kinds of supplies were short, and the whole world lacked sufficient cargo ships. In addition, the Royal Navy was not familiar with that administration of carriers in large numbers that had been developed by the United States Navy in the war years.

King emphasised that the British C-in-C would be an administrative and not operational designation; that the officer would report to King, who would in turn give him specific directives. King still held to the view that the British should operate as separately from the USN as possible. He intended that the BPF be given certain tasks to carry out independently, rather than integrated into the USN.

Fraser conducted a strenuous correspondence with Admiral Nimitz throughout the autumn of 1944, seeking to secure his agreement for the use of the BPF in the most advanced operations against the Japanese.

The break-through came after face-to-face meetings at Nimitz's HQ in Hawaii. After a record breaking flight from Colombo to Perth and then on to Pearl Harbor, Fraser and Nimitz reached an accord and signed off on NF-1. Fraser had Nimitz's agreement to shared strategic areas and the employment of what would amount to a Carrier Task Group though designated a TF at least in support of the main USN thrust through Okinawa and on to the Japanese home islands. Now he just had to make it happen.

Although the BPF would operate in support of but independent of the USN Fifth Fleet, the RN needed to embed personnel at all levels into the US command structure. The exchange of Liaison Officers [LOs] between the USN and the RN was a vital mechanism for not only the sharing of information and intelligence but also for the wider interoperability of the two navies. The Admiralty commented on their role and function writing:

> Upon them, and them alone the Admiralty and the War Cabinet relied for information as to how far the war in the Pacific was keeping step with American official reports on its progress, and the truth about the methods and the efficiency of the US Navy. They were also envoys of the British Pacific Fleet. They were in a position to gather thorough and intimate knowledge of not only the organization and methods of the US Fleet, but the outlook and psychology of the officers and men of their Service, so that British ships and units on joining would be able to fit themselves harmoniously into service with our Allies.[13]

---

[13]   UKNA: ADM 223/49, US Intelligence Organization in the Pacific,

For the BPF to be effective the fleet had to have the ability to inter-operate with the USN. Not just for replenishment or shore-based facilities, intelligence material was provided in vast quantities, intelligence about the enemy but also about USN methods. So much that it threatened to overwhelm the capacity of the meagre RN intelligence staff.[14] Being there and interacting with the USN was the order of the day. Adopting USN signalling practice, transferring to USN codes, adapting fleet train replenishment at sea methods, conforming to new USN cruising dispositions and tactical manoeuvres, wearing khaki uniform; there was a lot to learn in a short space of time.

Not everybody appreciated these efforts. Fraser identified that key to the success of the BPF lay in the relations established with the USN. Admiral Rawlings, who commanded the BPF at sea, also understood this and how dependent this was on a professionally competent performance at the tactical level. Admiral Vian, Commander Aircraft Carriers BPF, was perhaps cut from the British version of Ernie King cloth. Referred to as a 'sour-faced puss', he resented the change in status that the Pacific campaign represented. He refused to adopt USN-style khaki and was never slow in reminding colleagues and allies alike of the RN's long and proud history of dominance at sea, often adding that USN jealousy was therefore hardly surprising.

Overall however there was perhaps an attitude of resigned acceptance of the change in status. Understanding came more readily to those deployed, the scale of operations in the Pacific, of geographic distance, of ships, and aircraft, and men, and stores, and replacements, and reports and paperwork, could not be ignored.

Rawlings, like Fraser with Nimitz, secured agreement from Admiral Halsey (C-in-C USN Third Fleet) for the full integration of the BPF with the Third Fleet, after a successful face-to-face meeting. Halsey had been reluctant to accept the BPF until Rawlings convinced him of his good faith and the Fleet's ability. This in part was achieved during the BPF's support to the invasion of Okinawa.

Operation Iceberg was the British codename for the RN's participation in the American invasion of Okinawa. The BPF were tasked with neutralising airfields through which the Japanese could stage aircraft from Formosa to attack the USN invasion shipping. The airfields were located on the Sakishima Islands, part of the Ryukyu Islands chain and some 175 miles south-west of Okinawa. From late March 1944 through May, with a brief return to their forward operating base, the BPF achieved their principal task of denying the airfields to the Japanese by the sustained projection of naval air power. The BPF had been continuously at sea for thirty-two days, longer than any other fleet since the days of sail. Admiral Cunningham in London explicitly brought this fact to the attention of the War Cabinet in his regular summary of naval air operations, when he referred to

---

[14] For a fuller discussion see J Robb-Webb, 'Anglo-American Naval Intelligence Co-Operation in the Pacific 1944–45' in *Intelligence and National Security*, 25:5, (2007) pp.767-786.

Task Force 57 (the designation for the BPF when operating alongside Admiral Spruance's USN Fifth Fleet) as making 'British naval history'.[15]

Ultimately it was the capability at the tactical level, at sea, in the most advanced operations against the Japanese that permitted the full integration of the BPF into the USN's Third Fleet. The BPF had undergone a remarkable adaptation to USN methods and procedures in the short time from their establishment in October 1944 until the war ended in September 1945. New cruising dispositions designed to deal with an almost exclusive air threat from the Imperial Japanese Navy (IJN) had been mastered. New signal methods and codes had been incorporated in order to communicate with the USN. New arrangements for Replenishment at Sea (RAS) had been adapted to so that the fleet could sustain itself from both the Fleet Train and from USN resources. New strike tactics had been employed in order to conform to the USN's ideas concerning attack at source. All of these innovations and adaptations were essential if the BPF were to be integrated successfully and efficiently into the Admiral Halsey's Third Fleet. Demonstrating these competences gave the BPF's commanders the confidence to argue for a place at the operational and tactical planning tables.

This process of integration into the USN's planning was neither smooth nor inevitable but it was greatly assisted by a number of key individuals who had the foresight to recognise what the Pacific experience represented and the diplomatic nous to ensure British participation. In theatre Admiral Fraser established a good working relationship with Nimitz. He was able to move Nimitz's view of the British from one of barely repressed annoyance as to their presence to one where the American Admiral bestowed generous praise on the fleet in both official communications and personal correspondence.[16]

Admiral Rawlings, the BPF commander at sea, developed such a close friendship with Admiral Halsey that he was invited to be a pallbearer at the latter's funeral; only illness unfortunately preventing him from accepting. With notable exceptions such as Admiral Vian, this attitude of mind toward the USN ran through most of the Fleet. Cdr Michael Le Fanu, BPF Liaison Officer on board Admiral Spruance's flagship, *Indianapolis*, was a crucial link during the early stages of Operation Iceberg as Spruance and Rawlings had not had the opportunity for a face-to-face meeting. Their knowledge of each other to a great extent depended upon Le Fanu's reports and the impressions he conveyed in both directions.

Le Fanu, like Fraser and Rawlings, recognised how important it was to make the greatest impression on the Americans despite the relative weakness of the British contribution to the Pacific Campaign. During operations against the Japanese home islands, under Admiral Halsey's Third Fleet Command, Le Fanu suggested that Rawlings' next visit to discuss forthcoming action should be made in the flagship, *King George V*, instead of a destroyer as would have been usual.

[15] UKNA: ADM 199/1492 Summary of Naval Air Operations - May–August 1945, 1st Sea Lord's Memoranda to War Cabinet.

[16] See *Light Two Lanterns*, op cit.

The suggestion resulted in an enduring image of inter-allied naval cooperation; the USS *Missouri* and HMS *King George V* oiling either side of the tanker *Sabine*. Le Fanu also assisted in the staging of the Japanese surrender ceremony aboard the USS *Missouri* when he obtained the wardroom chairs from HMS *King George V*, arguing that those from the American battleship, folding metal ones, were hardly appropriate for the conclusion of the greatest conflict in human history. The chairs were presented as a gift to the USN battleship upon conclusion. For his work as a Liaison Officer the USN awarded Le Fanu the Legion of Merit.[17]

These personal relationships, the goodwill that was eventually demonstrated by officers and men of both navies obviously eased both the learning process of the BPF and their integration into the USN. The more that this process is examined the more apparent it becomes that an important aspect was the fact that in many respects the RN and the USN shared a similar outlook and intellectual heritage. Although by the time the RN returned to the Pacific the USN had effectively defeated the IJN at sea and achieved command of the sea both navies had similar conceptions of the role of seapower in military strategy and how this ought to manifest itself at the operational and tactical levels of war. This shared outlook created a basis from which operational and tactical plans could be developed. It allowed the British to slip more easily into an American planning framework. Although the major decisions were obviously being taken by the dominant player, the British were able to make their voice heard in language that the USN understood.

A vital aspect of ensuring a British voice was heard at the operational and tactical levels of planning, essential to the accomplishment of wider grand strategic objectives, was a demonstrated capacity to operate effectively in the type of naval campaign being waged by the USN. The BPF deployed a full range of capabilities albeit at much, much reduced scale. They provided a complete Carrier Task Group. Although the BPF were given the designation of a Task Force (TF57 under Spruance's Fifth Fleet or TF 37 under Halsey's Third Fleet), in reality it was only comparable to a Task Group, three or four of which would make up a Task Force in the USN. Nonetheless it deployed fleet carriers with attendant escorts, sustained by a fleet train capable of at sea replenishment. This capability, particularly in logistics sustainment, operated with very tight margins and on more than one occasion the BPF was forced to curtail operations and rely on support from the USN.

In material terms American industrial capacity allowed the USN to speedily adopt new ideas and procure the necessary assets to make a significant impact at the tactical level. This was something the British with their limited resources could not hope to do. However the capability deployed by the BPF ensured that they were accorded entry into the tactical and operational discussions.

The reduced scale of participation that a Small Navy brings to an operation or campaign does not, in itself, prevent innovation. This in turn can provide very

---

[17]   See Richard Baker, *Dry Ginger. The Biography of Sir Michael Le Fanu*, (London:W.H. Allen, 1977).

valuable leverage and influence. The British learned much from their time operating alongside the USN that would later influence the whole post-War Royal Navy. The BPF adopted American practices in radio procedures, in refuelling at sea, they attempted to emulate American strike tactics and conformed to new tactical cruising dispositions. However this learning process was not entirely one way. The BPF developed USN methods of refuelling at sea (abeam rather than astern) and applied them to the replenishment of ammunition; something which the USN then observed, studied and applied. The RN had been developing an integrated structure for fighting ships and aircraft known as the Action Information Centre, AIC, which centralised all information from the Task Group and controlled the tactical battle. This was the forerunner of the Combat Information Centre which was to become central to USN practice.

As well as innovating with procedures the British did bring at least one piece of equipment that the USN coveted: armoured fleet carriers. Often referred to as armoured flight decks in actuality it was the hangars underneath the decks that were armoured. Developed when British ideas about the air defence of carriers, unable to provide flight deck interception of attacking aircraft, was focused upon safely storing aircraft in their hangars and relying on anti-aircraft gunfire; the armoured hangars proved their worth when the carriers came under Kamikaze attack. The USN liaison officer aboard HMS *Indefatigable* is reported to have commented that 'When a kamikaze hits a US carrier it's six months repair at Pearl. In a Limey carrier it's a case of "sweepers man your brooms"'.[18]

Much discussion over the last twenty years has explored the way in which small, discrete, niche capabilities can provide influence in a coalition operation dominated by the US. The BPF experience suggests that niche capabilities have a role to play but are also dependent upon the degree of integration in the command structure. Making one's voice heard is complex and dependent upon issues at the grand and military strategic level, as well as operational and tactical competency. The British deployed both 'Highball bombers' and XE-craft to the Pacific as part of their contribution. Highball was the codename for a variant of the 'bouncing bomb' bomb, designed for use against shipping. No 618 Squadron RAF, flying Mosquitos, began trials in April 1943, finally reaching the Far East in January 1945. XE-craft were a type of midget submarine of 33 tons submerged displacement, a crew of four and an underwater endurance of around 80 miles. These submarines had carried out an attack on the *Tirpitz* in Norway and operated off the landing beaches in Normandy. Interestingly the Highball bombers were never employed and the squadron disbanded in July 1945. In contrast the XE submarines did attack and cut Japanese undersea cable communications and attack shipping in Singapore harbour. The issue with niche capabilities appears to be that they are niche, peripheral to the dominant partner's conception of how the war should be

---

[18] J Winton *The Forgotten Fleet* (London: Michael Joseph Ltd 1969) (reprint Douglas-Boyd Books Warhust 1991) p. 122

waged. As such, deriving influence from them, obtaining leverage during planning discussions as to their employment, is strictly limited.

Learning to be small involved an important change in attitude. For the British this was no easy mental adjustment. Ideas about who and what the Royal Navy now was, and should be in the future, had to recognise what the Pacific War represented: a new style of naval warfare which was dominated by the scale and technological sophistication of the USN. For a Navy which carried over a century of naval dominance on its shoulders, which operated under the long shadow of Nelson, Benbow, Collingwood, Anson and the whole pantheon of British naval heroes, this mental adjustment would at times be difficult and painful. Many in the RN looked at the USN, and whilst acknowledging their greater resources and size, viewed them as an institution which had only two years earlier won their first major naval battle. The War of 1812 had demonstrated an American capacity to fight and win frigate actions, the US Civil War had shown them capable of fighting a littoral campaign, the Spanish–American War had seen the decisive engagement at the Battle of Manila Bay but that had only involved a few protected cruisers and gunboats on each side, and the First World War saw USN sinkings of U-boats. But it was only with the great naval battles against the Japanese at Coral Sea and Midway that the USN truly came of age. Witnessing first-hand what the USN was deploying in the Pacific, experiencing their 'revolutionary' methods of sea warfare with the carrier task force at its heart, changed the Royal Navy's attitude to their now dominant ally and vice versa.

In the end the BPF marks the start of a process that would see the RN relinquish superiority in tonnage and numbers and replace it with a parity of professionalism and a capacity to seamlessly integrate into the USN. This was a process that would gather pace in the years following the end of the war and come to mark out the whole Navy.

Appendix A

Small Navies Conference: National University of Ireland Maynooth, 20–21 October 2012

List of contributors (in alphabetical order)

Hans Christian Bjerg, (Naval Academy, Copenhagen), *The Royal Danish Navy 1860–2010. A Study of the Political, Strategic and Technical Challenges of a Small Navy*

Ian Bowers, (King's College London) *The Republic of Korea Navy: Moving from the Littoral to the Regional*

Cdr Con Burns RN (EUNAVFOR), *Operation Atalanta: briefing*

Lt Col Wallace Camilleri, (Commanding Officer of the Armed Forces of Malta Maritime Squadron) *The Maltese Maritime Squadron*

Jonathan Chavanne (Texas A&M), *'A Slow, Dirty, Sandbar Kind of War' The US Navy's Brown Water Fleet in Vietnam, 1965–1973*

Timothy Choi, (Centre for Military and Strategic Studies, University of Calgary) *Nowhere May They Roam: Ottoman Area-Denial Operations and Lessons for the Strait of Hormuz*

Dr James Corum, (Baltic Defence College), *Small Navies in Counterinsurgency Operations: 1980–2012*

Dr Basil Germond, (Lancaster University), *Small Navies in Perspective. Deconstructing the Hierarchy of Naval Forces*

Niklas Granholm, (Swedish Defence Research Agency, FOI), *A Small High-Tech Navy in a Changing World. Challenges for the Royal Swedish Navy*

Dr Kostas Grivas, (Hellenic Military Academy), *Affordable Naval Power Projection. Geopolitical and technological factors favouring the development of small naval forces*

Prof Eric Grove, (University of Salford), *The Ranking of Smaller Navies Revisited*

Dr Serhat Guvenc, (Kadir Has University, Istanbul), *Turkish Naval and Amphibious Operations during the Cyprus War of 1974*

Ivo Juurvee (University of Tartu, Estonia), *Gaining Public Support While Maintaining Secrecy. The Experience of Estonian Navy in 1918–1940*

Dr Bernard Kelly (Edinburgh University), *Navies within the Navy: the relationship between British dominion naval forces and the Royal Navy, 1919–1939*

Prof Tom Kristiansen (Norwegian Institute for Defence Studies) & Capt. Roald Gjelsten, RNoN retd., *The Norwegian Navy 1807–2012*

Collin Koh Swee Lean, (Institute of Defence & Strategic Studies, Nanyang Technological University), *Modern Small Navies in the New Security Environment: the Case of the Republic of Singapore Navy*

Robert McCabe (NUI Maynooth), *Counter-piracy Operations in Southeast Asia 1980–1991: Small Navies – Big Problems*

Rear Admiral Mike McDevitt, USN retd. (Center for Naval Analyses, Virginia) *Small Navies in Asia: the Strategic Rationale behind Growth*

Commodore Mark Mellett (Flag Officer, Irish Naval Service) *Meeting requirements for innovation and enhanced service delivery while maintaining cost-effective running of fleets in a post-modern world.*

Professor Michael Mulqueen, Professor Mark Mellett & Dr Terry Warburton (Liverpool Hope University) *Small Navies. Enabling Innovation*

Dr Padraic O'Confhaola, *Neither Time Nor Money: Naval Procurement in the Irish State, 1922–1975*

Steven Paget (Strategic & Defence Studies Centre, Australian National University), *Changing Tides: the Re-aligned Royal Australian Navy at War in Vietnam*

Michael Peszke, *Polish Navy During WWII. A Small Navy on the Wide Oceans*

Chris Reynolds, (Director of the Irish Coast Guard), *The EU Coast Guard Forum*

Dr Jon Robb-Webb (King's College London & the UK Joint Services Command and Staff College), *A small fish big in a big pond: The British Pacific Fleet experience of working under the USN*

Dr Chiara Ruffa (Uppsala University/Harvard Kennedy School), *Maritime Power Today. The Use of Small Southern European Navies for Border Control and Humanitarian Support: Frontex Operations in the Mediterranean*

Dr Deborah Sanders, (King's College London & the UK Joint Services Command and Staff College), *Small Navies in the Black Sea. A Case Study of the Romanian Navy*

Dr Ian Speller (Centre for Military History and Strategic Studies, NUI Maynooth) *Conference introduction and concluding remarks*

Jacob Stoil (Worcester College, Oxford University), *Crossing the Red Sea and the Unsuitability of Amphibious Warfare Doctrines to Small Navies: The Israeli Case*

Professor Geoffrey Till (Corbett Centre for Maritime Policy Studies), *Small Navies. Are They Different?*

John Treacy (Mary Immaculate College, University of Limerick), *Administrative Difficulties During the Acquisition and Early Service of the Irish Naval Service Flower-Class Corvettes: Lessons for the Current Period of Defence Austerity*

Dr Christopher Tuck, (King's College London & the UK Joint Services Command and Staff College), *The Military Effectiveness of Small Navies: a case study of the Confederate States Navy*

Dr Carlos Alfaro Zaforteza, (King's College London), *Low-Cost Navy: Spanish Sea Power in the 1840s*

Bibliography

Adamson, Fiona B. 'Crossing Borders: International Migration and National Security' *International Security* 31, no. 1 (2006) pp. 165–199.

Adamson, Fiona B., Triadafilos Triadafilopoulos and Aristide R. Zolberge. 'The Limits of the Liberal State: Migration, Identity and Belonging in Europe', *Journal of Ethnic and Migration Studies* 37, no. 6, Special Issue (2011), pp. 843–859.

Agence France Presse. 'Singapore confirms talks with US over troops in Malacca Straits.' *Agence France Presse*, 5 April 2004.

Agence France Presse. 'Taiwan plans to buy four warships from the US: Report.' *Agence France Presse*, 22 April 2012.

Agence France Presse. 'Taiwan deploying more "carrier killers": report.' *Agence France Presse,* 14 May 2012.

Agence France Presse. 'Philippines May ask the U.S. for Air Surveillance.' *Agence France Presse,* 2 July 2012.

Agger, Ben. 'Critical theory, poststructuralism, postmodernism: Their sociological relevance.' *Annual Review of Sociology* 17 (1991) p. 109

Agrell, Wilhelm. *Bakom ubåtskrisen. Militär verksamhet, krigsplanläggning och diplomati i östersjöområdet.* Stockholm: Liber förlag, 1986.

Agrell, Wilhelm. *Fredens illusioner. Det svenska nationella försvarets nedgång och fall 1988–2009.* Malmö: Atlantis, 2010

Anderson, Bern. *By Sea and River: The Naval History of the Civil War.* New York: Da Capo, 1962.

Andersson, Per. 'Vad gjorde de här? Personliga reflexioner om den främmande undervattensverksamheten.' *Tidskrift i Sjöväsendet* nr 3 (2010). *Proceedings of the Royal Swedish Society for Naval Sciences*, no 3 (2010).

Andress, Jason, and Steve Winterfeld. *Cyber Warfare: Techniques, Tactics and Tools for Security Practitioners.* Waltham, MA: Syngress, 2011.

Andreas, Peter. 'Illicit Globalization: Myths, Misconceptions, and Historical Lessons.' *Political Science Quarterly* 126, no. 3 (Fall 2011) pp. 403–425.

Arbukle, James V. *Military Forces in 21st Century Peace Operations.* New York, NY: Routledge, 2006.

Aron, Raymond and Susan Tenenbaum. 'Reason, passion, and power in the thought of Clausewitz.' *Social Research* 39, no. 4 (Winter 1972) pp. 599–621

Associated Press. 'Military Base in Romania approved.' *Associated Press*, 7 December 2005.

Associated Press. 'Malaysia doesn't want outside help to patrol Malacca Straits, minister says.' *Associated Press Newswires*, 8 April 2004.

Australia, Government of Australia. 'Steven Smith, Minister for Defence – Speech to the Lowy Institute on the 2013 Defence White Paper.' http://bit.ly/1ibq

Baker, Richard. *Dry Ginger. The Biography of Sir Michael Le Fanu*. London: W.H. Allen, 1977.

Basescu, Traian. 'Black Sea cooperation is extremely important for Romanian economy.' *Hurriyet Daily News*, 26 June 2012.

Basescu, Traian. 'Tourism could be one of Romania's advantages in economic growth.' Permanent mission of Romania to the United Nations. *AGERPES*. http://bit.ly/1fjNz9o

Barber, Josh and Joe Sipos. 'The Future Maritime Security Environment.' in *The Future of Canada's Maritime Capabilities: the Issues, Challenges and Solutions in a New Security Environment*, by Robert H. Edwards, pp. 165–75. Halifax: Centre for Foreign Policy Studies, Dalhousie University, 2004.

Barta, Patrick. 'U.S., Vietnam in Exercises Amid Tensions With China.' *Wall Street Journal* (16 July 2011). http://on.wsj.com/18DVBbE

Bartra, Patrick and Vu Trong Khan. 'Clinton presses Vietnam on Human Rights Record.' *The Wall Street Journal* 10 July 2012. http://on.wsj.com/1c24UyD

Batty, Peter and Peter J. Parish. *The Divided Union: A Concise History of the American Civil War*. Stroud: The History Press, 2009 pp. 151–152.

BBC Radio 4. 'In Business.' *London: BBC Radio 4*, 11 October 2007.

BBC Monitoring Asia Pacific. 'Singapore seeks joint patrols of Malacca Straits, involving Japan.' *BBC Monitoring Asia Pacific*, 20 May 2004.

BBC Monitoring Asia Pacific. 'Maritime piracy declining in Malacca Straits – Malaysian daily.' *BBC Monitoring Asia Pacific*, 19 August 2009.

Becker, Markus. 'Monster Waves – Vessel Measures Record Ocean Swells'. *Der Spiegel*. 31 March 2006. http://bit.ly/18iXvAm

Beesley, Alan. 'The Negotiating Strategy of UNCLOS III: Developing and Developed Countries as Partners: A Pattern for Future Multilateral International Conferences?' *Law and Contemporary Problems* 46, no. 2 The Law of the Sea: Where Now? (Spring,1983) pp. 183–194.

Berteau, David J., Guy Ben-Ari, Joachim Hofbauer, Priscilla Hermann and Sneha Raghavan. *European Defense Trends 2012: Budgets, Regulatory Frameworks and the Industrial Base*. Washington DC: Center for Strategic & International Studies, 2012.

Black, Jeremy. *Naval Power: A History of Warfare and the Sea from 1500*. Hampshire: Palgrave Macmillan, 2009.

Bran, Mirel. 'Persistent drought in Romania threatens Danube's power.' *The Guardian Weekly*, 13 December 2011.

Brenthurst Foundation. 'Maritime development in Africa: An independent specialists' framework.' *Brenthurst Discussion Paper* 3 (2010).

Brzezinski, Zbigniew. *Strategic Vision. America and the Crisis of Global Power*. New York: Basic Books, 2010

Bulmer, Simon, and Martin Burch. 'Organizing for Europe: Whitehall, The British State and European Union.' *Public Administration* 76 (1998) pp. 621–608.

Buzan, Barry. *People, States and Fear: An Agenda for International Security Studies in the Post-Cold War Era.* Second edition. Hemel Hempstead: Harvester Wheatsheaf, 1991.

Buzan, Barry, and Ole Wæver. *Regions and Powers.* Cambridge: Cambridge University Press, 2003.

Buzan, Barry, Ole Wæver, and Jaap de Wilde. *Security: A New Framework for Analysis.* Boulder, CO: Lynne Rienner, 1998.

Camburu, Alexandru. 'Petrom and Exxon discover natural gas in Romania's Black Sea.' *Business & Macroeconomy*, 4 February 2012.

Campbell, R. Thomas. *Southern Thunder: Exploits of the Confederate States Navy*, Shippensburg, PA: Burd Street Press, 1996 pp. 139–140.

Campbell, R. Thomas. *Gray Thunder: Exploits of the Confederate States Navy.* Shippensburg, PA: Burd Street Press, 1996.

Calaprice, Alice (ed.). *The Expanded Quotable Einstein.* 2nd edn (Princeton NJ: Princeton University Press 2000)

Channel NewsAsia. 'S'pore committed to playing its part in international security operations.' *Channel NewsAsia*, 30 September 2010.

Channel News Asia. 'MINDEF signs contract with ST Engineering to construct naval vessels.' *Channel NewsAsia*, 30 January 2013.

China, Information Office of the State Council of the People's Republic of China. *China's National Defense in 2008.* (January 2009) p. 12.

Choong, William. 'US – It's not for us to police Malacca Straits.' *Straits Times*, 6 June 2004.

Chow, Jermyn. 'Singapore will reassess Gulf of Aden involvement.' *Straits Times*, 28 September 2012.

Chung, Eui-sung. *Ultramodern Conventional Submarine KSX As a Leverage for the Future Defense of the Korean Peninsula.* Seoul, 2007 pp. 141–142.

Churchill, Joan, Mary Sonnack, and Eric von Hippel. *Lead user project handbook: A practical guide for lead user project teams.* Cambridge MA: MIT Press, 2009.

Churchill, Winston. 'Speech by Winston Churchill to the House of the British Parliament.' *The Times of London.* 5 October 1938.

Clarke, Richard A., and Robert K. Knake. *Cyber Security: The next threat to national security and what to do about it.* New York: Ecco, 2010.

Commission on the Limits of the Continental Shelf. 'Statement by the Chairman of the Commission on the Limits of the Continental Shelf on the progress of work in the Commission Nineteenth session'. New York, 5 March–13 April 2007. http://bit.ly/1jzIzTa

Commission on the Limits of the Continental Shelf. 'Rockall Hatton Continental Shelf Submission to Commission on the Limits of the Continental Shelf (CLCS).' 2009a. http://bit.ly/1blS0LP

Commission on the Limits of the Continental Shelf. 'Rockall Hatton Continental Shelf Submission to Commission on the Limits of the Continental Shelf.' http://bit.ly/1blS0LP

Conrad, James Lee. *Rebel Reefers*: *The Organization and Midshipmen of the Confederate States Naval Academy*. Cambridge, MA: Da Capo Press, 2003.

Corbett, Julian. *Some Principles of Maritime Strategy*. London: Conway Maritime Press, 1972.

Coticchia, Fabrizio and Giampiero Giacomello, 'Helping Hands: Civil–Military Cooperation and Italy's Military Operation Abroad', *Small Wars and Insurgency* 20, no. 4 (2009).

Council of Europe. 'Frontex: Human Rights Responsibilities.' Parliamentary Assembly of the Council of Europe, 25 April 2013. http://bit.ly/18965Mq.

Council of Europe. 'Frontex: Human Rights Responsibilities', Parliamentary Assembly, Council of Europe, 8 April 2013, Doc. 13161. http://bit.ly/18965Mq.

Coutau-Bégarie, Hervé. *Traité de Stratégie*. Paris: Economica, 2002.

Cummins, Valerie. 'Opportunity in the face of adversity: The potential role of the military in contributing to Ireland's economic recovery with a focus on the Irish Naval Service.' *Defence Forces Review*, 2011: 7–12.

Cyrus, Allan. *Kungl Kustartilleriet 1902–1952. Vapenslagets historia utgiven av Kustartilleriinspektionen med anledning av Kungl Kustartilleriets femtioåriga tillvaro som självständigt vapenslag*. Stockholm: Viktor Petterson Bokindustrier AB,1952.

Dalsjö, Robert. *Life-Line Lost. The Rise and fall of 'Neutral' Sweden's Secret Reserve Option of Wartime Help from the West*. Stockholm: Santérus Press, 2006.

De Borchgrave, Arnaud. *Commentary: Alarm bells in the US,* Washington, *UPI*, May 29, 2012.

Defense Daily International. 'Singapore Naval Programs Could Face Problems.' *Defense Daily International*, 18 May 2001.

de Kay, James Tertius. *The Rebel Raiders: The Warship Alabama, British Treachery and the American Civil War*. Pimlico: London, 2003 pp. 230–232.

Der Derian, James and Michael J. Shapiro (eds), *International/intertextual relations: postmodern readings of world politics*. Lexington: Lexington Books, 1989.

Devetak, Richard. 'Postmodernism.' in *Theories of international relations*, by Andrew Linklater, Richard Devetak, Matt Paterson, Jacqui True Scott Burchill, pp. 179–209. Hampshire and London: Macmillan, 1996.

Dobbins, James, Seth G. Jones, Keith Crane, Christopher S. Chivvis, Andrew Radin, F. Stephen Larrabee et al. *Europe's Role in Nation-Building: From the Balkans to the Congo*. Santa Monica, CA: Rand, 2008.

Dougherty, Kevin. *Strangling the Confederacy: Coastal Operations in the American Civil War*. Havertown, PA: Casemate Publishers, 2009.

Douglas-Westwood. Marine Industry Global Market Aanlysis. 'Marine Foresight Series No.1' (2005). http://bit.ly/1c0Vas1

Durkin, Joseph T. *Confederate Navy Chief Stephen R. Mallory*. Tuscaloosa, AL: University of Alabama Press, 1954 p. 295.

Estonia, Eesti Kaitsevägi/Estonian Defence Forces, 'Estonian Long Term Defence Development Plan 2009 – 2018.' Talinn: Public Affairs Department of the Ministry of Defence, 2009.
European Union. 'Action Plan Atlantic Strategy'. http://bit.ly/1jAS4wd
European Union. *A Secure Europe in a Better World: European Security Strategy*. Brussels: European Union, 2003.
European Union. 'Speech of Commissioner Damanaki, Irish Presidency Dublin Castle.' 08 April 2013. http://bit.ly/1jAS6UF
European Union. 'Treaty of Lisbon Amending the Treaty on European Union and the Treaty establishing the European Community, signed at Lisbon, 13 December 2007'. *Official Journal of the European Union* C306 Vol 50. http://bit.ly/1aMnYES
Faist, Thomas. 'The Migration-Security Nexus.: International Migration and Security before and after 9/11.' *Willy Brandt Series of Working Papers in International Migration and Ethnic Relations*. 4, no. 03 (2004). Malmö: School of International Migration and Ethnic Relations, Malmö University.
Fältström, Herman and Olof Santesson (eds.). *På spaning efter det okända. Bilder från det kalla krigets ubåtsjakt*. Stockholm: National Swedish Defence College, Royal Swedish Academy of War Sciences, Royal Swedish Society for Naval Sciences, 2010.
Felgenhauer, Pavel. 'Moscow sees military threats from all directions.' *Eurasia Daily Monitor* 9 No. 58 22 March 2012.
Fellman, Sam. 'World Crises Challenge U.S. Navy Deployments.' *DefenseNews International*, 1 October 2012.
Fischer-Lescano, Andreas, Tillmann Löhr and Timo Tohidipur. 'Border Controls at Sea: Requirements under International Human Rights and Refugee Law.' *International Journal of Refugee Law* 21, no 2 (2009) pp. 256–296.
Foreman, Amanda. *A World on Fire*. London: Allen Lane, 2010.
Forslund, Johan (ed.). *Pansarbåtsinsamlingen 100 år. Symposium fredagen 9 november 2012*. Stockholm, 2012.
Forster, Andreas. *Armed Forces and Society in Europe*. Basingstoke, UK: Palgrave, 2006.
Forster, Stig and Jorg Nagler. *On the Road to Total War: The American Civil War and the German Wars of Unification, 1861–1871*. Cambridge: Cambridge University Press, 1997.
France Assemblée Nationale. *Avis n°1867 sur le projet de loi de finance pour* 2005. Paris: Commission de la défense nationale et des forces armées, 2004.
Franke, Nickolaus, and Eric von Hippel. 'Satisfying heterogeneous user needs via innovatoin toolkits: The case of Apache security software.' *Research Policy* 32 (2003) pp. 1199–215.
Franke, Nikolaus, and Frank Piller. 'Value creation by toolkits for user innovation and design: the case of the watch market.' *Journal of Product Innovation* 21, no. 6 (2004) pp. 401–15.
Fraser, Douglas. *Jobs for the Clyde Boys*. 19 March 2013. http://bbc.in/18yP3HM

Frazier, Emily. *Population Media Centre – Annual Report 2010–2011.* http://bit.ly/1gbbpnN
Friedman, Norman. *Seapower as Strategy. Navies and National Interests.* Annapolis, MD: Naval Institute Press, 2001.
Frunzaxverde, Sorin. 'Strategic defence in Romania.' *Defence Management Journal*, 36. http://bit.ly/197N0dy
Gallagher, Gary W. *The Confederate War: How Popular Will, Nationalism, and Military Strategy Could Not Stave Off Defeat.* Cambridge, MA: Harvard University Press, 1997, p. 115.
Gallagher, Tom. *Modern Romania.* New York: New York University Press, 2008.
Gallagher, Tom. *Romania and the European Union, How the weak vanquished the strong.* Basingstoke: Palgrave Macmillan 2009 pp. 132–151.
Gänzle, Stefan and Sens, Allen. *The Changing Politics of European Security: Europe Alone?* Basingstoke, UK: Palgrave, 2007.
Germany, Inspekteur der Marine, *Zielvereinbarung für die Deutsche Marine.* Bonn: Bundesmarine, 2003.
Germany, Inspekteur der Marine, *Transformation – Marine Auf Kurs!* Bonn: Bundesmarine, 2004.
Germany: Federal Ministry of Defence, *White Paper 2006 on German Security Policy and the Future of the Bundeswehr.* Berlin, 2006.
Germond, Basil. 'The European Union at the Horn of Africa: The Contribution of Critical Geopolitics to Piracy Studies.' *Global Policy* 4, no. 1 (2013) pp. 80–85.
Germond, Basil. 'Venus Has Learned Geopolitics: The European Union's Frontier and Transatlantic Relations.' in *The Routledge Handbook of Transatlantic Security*, by Jussi Hanhimäki, Georges-Henri Soutou and Basil Germond, pp. 206–17. Routledge: London and New York.
Germond, Basil. *Les Forces navales européennes dans la période post-guerre froide.* Paris: L'Harmattan, 2008.
Gheorghe, Constantin. 'Force Restructuring.' in *Romanian Military Reform and NATO Integration*, Larry L. Watts, The Centre for Romanian Studies, UK pp. 121–134.
Giddens, Anthony. *The Constitution of Society: Outline of the theory of structuration.* Cambridge: Polity, 1984.
Giegerich, Bastian. *European Crisis Management: Connecting Ambition and Reality.* London: The International Institute for Strategic Studies, Adelphi Paper 397: 2008.
Glasius, Marlies and Mary Kaldor, eds. *A Human Security Doctrine for Europe: Project, Principles, Practicalities.* London, UK, and New York, NY: Routledge, 2006.
Global Insider. 'Vietnam Seeks U.S equipment to close military gaps.' The Editors, *Global Insider,* 6 July 2012.
Goldrick, James and Jack McCaffrie. *Navies of South-East Asia: A Comparative Study.* London and New York: Routledge 2013 pp. 11–13.

Graham, Eric J. *Clydebuilt: The Blockade Runners, Cruisers and Armoured Rams of the American Civil War*. Edinburgh: Birlinn, 2006 p. 19.

Gray, Colin S. *The Leverage of Sea Power: The Strategic Advantages of Navies in War.* New York: The Free Press (1992).

Gray, Colin S. *Modern Strategy*. Oxford: Oxford University Press, 1999 p. 17.

Gray, Colin S. *The Sheriff: America's Defense of the New World Order*. Lexington, KY: University Press of Kentucky, 2004 p. 107.

Greene, Jack and Alessandro Massignani. *Ironclads at War: The Origin and Development of the Armored Warship, 1854–1891*. Conshohocken, PA: Combined Publishing, 1998 p. 46.

Griffin Jones, John. *Mississippi Writers Talking*. Jackson: University Press of Mississippi, 1982 p. 66.

Grotius, Hugo. *The Freedom of the Seas: or the Right Which Belongs to the Dutch to Take Part in the East Indian Trade*. (1609). Translated from Latin by Ralph van Deman Magoffin and edited with an introduction by James Brown Scott, New York: Oxford University Press, 1916.

Grove, Eric. *The Future of Sea Power*. Annapolis, MD: Naval Institute Press: Annapolis, 1990.

Gupta, J., Termeer, C., Klostermann, J., Meijerink, S., van den Brink, M., Jong, P., Nooteboom, S., Bergsma, E., (2010) The Adaptive Capacity Wheel: a method to assess the inherent characteristics of institutions to enable the adaptive capacity of society *Environmental Science & Policy* 13 no. 6 (2010) pp. 459-471

Gustafsson, Bengt. *Sanningen om ubåtsfrågan. Ett försök till analys.* Stockholm: National Swedish Defence College, Royal Swedish Academy of War Sciences, Royal Swedish Society for Naval Sciences, Stockholm, 2010.

Hables Gray, Chris. *Postmodern War: the new politics of conflict.* New York: The Guildford Press, 1997.

Haines, Steve. 'Third World Navies, Myths and Realities.' *Naval Forces*, April 1988.

Hall, Peter A., and Rosemary C.R. Taylor. 'Political Science and the Three New Institutionalisms.' *Political Studies* 44, no. 5 (1996) pp. 936–57.

Hand, Marcus. 'Indonesia, Malaysia pull back from joint patrols of Malacca Strait,' *Lloyd's List*, 5 July 2004.

Hattaway, Herman and Archer Jones. *How the North Won: A Military History of the Civil War*. Urbana: University of Illinois Press, 1991 p. 129.

Haydon, Peter T. 'Naval Diplomacy: Is it Relevant in the 21st Century?' in *The Politics of Maritime Power*, by Andrew T.H. Tan, pp.62–79. London: Routledge, 2007.

Hearn, Chester G. *The Capture of New Orleans, 1862.* Baton Rouge: Louisiana State University Press, 1995: pp. 188, 259.

HELCOM CHEMU. *Report on Chemical Munitions Dumped in the Baltic Sea.* Danish Environment Protection Agency, 1994.

Heuer, Richards J, and Randolph H. Pherson. *Structured Analytic Techniques for Intelligence Analysis.* Washington DC: CQ Press, 2010.

Hickey, Captain (N) Laurence M.'Enhancing the Naval Mandate for Law Enforcement: Hot Pursuit or Hot Potato?' *Canadian Military Journal* 7, no. 1 (2006) pp. 41–48.

Hill, J.R. *Maritime Strategy for Medium Powers.* Annapolis MD: Naval Institute Press, 1986.

Hisrich, Robert D. and Michael P. Peters. *Entrepreneurship.* New York: McGraw Hill, 2002.

Holden Reid, Brian. *The American Civil War.* London: Cassell, 1999.

Holmström, Mikael. *Den Dolda Alliansen. Sveriges hemliga NATO-förbindelser.* Stockholm: Bokförlaget Atlantis, 2011.

Hopkins, Nick. 'Cuts force Royal Navy to drop Somalia piracy patrol.' *The Guardian*, 8 May 2012. http://bit.ly/Jap6IB

Human Rights Watch. *The EU's Dirty Hands. Frontex Involvement in Ill-Treatment of Migrant Detainees in Greece.* Human Rights Watch, September 2011.

Hyllander, Jan. *Maritim samverkan. SOU 2012.* Stockholm: Fritzes, 2012 p. 48.

IMERC. *Irish Maritime Energy Resource Cluster Strategy 2011–2016.* Cork: IMERC, 2011.

IMO, UNHCR and International Chamber of Shipping. *Rescue at Sea: A Guide to Principles and Practice as Applied to Migrants and Refugees.* 2006. http://bit.ly/199A7Dj

International Institute of Strategic Studies. *The Military Balance 1975–1976.* London: International Institute of Strategic Studies, 1975.

International Institute of Strategic Studies. *The Military Balance 1995–1996* London: International Institute of Strategic Studies, 1995.

International Institute for Strategic Studies. *The Military Balance 2013.* London: International Institute of Strategic Studies, 2013.

International Maritime Organization (IMO). 'International Convention on Maritime Search and Rescue (SAR)', adopted 7 April 1979. http://bit.ly/Isqd6g

International Maritime Organization (IMO). 'Global Maritime Search and Rescue Areas', available from http://bit.ly/1glc0TU

Ireland, Anglo Irish Treaty (1921) Treaty of Independence http://bit.ly/1fCuxh9

Ireland, Department of Defence and Defence Forces, *Strategy Statement 2011–2014.* Newbridge: Department of Defence and Defence Forces, 2011.

Ireland, Department of Defence and Defence Forces. *Value for money review – Naval service vessel maintenance.* Newbridge: Department of Defence and Defence Forces, 2009. http://bit.ly/19VLwTp

Ireland, Department of the Taoiseach. *Building Ireland's smart economy: A framework for sustainable economic renewal.*Dublin: The Stationery Office, 2008.

Ireland, Government of Ireland. *Our Ocean Wealth. Towards and Integrated Marine Plan for Ireland.* 2012. http://bit.ly/1fCuxxm

Ireland, Department of Defence. *White Paper on Defence 2000–2010*. Dublin: The Stationery Office.

Irish Maritime and Energy Resource Cluster. *IMERC Strategy 2011–2016.* http://bit.ly/1hd4wFw

IRGA. 'India, Vietnam: Testing China's Patience.' *IRGA* 26 September 2011. http://bit.ly/1cpqlvV

Ismay, General Lord. *The Memoirs of Lord Ismay*. London: Heinemann, 1960.

Italy, Marina Militare Italiana. *Rapporto 2003.*Roma: Ministero della Difesa, 2004.

ITAR-TASS News Agency. 'Romanian interested in constructive relations with Russia.' *ITAR-TASS News Agency*, 11 August 2011.

Jackson, Aaron P. 'Keystone Doctrine Development in Five Commonwealth Navies: A Comparative Perspective.' *Papers in Australian Maritime Affairs* 33 (2010).

Jane's Defence Weekly. 'Republic of Singapore Navy: Chief of Navy Rear Admiral Ronnie Tay.' *Jane's Defence Weekly* 26 April 2007.

Jane's Defence Weekly. 'Jyri Hakamies, Finland's Minister of Defence, Interview.' *Jane's Defence Weekly,* 10 November 2010.

Jane's Defence Weekly. 'Briefing: Punching above its weight.' *Jane's Defence Weekly* 9 February 2012.

Jane's Intelligence Weekly. 'Romania to slash public sector spending for IMF deal.' *Jane's Intelligence Weekly*, 7 May 2010.

Jane's Intelligence Weekly, 'Ukraine calls for consultations with US over missile defence plans in Romania.' *Jane's Intelligence Weekly*, 20 May 2011.

Jane's Navy International. 'Singapore Navy passes milestone en route to area defence capability.' *Jane's Navy International*, 16 April 2008.

Jane's Navy International. 'Interview: Rear-Admiral Chew Men Leong, Chief of Navy, Republic of Singapore Navy.' *Jane's Navy International*, 23 April 2009.

Jane's Navy International. 'Romania's nascent naval helicopter force trains with US navy.' *Jane's Navy International*, 4 August 2011.

Jane's Underwater Warfare Systems. 'Romania's submarine forces.' *Jane's Underwater Warfare Systems*, 12 May 2011.

Jones, Archer. *Civil War Command and Strategy: The Process of Victory and Defeat*. New York, NY: The Free Press, 1992.

Joppke, Christian. 'Why Liberal States Accept Unwanted Immigration,' *World Politics* 50, no. 2 (1998): 266–93 (reprinted in:. *International Migration*, by Andrew Geddes. *London*: SAGE, 2011).

Joppke, Christian. 'Transformation of immigrant integration: civic integration and antidiscrimination in the Netherlands, France and Germany', *World Politics*, 59, no. 2 (2007a) pp. 243–73.

Joppke, Christian. 'Beyond national models: civic integration policies for immigrants in Western Europe.' *West European Politics*, 30, no. 1 (2007b) pp. 1–22.

Joppke, Christian. *Citizenship and Immigration*. Cambridge: Polity Press, 2010.

Jung, Sung-ki, 'Navy to focus on littoral warfare,' *Korea Times*, 9 September 2010, http://bit.ly/19Zvh7E

Kaldory, May and Andrew Salmon. 'Military Force and European Strategy.' *Survival*, 48, no. 1 (2006) pp. 19–34.

Kalmoukis, Antonios. 'Piracy in European Waters – A Novelty?' *Dalimbassieris Maritime*, 8 February 2012. http://bit.ly/IFk9am

Kalu, Kalu. 'Postmodern Citizenship, Logic and Praxis in State and Identity'. in *Citizenship, A Reality Far From Ideal*, by Andrew Kakabadse, Nada Kakabadse and Kalu Kalu. Basingstoke and London: Palgrave Macmillan, October 2009.

Karniol, Robert, 'Country briefing: Singapore – Diplomacy teams up with deterrence.' *Jane's Defence Weekly*, 20 April 1997.

Kearns Goodwin, Doris. *Team of Rivals: The Political Genius of Abraham Lincoln*. London: Penguin, 2009.

Keymer, Eleanor. *Jane's World Navies Issue Five May 2010* Jane's Information Group:, Surrey 2010, p. 278

Killhan, Edward L. *The Nordic Way: A Path to Baltic Equilibrium*. Washington DC: The Compass Press, 1993.

Kim, Samuel S. 'Korea and Globalization: A Framework for Analysis', in *Korea's Globalization*, by Samuel S. Kim, pp.1–28. Cambridge: Cambridge University Press, 2000.

Kirk, Donald. 'Seoul and Hanoi Eye a Glowing Partnership.' *Asia Times Online*, 10 November 2011. http://bit.ly/1c6rdaI

Klepp, Silja. 'A Contested Asylum System: The European Union between Refugee Protection and Border Control in the Mediterranean Sea.' *European Journal of Migration and Law* 12 (2010) pp. 1–21

Klingner, Bruce. *South Korea: Taking the Right Steps Towards Defence Reform*. Washington DC: The Heritage Foundation, 2011.

Koh, Swee Lean Collin. *'Seeking Balance: Force Projection, Confidence Building and the Republic of Singapore Navy.'* *Naval War College Review* 65, No. 1 (Winter 2012) pp. 75–92.

Krause, Keith and Michael C. Williams. 'Broadening the Agenda of Security Studies: Politics and Methods.' *Mershon International Studies Review* 40, no. 2 (1996) pp. 229–54.

Kuala Lumpur Security Review. 'Singapore Launched Fleet Support Vessel.' *Kuala Lumpur Security Review*, 8 June 2009.

Kuzio, Taras. 'Romanian-Ukrainian Espionage scandal exacerbates already poor relations.' *Eurasia Daily Monitor* 6, No. 51, 17 March 2009.

Lagerberg, Sven. *Kustinvasion – Kustartilleri. Årsberättelse i Kungl Krigsvetenskapsakademien avd. II den 17 februari 1959*. KkrVAHT nr 4/2003. Proceedings of the Royal Swedish Academy of War Sciences, Stockholm, 2003.

Landahl, Jan and Thomas Dawidowski. *Bemanningen av marinens och flygvapnets stående insatsförband*. Riksrevisionens rapport, 2012. Report by the National Audit Office, Stockholm 2012.

Lavinia Stan. 'Romania: in the shadow of the past.' in *Central and South East European Politics since 1989*, by Sabrina P. Ramet. Cambridge: Cambridge University Press, 2010 pp. 379–400.

Ledwidge, Frank. *Losing Small Wars: British Military Failure in Iraq and Afghanistan.* Yale: Yale University Press, 2011.

Lee, Seo-hang. 'Issues of Oceanic Navy and Complement of Naval Force after Warship Cheonan Incident.' *A Sejong Commentary* No.181, Seoul, 2010.

Leiev-Sawyer, Clive. 'Russia's message to Romania.' *The Sofia Echo*, 20 August 2010.

Lester, Richard I. *Confederate Purchasing and Finance in Great Britain.* Charlottesville, VA: University of Virginia Press, 1975 pp. 130–131.

Li, Nan and Christopher Weuve. 'China's Aircraft Carrier Ambitions: An Update.' *Naval War College Review*, Winter 2010 p. 15. http://bit.ly/1gemYuk

Lindberg, Michael S. *Geographical Impact on Coastal Defence Navies.* Basingstoke: Macmillan, 1998

Lindley-French, Julian and Wouter van Straten. 'Exploiting the Value of Small Navies: The Experience of the Royal Netherlands Navy.' *The RUSI Journal*, 153, no. 6 (2008) pp. 66–69.

Lithuania, Ministry of National Defence. 'White Paper: Lithuanian Defence Policy.' *Vilnius: Ministry of National Defence*, 2006: UDK 355(474.5) Vh-05.

LKBN ANTARA.'RI Navy rejects US presence in Malacca Straits.' *LKBN ANTARA*, 27 October 2005.

Lloyd's List. 'Littoral states "cannot protect Malacca Strait".' *Lloyd's List*, 27 April 2004.

Long, Viet. "China's Strategy of Widening Disputed Areas in East Sea." Quan Doi Nhan Dan Online. In OSC-SEP20110708178001, Hanoi (18 June 2011).

Lonsdale, David. 'Strategy.' in *Understanding Modern Warfare*, by David Jordan et al. Cambridge: Cambridge University Press, 2008 pp. 32–33.

Lungu, Serban. 'Joint Defence Planning.' in *Romanian Military Reform and NATO Integration*, by Larry L. Watts, The Centre for Romanian Studies, UK pp. 107–119.

Luraghi, Raimondo. *A History of the Confederate Navy.* London: Chatham Publishing, 1996.

Lyotard, Jean Francis. *The postmodern condition: A report on knowledge.* Manchester: Manchester University Press, 1984.

Maritime Analysis Operations Centre (Narcotics). *Maritime Analysis Operations Centre Narcotics Statistics.* 2013. http://bit.ly/1l9330y

McDevitt, Michael. 'PLA Naval exercises with International Partners.' in *Learning by Doing: The PLA Trains at Home and Abroad*, by R. Kamphausen, D. Lai, T. Tanner. Carlisle, PA: Strategic Studies Institute, US Army War College p. 102.

McDevitt, Michael and Frederic Vellucci. 'The Evolution of the People's Liberation Army Navy: the twin missions of area-denial and peacetime operations.' in *Sea*

Power and the Asia-Pacific: The Triumph of Neptune? by Geoffrey Till and P. C. Bratton. Oxon: Routledge, 2012.

McDonagh, Marese. 'Uproar after Smith denies axe for Navy and Air Corps.' *Independent* 10 August 1999. http://bit.ly/1jI1eKd

McPherson, James M. 'American Victory, American Defeat.' in *Why the Confederacy Lost*, by Gabor S. Boritt. Oxford: Oxford University Press, 1992 pp. 17–42.

Magnette, Paul. *Citizenship: The History of an Idea*. Essex: ECPR Press, 2005.

Mahadzir, Dzirhan. 'Interview: Ng Eng Hen, Singaporean Minister of Defence.' *Jane's Defence Weekly*, 31 January 2012.

Mahan, Alfred T. *The influence of sea power upon history: 1660–1783*. Fifth edition. New York: Dover Publications, 1987.

Maior, Gheorghe Cristian. 'Personnel Management and Reconversion.' in *Romanian Military Reform and NATO Integration*, by Larry L. Watts, The Centre for Romanian Studies, UK pp. 57–81.

Major, George Christian and Sebastian Huluban. 'From Hardware to Software Reforms in Romania's Civil–Military Relations.' *Baltic Defence Review* 8, No. 2 (2002) pp. 103–123.

Maritime Bulletin. 'Danube piracy a growing concern for regional shipping.' *Maritime Bulletin*, 20 January 2012.

Marolda, Edward J. Ready *Seapower: A History of the US Seventh Fleet*. Washington DC: Naval History and Heritage Command, Department of the Navy, 2012 pp. 40–52.

Mårtensson, Evorn, *Vart är marinen på väg? Behov av en ny plan*. Tidskrift i Sjöväsendet nr 1/2013. Stockholm: Royal Swedish Society for Naval Sciences, 2013.

Matache, Georghe. 'The New Procurement Concept.' in *Romanian Military Reform and NATO Integration*, by Larry L. Watts. The Centre for Romanian Studies, UK, 2002:

Maull, Hanns W. 'Germany and Japan: the New Civilian Powers.' *Foreign Affairs* 69, no. 5 (1990): pp. 91–106.

Mediafax. 'Romania urges Moldova closer to NATO and Russia to withdraw troops from Transnistria.' *Mediafax*, 10 October 2009.

Merlingen, Michael and Ostrauskaite Rosa. *European Union Peacebuilding and Policing*. London, UK: Routledge, 2006.

Metz, Steven. *Armed Conflict in the 21st Century: The Information Revolution and Post-Modern Warfare*. Carlisle, Penn: Strategic Studies Institute, US Army War College, 2000.

Micewski, Edwin R. 'Leadership responsibility in postmodern armed forces.' in *Civil–Military Aspects of Military Ethics (Volume 2): (Military) Leadership and Responsibility in the Postmodern Age*, by Edwin R. Micewski and Dietmar Pfarr, 5–12. Vienna: National Defense Academy, 2005.

Miller Beebe, Sarah, and Randolph H. Pherson. *Cases in Intelligence Analysis: Structured Analytic Techniques in Action*. Washington DC: CQ Press, 2012.

Minnick, Wendell and Paul Kallender-Umezu. 'Open Asian Market: Vessels, UAVs Sought for Coastal Security.' *DefenseNews International*, 14 January 2013.

Miranda, Army Sgt Mark. 'Romanian Forces End Mission in Iraq.' *American Forces Press Service*, US Department of Defence. http://1.usa.gov/1bcYcFE

Moon, Chung-in, 'South Korea Recasting Security Paradigms' in *Asian Security Practice: Material and Ideational Influences*, Muthiah Alagappa (ed.), Stanford: 1998. pp. 264–287

Morris, M.A. *Expansion of Third World Navies*. London: Macmillan, 1987.

Morris, Michael A. *Expansion of the Third World Navies*. London: The Macmillan Press, 1987.

Moskos, Charles C., John Allen Williams and David R. Segal, eds. *The Postmodern Military: Armed forces after the Cold War*. New York: Oxford University Press, 1999.

Mullen, Admiral Michael. 'What I Believe: Eight Tenets That Guide My Vision for the 21st Century Navy.' *US Naval Institute Proceedings* 132, no. 1 (2006), online version.

Mulqueen, Michael. *Re-evaluating Irish national security: affordable threats?* Manchester: Manchester University Press, 2009.

Mulqueen, Michael, and Terry Warburton. 'Breaking with tradition: Remodelling naval strategic thinking and outcomes using an open innovation approach.' *Administration* 60, no. 4 (2013): 89.

Mulvenon, James and David Finkelstein (ed.). China's Revolution in Doctrinal Affairs: Emerging Trends in the Operational Art of the PLA, *Conference Report*. Washington DC: Finkelstein, 2005 p 12.

Mussington, David and John Sislin. 'Defining Destabilizing Arms Acquisitions.' *Jane's Intelligence Review* 17, No. 2 (February 1995) pp. 88–90.

Nanto, Dick K. *Economics and National Security: Issues and Implications for U.S. Policy*. CRS Report for Congress, Washington DC: Congressional Research Service, 2011.

Natural Gas Europe. 'Romanian President: Black Sea Deep-water well may produce by 2015.' *Natural Gas Europe*, 6 March 2012.

Natural Gas Europe. 'Romania looks to natural gas to fuel energy needs.' *Natural Gas Europe*, 10 March 2012.

North Atlantic Treaty Organisation. 'The Alliance's Strategic Concept.' approved by the Heads of State and Government participating in the meeting of the North Atlantic Council in Washington, DC, April 23–24 1999, Press release. NAC-S 99, no. 65, 24 April 1999.

Neal, Andrew W. 'Securitization and Risk at the EU Border: The Origins of FRONTEX.' *Journal of Common Market Studies*. 47, no. 2 (2009) pp. 333–56.

Nelson, Daniel N. 'Romanian Security.' in *Romania since 1991 Politics, Economic and Society*, by Henry F. Carey. Oxford: Lexington Books, 2000 pp. 461–483.

Nelson, Larry E. *Bullets, Ballots, and Rhetoric: Confederate Policy for the United States Presidential Contest of 1864*. University of Alabama Press, 1980 p. 27.

New Straits Times. 'Local Firms Can Show their Power.' *New Straits Times*, 3 December 2009.
New Straits Times. 'Getting into its Stride.' *New Straits Times* 3 December2009.
Newslink Romania. 'Ukraine criticises US plans to deploy missiles in Romania.' *Newslink Romania*, 11 October 2011.
Ng, Eng Hen, Minister for Defence of Singapore. 'Emerging Risks to Global and Asia-Pacific Security.' *Military Technology* 37, No. 3 (2013) 27.
Norway, Forsvarsdepartementet, *The Further Modernisation of the Norwegian Armed Forces 2005–2008*, Proposition to Parliament No. 42. Oslo, 2004.
Ó Confhaola, Padhraic. *The Naval Forces of the Irish State, 1922–1977*. PhD thesis. Maynooth: National University of Ireland, Maynooth, 2009.
O'Dwyer, Gerard. 'Norway Eyes Next-Gen Submarine Acquisition.' *DefenseNews International*, 18 February 2013.
OSW Centre for European Studies. 'Ukraine loses the dispute over Snake Island to Romania.' *OSW Centre for Eastern Studies*, 3 February 2009.
Ó Tuathail, Gearoíd and John Agnew, 'Geopolitics and discourse: practical geopolitical reasoning in American foreign policy.' *Political Geography* 11, no. 2 (1992) pp. 190–204.
Official Records of the Union and Confederate Navies in the War of Rebellion (ORN), Series II, Vol. 2, 69.
Olsen, Jesper P., and James P. March. 'Institutional Perspectives on Political Institutions.' *Governance: An International Journal of Policy and Administration* 9, no. 3 (1996) pp. 247–64.
Olsen, S., J. Sutinen, L. Juda, M.Hennessey, T. Grigalunas, *A Handbook On Governance and Socioeconomics of Large Marine Ecosystems*, Coastal Resources Centre, University of Rhode Island 2006.
Opall-Rome, Barbara. 'Israel Eyes S. Korean OPVs for EEZ-Defense.' *DefenseNews International*, 14 January 2013.
Owens, Admiral William. 'America must start treating China as a friend.' *Financial Times*, 17 November 2009.
O'Reilly, Charles and Michael Tushman. 'Ambidexterity as a Dynamic Capability: Resolving the Innovator's Dilemma. *Research in Organizational Behaviour* 28 (2008): 185–206.
Park, Chang Kwon, 'The Long Term Impacts of Cheonan Sinking on the Alliance Naval Concepts and Operations' Paper prepared for the 5th Annual KIMS-CNA Conference 1–2 December 2011.
Pherson, Randolph H., and Katherine Hibbs Pherson. *Critical Thinking for Strategic Intelligence*. Washington DC: CQ Press, 2012.
Pinalez, Juan. 'Vietnam Representatives Visit USS George Washington.' *Navy News Service. NNS110309-12*, 9 March 2011. http://1.usa.gov/19EeWdk
Poku, Nana K. and David T. Graham (eds). *Redefining Security: Population Movements and National Security*, Westport, CT and London: Praeger, 1998.

Popescu, General Mihail. 'Military Interoperability with NATO.' in *Romanian Military Reform and NATO Integration*, by Larry L. Watts. The Centre for Romanian Studies, UK, 2002 pp. 151–167.

Popovici, Vlad. 'The Hidden Benefits of Southeast European Pipeline Politics.' *Balkanalysis.com,* 21 September 2010. http://bit.ly/19hkEl0

Price Waterhouse. *Report to the Steering Group on the Review of the Irish Naval Service and Air Corps*. Dublin: The Stationery Office, 1998.

Ragan, Mark K. *Submarine Warfare in the Civil War*, Cambridge, MA: Da Capo, 2002 p. 130.

Reed, Rowena. *Combined Operations in the Civil War*. Lincoln: University of Nebraska Press, 1993 pp. 133–224.

Regeringskansliet/Ministry of Defence Sweden. 'A functional defence: Government Bill on the future focus of defence.' Fact sheet summarising Bill 2008/09: 140. Stockholm, 2009.

Richard, John. S. 'The Learning Army, Approaching the 21st Century as a Learning Organization'. *USAWC Strategy Research Project*. Carlisle, PA: U.S. Army War College, 1997.

Richardson, Doug. 'Romania and Turkey agree to ABM deployments.' *Jane's Missiles and Rockets*, 26 September 2011.

Rijpma, J.J. 'Frontex: Successful Blame Shifting of the Member States?' Analysis of the Real Insituto El Cano. 69 (2010)

Robb-Webb, Jon. 'Light Two Lanterns the British are Coming by Sea: Royal Navy Participation in the Pacific 1944–45.' in *British Naval Strategy East of Suez, 1900–2000*, by Greg Kennedy. London: Frank Cass, 2005.

Robb-Webb, Jon. 'Anglo-American Naval Intelligence Co-Operation in the Pacific 1944–45.' *Intelligence and National Security* 25, no. 5, (2007) pp. 767–786.

Robb-Webb, Jon. *The British Pacific Fleet Experience and Legacy 1944–50*. Farnham: Ashgate 2013.

Roehrig, Terence. 'South Korea-China maritime disputes: toward a solution.' *East Asia Forum*, 27 November 2012. http://bit.ly/18DUQ2m

Ronzitti, Natalino. *Diritto Internazionale dei Conflitti Armati*. Torino: Giappichelli, 2006.

Romanian Ministry of Foreign Affairs. 'Priorities of Romanian Diplomacy in 2011.' Bucharest: Romania Ministry of Foreign Affairs. www.mae.ro/en/node/2147

Romanian Ministry of National Defence. 'Romanian Defence, 2004–2009, Five years of NATO membership.' Bucharest: Romanian Ministry of National Defence: 27.

Romanian Ministry of National Defence, Information and Public Relations Directorate. 'Romania's participation with forces in NATO operation to enforce arms embargo against Libya.' *Bucharest: Ministry of National Defence, Information and Public Relations Directorate*.

Romanian National News Agency. 'Ceremony is held as Regele Ferdinand frigate leaves on mission.' *Romanian National News Agency AGERPRES*, Permanent Mission of Romania to the United Nations. http://bit.ly/1gRBTxF

Rose, Lisle A. *Power at Sea Vol. 3: A Violent Peace 1946–2006*. Columbia: University of Missouri Press, 2007.

Rozoff, Rick. 'Romania: U.S. Escalates Missile Brinkmanship Against Russia.' *Global Research*, 1 July 2012.

Rudolph, Christopher. 'Sovereignty and Territorial Borders in a Global Age.' *International Studies Review*, 7 (2005) pp. 1–20.

Sabine, C. L., R.A. Feely, N. Gruber, R.M. Key, K. Lee, J.L. Bullister, R. Wanninkhof, C.S. Wong, D.W.R. Wallace, B. Tilbrook, F.J. Millero, T.H. Peng, A. Kozyr, T. Ono, A.F. Rios, 'The oceanic sink for anthropogenic CO2.' *Science* 305 pp.367–371 (2004).

Salmon, Trevor and Alistair J. K. Shepherd. *Toward a European Army: A Military Power in the Making?* Boulder, CO: Lynne Rienner, 2003.

Saunders, Stephen. *Jane's Fighting Ships 2012–2013*. Surrey: Jane's Information Group, 2010

Sava, Ionel Nicu. 'Romania-Russian Relations in the context of Euro-Atlantic integration process.' *Conflict Studies Research Centre*, September 2011.

Scharf, J. Thomas. *History of the Confederate States Navy*. Avenel, NJ: Gramercy, 1996.

Schivelbusch, Wolfgang. *The Culture of Defeat: On National Trauma, Mourning, and Recovery.* reprint St Martin's Press: 2004

Selden, Mark. 'Small Islets, Enduring Conflict: Dokdo, Korea–Japan Colonial Legacy and the United States.' *The Asia-Pacific Journal: Japan Focus*. http://bit.ly/1cqKbuB Shafir, Michael. 'Analysis: Serpents Island, Bystraya Canal, and Ukrainian-Romanian Relations.' *RFE/RL* 24 Aug 2004.

Sheehan, James J. *Where Have all the Soldiers Gone? The Transformation of Modern Europe*. Boston, NJ, and New York, NY: Houghton Mifflin, 2008.

Siegel, Matt. 'Ship of Asylum Seekers Capsizes off the Coast of Java', *The New York Times (global edition)*, 28 June 2012 p. 3.

Siggins, Lorna. *Once Upon a Time in the West.* Transworld Ireland, 2010

Simson, J.W. Naval *Strategies of the Civil War: Confederate Innovation and Federal Opportunism*. Nashville, TN: Cumberland House, 2001 p. 187.

Singapore, Ministry of Defence. Defending Singapore in the 21st Century. Singapore: January 2000.

Singapore, Ministry of Defence. Speech by Chief of Navy, RADM Lui Tuck Yew at the Opening of the Naval Platform Technology Seminar 2001 http://bit.ly/1fYD6D4 10 May 2001.

Singapore, Ministry of Defence. Keynote Address by Mr Peter Ho, Permanent Secretary (Defence), at the Naval Platform Technology Seminar 2003 11 November 2003. http://bit.ly/1hsDKcm

Singapore, Ministry of Defence. Speech by Chief of Navy, Rear-Admiral Ronnie Tay, at the Opening Ceremony of Changi Naval Base, 21 May 2004.

Singapore, Ministry of Defence. 'Minister visits RSN ship deployed to Gulf,' 25 February 2005.

Singapore, Ministry of Defence. Speech by Dr Ng Eng Hen, Minister for Manpower and Second Minister for Defence, for the Launching Ceremony of RSS Supreme, 9 May 2006. http://bit.ly/1dKPvdB

Singapore, Ministry of Defence. Speech by Mr Teo Chee Hean, Minister of Defence, at Ground-Breaking Ceremony of the Changi Command and Control Centre, 27 March 2007 http://bit.ly/1bDem1e.

Singapore, Ministry of Defence. Speech by Mr Teo Chee Hean, Minister for Defence, at the Commissioning Ceremony of RSS Intrepid, RSS Steadfast and RSS Tenacious, 5 February 2008. http://bit.ly/1fYDu4y

Singapore, Ministry of Foreign Affairs. Speech by Mr Lim Hng Kiang, Minister for National Development and Second Minister for Foreign Affairs, on 'The Challenges to Small Nations' Foreign Policies' at the Ministry of National Development (MND), 29 July 1995

Singapore, Ministry of Foreign Affairs. 'MFA Spokesman's Comments on an Exclusive Economic Zone around Pedra Branca.' 25 July 2008.

Singapore, Ministry of Foreign Affairs. Speech by Senior Minister Professor S Jayakumar at the S Rajaratnam Lecture 19 May 2010.

Singapore, Republic of Singapore Navy. *Onwards and Upwards – Celebrating 40 Years of the Navy,* Singapore: SNP International, 2007.

Singer, P.W. *Wired for War: The robotics revolution and conflict in the 21st century.* New York: Penguin, 2009.

Skocpol, Theda, and Paul Pierson. 'Historical institutionalism in contemporary political science.' in *Political science: State of the discipline*, by Ira Katznelson and Helen Milner, pp. 693–721. New York and London: W.W. Norton & Co., 2002.

Smith, Laurence C. *The New North. The World in 2050.* London: Dutton Books, 2010.

Smith, Steve. 'Reflective and constructive approaches.' in *The globalisation of world politics*, by John Baylis and Steve Smith, 224–51. Oxford: Oxford University Press, 2001.

Smith, Steven, Minister for Defence – Speech to the Lowy Institute on the 2013 Defence White Paper, http://bit.ly/1ibqSIM

Sobéus, Urban. *Havsbandslinjen i Stockholms skärgård 1933–1945.* Bohus: Militärhistoriska Förlaget, 2000.

Söderberg, Hjalmar. 'Generalkonsulns F-båtsmiddag.' in *Den talangfulla draken.* Stockholm: Bonniers, 1913.

Söderlindh, Håkan, Carl-Johan Engström, and Bo Fahlander (eds.). *Kustförsvar. Från kustbefästningar till amfibiekår.* Västervik: Marintaktiska Kommandot, 2002.

Soh, Felix. 'Course set for the Best Little Navy in the World.' *Straits Times,* 5 May 1992.

Soh, Felix. 'S'pore navy is No 1.' *Straits Times,* 11 June 1999.

Song, Sang-ho,'Navy pushes blue-water operations', *The Korea Herald*, 7 February, 2013

South Korea, Republic of Korea Ministry of National Defense. Defense White Paper 2006, Seoul, 2006 p. 53.

South Korea, Republic of Korea Department of Defence. 'Speech by L.N. Sisulu, Minister of Defence and Military Veterans, on the Occasion of the Department of Defence Budget Vote.' Good Hope Chamber, Capetown, 13 April 2011. www.info.gov.za/speech

South Korea, Republic of Korea Navy ROKN Headquarters, Navy Vision 2020 (해군 비전 2020). Gyeryon-dae, 1999 p. 80.

South Korea, Republic of Korea Navy, ROKN Headquarters. Navy Vision 2030 (해군 비전 2030). Gyeryon-dae, 2008 p. 8.

South Korea, Republic of Korea Navy, Construction of the 7th Flotilla one step closer (해군 제기동전단 창설, 품 한절음더). Seoul, 2010. Republic of Korea Navy News Release.

Spain, Ministerio de Defensa. *Revisión Estratégica de la Defensa*. Madrid: Secretaria General Técnica, May 2003).

Spulber, Nicolas. 'The Danube-Black Sea Canal and the Russian Control over the Danube.' *Economic Geography* 30, No. 3 (July 1954) pp. 236–245.

Stacey, Ralph. D. *Complexity and Organizational Reality: Uncertainty and the need to rethink management after the collapse of investment capitalism*. 2nd Ed. New York: Routledge, 2010.

Starck, Magnus. *Allmän sjökrigshistoria 1945–1965*. Stockholm: Bonniers, 1975.

Stefan, Laura, Dan Tapalaga and Sorin Ionita. 'Romania.' *Nations in Transit*. Freedom House 2010.

Stefan, Laura and Sorin Ionita. 'Romania', *Nations in Transit*. Freedom House 2011.

Stern, Lewis and Michael McDevitt. 'Vietnam and the South China Sea.' in *The Long Littoral Project: the South China Sea: A Maritime Perspective on Indo-Pacific Security*, by Michael McDevitt. CNA 2013): pp. 61–72. www.cna.org

Stewart, Cameron. 'Obsolete Collins fleet a lost cause.' *The Australian* 21 April, 2012, http://bit.ly/IfkfVu

Stewart, Joshua. 'Mideast Crises Force U.S. navy to keep carriers at sea longer.' *Defense News*, 30 July 2102.

Still Jr, William N. *Iron Afloat: The Story of the Confederate Armorclads*. Columbia, SC: University of South Carolina Press, 1988 p. 7.

Still, Jr, William N. *Confederate Shipbuilding*, Columbia, SC: University of South Carolina Press, 1987

Stokes, Mark. 'China's Quest for Joint Aerospace power: Concepts and Future Aspirations.' in *The Chinese Air Force: Evolving Concepts, Roles, and Capabilities*, by R. Hallion, R. Cliff and P. Saunders. Washington DC: Center for Study of Chinese Military Affairs, Institute for National Strategic Studies, National Defense University p. 38.

Strasser, Stephen. *Understanding and explanation: Basic ideas concerning the humanity of the human sciences*. Pittsburgh: Duquesne University Press, 1985.

Strachan, Hew, 'Making Strategy: Civil–Military Relations after Iraq.' *Survival*, 48, no. 3 (2006) pp. 59–82.

Straits Times. 'Fall of Kuwait "shows S'pore has right defence policy".' *Straits Times*, 12 August 1990.

Straits Times. 'Investment in defence small price to pay to protect assets: Dr Yeo.' *Straits Times*, 26 May 1991.

Stratfor. 'Romania's political crisis.' *STRATFOR Global intelligence*, 6 July 2012.

eeSweden, Government of Sweden. *Ett användbart Försvar. Regeringens proposition 2008/2009.* Stockholm, 2009.

Symonds, Craig L. *Lincoln and His Admirals*, Oxford: Oxford University Press, 2008.

Symonds, Craig L. T*he Civil War at Sea*. Santa Barbara, CA: ABC-Clio, 2009.

Taipeh Times. 'Taiwanese flotilla sails to Diaoyutais.' *Taipeh Times*, 25 September 2012.

Taipeh Times. 'Chinese ships spotted near disputed islands.' *Taipeh Times*, 25 September 2012.

Teece, David .J., Gary Pisano and Amy Shuen. 'Dynamic capabilities and strategic management'. *Strategic Management Journal* 18(7), 2008 pp. 509–53.

Teo, Chee Hean. 'Total Defence for Singapore,' *Military Technology* 32, No. 2 (2008) p. 14.

Teo, Chee Hean. 'Meeting the Challenges of Singapore Defence.' *Military Technology* 34, No. 2 (2010) pp. 16–18.

Thayer, Carl. 'The Tyranny of Geography: Vietnamese Strategies to Constrain China in the South China Sea.' *Contemporary Southeast Asia: A Journal of International and Strategic Affairs* Vol. 33, no. 3 December 2011 pp. 348–369.

The Chosunilbo. 'Navy to Build up Strategic Fleet with Six Aegis War Ships'. *Chosun Media*, 2007. http://bit.ly/1fG3Jwq

The Economist: 'Romania's economy: Buckle up, A tight budget and a credit squeeze will make 2012 a tough year.' *The Economist*, 10 December 2011.

The Economist. 'Next! A country where governments have the longevity of mayflies.' *The Economist*, 5 May 2012.

The Economist. 'Gold-hunting in a frugal age.' *The Economist*, December 2012 p. 62.

The Finnish Defence Forces, 'Facts about National Defence.' Helsinki: Public Information Division of Defence Command, 2008.

The Jakarta Post. 'Military chiefs sign key pact on Strait of Malacca.' *The Jakarta Post* 22 April 2006.

Thompson, Mark. 'Confusion Down Under: Australia and the US Pivot to Asia.' *East-West Center, Asia-Pacific Bulletin 180* 18 September 2012. www.EastWestCenter.org/APB

Till, Geoffrey. *Seapower: A Guide for the Twenty-First Century.* London: Frank Cass, 2004.

Till, Geoffrey. Asia's Naval Expansion. An Arms Race in the Making? London: International Institute for Strategic Studies, 2012.

Till, Geoffrey. *Seapower: A Guide for the Twenty-First Century*. Third edn. Routledge, 2013.

Torode, Greg. 'Vietnam buys submarines to counter China.' *South China Morning Post*, 17 December 2009. http://bit.ly/1bRJZPk

Tran, Pierre. 'Hollande to review 'Survival', 'Apocalyptic' Budgets.' *DefenseNews International*, 1 April 2013.

Tucker, Spencer C. *Blue and Gray Navies: The Civil War Afloat*. Annapolis, MD, Naval Institute Press, 2006.

Tunberger, Johan and Jan Blomqvist. 'Strategisk Vindkantring.' in *För Sveriges säkerhet*, by Tommy Jeppsson, pp. 45–82. Stockholm: Royal Swedish Academy of War Sciences, 2012.

Turnock, David. 'The Danube–Black Sea Canal and its impact on Southern Romania.' *GeoJournal* 12, No. 1 (1996) pp. 65–79.

Tzalel, Moshe. *From Ice-breaker to Missile Boats: The Evolution of Israel's Naval Strategy*. Westport,CT: Greenwood Press, 2000.

Urquhart, Donald. 'S'pore welcomes joint patrol proposal.' The Shipping Times, 21 June 2004.

UK Admiralty Board. Future Navy – Operational Concept. London: Admiralty Board, 2001: NAVB/P(01)13.

UK Ministry of Defence. *The Cod War: Naval operations off Iceland in Support of the British Fishing Industry (1958–1976)*. Naval Staff History, BR 1736, No. 57. London: Ministry of Defence, 1990.

UK Ministry of Defence. 'Innovative ways sought to improve the security of maritime operations.' www.gov.uk. 28 January 2013. http://bit.ly/18yQJBb

UK Ministry of Defence. *Defence White Paper: Delivering Security in a Changing World*, presented to Parliament by the Secretary of State for Defence by Command of her Majesty. London: Crown TSO, December 2003).

UK Ministry of Defence. *Joint Doctrine Publication 0-10: British Maritime Doctrine*. Shrivenham: Ministry of Defence.

Underwood, Rodman L. *Stephen Russell Mallory: A Biography of the Confederate Navy Secretary and United States Senator*. Jefferson, NC: McFarland and Company, 2005 p. 96.

UPI. 'Chile advances plan to build submarine.' *UPI*, 17 May 2012.

UPI. 'US Braces itself for Action in Persian Gulf.' *UPI*, 11 June 2012.

UPI.com. 'Defence cuts threaten Australian subs.' *UPI.com*, 7 March 2013, http://bit.ly/1emR9OM US Government. 'US Military Engagements to Romania.' Embassy of the United States, Bucharest, Romania, 27 May 2008.

US Government. 'Memorandum of Discussion at the 208th Meeting of the National Security Council, July 29 1954. Foreign Relations of the United States, 1952–54. V. XV, Korea Part 2.'.

US Navy, Marine Corps and Coast Guard. Naval Operations Concept 2010: Implementing The Maritime Strategy, http://1.usa.gov/18jWk3o

US Operations Coordinating Board. 'Second Progress Report by the Operations Coordinating Board to the National Security Council on NSC 170/1: United States Objectives and Courses of Action with Respect to Korea, 29 December 1954.' Foreign Relations of the United States, 1952–54, VXV, Korea Part 2. Washington DC (1984): 1943–1956.

USA Today. 'Romania a golden opportunity.' *Our World, USA Today*, Thursday 22 September 2011.

Vendil, Carolina (ed.). *Russian Military Capability in a Ten-Year Perspective*. Stockholm: Swedish Defence Research Agency, 2012).

Vian, Admiral of the Fleet Sir Philip. *Action This Day*. London: Frederick Muller Ltd., 1960.

von Clausewitz, Carl. *On War*, translated and edited by Sir Michael Howard and Peter Paret. Princeton, NJ: Princeton University Press, 1976.

von Hippel, Eric. *The sources of innovation*. Oxford: Oxford University Press, 1995.

von Hippel, Eric. *Democratizing innovation*. Cambridge MA: MIT Press, 2007.

von Hippel, Eric. 'Horizontal innovation networks – by and for users.' *Industrial and Corporate Change* 16, no. 2 (2007) pp. 298–315.

Von Hofsten, Gustaf and Frank Rosenius (eds.). *Kustflottan. De svenska sjöstridskrafterna under 1900–talet.* Stockholm: Marinlitteraturföreningen, 2009.

Wanski, Tadeuz. 'Ukraine- Romania: a sustained deadlock.' *OSW Centre for Eastern Studies*, 30 December 2011.

Waterfield, Bruce. 'Activist accused of waging net war from bunker.' *The Sydney Morning Herald*, 30 March 2013.

Watts, Larry L. 'Democratic Civil Control of the Military in Romania: An Assessment as of October 2001.' Conflict Studies Research Centre, December 2001 p. 15.

Watts, Larry L. *Integration*. The Centre for Romanian Studies, UK pp. 135–150

Watts, Larry, L. 'The Transformation of Romanian Civil–Military Relations: Enabling Force Projection.' *European Security* 14, No. 1 (2005) pp. 95–114.

Watts, Larry L. 'Introduction the Convergence of Reform and Integration.' in *Romanian Military Reform and NATO Integration*, by Larry L. Watts, 9–20. UK: The Centre for Romanian Studies, 2001.

Watts, Larry. 'Romanian Public Attitudes to Defence and Security Sector Reform.' in *Public Image of Security: Defence and the Military in Europe*, by Marie Vlachová, 266–283. Geneva: Center for the Democratic Control of Armed Forces in Geneva, 2003.

Watts, Larry L. 'Stressed and strained civil–military relations in Romania, but successfully reforming.' in *Civil Military Relations in Europe: Learning from Crisis and Institutional Change*, by Hans Born et. al. 21–35. London: Routledge, 2006 pp. 21–34.

White, Hugh. *The China Choice: Why America Should Share Power*, Black Inc: Melbourne Australia 2012

Williams, John Allen. 'The Postmodern Military Reconsidered.' in *The Postmodern Military: Armed forces after the Cold War*, by John Allen Williams, David R Segal, Charles C. Moskos, pp. 265–88. New York: Oxford University Press, 1999.

Willmott, H.P. *Just Being There*. Paper presented to the Institute of Historical Research for the Julian Corbett Prize in Modern Naval History, 1986.

Winton, John. *The Forgotten Fleet*. London: Michael Joseph Ltd., 1969 (re-print Douglas-Boyd Books Warhust 1991).

Winter, Sidney. 'Understanding Dynamic Capabilities'. *Strategic Management Journal*. 24, no 10, Special Issue: Why Is There a Resource Based View? Toward a Theory of Competitive Heterogeneity (October 2003) pp. 991–995.

Wise, Stephen R. *Lifeline of the Confederacy: Blockade Running During the Civil War*. Columbia, CS: University of South Carolina Press, 1988.

Wolff, Sarah 'Border management in the Mediterranean: internal, external and ethical challenges.' *Cambridge Review of International Affairs* 21, no. 2 (2008) pp. 253—271

Wolff, Sarah, Wichmann, Nicole and Gregory Mounier 'The External Dimension of Justice and Home Affairs: A Different Security Agenda for the EU?' *Journal of European Integration*, 31, no. 1 (2009) pp. 9–23.

Zulean, Marian. 'Professionalisation of the Romanian Armed Forces.' in *The Challenge of Military Reform in Postcommunist Europe*, by Antony Forster, Timothy Edmunds and Andrew Cottey. Basingstoke: Palgrave Macmillian, 2002: 115–133.

Index

A2/AD (Anti-Access/Area Denial) strategy 28, 82
Adamson, Fiona 135, 136
adaptive dynamic capabilities, and innovation 67–80
AEGIS air defence system 91
AEGIS-equiped KDX-III destroyer class 85, 102, 104, 105
AFM (Armed Forces Malta) 4
AFM Maritime Squadron 4
    anti-piracy 113*(ill.)*
    Frontex operations 134, 144, 145, 146
    and Operation Atalanta 4
Air-Sea Battle concept 178
Algerian Navy, classification 18
Alvaro de Bazan 91
Amazing Trinity 72, 75, 76
An Byeong-tae, Admiral 99
Andreas, Peter 136
anti-piracy *see* piracy
APS (Africa Partnership Station) 3–4
Archer class submarines 124–5
Arctic ice-melt 178
Argentinian Navy, classification 16, 18
ASCM (anti-ship cruise missile) (supersonic) capability 124
ASEAN (Association of Southeast Asian Nations) 120, 125, 128–9
ASPI (Australian Strategy Policy Institute) 91
asylum seekers 134–8, 141, 142, 148
Asylum Support Office 142
asymmetric technology 27
Atlantic Strategy 68, 70–1
austerity policies 51–66
Australia
    budget cuts 90–1
    Defence White Paper 90
    maritime strategy 90–3, 94
    submarines 92
    threat from Chinese navy 83
Australian Navy
    classification 11, 17
    ship expansion programme 90–1
    size 93
autonomy criteria 41
AWD (Air Warfare Destroyers) 90, 91

Baconschi, Teodor 164
Bahrain Navy, classification 18
Ban Ki Moon 29
Bangladesh Navy, classification 16, 18
Barber, Josh 37–8, 39
Basecu, President Traian 161
Bastion Coastal Defence System 90
Beauregard, P.G.T. 187, 198
Beesley, Alan 68
Belgian Navy
    and APS 4
    classification 16, 17–18
    and Operation Atalanta 4
Belgium
    Frontex operations 145
    GDP from maritime sectors 68
Belize Navy, classification 19
Benin Navy, classification 19
binary identities 49
Black Sea navies 151–6
blockade running 185–201
BNS *Godetia* 4, 114*(ill.)*
boarding operations training 4
boat people 135
Booth, Ken 6, 15
border control operations, Mediterranean 133–50, *see also* Frontex
Borresen, Jacob 9
Bowers, Ian xi, 11–12, 95–107
Brazilian Navy, classification 16, 17
Britain *see* Royal Navy; United Kingdom

British Maritime Doctrine 15
Brunei Navy, classification 19, 25
BSEC (Black Sea Economic Cooperation) 152
Buchanan, Franklin 193
Bulgarian Navy, classification 18
Burma *see* Myanmar
Buzan, Barry 53

Cambodian Navy, classification 25
Cameroon Navy 114*(ill.)*
Canadian Navy, classification 16, 17
Canberra class amphibious ships 91
CARAT (Cooperation Afloat Readiness and Training) 110
Caribbean Naval Force, classification 19
categorization system *see* classification; rankings
Centre for Applied Research in Security Innovation (Liverpool Hope University, UK) 1
Centre for Military History and Strategic Studies (Maynooth, Ireland) 1, 2
Changi Naval Base 121
Charleston Mercury 194
Cheonan sinking 85, 105
Chilean Navy
   classification 16, 18
   fast attack craft 115*(ill.)*
China *see* People's Republic of China; PLAN (People Liberation Army Navy)
China threat theory 28
Churchill, Joan 64
Churchill, Winston 203, 204
Cioflina, General Dumitru 156
CISE (Common Information Sharing Environment) philosophy 78
CIT (Cork Institute of Technology) 77, 78
civilian business models 58
classification 18
   criteria 38
   see also rankings
Clinton, Hillary 164
coalitions 46–9
   specialisation in 48
coastal forces 40, *see also* ranks
Coastal Marine Research Centre 77, 78

coastguards 25–6, 36
collaborative research 60
Collins class submarines 92
Colombia Navy, classification 18
COMFORPAT 147
Connect and Develop system 63
Constantinescu, President Emil 155, 156, 157
cooperation/interoperability criteria 41
Corbett Centre for Maritime Policy Studies (King's College, UK) 1
Corbett, Sir Julian 70
corporate innovation 8
counter intervention operations 82
County class LSTs 121
Coutau-Bégarie, Hervé 36, 38
CPV (Communist Party of Vietnam) 88
crisis management team, Formidable-class multi-role frigate *(ill.)* 110
Croatian Navy, classification 18
CSN (Confederate States Navy) 13, 185–201
   coastal defence 194
   commerce raiding 187
   operational effectiveness 186–8
   organisation effectiveness 186–8
   river defences 187, 191
   size of 186–7
   strategic effectiveness 188–90
   strategic performance 190–9
   torpedo development 198
CSS *Alabama* 197
CSS *Arkansas* 187
CSS *Atlanta* 193
CSS *Chicora* 187, 194
CSS *Hunley* 191
CSS *Huntsville* 193
CSS *Louisiana* 192
CSS *Mississippi* 192
CSS *Nashville* 193
CSS *Palmetto State* 187, 194
CSS *Shenandoah* 189
CSS *Stonewall* 197
CSS *Tennessee* 191
CSS *Tuscaloosa* 193
CSS *Virginia* 187, 191, 193–4
Cunningham, Admiral Andrew Browne 208

Cyprus Navy, Frontex operations 134

defence budgets 2
Defending Singapore in the 21st Century 118
Degeratua, General Constantin 156
Denmark
    GDP from maritime sectors 68
    Navy, classification 18
DF-21D missile 24
division of labour 58
Dodko/Takeshima dispute 87, 104
DOKDO LPD 102–3
drug trafficking 69

East Timor intervention 129
Ecuador Navy, classification 18
EEZ defence 31
Egyptian Navy, classification 18
Endurance class LPDs 121, 129, 130
European Fundamental Rights Agency 142
Exocet ASCM 125
Expansion of Third World Navies 15
expeditionary forces 40, *see also* ranks
expeditionary warfare 40

F-35B STOVL fighters 91
FFX/ULSAN class frigates 103
Fillon, Francois 148
financial austerity, implications for navies 51–66
financial crisis (2008) 2
Finnish Navy
    classification 18
    development of 30
flexibility criteria 41
Foote, Shelby 189
force projection 15
Formidable class frigates 110*(ill.)* 123, 130
Forum of Small States 29
France
    Frontex operations 133, 148–9
    Gendarmerie Maritime 134, 148, 149
    maritime rescue/border control agencies 148
Fraser, Admiral Sir Bruce 203, 206, 207, 208, 209
Frattini, Franco 148

French Navy
    classification 16
    search and rescue/border control duties 148–9
Friedman, Norman 168
Frontex
    humanitarian support 141
    joint operations 142
    mandate/regulations 140–2
    operations 12, 133–50
    operations data 144–6
    problems with 139–43
fuel starvation 54
The Future of Sea Power 15

Gabriel missile 8
Gambia Navy, classification 19
GDP from maritime sectors 68
Gearing class destroyers 97
Georgia Navy, classification 19
Gepard class corvettes 90
German Navy (modern)
    classification 17
    Frontex operations 145
Germond, Basil xi, 10, 33–50
Ghana Navy, classification 19
Giacomello, Giampiero xi, 12, 133–50
global maritime system 169
global navies 40, *see also* rankings
global strategic pattern, changes to 177–9
Gotland class submarines 176
Granholm, Niklas xi, 12–13, 167–84
Greece, Frontex operations 134, 144, 145, 146
Greek Navy, classification 16, 18
Grove, Eric xi, 6, 7, 10, 15–20, 25, 35–6, 38, 117
Guadiamarina Riquelme 115*(ill.)*

Haines, Steve 15
Halpin Research Centre 79
Halsey, Admiral William 208, 209
Hamidi, Dr Ahmad Zahid 29–30
Harrier STOVL fighters 91
Hattendorf, John B. 1
Haydon, Peter T. 38, 39
HDMS *Iver Huitfeldt* 114 *(ill.)*
Helsinki Accords 172

Highball bombers 211
historical institutionalism 60
HMNLS *Johann De Witt* 4
HMNLS *Zuiderkrui* 4
HMNZS *Canterbury* 18
HMS *Indefatigable* 211
HMS *King George V* 209, 210
Hobart class destroyers 91
Hsiung Ffeng (Brave Wind) III missiles 28
HSwMS *Carlskrona* 113 *(ill.)*
Human Rights Watch 139–40
humanitarian support operations 133, 134–5, 141

ICC (International Coordination Centre) 142
Icelandic Navy
    classification 19
    Cod wars 27
IKC2 (Integrated Knowledge Command and Control) 123
illegal immigration 135–6, 141, 143
illicit globalisation 136
IMERC (Irish Maritime and Energy Resource Cluster) 78, 79
IMO (International Maritime Organisation) 137
Incheon class frigates 106
Indian Navy
aircraft carriers 91
classification 16, 17
Indonesian Navy, classification 16, 18, 25
innovation *see* systematic innovation
INS (Irish Naval Service)
    campaign plan perspectives 72–3
    classification 19
    collaborative research 60
    Defence Forces programmes/policy 71–2
    development of 71
    drug operations/trafficking 3, 69
    dynamic capabilities 73–4
    Frontex operations 134
    illegal arms shipments 69
    innovation in 11, 62–3
    service delivery ethos 72–3
    size of navy 1, 3, 54
    training facilities 8–9

Internal Look war games 27
international migration 135–9, 141, 143–50
Iranian Navy 5
    classification 16
    small craft threat*(ill.)* 112
    threat from 24, 27–8
Iraqi Navy 27
    classification 16, 19
Ireland
    Atlantic Strategy 71
    and Continental Shelf limits 68
    Defence Enterprise Committee 77
    Defence Green Paper 68
    Defence White Paper 68
    fisheries 69
    GDP from maritime sectors 68, 74
    hydrocarbon/mineral resources 69
    ICT strategy 78
    Integrated Marine Plan 68
    maritime jurisdiction 68, 69, 74–5
    Public Service Reform Plan 78
    Treaty of Independence and naval protection 68
    see also INS (Irish Naval Service)
Israeli Navy
    classification 16, 18
    development of 30
    Gabriel missile 8
Italy
    Frontex operations 133, 144, 145, 146–8
    Guardia di Finanza 143, 146, 147–8
    Guardia Costiera 134, 146–7
    MRCC 143
    SAR operations 146–7
Italian navy *see* Marina Militare
ITS *Borsini* 143

Japan
    and ROKN (Republic of Korea Navy) 87
    threat from China 82
Japanese Navy, classification 16, 17
JCB (Joint Coordinating Board) 142
joint exercises 9
Jones, Virgil Carrington 199
Joppke, Christian 136
Juan Carlos I 91

KDX-I destroyer class 85, 102, 104
KDX-II destroyer class 85, 102, 104, 105
KDX-III destroyer class 85, 102, 104, 105
Kearsley, Harold J. 44
Kenya Navy, classification 19
Kilo class submarines 28, 89, 157
Kim Dae-jung 99
Kim Young-sam 98, 100
King, Admiral Ernest 202, 203, 206–7
King Ferdinand 159
Klepp, Silja 136–7
knowledge and power 33–4
Koh, Swee Lean Collin xii, 12, 117–31
KPI (key performance indicators) 48
KPN (Korean People's Army Naval Force)
   classification 16, 17
   threat from 84–6, 95–7, 100–1, 106
KSS-II submarines 103
KSS-III submarines 103–4
Kuwait Navy, classification 18
KV *Tor* coastguard patrol boat*(ill.)* 109

La Gloire type ironclads 193
LACM (land-attack cruise missile) 124
Lampedusa migration 143, 148
large navies commitments 24
Latvia, Frontex operations 145
L.É. *Emer* 116*(ill.)*
L.É. *Niamh* 116*(ill.)*
Le Fanu, Commander Michael 209, 210
lead users 52–3, 62, 64
Lee Myung-bak 105
lesser African and Asian navies 17
LHD (landing helicopter dock amphibious
   ships) 90, 91
Libyan Navy 27
   classification 19
Lindberg, Michael S. 36, 38
logistics/support forces 40, *see also* ranks
*The Lost Cause: A New Southern History
   of the War of the Confederates* 189
Luraghi, Raimondo 185, 197

McDevitt, Rear-Admiral (retd.) Michael
   xii, 11, 81–94
Mahan, Alfred T. 15
Malaysian Navy *see* Royal Malaysian
   Navy

Mallory, Stephen 186, 188, 190, 193, 194,
   196, 198, 199
Maltese Navy *see* AFM Maritime
   Squadron
MAOC-N (Maritime Analysis Operations
   Centre Narcotics) 69
Marina Militare
   classification 16
   and illegal migrants 143–8
marine ecosystems 70
maritime jurisdictions 67
maritime patrol aircraft 8
Maritime Safety Committee 137
Maritime Security 3–4, 25–7, 45–6, 75
maritime strategy
   and small navies 2
   see also individual countries/navies
Maury, Matthew Fontaine 198
Maynooth conference (2007) 1, 2–3,
   212–14
Mediterranean SAR Zones 138–9
medium navies *see* rankings
Medium-light-navy 181–4
Mellet, Rear-Admiral Mark xii, 11, 57,
   67–80
Membership Action Plan (NATO) 157
Mendez Nunez 143
Mexican Navy, classification 18
Micewski, Edwin R. 58
migration, and small navies 135–9, 141,
   143–50
Mischief Reef 22
MOOTW (Military Operations Other Than
   War) 83
Moroccan Navy, classification 18
Morris, Michael A. 6, 25, 34–5, 38
Mosquito Fleet 198
MRCC (Maritime Rescue Coordination
   Centres) 137, 143
MSP (Malacca Strait Patrols) 127–9
Mulqueen, Michael xii, 11, 51–66
multinational operations 46–9
Munmu the Great destroyer *(ill.)* 111
MV *Faina* 112 *(ill.)*
Myanmar Navy, classification 19, 25

Nae Dyong submarine *(ill.)* 111
Napoleonic paradigm 195

national defence industries 29
nations of no account 1, 3
NATO 16
naval multilateralism 46–9
naval power hierarchies *see* rankings
NAVFOR 4
Navy Vision (2020) 100
Navy Vision (2030) 100, 101
Netherlands Navy
    classification 16, 17–18
    Frontex operations 145
    and Operation Atalanta 4
Network-Centric Warfare 43
New Zealand navy *see* Royal New Zealand Navy
niche capabilities 29
Nigerian Navy, classification 16, 19
Nimitz, Admiral Chester 206–7, 209
NMCI (National Maritime College of Ireland) 77, 79
non-state actors 45
Nordic Balance 170–1
Nordic Defence League 170
North Korean Navy *see* KPN
Norway, GDP from maritime sectors 68
Norwegian Navy
    classification 18
    inshore/SSK experience 29
    Penguin missile 8
nuclear submarines 16, 17

Ocean Governance 67–8, 70
offshore estates 31
Oman Navy, classification 18
open source innovation 52–3, 63, 64
Operation Active Endeavour 159
Operation Atalanta 4, 117, 176
Operation Blue Orchid 129
Operation Blue Sapphire 130, 131
Operation Indalo 149
Operation Iraqi Freedom 164
Operation Tungsten 205
order of battle criteria 41
order of effect criteria 41

Pacific campaign, WW2 202–12
Pakistan Navy, classification 16, 18
Partnership for Peace 173

path dependencies 60–1
peacekeeping 40
Penguin missile 8
PEOP (Pan European Oil Pipeline) 152
People's Republic of China
    Century of Humiliation 81–2
    China threat theory 28
    counter intervention operations 82
    defence perimeter 82
    navy *see* PLAN
    and Taiwan 82
Peruvian Navy, classification 16, 18
Philippines Navy 21
    classification 16, 18, 25
    coastguard 26
    Maritime Security 25
Phung Quang Thanh, General 88
piracy
    anti-piracy operations 3, 10, 45, 46, 83–4, 113*(ill.)* 127, 130, 134, 177
    Danube river 154
    Somalia/Gulf of Aden 4, 26, 112 *(ill.)* 127, 130
    trends in 70
PKX/GUMDOKSURI class patrol boats 103
PLA Defence White paper 83
PLAN (People Liberation Army Navy) 28
    anti-piracy operations 83–4
    classification 16, 17
    coastguard 25
    MOOTW (Military Operations Other Than War) 83
    surface/submarine components 83
    threat from 5, 11, 20, 23, 24, 25, 81–4, 177
PME (professional military education) systems 24
police/constabulary forces 40, *see also* ranks
Poland, Frontex operations 145
Polish Navy, classification 18
Pollard, Edward A. 189
Ponta, Prime Minister Victor 161
population growth 70
Portuguese Navy
    classification 16, 18
    Frontex operations 145

Proctor and Gamble 63
production of knowledge 10
projection forces 40, *see also* ranks
projection operations 46, 47
PS *Gregorio del Pilar* 26

R&D (research and development) 62
range/sustainability criteria 41
rankings 15–20, 24–5, 43–5, 50
    criteria and indicators 35, 39–43
    literature on 34–9
rank 1 (global major operations without support) 37
rank 1 (Global Navies) 36
rank 1 (Global Power Projection Navy) 36
rank 1 (Major Global Force Projection Navy – Complete) 6, 16, 36
rank 1 (major naval powers) 38
rank 1 (SE Asia)(Adjacent Shipping Protection) 25
rank 1 (symbolic navies) 42
rank 1 (Third World token navies) 35
rank 2 (Global Navies) 36
rank 2 (Major Global Force Projection Navy – Partial) 10, 16, 17, 36
rank 2 (medium naval powers) 38
rank 2 (one major out-of-area operation) 37
rank 2 (police/constabulary/coastal defence navies) 42
rank 2 (Regional Power Projection Navy) 36
rank 2 (SE Asia)(Offshore Territorial Defence) 25
rank 2 (Third World police/constabulary navies) 35
rank 3 (Coastal Defence Navy) 36
rank 3 (coastal defence/limited projection operations) 42
rank 3 (limited independent global expeditionary operations) 37
rank 3 (Medium Global Force Projection Navy) 16, 17, 36
rank 3 (Regional Navies) 36
rank 3 (SE Asia)(Inshore Territorial Defence) 25
rank 3 (small/coastguard navies) 38
rank 3 (Third World coastal/defensive navies) 35
rank 4 (Constabulary Navy) 36
rank 4 (limited force projection/medium intensity operations) 37
rank 4 (limited projection/joint high intensity operations) 43
rank 4 (Medium Regional Force Projection Navy) 16, 17, 18, 36
rank 4 (Regional Navies) 36
rank 4 (SE Asia)(Constabulary Navy) 25
rank 4 (Third World offshore/defensive navies) 35
rank 5 (Adjacent Force Projection Navy) 7, 16, 36
rank 5 (Coastal Navies) 36
rank 5 (leading multinational high intensity operations) 43
rank 5 (miscellaneous "all the rest") 37
rank 5 (Third World operations beyond EEZ navies) 35
rank 5 (Token Navy) 36
rank 6 (any sustained operations) 43
rank 6 (Coastguard Navies) 36
rank 6 (Offshore Territorial Defence Navy) 16, 36
rank 6 (Third World regional theatre operations navies) 35
rank 7 (Inshore Territorial Defence Navy) 16, 19
rank 8 (Constabulary Navy) 6, 16, 19, 36
rank 9 (Token Navy) 6, 7, 16, 19, 36
RAS (Replenishment at Sea) 209
Rawlings, Vice-Admiral Sir Bernard 208, 209
RCC (Rescue Coordination Centre) 138
Regina Maria 159
Republic of Ireland Navy *see* INS
resource constraints 8
RIB (Rigid Inflatable Boats) 62
Richmond Examiner 194
RIMPAC (Rim of the Pacific) exercises 111
RMSI (Regional Maritime Security Initiative) 127–9
Robb-Webb, Jon xiii, 13, 201–12
Roh Moo-hyun 99, 105
ROK (Republic of Korea)
    Defence Reform 307 106
    post-democracy policy changes 98–9

regional policy implementation 100–6
sunshine policy 84, 99
threat from China 82, 84, 86
threat from North Korea 84–6, 95–7, 100–1, 106
ROKN (Republic of Korea Navy)
classification 16, 17
development hindrances 105–7
development of 95–106
fleet command structure 104
maritime strategy 84–7, 93, 99–105
modernisation of 11–12
Navy Vision (2020) 100
Navy Vision (2030) 100, 101
relations with Japan 87
relations with naval strategy 84–7
relations with US/US Navy 96–7, 103
sea lane security 86
submarines 98
Romania
Black Sea interests 152–4
Black Sea tourism 152
and Danube river 153–4, 162
economic problems 155, 160–1, 166
foreign relations 151–2
military reform 154–8
missile sites 164–5
oil/gas interests 152–3
political instability 156, 160
relations with Russia/Ukraine 161–5, 166
Romanian Navy 12
building of 154–61
classification 18
Danube piracy 154
downsizing 157
Frontex operations 145
modernisation 157
NATO membership 157, 158, 159, 160
professionalism 158, 166
reform 157–8, 160
relations with US Navy 158–9, 165, 166
size of 157
submarines 157
Rose, Lisle A. 201
Royal Malaysian Navy
classification 16, 18, 25

size 23
submarines 125
Royal Navy
British Pacific Fleet (BPF)(1944–45) 7, 13, 201–12
classification 16
effects of association with 30
expenditure cuts 53–4
Icelandic Cod wars 27
Response Force Task Group 17
and US Navy 29
Royal New Zealand Navy 5, 23
capability of 118
classification 16, 18
size 23
small boats 29
RPL (recognition of prior learning) 77
RSN (Republic of Singapore Navy) 12
anti-piracy operations 127, 130
capability of 117, 118
classification 17, 25
force structure developments 121–5
geopolitics 121–5
Malacca Strait patrols 127–9
Operation Atalanta 117
squadron mergers 123
technology 121–5
RSwN (Royal Swedish Navy) 4–5
classification 18
coastal defence 171–2, 174, 177
in Cold War 170–3
financial planning constraints 167–8
inshore/SSK experience 29
light naval concept 171
Medium-light-navy 181–4
Naval plan 60 171
Operation Atalanta 4
operational patterns 175–7
overseas operations 12
peace-keeping duties 176, 179
range of operational tasks 180
restructuring options 180
seapower 168–70
seapower design 179–80
security needs 12–13
size of 174
Steady-as-she-goes-navy 181–4
structures/tasks matrix 181–4

Ultra-light-navy 181–4
Rudolph, Christopher 136
Ruffa, Chiara xi, 12, 133–50
Russian Navy 12
   concerns over 31

SAAB 175
SAF (Singapore Armed Forces) 121, 123
Sanders, Deborah xiii, 12, 151–66
SAR (International Convention on Maritime Search and Rescue) 62, 137–9, 149
SAR (Search and Rescue) 134
SAR Zones, Mediterranean 138–9, 146–7
Saudi Arabian Navy, classification 16, 18
Scarborough Shoal 22
Schengen External Borders Code 142
Scorpene class submarines 125
scrapping 54
sea, attributes of 169
sea environment, characteristics 136
seapower 168–70
Seapower – a Guide for the Twenty-First Century 37, 169
Seapower as Strategy 168
security dilemma 82
security interconnections 59
Siggins, Lorna 69
SIGMA class corvettes 90
significant regional navies 17
Simson, J.W. 197
Singapore
   Defence White Paper 118
   diplomacy and defence 125
   external security cooperation 125–7
   fertility rate 121, 122
   foreign policy 118–19
   international security operations 129–30
   naval/defence policy 118–21
Singapore Navy *see* RSN
Singer, P.W. 58
Sipos, Joe 37–8, 39
SKJOLD guided missile craft *(ill.)* 109
SLA (service level agreements) 72
SLOC (Sea Lines of Communication) 40, 45, 100, 104, 119, 172
small naval assets 61

small navies
   in Asia 81–94
   aspirations and size 199
   association with Royal Navy 30
   capacity to matter 28–9
   classification *see* classification; rankings
   cooperative practices 29
   definition 5–7, 33, 118
   dependence of 21–2
   different forms of 30–1
   dilemma of 49–50
   distinctiveness 21–4
   diversity of 21–31
   evolution 45
   and Frontex *see* Frontex
   historical perspective 13
   humanitarian operations 12
   importance of 26–7
   and international migration *see* international migration
   and PME systems 24
   protecting national interests 67–80
   reliance on other countries 21
   requirement for 70
   seapower 168–70
   significance of size 7–9, 10
   strategic effectiveness 188–90
   and strategic policy 23–4
   structures/tasks matrix 181–2
   systematic innovation 59–64
   vulnerability to austerity 54–6
   see also classification; individual countries/navies; rankings
Small Navies Conference, Maynooth, Ireland 7, 213–14
Small Navies Project 1–2
Söderberg, Hjalmar 167
SOLAS (International Convention for the Safety of Life at Sea) 137
Somali piracy *see* piracy
Sonnack, Mary 64
South African Navy, classification 16, 18
South China Sea 21–2
South Johnston Reef clash 90
South Korea *see* ROK
South Korean Navy *see* ROKN
South Pacific Naval Force, classification 19

Soviet Union Navy 10, 16, 17
Spain
    Frontex operations 133, 144, 145, 146, 149
    Guardia Civil 134
Spanish Navy
    classification 16
    maritime surveillance/security duties 149
Speller, Ian xiii
Spruance, Admiral Raymond 209
Sri Lankan Navy, classificaton 18
SSK *Delfinul* 157
Steady-as-she-goes-navy 181–4
strategic deterrent forces 40, *see also* ranks
strategic effectiveness 188–90
SU-27/30 aircraft 90
Sumner class destroyers 97
sunshine policy 84, 99
surveillance/SLOC protection forces 40, *see also* ranks
Sweden
    Arctic ice-melt 178, 180
    Cold War strategy 170–3
    Defence Bill (1958) 171, 172
    Defence Bill (1972) 172
    Defence Bill (2009) 174
    defence industry 174–5
    Frontex operations 145
    geostrategic role 178, 180
    in NATO 173
    non-alignment policy 170
    post-Cold War strategy 173–7
    seapower design 179–80
    Whiskey on the Rocks crisis 172
Swedish Navy *see* RSwN
systematic innovation 11, 51–66
    adaptive dynamic capabilities 67–80
    implications for military role 59–61
    inertia 61
    locating 57–9
    R&D (research and development) 62
    in small navies 59–64
systemic economic meltdown 59–60

Taiwan Navy
    classification 16, 18
    Maritime Security 25
    size 23
Taiwan, and People's Republic of China 82
Taiwan Relations Act 23
Tattnall, Commodore Josiah 192
technical assistance 21
Teniente Orella 115 *(ill.)*
Teniente Serrano 115 *(ill.)*
Teniente Uribe 115 *(ill.)*
Teo Chee Hean, Commodore 117
terrorism 27, 45, 46
Thailand Navy, classification 16, 18, 25
Thayer, Carl 89–90
Third World Navies, Myths and Realities 15
Till, Geoffrey xiii, 6, 7, 8, 9, 10, 21–31, 37, 39, 169
Traité de Stratégie 36
Tuck, Christopher xiii, 13, 185–201
Tunisia, migrants from 148
Turkish Navy, classification 16, 18
Type 22 frigates 157
Type 45 destroyers 53
Type 209 submarines 85
Type 214 submarines 85
Type 214/KSS-II submarines 103
A Typology for Navies 15

UAE Navy, classification 18
UCC (University College Cork) 77, 78, 79
Ukraine 12
Ultra-light-navy 181–4
UNCLCS (United Nations Commission on the Limits of the Continental Shelf) 68
UNCLOS (United Nations Law of the Sea) 68
UNHCR (United Nations High Commissioner for Refugees) 138, 142
UNIFIED PROTECTOR 143
United Kingdom
    GDP from maritime sectors 68
    navy *see* Royal Navy
United Nations river squadrons 28
United States Navy
    and APS 3–4
    classification 16
    commitments 24

In WW2 Pacific Theatre 202–12
increased role in strategy 177
and Iranian Navy 5
Maritime Strategy (2007) 3
size of 5, 16, 202
Vietnam fleet 7
see also CSN (Confederate States Navy)
Uruguay Navy, classification 19
USNS *Impeccable* 25
USS *Bunker Hill* 204
USS *Chafee* 115*(ill.)*
USS *Cole* 27
USS *Essex* 204
USS *Independence* 204
USS *Indianapolis* 209
USS *Missouri* 210
USS *Monitor* 192
USS *Princeton* 204
USS *Sabine* 210
USS *Saratoga* 204
USS *Whidbey Island* 159
utility of users 52

Venezuelan Navy, classification 18
versatility criteria 41

Vessel Protection Detachments 4
Vian, Admiral Sir Philip 203–4, 208, 209
Vietnam
    Defence White paper 88
    threat from China 82, 89–90
Vietnamese People's Navy 11, 21, 22
    classification 18, 25
    Maritime Security 25
    maritime strategy 88–90, 93–4
    search and rescue 115 *(ill.)*
von Clausewitz, Carl 72, 73, 75, 76
von Hippel, Eric 52, 62, 64
VUCA (volatility, uncertainty, complexity and ambiguity) environment 77–80

Waever, Ole 53
Warburton, Terry xiv, 11, 51–66
WBL (work-based learning programme) 77
Welles, Gideon 186, 194
West German Navy, classification 16, 17,
    see also German Navy
West Philippine Sea 21–2
Whiskey class submarines 172
Whiskey on the Rocks crisis 172

Yoon-young-ha patrol boats 106